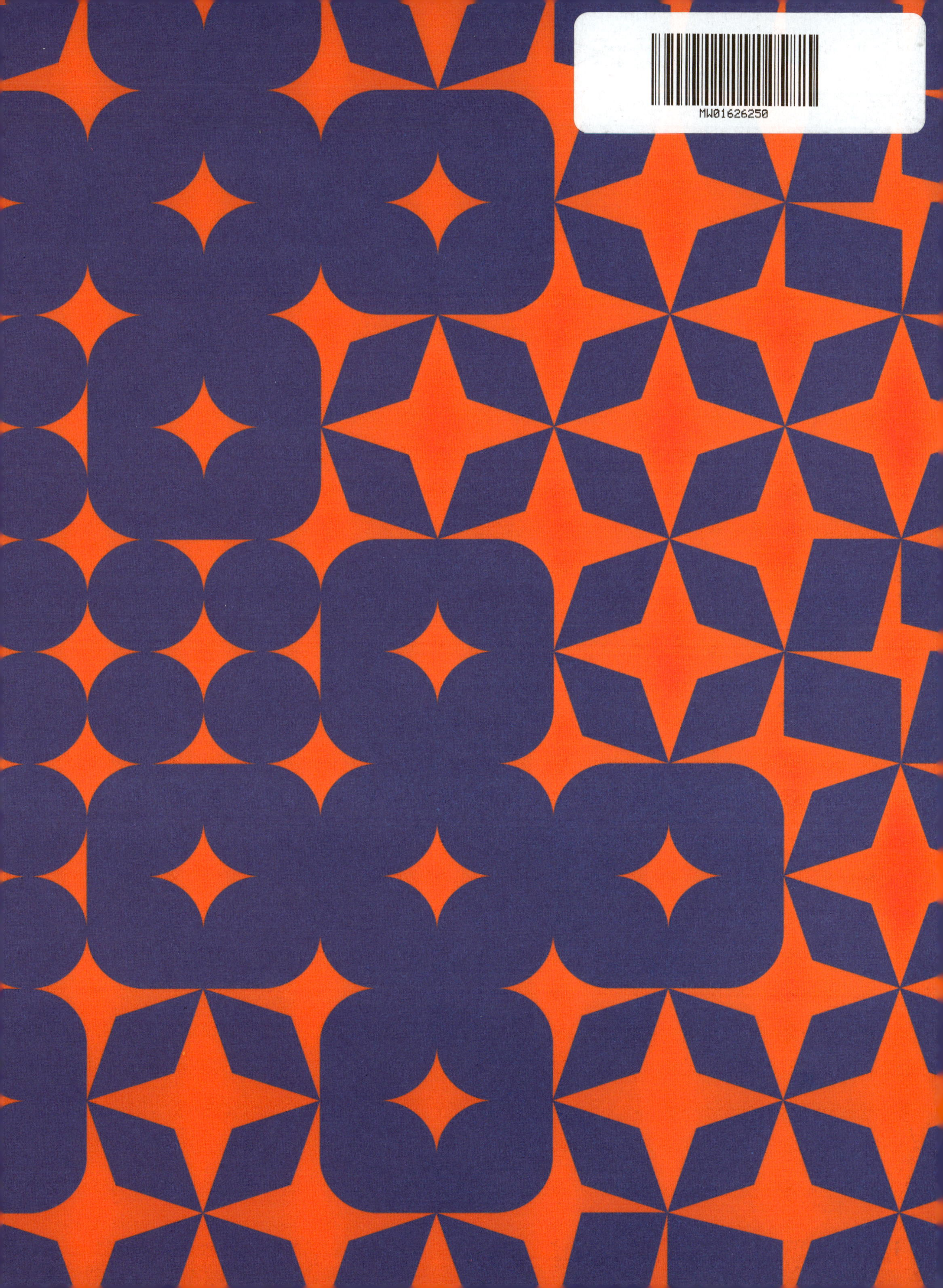

JIM ISERMANN
CARPET DESIGN FOR THE EXHIBITION SPACE AT THE KÜNSTLERHAUS GRAZ

PHOTO BY VENTURI, SCOTT BROWN & ASSOCIATES (MATT WARGO)

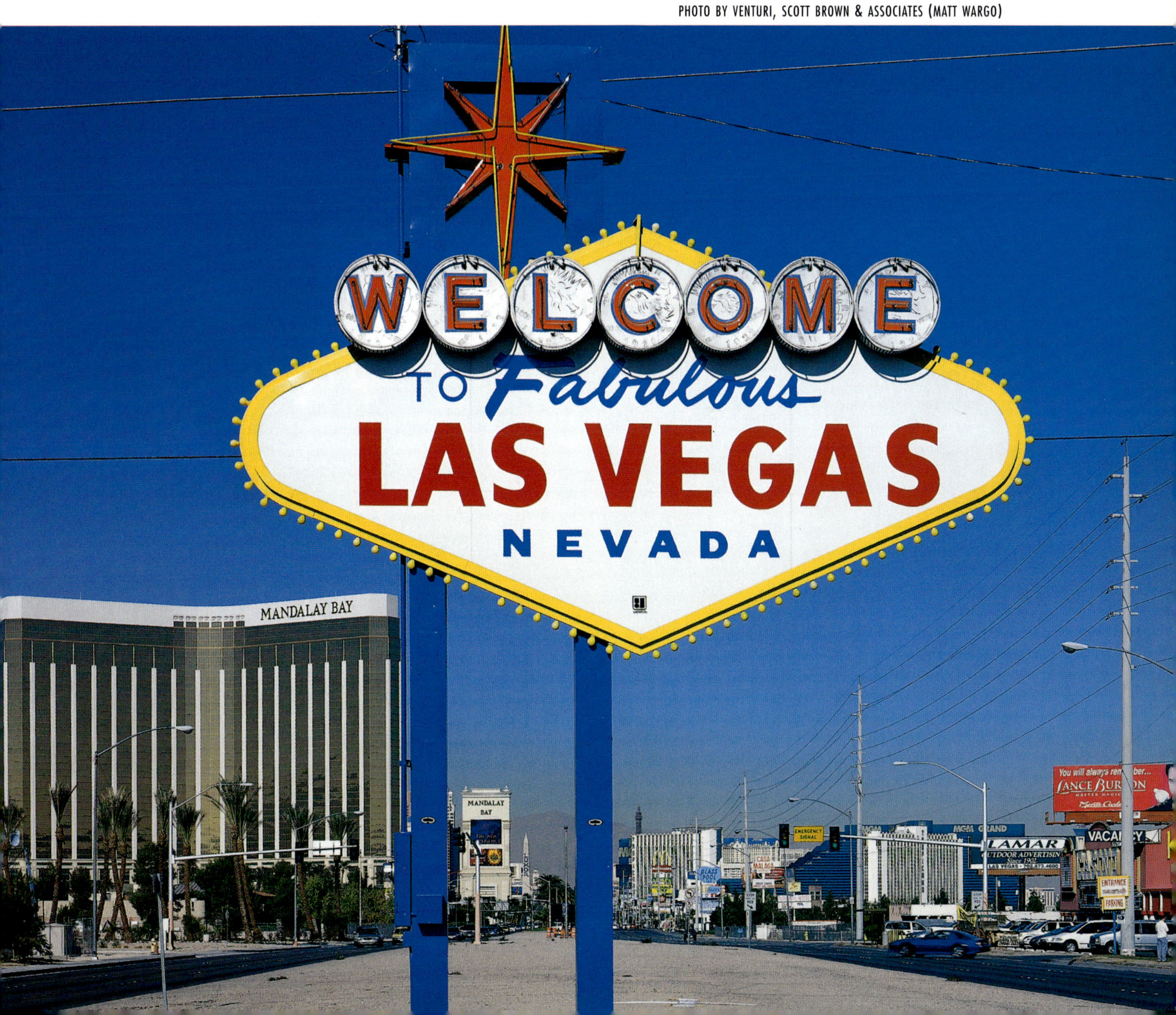

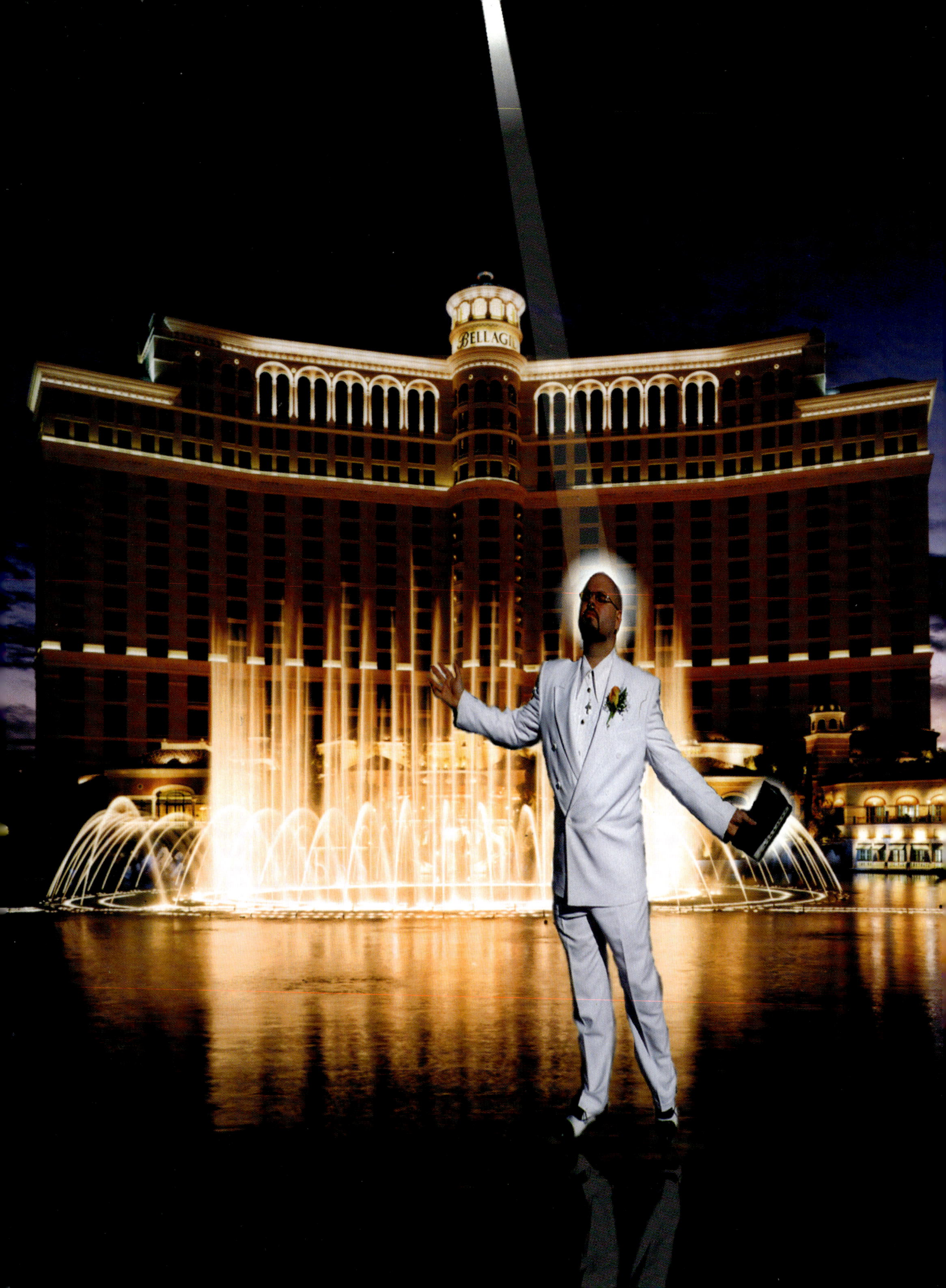

The Magic Hour

A Blessing by Reverend Ethan Acres

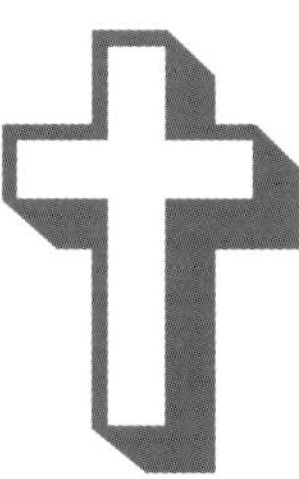

My brothers and sisters, friends and neighbors, I have been blessed with a lot of magic in my life. I have had a lot of magic moments, if you know what I'm talking about. Yes, oh sweet Jesus, yes, beloved, I think you do know, I can feel the knowing in your hearts. I'll say it again. I can feel the knowing in your hearts. Uh huh, YYYYEESSSSSuuuum, that's right, my children, we're talking about those special moments when time seems to just slow down ever so slightly ... moments when the fabric of time and space seems to fray just a tiny little bit. A time when all is possible: wooden staffs can become serpents, water can become wine, five dollars can become a fortune, and Elvis can live again. Let us give it a name, dear hearts. Let us call it 'The Magic Hour.'

REV. ACRES WALKING ON STEVE'S WATER
DIGITAL PHOTOGRAPH 21.5 x 27.9 CM
COURTESY OF THE ARTIST

Now, as I said, there have been many moments in my life that I could describe as magic: my first kiss, the moment I first saw my wife Lisa, the birth of my son. But today, beloved, a particular time stands out as most relevant. I think, my lambs, that you will agree.

I had left Texas blindly ... following nothing more than curiosity and faith. And let me tell you, after so many hours with my big, corn-fed, southern fried butt squeezed into a little tiny seat, flying 'Air Lilliputia,' sweet Jesus, curiosity and faith really didn't seem enough.

But twenty minutes or so before my plane was scheduled to land, I opened my window, and, with a few sparks of hope still jumping and jiving down deep in my soul, I peered longingly into the darkness. I remember looking out my window as the little plane careened over a desert shrouded in night, and seeing nothing ... nothing. Simply a black hole. Now, my children, I have made my life one of faith, but I'll tell you here and now that that doesn't mean I never falter. On the contrary, my friends, I believe that the candle placed closest to the door always goes out the most, if you catch my drift.

But, at that moment, looking out that little window and seeing nothing, well, I would be a real skunk if I stood here and told you that all was right in your pastor's world.

So friends, with the devil's laughter echoing in my ears, I remember reaching up, and slowly pulling down the shade. I was giving up, throwing in the towel, cashing in my chips. But then, praise God, just as I was about to turn my eyes away for good, surrendering my dreams to he that will remain nameless, a flicker of light caught my eyes.

I looked.

And I was saved.

Below me, bright patterns of light split the darkness. And there was form in the pattern, and the form was beautiful. Giant electric snow flakes drifting through the void. My hour was beginning. The plane began to descend, and the pattern beneath me grew ... reaching for my chariot, reaching up for me. I closed my eyes, and leapt from the sky, and the power caught me in its embrace, pulling me down into its arms. An airport at three in the morning, but like no airport I had ever seen: forests of pink, fiberglass palm trees accented by the sound of electric ditties, and the plink, plink, plink of coins falling into cups.

Moving sidewalks, and the voices of angels disguised as Siegfried and Roy, Tom Jones, and Don Rickles, reminding me not to leave my bags unattended, and then, with a swoosh of automated doors and a hot wind in my face, the cool interior of a car.

I remember, vaguely, that first hour, beloved. I spent most of it in a taxi. I just told the driver to, well, you know, DRIVE. And that is just what he did. Through my window I stared out at the neon, the garishly painted steel. There were tears in my eyes, my friends, and I didn't know if they were tears of joy or tears of horror. But even with my vision blurred and stung by salt, I couldn't stop looking. I could not tear my eyes away. I had to understand this place. I was Moses standing before the burning bush ... but this bush wasn't talking.

Finally, the cab deposited me in front of The Flamingo, and I stepped out into the hot desert night. Fifty-nine minutes had passed since I had looked down from the darkness and seen something new, and already I was beginning to get my equilibrium back. Already, the 'newness' was slipping away. "Las Vegas. So this is what all the fuss is about," I muttered conspiratorially under my breath.

And then, my sweet lambs, someone bumped into me. Actually two someones. I turned. I looked. And the world dropped out from under me a final time.

There were two Elvis impersonators walking down the sidewalk, holding hands.

The one who bumped me, turned, grinning and said "Smile, handsome, you're in Vegas."

My friends, since the beginning of time, men and women have gone out into the desert to find God. One night, at three in the morning, God found me. Las Vegas waits for all of us, my children. It sits there in the desert and promises that all things are possible.

But you must be willing to take a chance.

You must be willing to make a leap of faith.

AMEN.

In memory of Steven Izenour

The Magic Hour

The Convergence of Art and Las Vegas
Die Konvergenz von Kunst und Las Vegas

Alex Farquharson (Ed.)

Hatje Cantz
Neue Galerie Graz am Landesmuseum Joanneum

Vorwort
Foreword

von Günther Holler-Schuster und Peter Weibel

Günther Holler-Schuster erfuhr 1999 von Patricia Faure in deren Galerie in Santa Monica erstmals von Alex Farquharson und seinem geplanten Las Vegas-Projekt. Die Neue Galerie Graz zeigte sich sofort daran interessiert, weil am Beispiel der Las Vegas-Phänomenologie grundlegende Probleme der zeitgenössischen Kunst demonstriert werden können, nämlich die Stellung der Kunst in der Gesellschaft des Spektakels. Um dies zu verdeutlichen, hat die Neue Galerie in Eigenverantwortung dem Katalog des Kurators einen Epilog angefügt, in dem ein Spektrum von Positionen vorgeführt wird, das zeigen soll, was am Beispiel der Konvergenz von Las Vegas und Kunst allgemein interessant und relevant ist.

Wird Las Vegas, die Kapitale der westlichen Unterhaltungsindustrie, auch zur Hauptstadt der Kunst? Im historischen Moment, wo die Kunst die visionäre Kraft verliert, die sie immer beansprucht, weil die Kunst insgesamt sich den Formen der Unterhaltungsindustrie (vom Lifestyle bis zur Gameshow) annähert und in diesem Bestreben dieser sogar nachhinkt, wird Las Vegas in einer paradoxen Wendung auch zur Kapitale einer künftigen Kulturindustrie.

Als neueste radikale Phase der Entwicklung ist die Errichtung der Museen 'Guggenheim Las Vegas' und 'Hermitag-Guggenheim' von Rem Koolhaas zu betrachten: die Inklusion von Kunst in den Entertainmentkomplex, was bedeutet, dass die Kunst offensichtlich für die Unterhaltungsindustrie anschlussfähig geworden ist.

'The Magic Hour' ist eine Ausstellung, die die Unterhaltungsmetropole Las Vegas im amerikanischen Bundesstaat Nevada als Phänomen zwischen Realität und Fiktion und seine Wirkung auf die Kunst zeigt. Es ist dies die erste Museumsausstellung, die sich diesem Thema annimmt und versucht, die grundlegenden Aspekte zu analysieren, die zur Einzigartigkeit dieses Ortes beitragen. Es ist nicht zufällig, dass heute eine große Anzahl von KünstlerInnen Las Vegas besucht oder dort lebt. Seit dem 1972 erschienenen Buch von Venturi/Scott Brown/Izenour, 'Learning from Las Vegas', hat sich vieles verändert, sowohl in der Kunstentwicklung, als auch im gesellschaftlichen Leben allgemein.

Unterhaltung scheint zu einem Fetisch geworden zu sein, zu einer Matrix für alle Lebensformen. Diese Ausstellung versucht auch zu ergründen, was man nun von Las Vegas gelernt hat und wie sich das gesellschaftlich ausgewirkt haben könnte. Der Bereich zwischen Kunst und reiner Unterhaltung, egal auf welchem Niveau, ist so fließend, dass man ihn kaum mehr orten kann. Die Ausstellung wird somit sowohl Teil eines Casinos als auch Museums sein. Im tatsächlichen Las Vegas verhält es sich nicht anders. Venedig ist dort in den gleichen Dimensionen mit den gleichen Materialien teilweise nachgebaut und dient als Hotel. Das Resort und Casino Bellagio beherbergte eine Kunstsammlung mit Exponaten von El Greco bis Picasso, die beworben wurden wie Frank Sinatra oder die Beach Boys.

Die beiden Eckpunkte in der Diskussion sind mit Venturi, Scott Brown and Izenours Buch 'Learning from Las Vegas' auf der einen Seite und Dave Hickeys Lehrtätigkeit an der University of Nevada in Las Vegas auf der anderen Seite gegeben.

'Learning from Las Vegas' war theoretisch eine Schnittstelle zwischen Modernismus und Postmodernismus. Als der Theoretiker und Allrounder Dave Hickey und die Kunsthistorikerin Libby Lumpkin zu Beginn der 1990er Jahre nach Las Vegas zogen, entwickelte sich eine neue Interessensebene innerhalb der Rezeption der 'Vegas-Phänomenologie'. Für Hickey funktioniert der Strip als Plattform für seine Kritik an der elitären und puristischen Wertestruktur innerhalb der Kunstwelt. Außerdem brachte Hickey führende Künstler wie David Reed, Jim Isermann, Jim Shaw oder Jeffrey Vallance nach Las Vegas und zog durch seine Lehrtätigkeit viele junge Künstler in diese Stadt. Libby Lumpkin war von 1997-99 als Kuratorin in den Diensten des Casino-Visionärs Steve Wynn in der museumsähnlichen Galerie des Casino Hotels Bellagio tätig.

Selbstverständlich werden in 'The Magic Hour' alle Sparten (bildende Kunst, Design, Architektur und Showbusiness) vertreten sein. Als Kurator für dieses Projekt steht mit dem aus London kommenden Alex Farquharson ein junger engagierter Theoretiker zur Verfügung, der sich seit langem intensiv mit der Situation beschäftigt.

Auf allen gesellschaftlichen Ebenen breitet sich global ein Entertainment-Komplex aus, der auch die Kultur insgesamt erfasst. Die 'Gesellschaft des Spektakels' (Guy Debord, 1967) ist Wirklichkeit geworden. Die Massen, die Politik, das Spektakel bilden eine Allianz. Sogar die Kultureinrichtungen peripherer Orte wie Graz werden von dieser mächtigen Allianz deformiert. Das Phänomen Las Vegas zeigt die Konvergenz von Entertainment-Komplex und Kultur-Industrie. Wenn im Zuge der Globalisierung die Konvergenz weltweit dominiert, kann am Beispiel Las Vegas die Zukunft der Kunst im globalen Entertainment-Komplex transparent gemacht werden. Las Vegas wirkt wie eine Lupe, die bereits mikroskopisch die künftigen Praktiken und Probleme der Kunst erahnbar macht.

In Zeiten des globalen Amusements geht die Neue Galerie am Landesmuseum Joanneum den Dingen auf den Grund und beginnt bei den Wurzeln – 'The Entertainment Capital' – Las Vegas, Nevada.

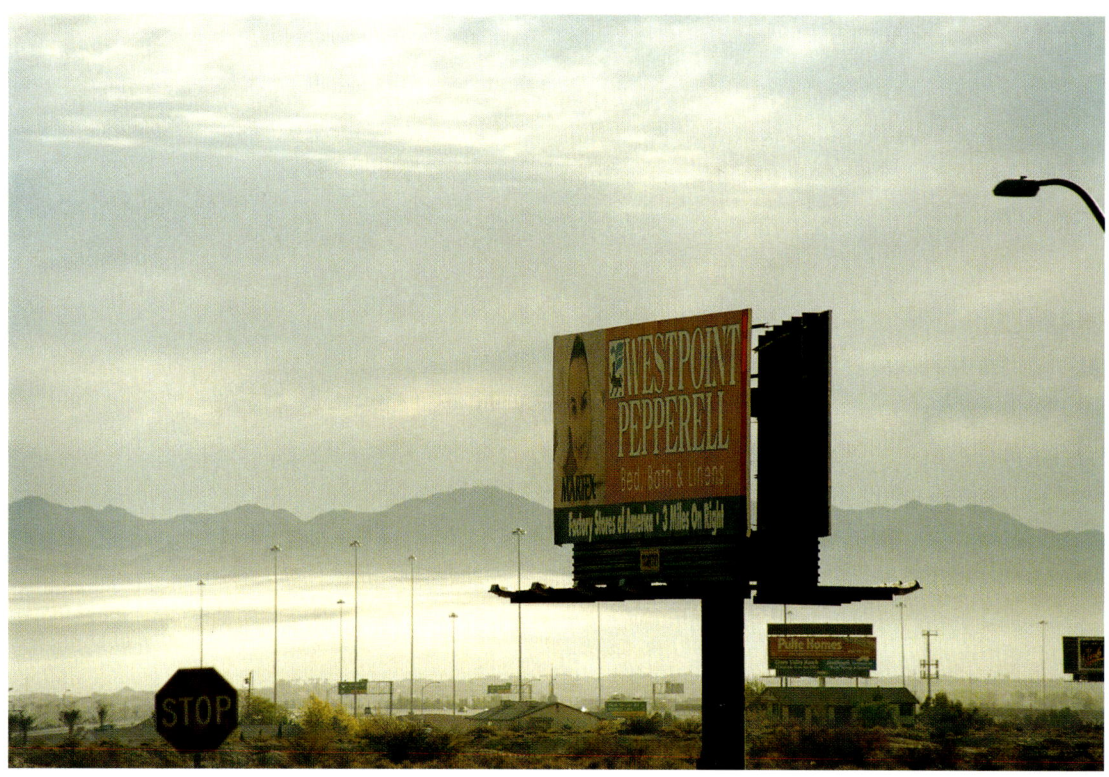

JEAN BAUDRILLARD
LAS VEGAS 1996

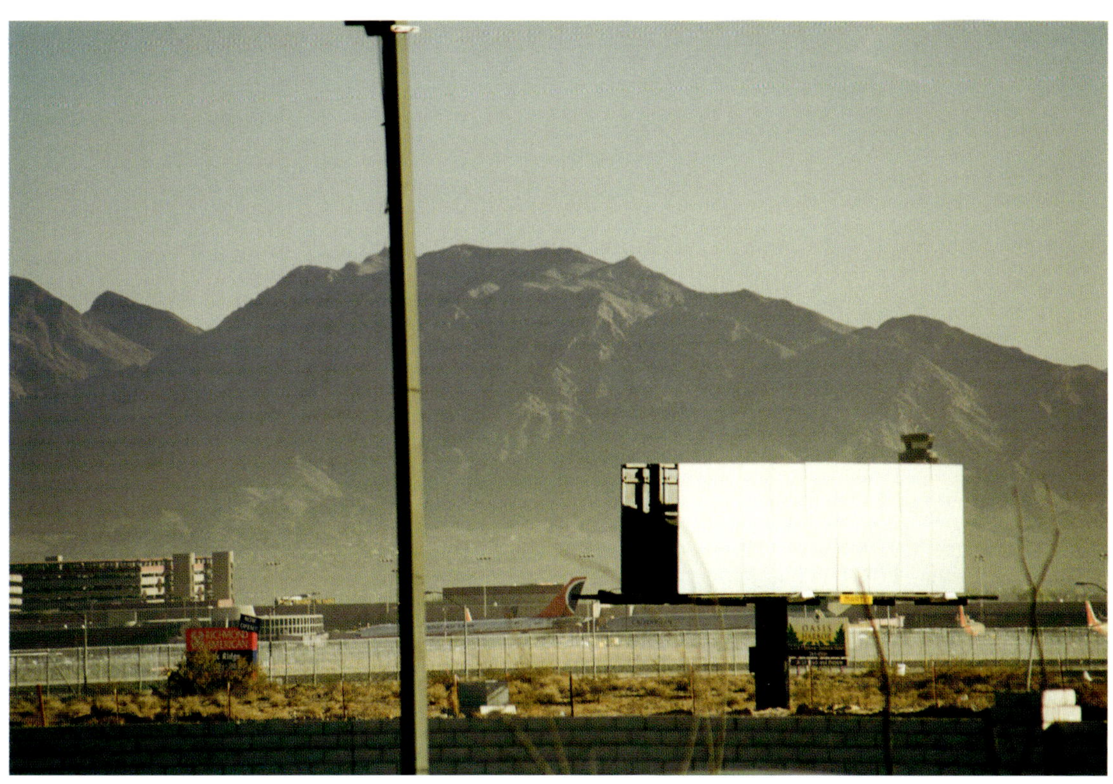

JEAN BAUDRILLARD
LAS VEGAS 1996

by Günther Holler-Schuster and Peter Weibel

It was Patricia Faure in her gallery in Santa Monica who introduced Günther Holler-Schuster to Alex Farquharson and his Las Vegas project. The Neue Galerie Graz was immediately interested. With the example of the Las Vegas phenomenology fundamental problems of contemporary art – that is, the position of art in the society of spectacle – can be demonstrated. In order to elucidate this, the Neue Galerie has added on its own authority an epilogue to the catalogue book of the curator. This epilogue presents a spectrum of positions, which demonstrate what is generally interesting and relevant in the example of the convergence of Las Vegas and art.

Is Las Vegas, capital of the western entertainment industry, also set to become the capital of art? At this historic moment, art is losing the visionary power to which it used to lay claim; art in general is drawing closer to the forms of the entertainment industry (from lifestyle to game shows) – and even in this respect its efforts are lagging behind. So, in a paradoxical turn of events, Las Vegas is also becoming the capital of the future cultural industry. The construction of the museums 'Guggenheim Las Vegas' and 'Hermitage Guggenheim' by Rem Koolhaas can be seen as the latest radical phase in this development: the inclusion of art in the entertainment complex, meaning that art is obviously ready for integration into the entertainment industry.

'The Magic Hour' exhibition shows the entertainment metropolis of Las Vegas in the American state of Nevada as a phenomenon existing between reality and fiction and how this has influenced art. It is the first museum exhibition to adopt this theme and to attempt an analysis of the fundamental aspects contributing to the unique nature of the place. It is no coincidence that a large number of artists today live in or are visitors to Las Vegas. Since the publication of 'Learning from Las Vegas' (Venturi/Scott Brown/Izenour) in 1972, much has changed, both within the art world and more generally in terms of life in society. Entertainment appears to have become a fetish, a matrix for all forms of life. This exhibition aims to uncover what we have now learnt from Las Vegas and what kind of effect this could have had on society. The area between art and pure entertainment, on whatever level, is so fluid that it is difficult to locate. So the exhibition is to be both part of a casino and a museum. No different from the real Las Vegas. Venice has been partially reconstructed there, in the same dimensions using the same materials, and serves as a hotel. The Bellagio resort and casino housed an art collection that included paintings from El Greco to Picasso, promoted in the same way as Frank Sinatra or the Beach Boys.

The two sides of the discussion are given on the one hand with Venturi, Scott Brown and Izenour's book 'Learning from Las Vegas' and on the other hand by Dave Hickey's teaching at the University of Nevada in Las Vegas.

In terms of theory, 'Learning from Las Vegas' served as an interface between modernism and post-modernism. When the theoretician and all-rounder Dave Hickey and the art historian Libby Lumpkin moved to Las Vegas at the beginning of the 1990s, a new level of interest within the perception of the 'Vegas phenomenology' developed. For Hickey, the Strip served as a platform for his critique of the elitist and purist structure of values within the art world.

Apart from this, Hickey brought leading artists such as David Reed, Jim Isermann, Jim Shaw or Jeffrey Vallance to Las Vegas and his teaching drew many young artists to this city. Libby Lumpkin was working for casino visionary Steve Wynn as curator in the museum-style gallery of the Bellagio casino hotel from 1997-99.

'The Magic Hour' will of course cover all areas (fine art, design, architecture and show business). The project's curator, Alex Farquharson, a young and committed London-based theoretician, has been studying the situation for a long time now.

An entertainment complex spreads globally on all levels of society, including culture as a whole. The 'society of spectacle' (Guy Debord, 1967) has become a reality. The masses, politics and the spectacle form an alliance. Even cultural institutions in marginal places like Graz are disfigured by this powerful alliance. The Las Vegas phenomenon demonstrates the convergence of the entertainment complex and the culture industry. If, in the course of globalisation, the convergence dominates world-wide, the example of Las Vegas can be used to elucidate the future of art in the global entertainment complex. Las Vegas serves as a magnifying glass, making the future practices and problems of art imaginable on a microscopic level.

In the age of global amusement, the Neue Galerie gets to the bottom of things and starts from the roots upwards – 'The Entertainment Capital' – Las Vegas, Nevada.

Las Vegas at the Magic Hour

☞

(Some Representations)

by Alex Farquharson

In January last year I was talking to one of the managers at Young Electric Sign Company's Las Vegas plant, with the view to borrowing a thing or two for this exhibition in Graz, and mentioned in passing that I liked Vegas's neons best soon after they're first switched on as the sun starts to set. "O yeah", he by-the-way'd, "we call that 'the magic hour'." It stuck.

Sunset is the only part of the day in Las Vegas when you are at all aware of time: by day the Strip's towers look almost bleached against a brilliant, evenly blue sky; at night the sky does little more than provide a flat black ground for the rolling calligraphic play of its unrivalled lights. To begin with, the gargantuan polychromatic pop sculptures that line the Strip do little more than shimmer against the still overwhelming desert daylight. Slowly, in time, the colours and forms of their supporting structures start to fade and the neons become more insistent, increasing in intensity until their colours flow like molten lava or pulse like chords. At some point in the magic hour object and image attain a fragile state of equivalence, before pivoting towards flat, animated luminosity and all out night. For around a magic hour Las Vegas takes on a cinematic feel, as if embroiled in the drama of consequential story-lines – as if anything might happen.

Appropriately, cinematographers, as well as neon artists, use the phrase 'the magic hour' (Terrence Malick filmed 'Days of Hope' entirely during this most fugitive time of day). Inside the new Forum, a faux Roman street of shops and restaurants in Caesars Palace, the painted ceilings simulate the turn of sunset every ten minutes. This effect seems to transform its tourist pedestrians into characters out of a Tiepolo celestial allegory. If ever one needed an allegory for the triumph of art, or artifice, over nature, the Strip on its way to the magic hour would be it.

And allegories, myths and legends cling hard to Las Vegas, often taking the form of arrivals, endings, epiphanies, apotheoses, calamities or apocalypses. Sometimes, as in movies like 'Leaving Las Vegas', or the photographs of Jack Pierson and the collages of Alexis Smith, or the careers of Sinatra, Elvis and Liberace, the city acts as the point at which the promises of the American Dream come home to roost, spectacularly or anticlimactically. Sometimes this narrative, already a little teleological, gets blown up to supernatural or biblical dimensions, as Sin City (America's Babylon, Babel, Sodom and Gomorrah) gets its divine comeuppance. In Jeffrey Vallance's 'Vegas Apocalypse' drawings the iconography of the Strip's resorts are transfigured into signs of the Second Coming – showgirls are beasts, rollercoasters serpents, porte cochères mouths of hell. Tim Burton's retro aliens in 'Mars Attacks!' choose the upper section of the Strip to launch their invasion of Planet Earth, their lasers rhyming nicely with the majestic lights of the Stardust pylon. On first encountering the Strip, you could be forgiven for imagining you saw the spectre of E. Chen's bogus billion dollar resort, 'Titanica', sailing through the desert sky, striking the tip of the Stratosphere – the tallest structure west of the Mississippi – before falling, broken, onto the next available lot just down from Mandalay Bay.

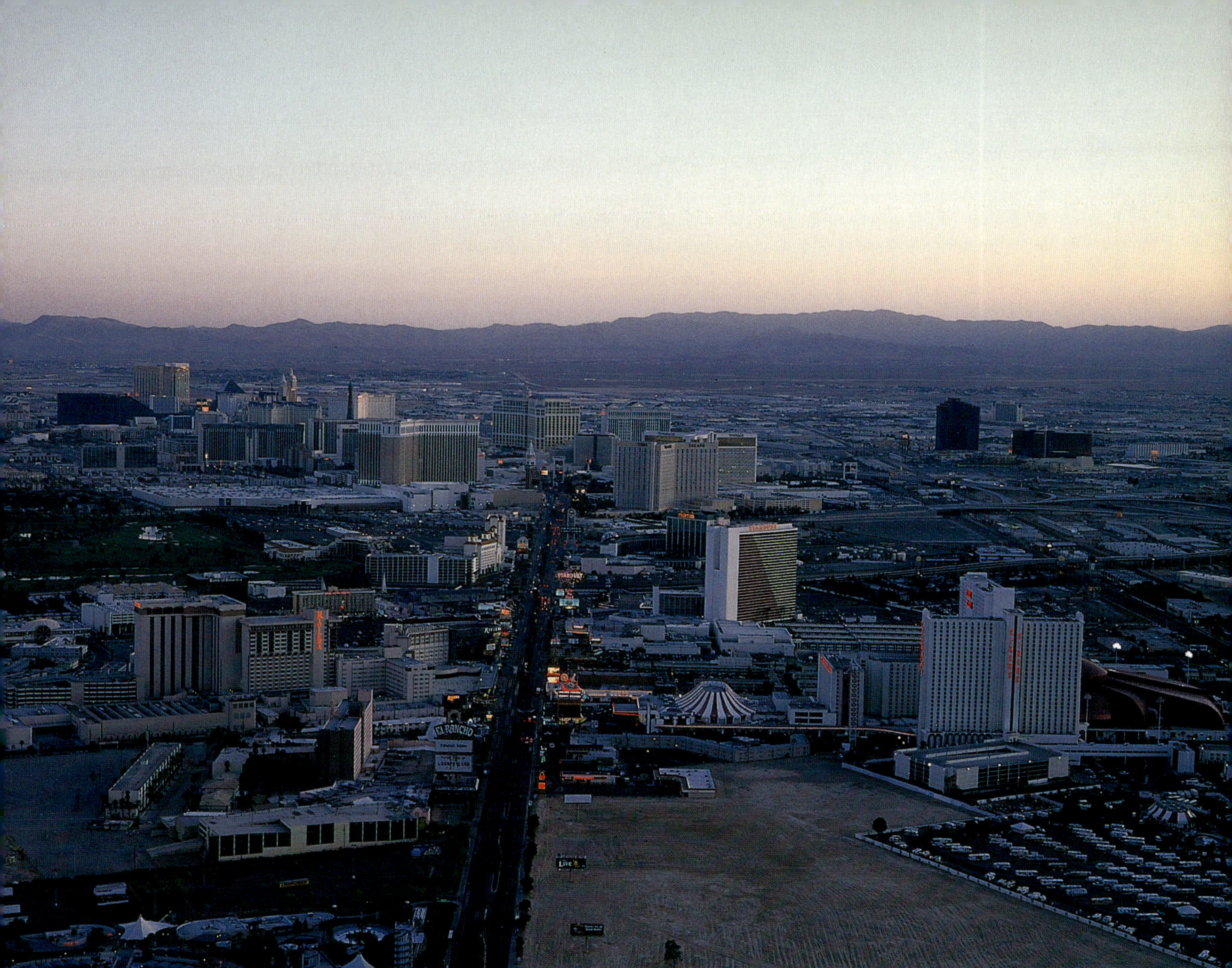

BRIDGET SMITH
STRATOSPHERE II 1999
C-PRINT MOUNTED ON ALUMINIUM 150 x 193 CM
COURTESY OF FRITH STREET GALLERY, LONDON

Hellfire is evoked by the opening credits of Martin Scorsese's 'Casino', which show Robert de Niro tumbling through a collage of the pink and coral neon feathers of The Flamingo's porte cochère and the leaping flames that erupt from the car bomb we presume has sent him to his afterlife. At the end of the movie, the journey to the underworld becomes collective: as the Joe Pesci gangster character mourns the corporate take-over of Mob city we see a crowd of mesmerised senior citizens in tracksuits ascending an escalator, under spectral light, seemingly being devoured whole by the casino floor of one of today's mega-resorts.

But as often, and sometimes simultaneously, Las Vegas is represented as a kind of bittersweet Baudelairian artificial paradise: Paradise, after all, runs parallel to the Strip. Jack Pierson's biggest neon word piece, over forty feet in length, spells out 'Paradise' in giant letters derived from a variety of dismantled casino signs and facades. Usually these artists' and movie directors' treatments of Las Vegan epiphanies and catastrophes have an air of travesty that is in keeping with the comedy of the Strip itself – where else would you find a life-size British galleon sinking on the hour, a volcano blowing its top every fifteen minutes, and street parties marking the implosion of another vintage resort? Besides the age-old association of Las Vegas with sinning and carnal appetites, there is something profane about the Strip's audacious burlesques of various civilisations' greatest hits – today's Strip, not content with at least seven wonders of the world, seems to be sending up the very notion that it could all end tomorrow. (Is this post-Cold War triumphalism? The first of the Strip's new resorts, The Mirage, coincided with the collapse of the Soviet block. Mandalay Bay has its own Red Square-themed restaurant with a giant, faux-bronze, decapitated Lenin on guard).

Add to this 'end of history' routine Las Vegas's tendency to better Nature (or 'Creation') by putting giant lakes, lawns, fountains, rainforests, shark reefs and sprinklered suburbs where there was once just scrubby desert. Nothing in Las Vegas personifies Promethean hubris better than Siegfried & Roy, its resident eco-sorcerer superstars: while white tigers are extinct in the wild, several dozen thrive in the magicians' ownership. The highlight of their nightly show at The Mirage is the part where they make their ghost-white tigers vanish and then re-appear, as if scorning abject nature.

Art, like nature, despite their age-old antagonisms, has a tendency to stand for truth, beauty and eternity, but big art's recent arrival on the Strip – in the form of Steve Wynn's Gallery of Fine Art at the Bellagio and the Guggenheim at the Venetian – has played havoc with these denotations. Where else would people wonder whether paintings on display are real, to the extent that this becomes part of the draw? In a city of 'authentic replicas' (official terminology in Las Vegas) – Luxor's tomb of 'King Tut' as Howard Carter found it, or Caesars' 'David' in Carrara marble like Michelangelo's own – where the notion of originals is a red herring, it is perhaps forgivable that the ontological status of diminutive miracles by Picasso, Rubens and Monet was ever held in doubt. (Steve Wynn, as ever, had the last laugh when it was revealed that he'd been the international art market's highest high roller in the late 1990s.) Las Vegas's genuine paintings and tigers don't undermine today's resorts: just as the white cube, with the discursive authority it symbolises, can transform any ordinary object within its walls into art, so art in a Las Vegas casino takes on the purposes and associations – the rare and glamorous incarnation of untold wealth – of the Strip's other competing attractions. Casino bosses grasp this more easily than the disorientated art historian. 'Now appearing: van Gogh. Monet. Cézanne. Picasso' declared the Bellagio's pylon where one would normally expect the names of a lavish magic act or showgirl revue.

Oddly, the monumental pastiches that line today's Strip have had the effect of shunting the neon casinos of yore up the old true/false metaphysical scheme. In their self-evident artifice, the Strip's vintage, candy-coloured, neon-festooned casinos "shine with a crisp, pop authority" (to quote Dave Hickey on Liberace's glittering cars and costumes in 'Air Guitar') that's quintessentially, indigenously Las Vegas, despite the far-away places they often pointed to. Neon, no longer the principle weapon in the survival of the fittest, is now a preservation issue, and the old Las Vegas Strip's unique, towering concoctions of luminosity, colour, movement, text, image and pattern are now appreciated in academic circles for their imaginative and formal daring. The "decorated sheds" of 'Learning from Las Vegas', although still underrated by culture at large (why aren't the renderings in the Met or Lacma?), have entered the history books.

Of course history is as much an oxymoron in Las Vegas as art and nature, since its entire raison d'être is the immediate future: the next shuffle of the deck, the next roll of dice, the next positioning of the ball. When the old

Las Vegas disappears altogether it will probably re-appear from the future as a Vegas-themed resort in Las Vegas in the manner of the New York, Paris and Venetian ones already there (the replica 1950s Las Vegan decor of the Hard Rock resort's A.J.'s Steakhouse is a sign that this process is underway).

Like Vegas's neon, much of the art made in or about Las Vegas in the last ten years has existed in a kind of twilight zone between resort and museum culture – artists have few exhibiting opportunities either in Las Vegas. Jeffrey Vallance's response to the absence of dedicated art spaces in Las Vegas was to invite other Vegas artists to custom-make art to the dictates of museums devoted, respectively, to Liberace, Debbie Reynolds, magic, cranberry juice and clowning. Vallance's museum shows popularise – and paranormalise – the somewhat tired, moralistic notion of the site-specific. Dave Hickey, under whose aegis at UNLV the art scene in Vegas emerged, reversed the terms of the site-specific altogether by adapting sites to art, instead of art to sites, using colour and 'skateboard technology' to invert the obligatory straight white walls in his series of 'Ultralounge' exhibitions in Las Vegas, Housten and Florida. These curating strategies reflect the sympathies of Vegas artists, for whom the permission and extravagance of the Strip holds no threat: a luminous, abstract, shaped painting by Yek, for example (part neon sunset, part potent cocktail), or the ecstatic sermons and expositional aids of the divine Reverend Ethan Acres, are some way off average Kunsthalle fare. For all the postmodern art world's supposed pluralism and license, Las Vegas illuminates the particular prejudices that habitually determine the presentation and reception of art today. Nowhere is this more evident than in the stark contrast between the cool white boxes we use to show art and Las Vegas's opulent, eye-popping casinos.

This exhibition attempts to operate on three levels: firstly, as a multi-faceted portrait of a city and its mythologies through the eyes of artists; secondly, as a selective survey of 1990s art engaged with Las Vegas, either by Las Vegans or by visiting artist-admirers; and thirdly, as a fictional space for these first two endeavours somewhere between the visual, social and conceptual realm of the 'white cube' gallery and the Las Vegas casino – a space, that might, in an abstract manner, evoke something of the Strip at that metamorphic magic hour of promise and permission.

"An Anomaly in the Desert"

☞

Joel Bergman in conversation.

***Alex Farquharson:** You talk of architecture in Las Vegas as though it were a gradual evolution, but from the outside it appears to have changed a lot in the last ten years with the injection of big corporate money. Whole buildings are now engulfed by themes.*

Joel Bergman: There were themes in the beginning. Something called the El Rancho [1941], which is long gone, and the Last Frontier [1942]. These were both Western-themed. It was topical. It was very appropriate for Las Vegas at that time, having gotten started because it was a crossroads for the Mormon Trail into California and the Southern Trail. So there had been gambling and prostitution in this general area and it was mostly clustered Downtown.

Then Eastern money came out here and created these tiny little mini-resorts. They didn't have very many rooms and the casino wasn't very big. But I can remember as a kid being brought here. I was probably nine or ten years old, so we're going back 53 or 54 years. My parents brought me here and we stayed in a little motel out in the middle of nowhere, halfway between what's now the Sahara and Fremont Street [Downtown]. I remember being taken to breakfast at the El Rancho because they had this marvellous buffet, which was probably all of 79 cents or something. And my father won five dollars at the craps table to pay for breakfast. That was my first impression of Las Vegas.

Then what happened was a character named Billy Wilkerson decided he wanted to do a very posh resort and he started something called the Flamingo [1946], which Benjamin 'Bugsy' Siegel bought and took over. (I think the movie 'Bugsy' is pretty accurate as to how the thing developed). And that sat there for a while and a few smaller hotels got going. These were true resorts in the sense that you came here, usually by car from Los Angeles, and you stayed there for two, three or four days. They had really fabulous entertainment and wonderful rooms and great food, but the real intent was to gamble. They had a marvellous pool in those days. All the hotels had high-dives, so the show-offs could really show-off. Anything you would have seen or heard about those days is pretty much accurate or wonderful myth – I kinda enjoy the myths to tell you the truth.

Then in 1966 the mega-resort was created. As much as 'Bugsy' Siegel gave us presence and had tremendous vision, the next man to come along that had an order of magnitude as a visionary was a man named Jay Sarno. When he created Caesars Palace he was playing to the decadence of the potential gambler, and like the Flamingo, he was creating a real resort. As fabulous as the Flamingo might have been in its time – and I can remember staying there early on – Caesars was ten times better. They had gorgeous girls who wore these false head-dresses. They looked just marvellous in their little skimpy costumes – every bit as good as anything Hugh Heffner ever did for Playboy. It was the place for every high-roller all around – not just from the USA, but the whole world. And he had a made audience, because anybody who wanted the best came to Caesars.

By the late 1960s other hotels had started to develop: Thunderbird; Sands; the Sahara had grown from a little motel to a real gambling hotel; the Hacienda; the Flamingo had grown; the Stardust had been built (I did re-models to the Stardust and Flamingo). Most of the hotels did a special buffet on Sundays. Caesars did it in the showroom,

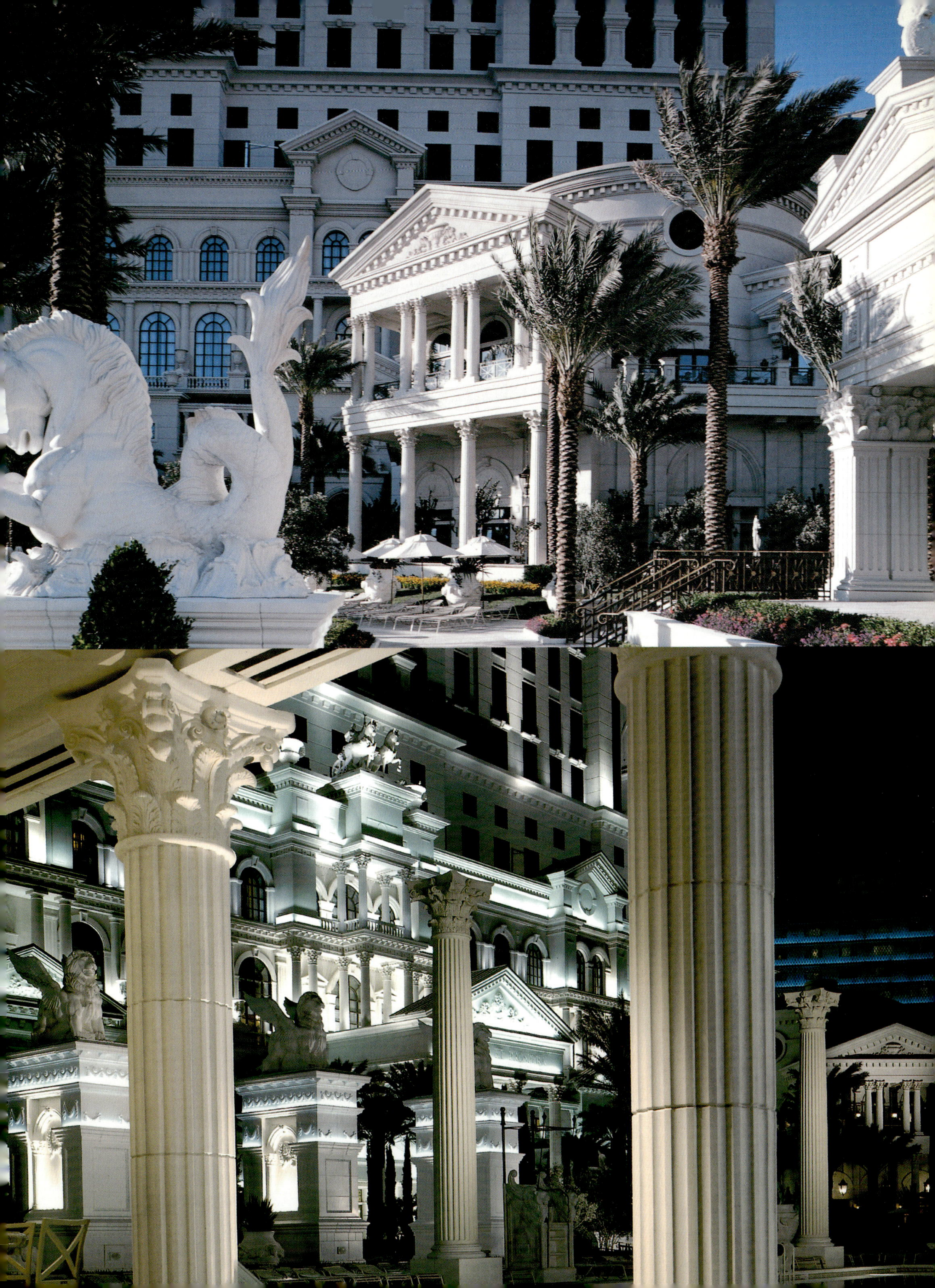

which was a fabulous experience to get your food and sit in these sumptuous, overly ostentatious booths. (There's a myth that currently we are introducing light into the casinos for the first time. Well, the truth of the matter is almost all the casinos, the exception being Caesars, had light. They all opened on to the swimming pool via glass doors. Some even had full-length windows. It's nothing new what we're doing now. It's kind of been re-discovered). So these other hotels that existed were all pretty much of the same genre. They catered strictly for gamblers. They tried to provide the best food at a reasonable price. Some of them had drop-dead suites. Because most of the early buildings in these joints were low-rise, it was easy to create bungalows, like the way old movie backlots used to have bungalows, only ours were likely to be 5,000 to 12,000 square feet. It was just a more relaxed atmosphere and totally dedicated to gambling and entertainment – the era of Frank Sinatra, and that whole group of entertainers, most of whom are gone now.

In the late 60s, a man named Kirk Kerkorian came to town, and if Caesars had been a mega-resort, he paled it in size. With the International [1969], he created the world's largest. That was when I went to work for the architect Martin Stern, so I was a junior detail designer on that – the real designers are in that office behind you. The International set a new standard because it was off the Strip. It was a self-contained environment, and it was positioned next to a small convention hall. It also had a large amount of meeting and exhibition space by the standards in 1969, which, by the way, have increased six or seven fold under Hilton's leadership – it's now the headquarters for many conventions.

Then Kerkorian bought a little place called the Bonanza, which, by the way, had a twenty or twenty-four storey log high-rise. I was the project architect. We tore down what was there, moved one building, and created the next mega-resort, even bigger than the International Hilton. This was the MGM Grand hotel [1973]. After that, building kind of petered out. It had played its role.

In 1973 or 74, a young man called Steve Wynn arrived, who I rank as the third great visionary in this town. (Although Kerkorian was a bit of a visionary, he was kind of like Howard Hughes. He was a recluse and he was a sound businessman. He was a little more prudent in his investments). Steve was brash and had balls the size of an elephant. He once told me, "sure, I'm scared, but I'm scared running straight ahead". And he took risks. Steve had something Jay had, which was the ability to understand what would attract people. Not many people have that. It was kind of, 'build it and they will come.'

He took an old joint Downtown called the Golden Nugget and he added some rooms, and as time went on he completely changed the facade. He eliminated all the neon. Vegas was known for neon. How the hell could anyone presume to take away the glitz? What he did was he added sophistication. He knew that the gamblers that went Downtown to his Golden Nugget liked the sophistication, even to the extent that many of the players who went to places like Caesars liked going Downtown, because they liked the suites, they liked the feeling in there, the homeliness, the cosiness. I went to work directly for Steve Wynn in 1978 and created a project in Atlantic City for him and later came back to do additions to the Golden Nugget. But Steve had a vision about what could be on the Strip.

Now themes, as I said, existed from the get-go. Some places had less of a theme than others – Sands had no strong theme, the Thunderbird had no strong theme other than it had a neon ceiling for a period. But Steve said, "Let's create an anomaly in the desert. People don't come out here for the desert. They come to the desert for what we do differently." And so, in 1989, we created The Mirage, with six acres of water right on the Strip. We created a

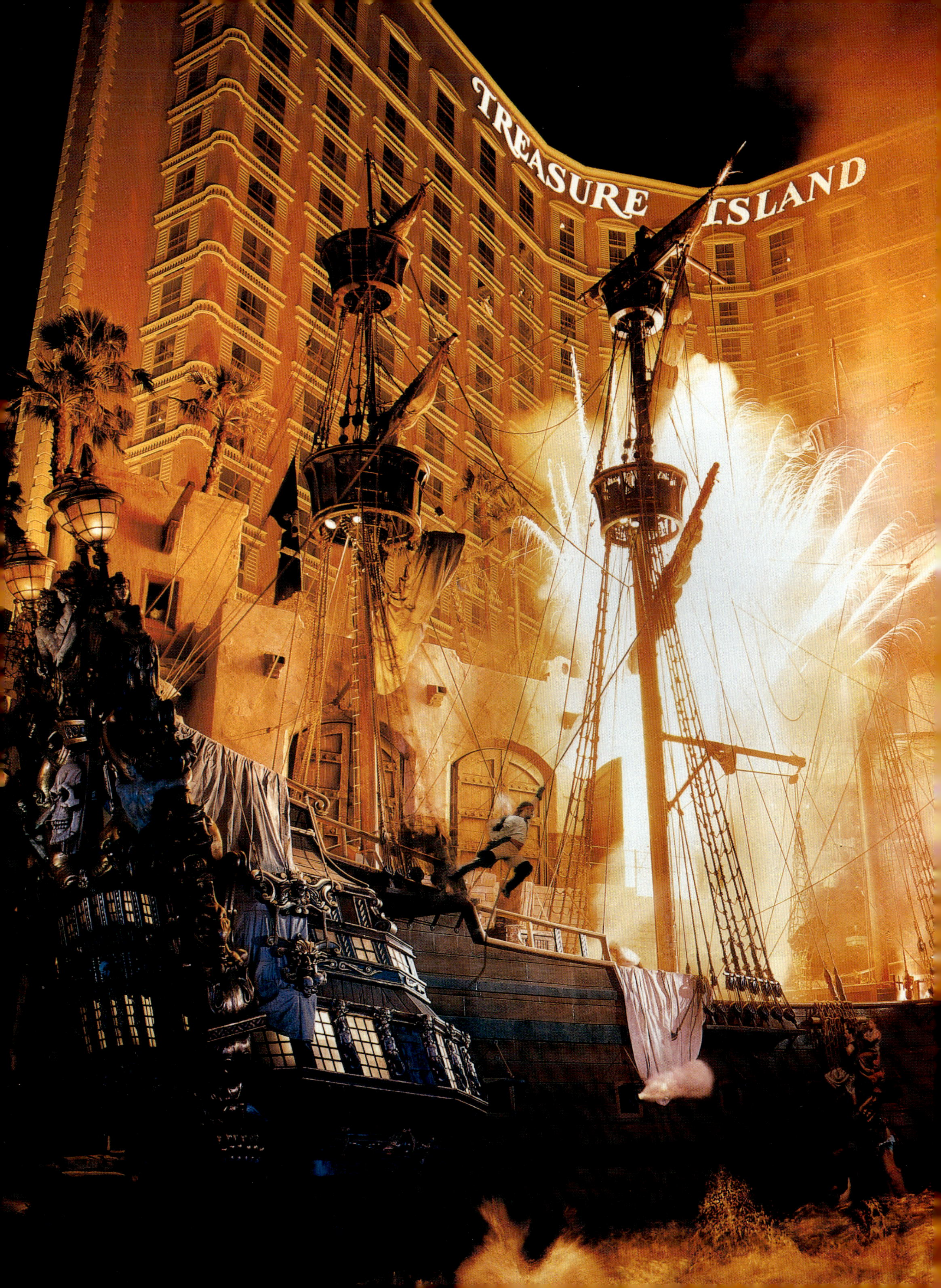
TREASURE ISLAND

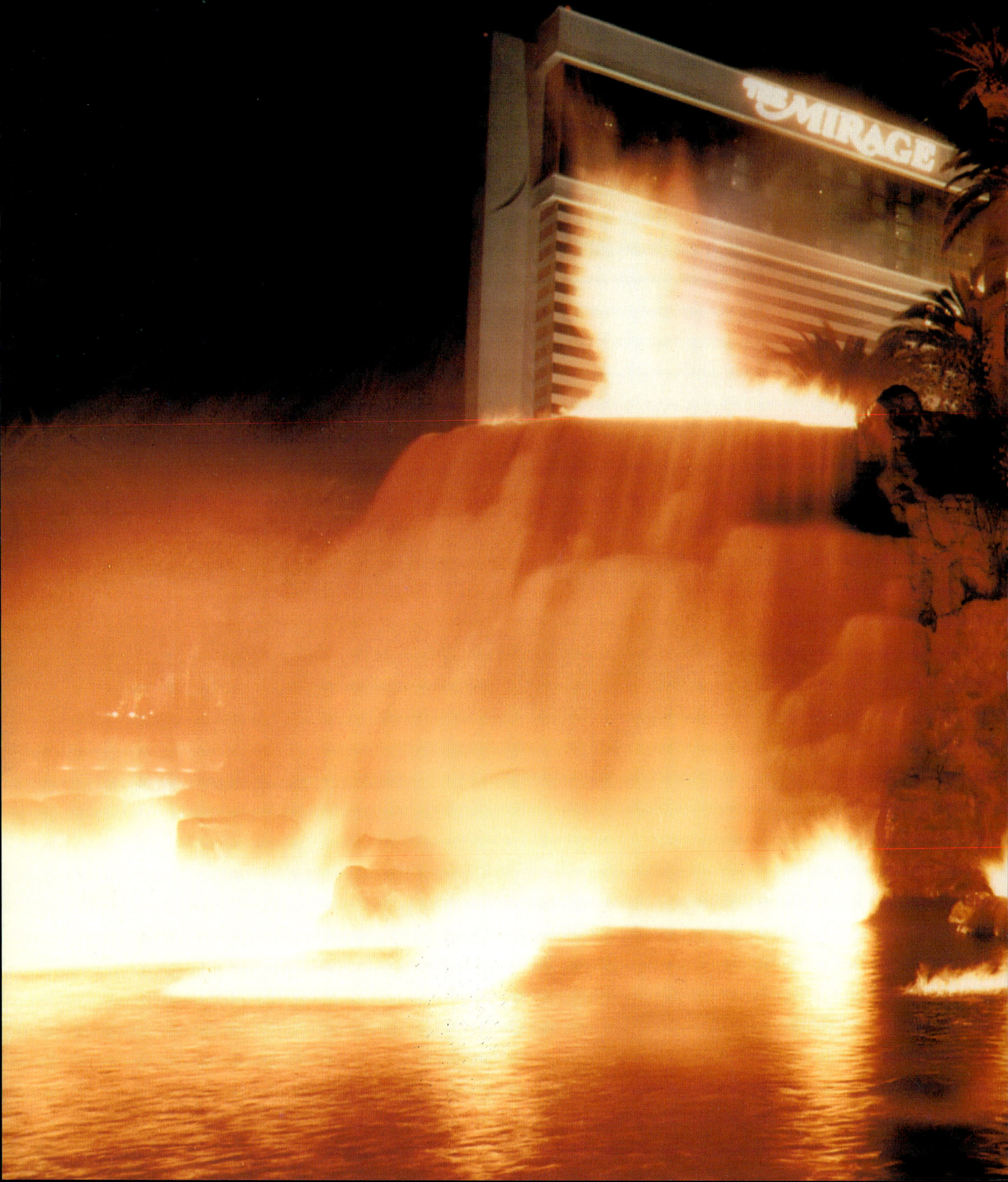
MIRAGE

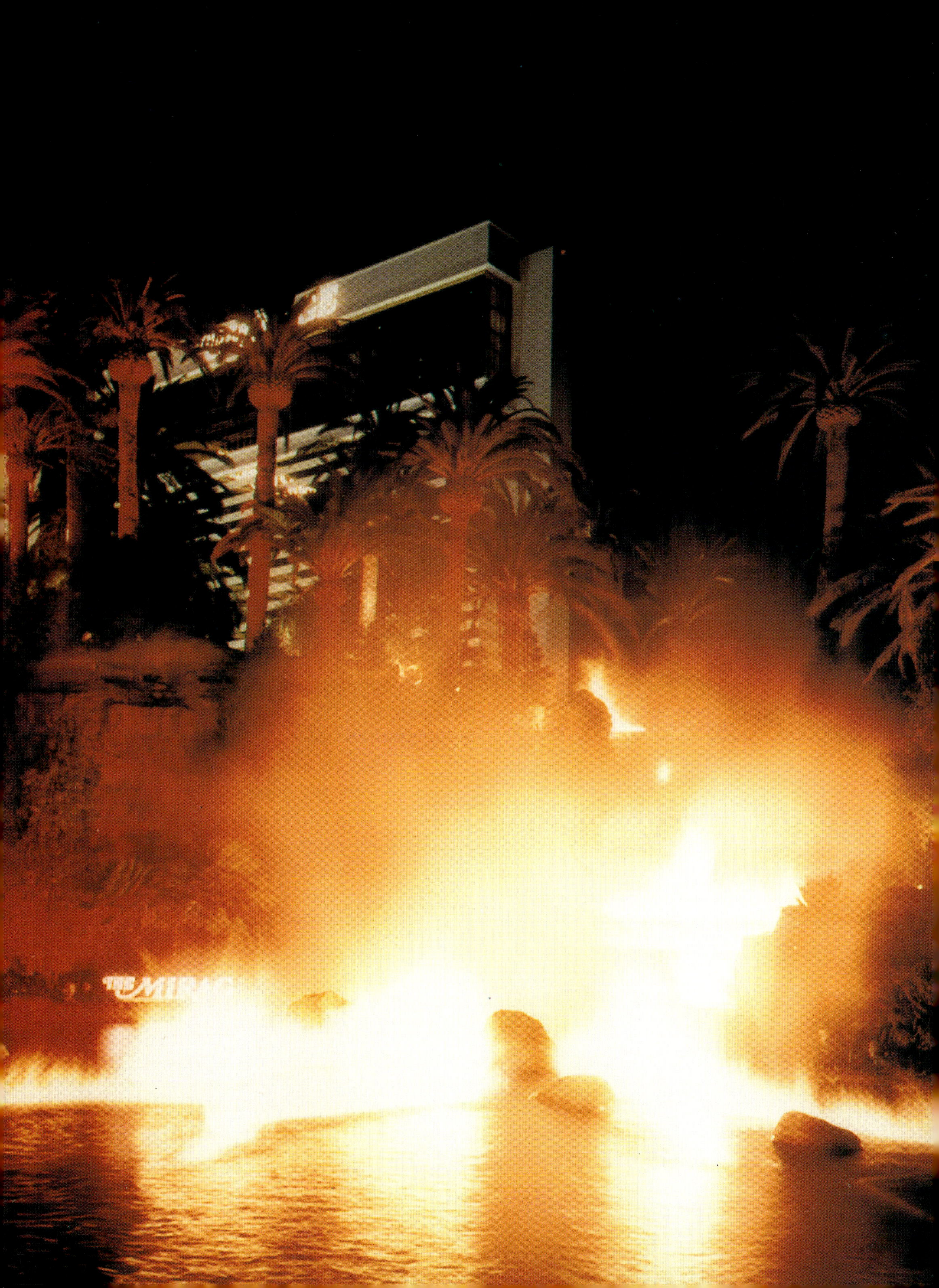

volcano. Every twenty minutes, when the volcano went off, traffic stopped. I guess we had 2,500 to 3,000 people watching it go off at any one time.

Most of the tropical plants you see in The Mirage are real. Everything you see on the outside is real; some of the stuff you see on the inside is fossilised. No matter what you brought into the desert, it wouldn't survive the trip. You get the climate you create.

And Steve brought light back into the casino with that huge atrium. He created a pool area that would hold 1,500 people and yet it wouldn't look like more than a few hundred people at any given point. He introduced the idea of cabanas at the pool. People loved them, the high-rollers loved them, and it turned out to be another profit centre – cabanas rent for as much as the guest rooms for a day. And he did service; he created a fun place. It's a huge casino that doesn't look huge.

Next we created Treasure Island. Instead of a place we decided to do a story. A friend of Steve Wynn's came up with Treasure Island, but we explored all kinds of hair-brained schemes before we got to that. And Treasure Island was perfect. Steve said, "let's have a pirate battle – we're gonna have a body of water here". And then he decided he wanted to sink a ship. That show was consistently drawing 2,500 to 3,000 people without a bat of an eye and it went on every hour and a half, starting around dusk, because the best part of the show is the flames and the smoke and all of that which shows off best at night. And since October of '93 when we opened that place, every hour and a half in the evening, that ship sinks. And it was very successful. Again, it has a sense that the other joints haven't managed to pick up on – and that's cosiness. People like being there; they like being part of the story. Some of the things are kinda silly: the women's shop in there is called 'A Damsel in dis Dress'. Hey, you put your tongue in your cheek and you have a good time with those things! But it was well done. There are many other places like Circus that are two-dimensional. The stuff we created was in three dimensions. They really had a fourth because they had that feeling; that something that you can't touch but you can feel. They're fun to be at.

An example of someone not getting with the programme is Luxor. At the time that we heard they were doing a pyramid we were researching Treasure Island, and we ran into the Circus people at a convention in Florida or someplace. I was with Steve and a couple of other guys from the company and they started to tell us about a new project they had which was a pyramid. Steve and I looked at each other and said "God, I wish to hell we'd thought of that!" It was such a fetching idea and it ended up a piece of shit – a horrible black box that hasn't been improved by all the additions they've done to it; a miserable volume of space that lacks any sense of charm or grace or cosiness. Horrible. I think Circus somewhat learned their lesson because the next joint they created was Mandalay Bay, which has a lot better feeling and their business has grown. It's probably one of the few places outside of the Rio where I'd go to for lunch or dinner.

An interesting phenomenon took place during this period of the 90s. The local casinos had started as these small little grind-joints to service the people in the neighbourhood around the perimeter of Vegas. As the population of this town has grown – and it has grown tremendously throughout the 90s, adding five or six hundred thousand people to our population – their audience grew. The locals used to go Downtown for their entertainment and gambling, but then began to go to these other places in large masses to the point where Downtown suffered. (Hence they created this monstrosity called The Fremont Street Experience to attract people away from the Strip. A lot of the locals go down there to see the show, which is hokey, it's yesterday's technology and it's an ugly structure. I might also add that there's a little bit of sour grapes because I had this scheme for four blocks of canals

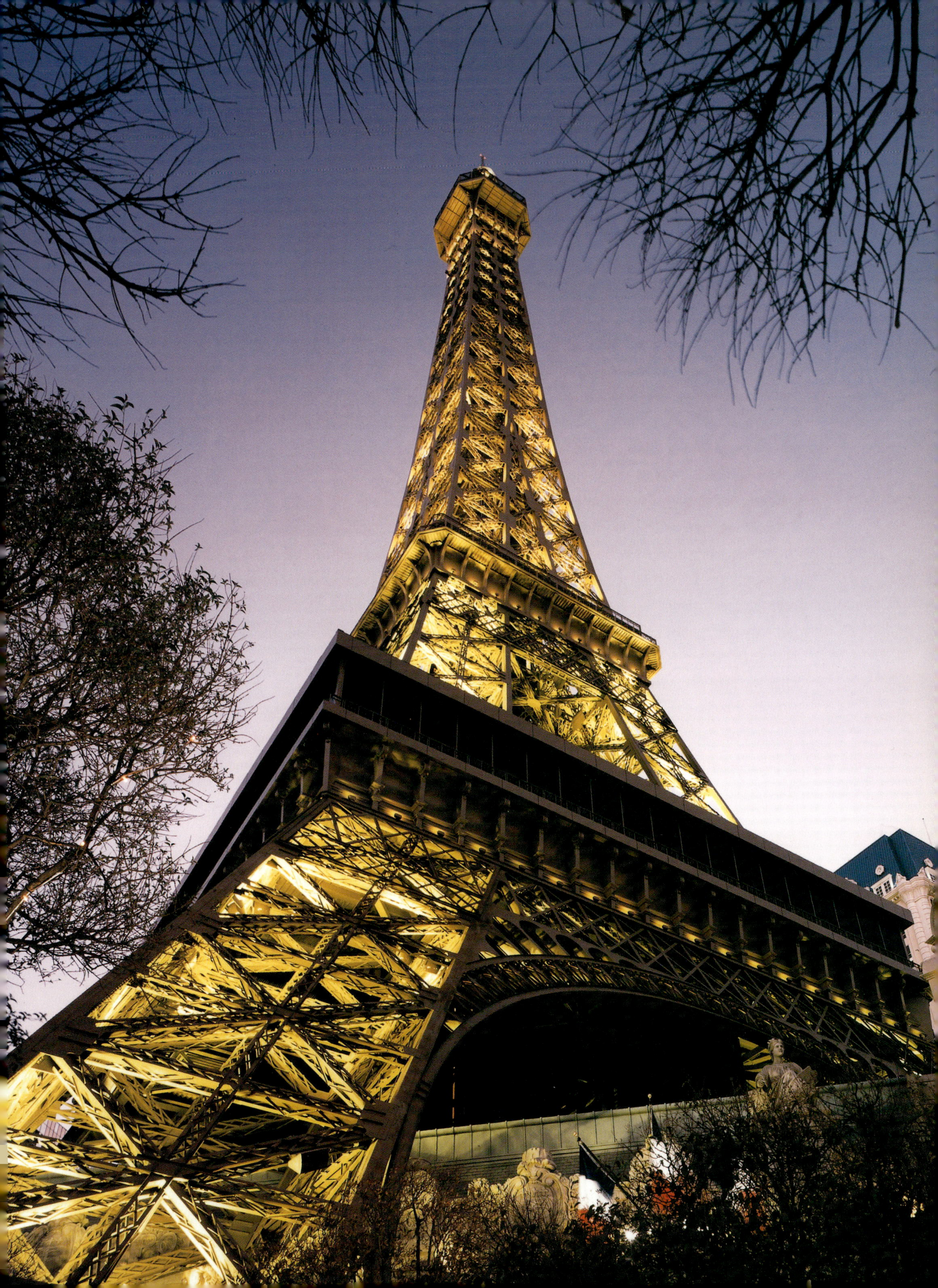

with boats and planting through Downtown). In any case, these local places began to grow by leaps and bounds. I don't remember when the legislation was passed, but we had an ordinance in Clark County that says if you want to have a casino with tables and anything over fifteen slots you have to have three hundred guest rooms. So these local places were all added to the population of casinos and had three hundred, sometimes four or five hundred guest rooms, so they could qualify to have casinos. The guest rooms were tertiary, they weren't even secondary. And lo and behold we found out that people were staying there. People like me who have guests from out of town. I put people up in the local joints. I don't send them to the Strip. Why? because it's convenient for me to get to the Orleans or the Palace Station so I don't have to go on the Strip to pick them up. Plus they developed their own market. They offer usually less expensive rooms, the food is generally good. The Rio is probably the best example – it has the best food in Las Vegas across the board. They also treat their customers very well. So these places became cross-over: mostly local, but they were getting a lot of tourist business as well. Again, the most successful of that genre is the Rio, with its outlandish kidney-bean shaped tower with purple and red and blue neon. If you stand back and look at it, it's terrific. It's part of the complexion of Vegas. Most of the local joints, though, have some kind of a South-Westernised theme.

Most recently we started directly with cities, such as Paris, which was a project we did here. I think it has probably been the most successful of all. The client on Paris started out to be Ballys, which was bought by the Hilton and has subsequently changed its name to Park Place Entertainment, and will probably change its name again to incorporate the Caesars name because they have recently acquired Caesars. They are the world's largest. They have the Caesars brand, the Flamingo brand, the Hilton gaming brand, they have Ballys, they have Park Place. In fact they own a hotel now which I originally designed as the Golden Nugget in Atlantic City. It's now called the Atlantic City Hilton. It's an incestuous community.

After Paris [1999] came the Venetian. It probably opened too soon. It was on the site where the Sands had been and it is a convention hotel. It was very poor planning. It's not a terribly appealing building outside of the little forecourt which is based on St. Marks Square in Venice. In any case this current genre continues. We have on our boards a project called The City by the Bay, which is a San Francisco-based theme, and there are a couple of other projects also based on places or cities.

Alex Farquharson: *Where did this concept of compact versions of famous cities come from?*

Joel Bergman: I had just formed my own company. I had retired from The Mirage in late '93 and we were hired by Caesars to create some additional space for them – the tallest of their high-rises that has a real Roman flavour. We have plans to re-clad all the others.

Alex Farquharson: *Oh, I rather like the mix of styles and the honeycomb skin.*

Joel Bergman: That old stuff is horrible. We call it Sarno-block. It was just an off-the-shelf concrete block that Jay [Sarno] liked and you hear all this bullshit about how it was created for him. It wasn't. The problem is the stuff is very dated. It's arabesque, not Roman, and we've been trying to truly Romanise Caesars. Aside from the girls in Roman costumes, and Cleopatra walking around the casino, it wasn't really Roman until we did all this

stuff. Ultimately, what we've done here on the Strip is we've turned gambling into an entertainment; we've turned food into an entertainment. Along the way we've become a shopping Mecca and that's entertainment. When you go to the Forum at Caesars, for example, it's showtime. Every half hour or hour you can watch Bacchus do a little schtick, and then you can go down and watch some Amazons or Atlantisians at Atlantis. And of course in the centre they have this marvellous horse sculpture, but I forget what in the world that's based on.
And we've turned our buildings into entertainment. When Vegas first got started people would drive here, usually from Southern California, park their car and stay at the hotel. Well, now they fly in – 32 million people this year will come here, and most of them come by air. They have a limited amount of money to spend, whatever that is, and they want to give it to us – they just want to do it their way. But prices have gone up: the rooms cost more, the gambling is faster – the slot machines are no longer just nickels, and if you're really risky, a quarter. You can play a $500 or $1000 slot machine in some places. So people have more time for their time increment to stay here. The average stay is now about four days. So they walk. Very few of the little junk shops that used to line the Strip between the hotels are left. People can start walking from the Fashion Show mall, and except for a short stretch on the west side of the street, they are almost always in front of an event. So the buildings become entertainment and that's where we are today. I'm rather proud of the Paris building. If you're at all familiar with Paris – I have to assume you've been there at least once in your young life.

***Alex Farquharson:** I know the old one better than the new one.*

Joel Bergman: I do too. I don't speak French, but I've spent many, many days there over the course of the last thirty years. What we were trying to capture – as well as the icons – is the flavour and the feeling of Paris, and I think we've done a pretty good job. Certainly it meets and exceeds the expectations of the average person who comes here, who outside of a movie or a National Geographic on T.V., only have an image of Paris. They've never tasted it, if you will. And I think Paris Las Vegas does a pretty good job of that. I think that's where we're gonna go for the next four or five years. Maybe we will be the architects; maybe someone else will be the architect who gets an owner with balls bigger than an elephant who says, "We're gonna go off in this direction".

***Alex Farquharson**: It seems the reason you and your colleagues have been working here so long is that an architect has to absorb the whole psychology of Las Vegas in order to be successful here. You can't be a purist who puts their buildings up all over the U.S. irrespective. Being an architect of Vegas casinos seems to be a different discipline altogether.*

Joel Bergman: It is. There are people who go to architecture school who are as up to speed as you could possibly be on computers and current trends, they read every magazine and know the histories of all the great architects, but they are not architects. They're people who do architecture.
There's an emotional response that we get from people here. To some extent, we can control it. To a large extent, I pander to it. If I'm able to do something that makes them go 'wow!' and keep going 'wow!' all the way through, I'm successful. For whatever reason, I'm able to do that. And once in a while I try to figure it out, but most of the time I don't give a damn – it just happens. I never lose sight of what it is I'm trying to achieve and that is that

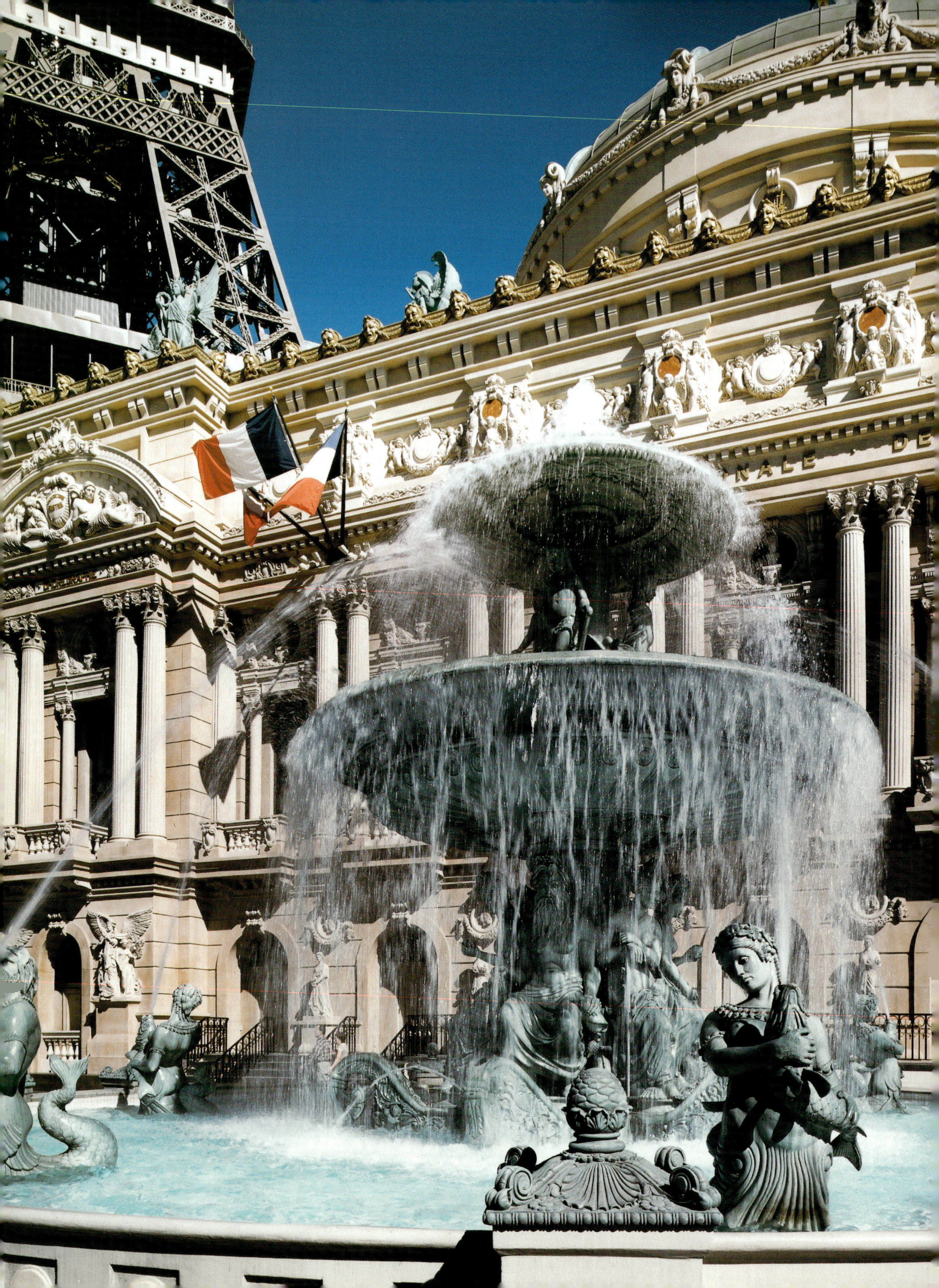

the people who use the building, whether they work there or are guests there, have a great experience. I've been very lucky. For 32 years I've been involved in this aspect of architecture. I haven't always been popular; I don't know whether I'm popular today to tell the truth.

I was embarrassed when I first started doing this sort of thing because the people who taught me in school and that I worked for early on, were all doing these very modern buildings 'with integrity'. If there was a structure, it was exposed. They weren't just forms and shapes and places and things because they looked good or felt good. So I didn't tell people. Then one day I discovered that they knew anyway and that they all wanted to do what I was doing! Meantime I'd been feeling sorry for myself: I'd been relegated to this and I really wanted to do what they were doing.

When I started work in Vegas, in 1968 under Martin Stern, I didn't even like what I designed. I was embarrassed by it. So, after about a year and a half I stopped being a designer. I was pretty good with dealing with contractors and clients and so I became a bullshit merchant: a project architect. I did that for eight years until I met Steve Wynn, and he said "I want you to design my buildings." I've got pretty good-sized balls too, and I didn't tell him I hadn't designed a real building in eight years, but hey, I just jumped in and did it and it took off from there. I've been lucky; I've had a lot of mentors in my life.

For ten years I was a church architect, and, by the way, more people pray in my casinos than ever prayed in my churches. We did that kind of very pure architecture where the structure was exposed, and, yes, when I think back on it, very naive, because I was as contrived then as I am now.

But this is a blast. I love it. I'm usually here by seven in the morning and most times I'm here at seven or later at night. Sometimes I take stuff home. I have a full office at home as well just in case I get an idea. It's just fun. And it's fun watching other people having fun. One of the things I do is I go back to my buildings. I look at the buildings and I see things I want to do differently. I go talk to people and they don't know who I am – you see the way I'm dressed today? This is me in my working outfit – at home I wear a tuxedo. I want to hear what people have to say about the place. I fly a lot, and when I'm coming back to Vegas I talk to people: "where are you going? where are you staying? what do you like there?" I want to hear what their expectations are. Sometimes, if I can get them in the right frame, I ask them why they like it. It all filters inside my little work brain and it comes out in the next project.

Photos by Peter Malinowski except The Mirage and Treasure Island (unknown photographer)

The Summit

the players –

Dave Hickey (DH)
Libby Lumpkin (LL)
Ralph Rugoff (RR)
Robert Venturi, Denise Scott Brown & Steven Izenour (VSBI)

questions dealt by Alex Farquharson (AF)

AF *Today's Strip seems to be the quintessential Post-modern environment, persuading its visitors that they are anywhere other than a desert town, whether that be Paris or Polynesia, Outer Space or Ancient Rome. Is Vegas a model of virtuality, or does it – or did it? – possess its own indigenous, authentic culture?*

RR Why would the Strip be seen as persuading visitors they are somewhere else other than a desert town, when Vegas isn't really a desert town to begin with, but a booming city – the last time I checked it was the fastest growing urban center in the U.S., with the lowest unemployment rate. Silicon Valley may be on the skids, but Vegas is still going strong.

Besides, the Strip's casino-resorts don't really try to convince us that we're somewhere else. Rather than constituting some kind of VR simulation experience, these environments brazenly parade their theatricality. Beyond the promise of hitting it big, they don't seduce visitors with escapist promises, so much as they appeal to our sense that in today's shrinking world, real escape is an impossibility for most of us, a notion that can only be parodied.

VSBI Popular resorts have always used symbols and images of more exotic and remote places than where you are, e.g. William Price's Byzantine fantasies in Atlantic City a hundred years ago or the Brighton Pavilion of more than 150 years ago. The 'authentic' culture of popular resorts is always an 'inauthentic' one.

LL I agree with VSBI that Las Vegas's popular resort design is authentic. Little wonder Las Vegas sent postmodern continental theorists blithering on about hyper-realities. They couldn't understand the absence of pretense.

NEON MUSEUM'S BONEYARD, PHOTO BY ALEX FARQUHARSON
BINION'S HORSESHOE, PHOTO BY ROLF RICKE

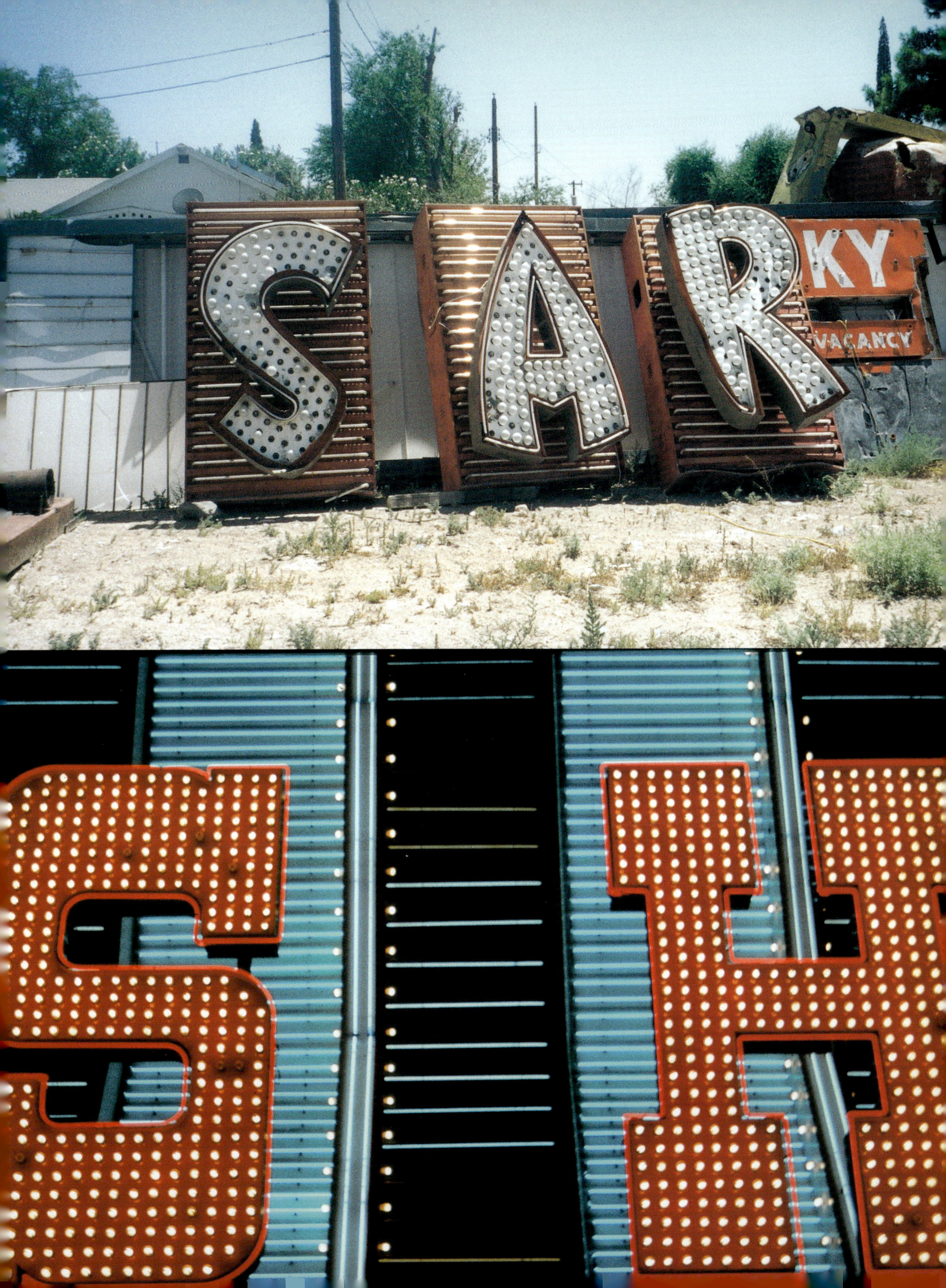
SAR
KY
VACANCY

DH Las Vegas is a gambling town, first, last and always. It is as tough, abstract, cosmopolitan, gregarious and optimistic as any other gambling town. It is also a 24-7 mercantile city in the middle of a desert in the middle of the American West – a town without a white Protestant upper-middle-class, whose manners and mores derive from its conglomeration of marginal cultures: Jews, Italians, Cubans, Armenians, Chinese, Portuguese and Mormons. As to its 'authenticity,' the word means nothing to me.

AF *Isn't it the relationship between the Strip and the desert that has made Vegas unique? (as against Atlantic City or Times Square, for example). How would you describe the desert / Strip dynamic?*

VSBI Yes and no. There is something magical to the image and symbol of the exotic oasis in the desert and mountain backdrop, both formally and symbolically, but Atlantic City has the ocean and Times Square has skyscrapers instead of mountains. The key is the scale jumps – big and little juxtaposition.

LL Yes, it is unique because of the extreme visual contrast between the organic and the artificial. The Las Vegas valley is vast, with the Strip occupying its lowest point. Consequently, from almost any direction you approach, the spectacle of lights stands out as something peculiarly foreign to its surroundings. The city makes no attempt to disguise its artificiality or to harmonize with the landscape, in the way, for example, classical architecture rhymes with the landscape and is made to appear to share a fundamental logic with nature in the paintings of Nicolas Poussin, or the way adobe structures seem to grow organically out of desert terrain in Santa Fe, New Mexico, and other desert habitats around the world. Consequently, the city of Las Vegas as an entity has easily lent itself as a visual trope to traditional allegories of the ethical distinction between nature and culture. In fact, I think the contrast of the city with its surroundings, as much as the goings on here, have contributed to its widespread use in literature and cinema as an emblem of the 'evils' of civilization. Now that the concept of civilization as evil is being challenged, Las Vegas's character as an emblem is changing.

RR The desert is important not so much as a specific type of environment, with its attendant mythological associations (mirages, delirium, etc), but because there is so much of it that it effectively cuts Las Vegas off from a sense of being connected to a sprawling continuum of 'civilization.' The Mohave desert acts as a kind of psychological prophylactic barrier, isolating you from the larger cultural community of the world. The moment you arrive in Vegas, you feel marooned from all that you've left behind, including your 'normal' range of values. If they'd built Vegas in the middle of a vast and impenetrable forest, the effect might be similar, though the inhospitable character of the desert is also useful, in that it doesn't offer much in the way of recreational distractions, and leaves you happy to enjoy the shelter of air-conditioned casinos.

DH Las Vegas is an oasis – a refuge from nature (the desert most prominently), but also from culture, from Protestant values and American ennui.

AF *Las Vegas has been getting 'high culture' of late: a Guggenheim, paintings from the Hermitage, structures by Gehry and Koolhaas, Galleries of Fine Art, the world's finest chefs, haute couture, etc. What is going on here, and* *is Las Vegas turning its back on the outstanding contribution it has made to post-War American Pop culture by imploding its neon signs and facades?*

DH First, high culture follows the money. It does not seek out virtue in the desert. Second, Las Vegas, in most of its incarnations, is a town devoted to the visible and the physical. Without the chaotic contingency of the visible and the physical world, there is nothing to gamble on, nor is there any art, haute couture or gourmet dining. Vegas has always aspired to the condition of art, now it is achieving that aspiration. The question in Vegas is not: Is it art? Or: Is it real art ('real' is not in the Vegas lexicon), but: Is it better art? Is the Cézanne better than the fake Augustus? Art makes Vegas more like it is: more physical and visible; Vegas makes art more like it was: an occasion for speculation on visual pleasure.

LL Soon after Dave and I arrived in Las Vegas in 1990, the lettering on the famous Stardust sign was changed from the original, charming sort of 'Jetson's' script to a rather banal contemporary design. We were heartbroken. Then, great old populuxe motels started to go; then landmark facades. Finally, we were forced to make a pact: "no nostalgia". Of course, this kind of ruthless change would happen in any place that remained the fastest growing city in the nation for ten years, as Las Vegas has. One might wish that in 1990 the economy had turned down instead of up, so that more of the Las Vegas of the 1960s and 70s could have been preserved, in the way much of 19th century Galveston remains intact because its economy went flat at the turn of the century. Sadly, the eradication of older Las Vegas has been so complete it makes Georges Haussmann's brutal modernization of 19th century Paris seem like a preservation campaign. There's no question the heritage of this city has been lost to unrestrained development. But the absence of restraint is one of this city's defining characteristics.
As it happens, it is not the new but the lost Las Vegas that is having greater influence in the arts now, despite all the attention the new Las Vegas has received. For all its ornamental excess, the new Las Vegas is less imaginative than the old, and somewhat bland for relying on conventional themes and designs. Observing development here over the last ten years has been a bit like watching a high-speed comedic replay of the development of pre-20th century America. The architecture has been modeled on that of old-world Europe, and the cult of nature embraced, albeit in the form of faux volcanoes, jungles, and lakes. The Strip now parodies the aristocratic Grand Tour, with stops in Egypt, France, Italy, and various loosely identified islands. Of course, no Grand Tour is complete without its museums of fine art. Nothing wrong with that. We can only hope the Paris resort follows the example of its Italian counterparts, and cuts a deal with the Louvre.

RR If we can mention the Guggenheim museum and 'high' culture in the same phrase, then we're already assuming that exhibitions of motorcycles, Armani clothing, and the paintings of Norman Rockwell are also worthy of that same label. In which case, I don't feel it's at all absurd to say that Las Vegas is high culture today. Opera, by contrast, is clearly kitsch (though it obviously wasn't in the 19th century). And compared to the imagination and craftsmanship – not to mention the self-conscious references and brazen appropriations – that characterizes the design of the Strip's successes, most contemporary art looks pretty anaemic. Las Vegas may not be the work of any single identifiable genius or group of geniuses, but that doesn't mean it's not high culture. I think Reyner Banham said it best when he called the Strip "one of the great works of collective art in the Western world."

VSBI There's no such thing as preservation in an environment as hyper as Las Vegas. One decade's popular culture will be devoured and consumed by the next. So take your photos while you can because the only sure thing is that it will be gone when you turn around. This is a comforting thought when Vegas is as banal as it is right now. Maybe if we just close our eyes for a minute the visual excitement of the 1960s will reassert itself.

***AF** Vast palaces used to be built for absolute monarchs, while in Las Vegas today, Bourbon-esque resorts accommodate thousands each night. Does Vegas offer a new model of egalitarianism in our age of commerce?*

DH Vegas palaces prove what we have known all along, that non-aristocrats want the same things aristocrats do – nice spaces, visual excitement, elegant gesture and ebullient adornment. These spaces, in their success, put paid to the ideological assumption of 'workers' housing' – the premise that working people, once liberated, will seek out something cleaner and simpler, something more rigorous, puritanical and intellectual than vulgar aristocrats do. Not so.

LL Oddly, Las Vegas is a place where 'commoners' can imagine themselves aristocrats and aristocrats can slum. It's a full service destination.

VSBI Aspiring is the name of the game in resorts. Always has been, always will be. The Bellagio tests the limits of the high end taste culture. Did they overshoot their audience? The Venetian accommodates various taste cultures – like the Marlborough-Blenheim and the Traymore in Atlantic City, the swells can sit on their palazzo balconies and watch the hoi polloi on the Grand Canal below.

RR Las Vegas is probably less egalitarian than Disneyland and other themeparks, where – as far as I know – they don't have special rides or deluxe rollercoasters exclusively reserved for the use of high-rollers. The casinos are egalitarian primarily in the sense that everyone, no matter what their income bracket, is free to put their money on the tables, but clearly there's a very distinct money-based class system in place in the casinos. Only it's not always very visible.

***AF** By embodying Robert Venturi's maxim "Less is a Bore" – and Liberace's maxim "Too Much of a Good Thing is Wonderful" – does the Strip still challenge the haute bourgeois tastes of the Academy or Kunsthalle? Have we come round to accepting symbol, ornament, colour, narrative, eclecticism, the exotic and excess in art and architecture? Or is the puritanical 'White Cube' still the order of the day?*

VSBI Yes and no. Designers of 'good taste' are still offended by the 'lower' taste cultures. All they have done is substitute abstract titanium potato chips and incandescent white cubes for white cubes. They're still offended by representation, sign and symbol, perhaps because they can't control the content or the interpretation of symbols and signs, and it's impossible to be exclusive, which is the goal of high culture. High culture disdains the commercial vernacular, therefore ignores the true vitality of our time – VIVA THE VITALITY OF VULGARITY!

RR As far as I can tell, the Academy and the Kunsthalle are in love with Vegas. And the Mc-mansions in Silicon Valley seem to suggest an affinity with the Strip's fantasy-fueled ethos of excess. No doubt, as Steve, Bob and Denise point out, there are still plenty of postmodern modernists out there, lobbying for a white cube world. And the art world, of course, has so heavily bought into the white cube as a kind of rhetorical scaffolding and aesthetic prop that it may take a few more decades before it starts to see this as merely another variety of fantasy architecture.

LL Popular design and fine art exist as different genres. Pop Art was inspired by and embraced popular design, but it did not become popular design, even though it enjoyed great popularity. Las Vegas poses no challenge to the Kunsthalle. It poses a considerable challenge to artists interested in understanding the effect on the body of visual spectacle. Lately, it has become a touchstone for artists who would redeem the power of the visible, but it has not become a model for fine art practice.

DH Architecture in Las Vegas embodies the natural inheritance of 19th century eclectic, beaux-arts American architecture, only writ large. The bridge between Sanford White and the Bellagio probably resides in the practice of Morris Lapidus. To his credit, Morris understood from the first that modernism was not a religion but a permeable style like any other. He founded the idiom of 20th century American commercial architecture on this premise and was punished for his wisdom and insight. Morris wins.

***AF** I guess Vegas is commonly considered an architectural and social aberration, but briefly, what are the historical precedents for Vegas casinos?*

VSBI The original Fremont Street casinos were gussied-up Western salons with a whole lot of neon, located on a typical Western main street, Fremont Street, i.e. our Learning from Las Vegas Nolli map of Fremont looked like Nolli's Rome adapted to a 20th century American gridiron city and main street, just gaudier. The Strip casinos started life as glorified motel/lounges located along the highway from L.A. but being Vegas they had bigger and brighter signs, like the great Stardust sign of the 1960s. In the late 1960s, starting with Caesars and Circus Circus, these glorified motel/lounges began to evolve into the 'themed' resort/malls we see today. The themed resort lineage goes back to 18th-19th century European spas like Bath, and middle-class American resorts like Atlantic City. If the major come-on in themed resorts is to evoke some place more remote and exotic than where you are, the Strip resorts did just this, but at a very much larger scale. As they grew bigger and bigger, the Strip evolved into the 'New Urbanist's' worst nightmare: a mega pedestrian 'Main Street.' The model for these themed resorts is really Disneyland and themed, regional malls, but the theming is grander and more monumental than the mall back home. Our 1960s Nolli map of the Strip showed Strip/parking/casinos located like pearls strung along the linear necklace of the Strip. The new Nolli map shows giant public/private 'malls,' like amoebas with glandular problems, devouring the Strip.

RR Historical precedents could probably include all kinds of themed design environments, including Marie-Antoinette's peasant themepark; Orientalist design schemes in 19th century European salons; and the facades of

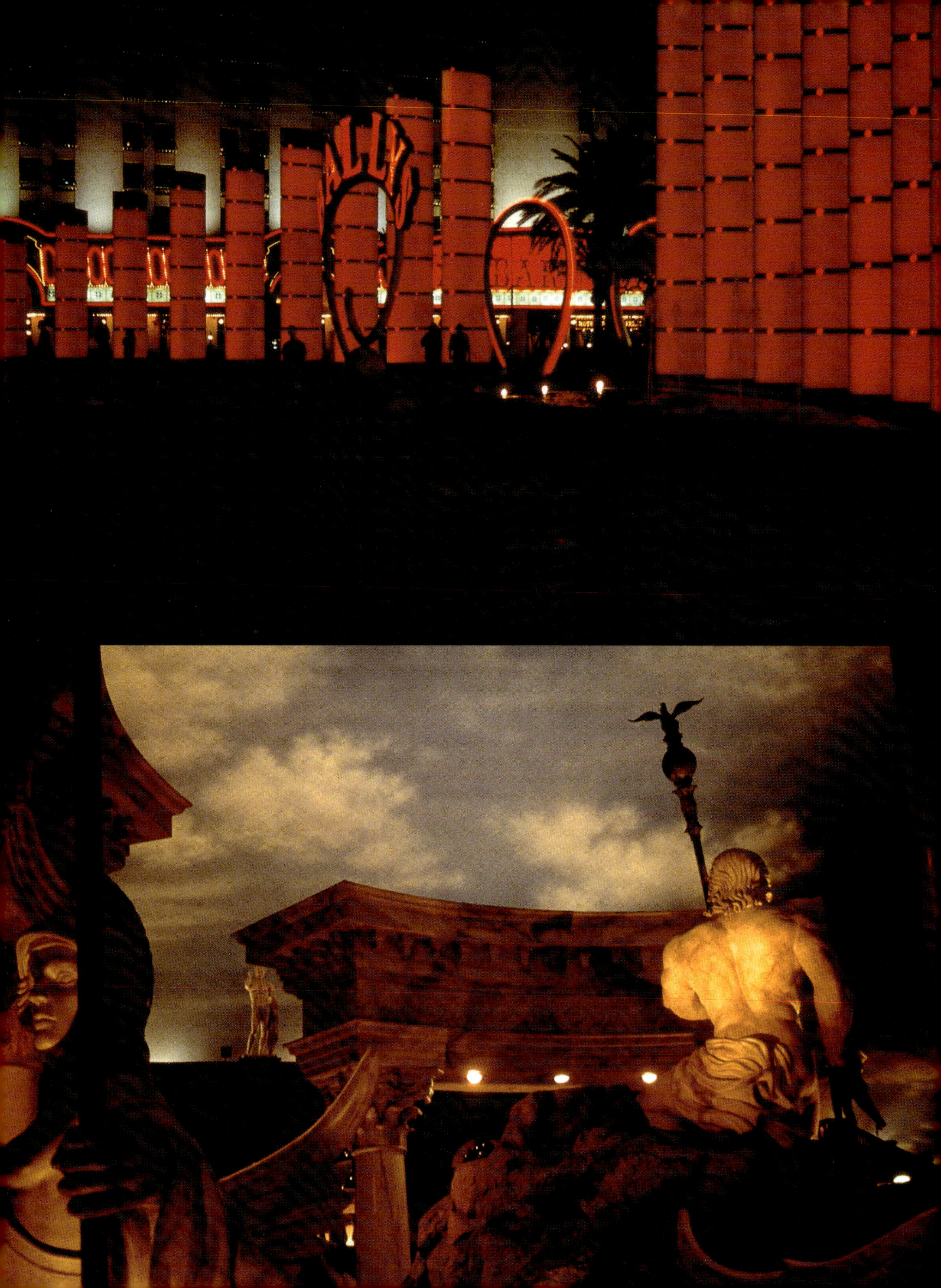

small town buildings that, as Alan Hess has written, were used by railroads to make the desert west look more inviting to prospective settlers looking out the windows of their train compartments. The Strip's identity as a place where every locale in the world, and their respective design traditions, deliriously converges is also probably part of an aesthetic common to empire cultures. More specifically, I think Dave Hickey has pointed out the casino's relationship to the interiors of Mannerist cathedrals, with their painted ceilings (cf. Caesars shopping Forum). In their aesthetic of total immersion, of comprising labyrinths of incompatible parts, the contemporary themed casino in Vegas definitely corresponds to definitions of Mannerist art.

DH In general, I think most casino spaces aspire to some kind of Italian grandeur: I mean, who built these places? Italians or what? More to the point, it helps to remember that nearly all pre-industrial Mediterranean cities were 'themed' or self-consciously 'styled' cities, and for the most part remain so. Given the very possibility that the industrial age, like the dark ages, was more an aberration than a future, the continuity between Las Vegas and Rome, in which the 'high' buildings are simply elaborations of the 'low,' may actually define the prevailing historical mainstream – after a short divagation into industrial regimentation.

AF *Tom Wolfe famously wrote of Vegas's neon signs that "they revolve, they oscillate, they soar in shapes before which the existing vocabulary of art history is helpless". Could you attempt to codify the sign art of Vegas, and does it fit into any aesthetic lineage?*

VSBI The vivid imagery by night and day that characterizes this urban and rural phenomenon is artfully perceived from the moving car via its bold scale in our Automobile Age, while its Pop iconography involving signs and symbols vitally engages the hype-sensibility that predominates in our Information Age.
And the commercial content that distinguishes the American vernacular architecture of the 20th century parallels the persuasive content that distinguishes an iconographic architecture that is maintained within a long historical tradition that includes ancient Egyptian pylons (are they hieroglyphic billboards?), ancient Greek temples (whose sculptural pediments proclaim gods galore), ancient Roman triumphal arches (whose sculptural reliefs promote patriotic history), the interiors of Early Christian and Byzantine basilicas (whose mosaic murals teem with hierarchies of saints that promote theology and educate thereby a mostly illiterate public), (the same goes for those interiors of Gothic cathedrals – think what those stained glass artisans could have crafted if they'd had neon!), and the churches of the Baroque period (whose whammo ceiling murals exude Counter-Reformation propaganda as well as art). In this context is our commercial/advertising-dominated architectural culture really so base – despite its vigor? Not all great art has been highfalutin'! In imagining future evolutions, could it be that our American-inspired, commercial-vernacular art and architecture of the 20th century will be transformed in the 21st century via the LED medium of electronic technology into forms of artistry even more glorious?

DH Vegas signs do for words what Ed Ruscha's paintings do: they force us to read the meaning of words as we read the meaning of colors and abstract configurations – through the modality of memory, similitude and analogy, rather than through the standard modality of linguistic reference and representation. This is old news.

THE BALLY'S, PHOTO BY ROLF RICKE
CAESARS PALACE, PHOTO BY ROLF RICKE

LL 1960s and 70s Las Vegas signage has seemed to exist as the mercantile analog of Pop fine art painting, and the antithesis of contemporaneous Minimalist sculpture. From today's perspective, however, the reverse seems closer to the truth. Despite the presence of figuration, ornamentation, and sequential light configurations, vintage Las Vegas signage (which simply is a more ebullient version of vintage mainstream American mercantile signage) is grounded in constructivist principles. This analogy has become apparent only with the profound transition in signage that occurred gradually in the 1980s and 90s, from the 'hard' sculptural object to the 'soft' narrative images of the LED. The huge LED screens that now dot the strip, featuring singers singing, dancers dancing, dolphins leaping, tourists eating, and so on, are objects also, of course. But in their present first generation, the physical aspects – size, shape, color, screen quality – are invisible. We have seen a parallel and analogous transition in fine art, as artists have exploited images, first in appropriated photographs, which carried the day in the 1980s, and more recently in ubiquitous video projections. When appropriation was new, critics saw only the narratives, and not the forms. Consequently, the distance between vintage signage and Pop, which could be said to have spawned, through gross misinterpretation, the soft-image industry, now seems greater than the distance from the 'hard', if figurative, classic signs to refined Minimalist objects. Vintage signage took its cue from architecture, as did Minimalist sculpture. Images take their cues from the narratives of the human body. Big difference.

***AF** Why has the art world only just become interested in Las Vegas? Specifically, why do you think no Pop Artists made work about Las Vegas?*

DH Artists since de Kooning and Duchamp have been interested in Las Vegas. Pop artists, conceptual artists and light and space artists did in fact make works evoking Las Vegas. It is only recently that arts administrators and art academics have become interested in Las Vegas. I don't know why but I wish they hadn't.

RR Pop artists were interested in common images, images people took for granted because they were ubiquitous or appeared in familiar contexts. Las Vegas in the 1960s stood for the opposite – a renegade glamour. It didn't need to be redeemed by contemporary artists looking to call our attention to neglected cultural icons.
Nowadays, artists have given up the idea of possessing redemptive powers. Instead, they have developed the habit of stealing from, or riding piggyback on, more complex works of art. Such as Las Vegas, which is far more fascinating, nervy, paradoxical, and contemporary than the great majority of what passes for contemporary art.

VSBI It's probably because places like the Strip and Times Square are so 'perfect' in their ad hoc excess that they don't leave much room for the artists to comment beyond saying, "Wow!", and, if they're lucky, "Learn from..."

RV Denise discovered Ed Ruscha when she taught at UCLA in the mid-1960s and we both had been learning from the Pop artists and their appreciation of the Everyday from the late 1950s on. Denise would expand this list of influences on 'Learning from Las Vegas' to include 1940s and 50s Pop artists in England and African popular art in South Africa.

***AF** Despite the psychedelia of its lights, and the spectacle of its mega-resorts, is Vegas really a conservative town? – its typical entertainment fare would seem to bear this out. Does Vegas function as Middle America's Saturnalia / Carnival? – a controlled, three day release from the Protestant work ethic.*

LL The Strip is conservative. Midway through his nightly show at the Stardust, Wayne Newton pauses to salute America's veterans. The Showgirl revues were already antiquated when they arrived here in the 1950s, and now are merely quaint. Only a few experimental venues feature comedians as transgressive as those that can be found on prime-time TV. Las Vegas entertainment is geared primarily to those nostalgic for earlier forms of transgression that have now become safe. Consequently, all venues feel a bit like museum showcases, a phenomenon that has an analogical relationship with the new music museums, such as the Rock and Roll Hall of Fame in Cleveland and the Experience Music Project in Seattle. When performers such as Newton, Liza Minelli, or Debbie Reynolds play, it is less an occasion to be entertained by them than an occasion to celebrate the memory of having been entertained by them. Even performers who still deliver, such as Merle Haggard or the Allman Brothers, are enveloped in the atmosphere of nostalgia. These can be sweet affairs; love truly is in the air. But there's no edge here. Reputations are built elsewhere, except among magicians.

DH In its secular, political configuration, Las Vegas is a hard-working, high-employment, labor-liberal city, one of the last, along with Brooklyn. We have lots of joints with a wide choice of live entertainment that stay open all night.

RR Vegas is like a Saturnalia where you don't have to enter the riptides of a group unconscious. Nobody wears costumes in Las Vegas, after all, except the hired help. Legalized gambling, round-the-clock drinking, and legalized brothels just over the city limits may suggest a sense of a city operating beyond the mores of Middle America, but in the end Vegas is less a social aberration than the epitome of the puritanical imperative to 'enjoy' that rules American commercial culture. Enjoy yourself 24 hours a day! That's a tall order, and it produces a fairly grim recreational style. Saturnalia is characterized by unlicensed behavior and wild joy, but obviously that is not what you find in casinos.

VSBI Saturnalia: you've got that right. All you have to do is suffer through a flight to Las Vegas and watch people lose their inhibitions by the hour. Dave Hickey describes Las Vegas as "an aesthetic desert in the desert." Las Vegas may be the last place to 'learn from Las Vegas.' They are planning to build a sign museum where the signs are hidden behind trees – only rusting signs will be exhibited in a 'Sign Boneyard.'

***AF** Has Vegas become a corporate, Disney-esque über-mall for ubiquitous big brands (Gap, Warner, Starbucks, Nike et al)? Is its spectacle pacifying or coercive – like sitting in a movie theatre – at worst producing what Mike Davis calls "Casino Zombies"?*

DH It would take me two weeks to unload this loaded question. It smacks of elitist philistinism. In general, I might observe that Guy Debord is dead, and, Mike Davis notwithstanding, we don't talk like this anymore.

VSBI This is the old 'chicken and egg' argument: which comes first, the manipulation or the taste culture? It's an endless circular argument and one way 'high' culture tries to lord it over 'low' culture. We agree with Herb Gans that people are much more competent and able to define their social needs and aesthetic tastes than their critics from high culture give them credit for.

RR The spectacles of Las Vegas are no more or less coercive than any other form of spectacle – whether it's watching TV or watching the mall. They're probably just more entertaining. And who's to say those "casino zombies" Mike Davis speaks of weren't zombies before they got to Vegas?

LL Las Vegas has become the world's grandest convention center, in every sense of the term. But this is less surprising than the fact that New York is beginning to seem like a big convention center itself, as indigenous industry, and workers, are squeezed out of Manhattan to make room for marketing and tourists.

***AF** Now that Vegas's population is well over a million, is it becoming a typical American city?*

LL Today there is a vast Middle American underground that threatens the very stability of Las Vegas's cool culture. With no sound immigration policy in place during the recent economic boom, Las Vegas allowed refugees from California real estate inflation and East Coast stagnant job markets to infect the city. They go hiking and wear khaki even at night. New schools for their children strain the tax base, and sales of Martha Stewart off-white paint have grown exponentially. Many of these intruders view the Strip as a necessary evil. I believe it is the guilt this conflict produces that makes them defensive, cranky, and peculiarly intolerant of privacy, eccentricity, and bad habits. However, they haven't succeeded in spoiling the fun yet. Las Vegas is still pretty cool.

RR A typical American city? I wish! San Francisco (to name another popular tourist town), could definitely use a few exploding volcanoes to liven up its drab Victorian stageshow. Unlike almost any city I can think of, Las Vegas possesses a central drag – the Strip – that has a sense of humor. Steve Wynn [the Las Vegas casino tycoon], in explaining the charms of The Mirage, invoked the idea that you can't have comedy, or humor, without conflict. The state of constant cultural tension in the multi-themed resorts is basically a kind of spectacular comedy. And as visitors, we're always in on the gag. That may be the most egalitarian aspect of the Strip – its humor is very inclusive. Of course, that's a useful set-up for the sucker-punch delivered at the gambling tables ... but that's another matter.

VSBI It always was. Being a destination resort, it's an exaggeration of the typical, which is why we went there to begin with. It was easier to see and understand typical strips, malls, or suburban subdivisions after seeing a resort like Vegas, i.e. a commercial environment where the volume is turned up and where the desert is the only context. 'Learning from Las Vegas' was a primer for learning about Los Angeles – the archetypal automobile city.

DH Typical American cities are boring, ugly and repressive. Las Vegas, in my view, is not.

28th & 29th July 2001. Via electronic mail

STARDUST, PHOTO BY ROLF RICKE
NEON MUSEUM'S BONEYARD, PHOTO BY ALEX FARQUHARSON

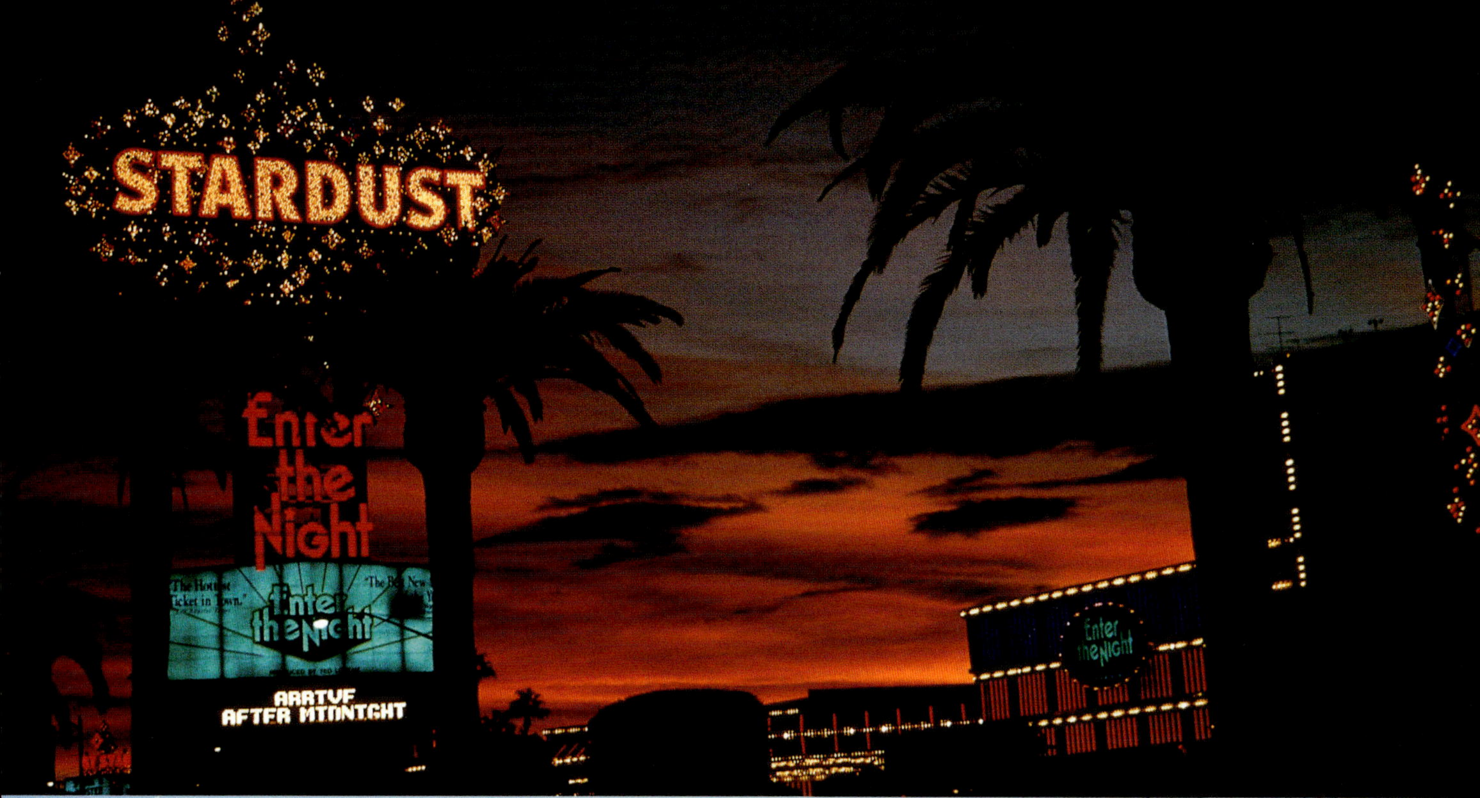

STARDUST
Enter the Night
Enter the Night
ARRIVE AFTER MIDNIGHT
Enter the Night
Sassy Sally's

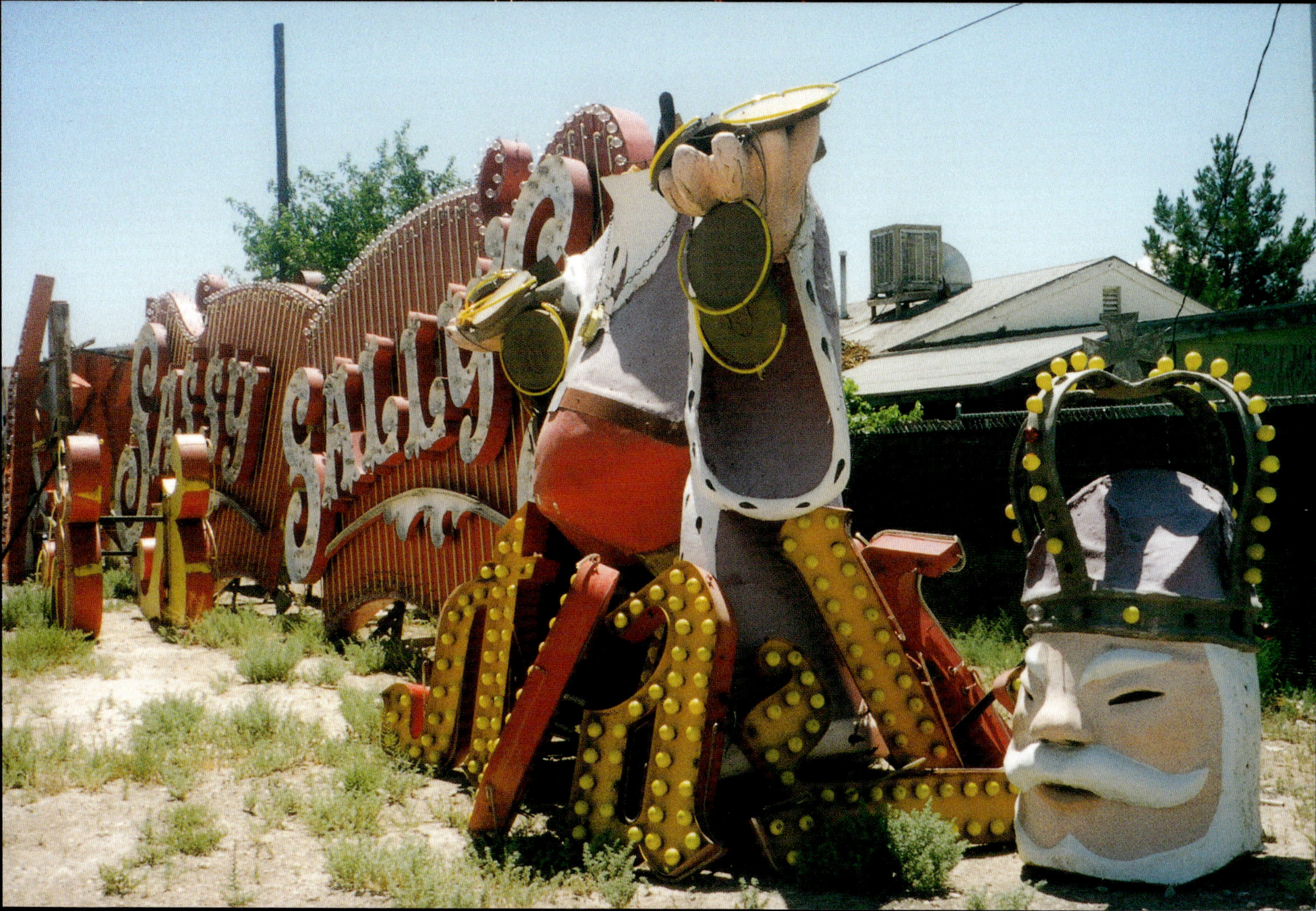

Catalogue

Rev. Ethan Acres

1970 Born in Ft. Payne, AL
1980 Born Again, 'Flat Rock Primitive' Baptist Church, Flat Rock, TN
1996 M.F.A. University of Nevada, Las Vegas, NV
1995 Ordained, World Christianship Ministries, Fresno, CA
Lives in Las Vegas, NV

2001
FRESH: The Altoids Curiously Strong Collection, The New Museum, New York, NY
2000
Faith: The Impact of Judeo-Christian Religion on Art at the Millenium, Aldrich Museum, Rigdefield, CT
1999
Reverend Acres' Rockin' Millenium Countdown, Bronwyn Keenan Gallery, New York
Jesus Freak, Patricia Faure Gallery, Santa Monica, CA
1998
The Reverend Ethan Acres' Holy War, Lisa Livingstone Gallery, Las Vegas, NV

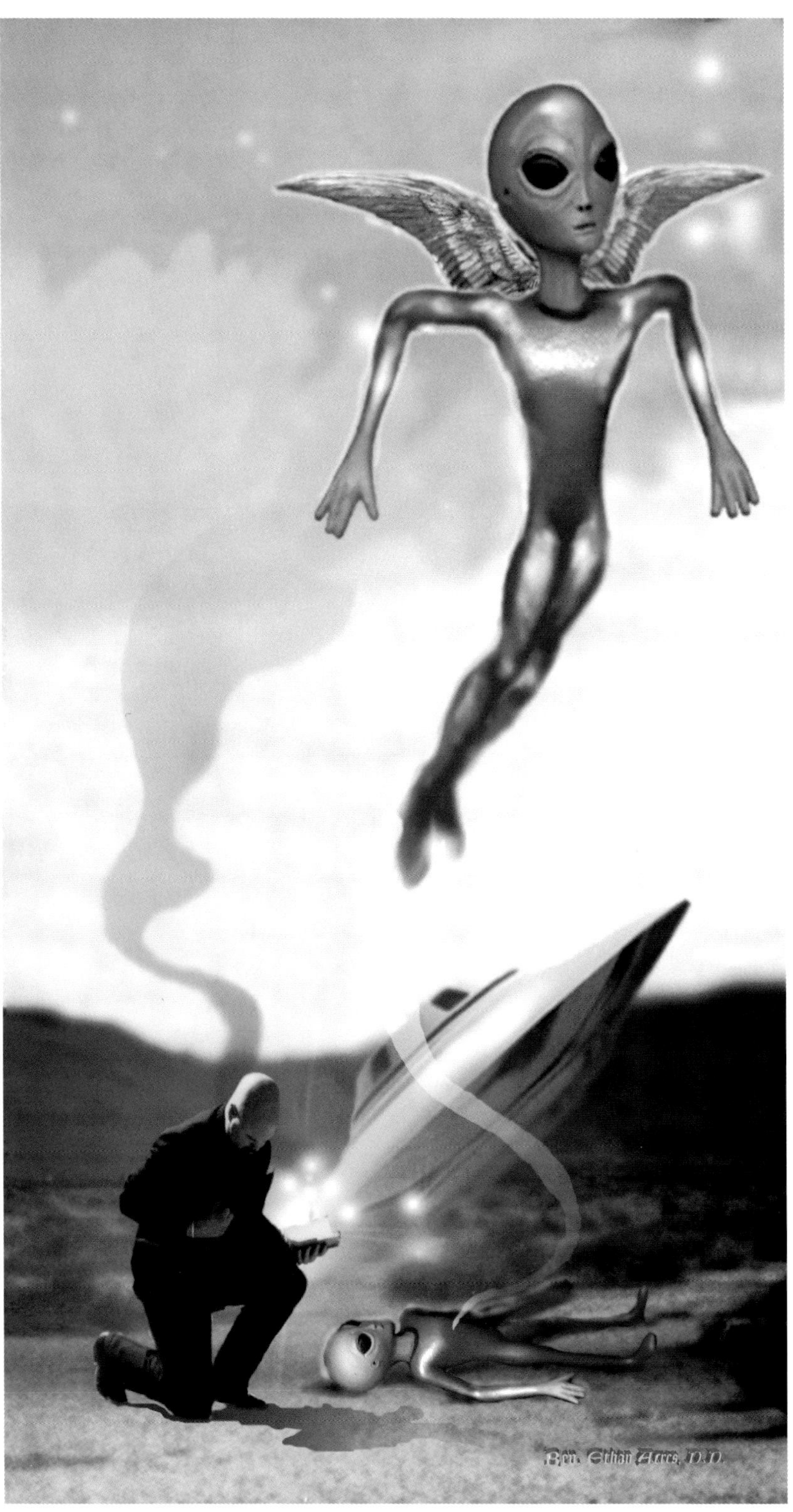

E.T. GO HOME 1999
DIGITAL PHOTO ON MYLAR
152.4 x 76.2 CM
COURTESY OF PATRICIA FAURE GALLERY, SANTA MONICA, CA

DRAWING FOR 'TRUE LOVE CHAPEL' 2001
MIXED MEDIA 365.7 x 203.2 x 365.7 CM
SHOWING VIDEO 'THE STRAIGHT OR CROOKED WAY' 1997, 32'
COURTESY OF THE ARTIST

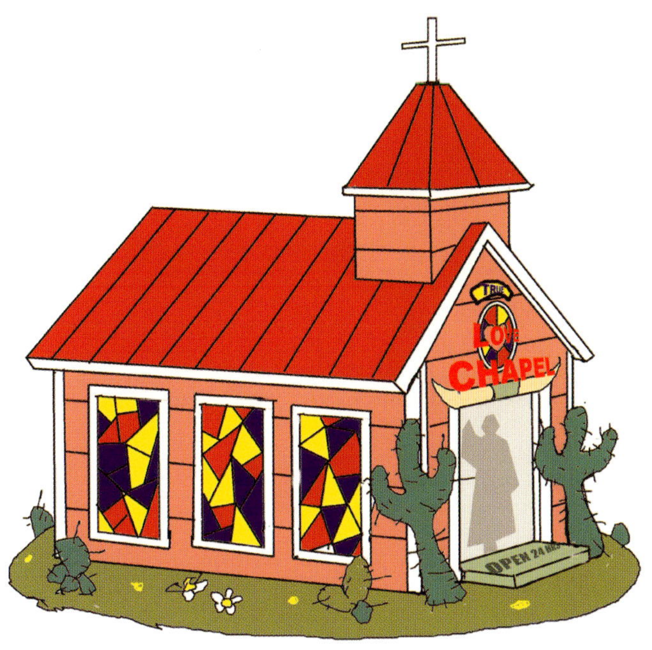

THE HIGHWAY CHAPEL AT THE END OF TIME AND SPACE 2001
INK JET ON CANVAS 121.9 x 152.4 CM
COLLECTION OF THE ARTIST

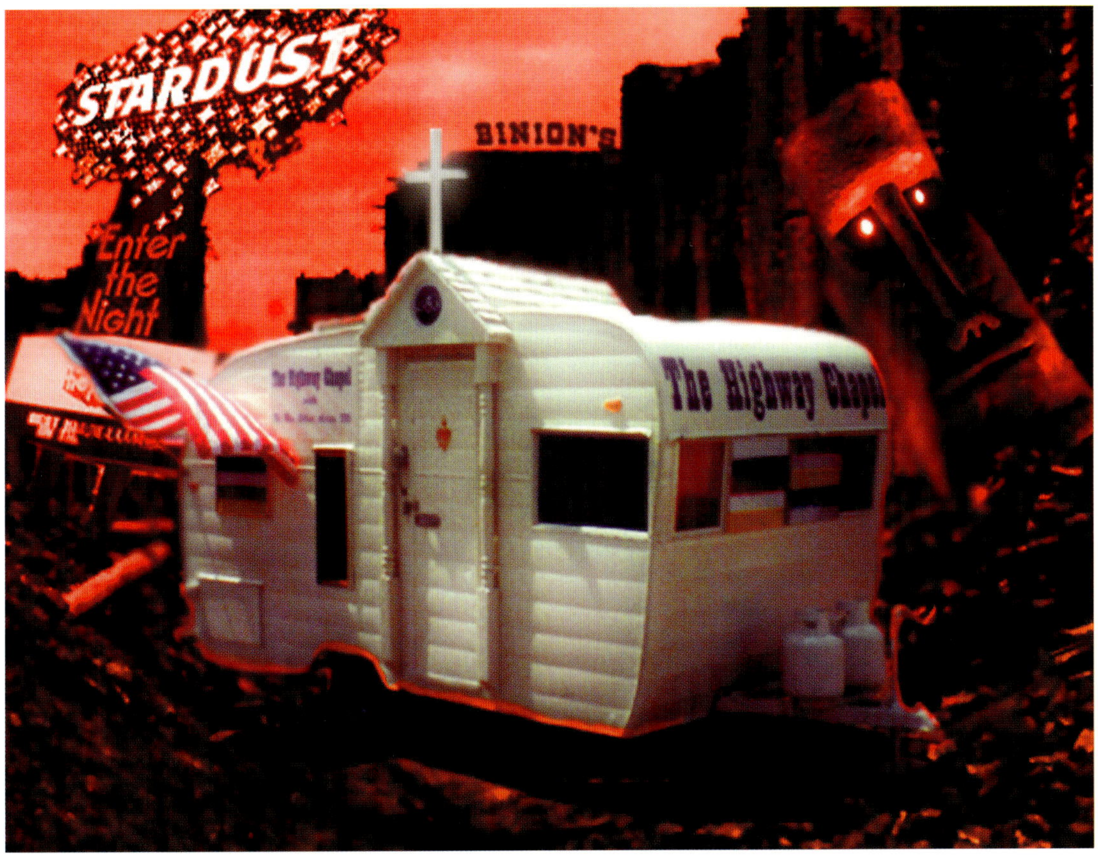

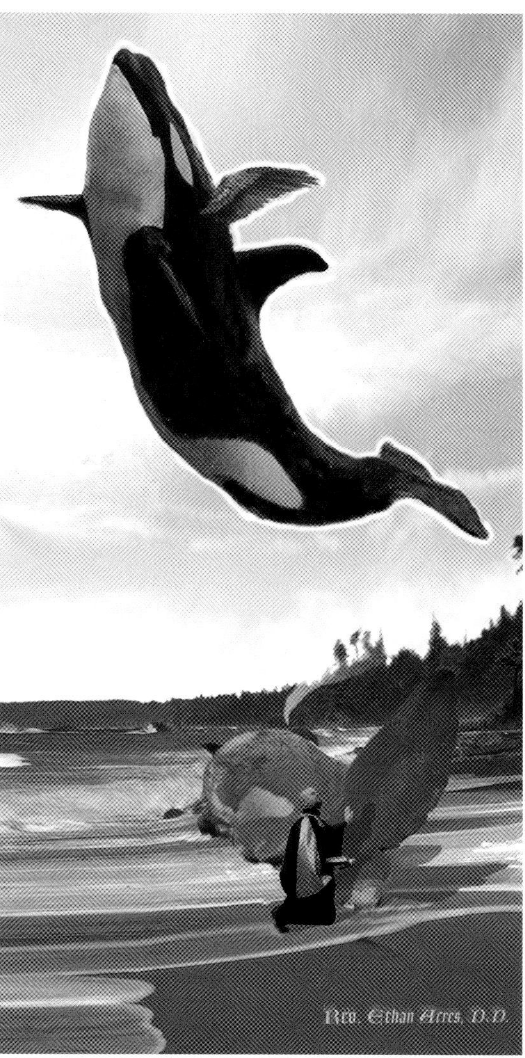

ASCENSION OF SLAMOO 1999
DIGITAL PHOTO ON MYLAR
152.4 X 76.2 CM
COURTESY OF MARK PALEY

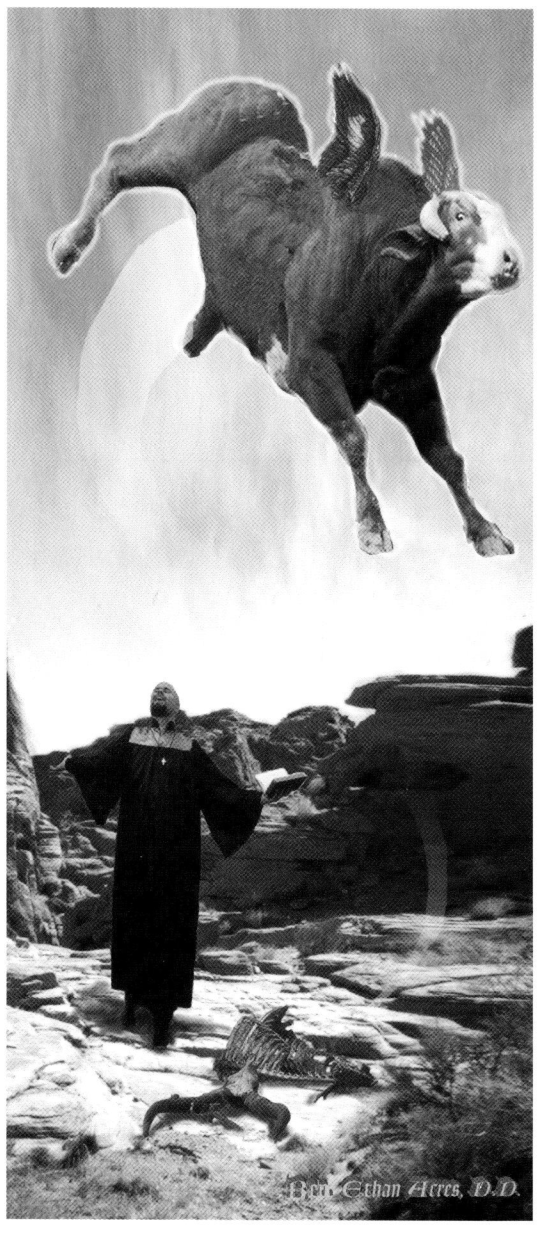

RISING BULL 1999
DIGITAL PHOTO ON MYLAR
182.8 X 121.9 CM
COURTESY OF GOLLINELLI COLLECTION,
VENICE, ITALY

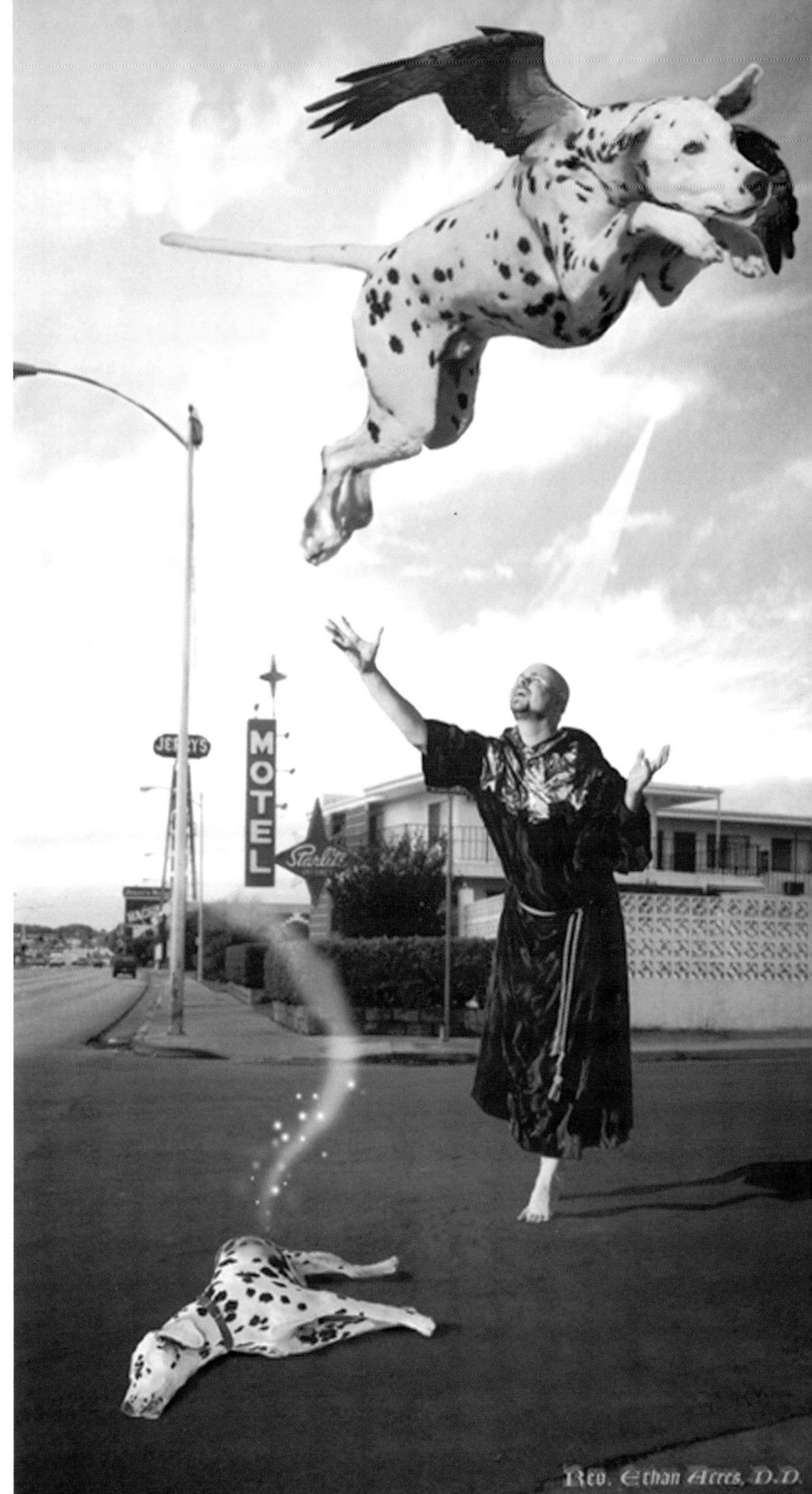

OUT SPOT 2001
DIGITAL PHOTO ON MYLAR
152.4 X 76.2 CM
COURTESY OF
PATRICIA FAURE GALLERY,
SANTA MONICA, CA

Philip Argent

1962 Born in Southend-on-Sea, Essex, GB
1985 B.A. (Hons) Cheltenham School of Art, GB
1994 M.F.A. University of Nevada, Las Vegas, NV
Lives in Santa Barbara, CA

2001
Philip Argent, Shoshana Wayne Gallery, Santa Monica, CA
The Dreams Stuff is Made Of, Frankfurt Art Fair, D
2000
Ultralounge, Contemporary Art Museum, University of South Florida, Tampa, FL
1999
Millenium, Tate, New York, NY
1998
Painting From Another Planet, Deitch Projects, New York, NY

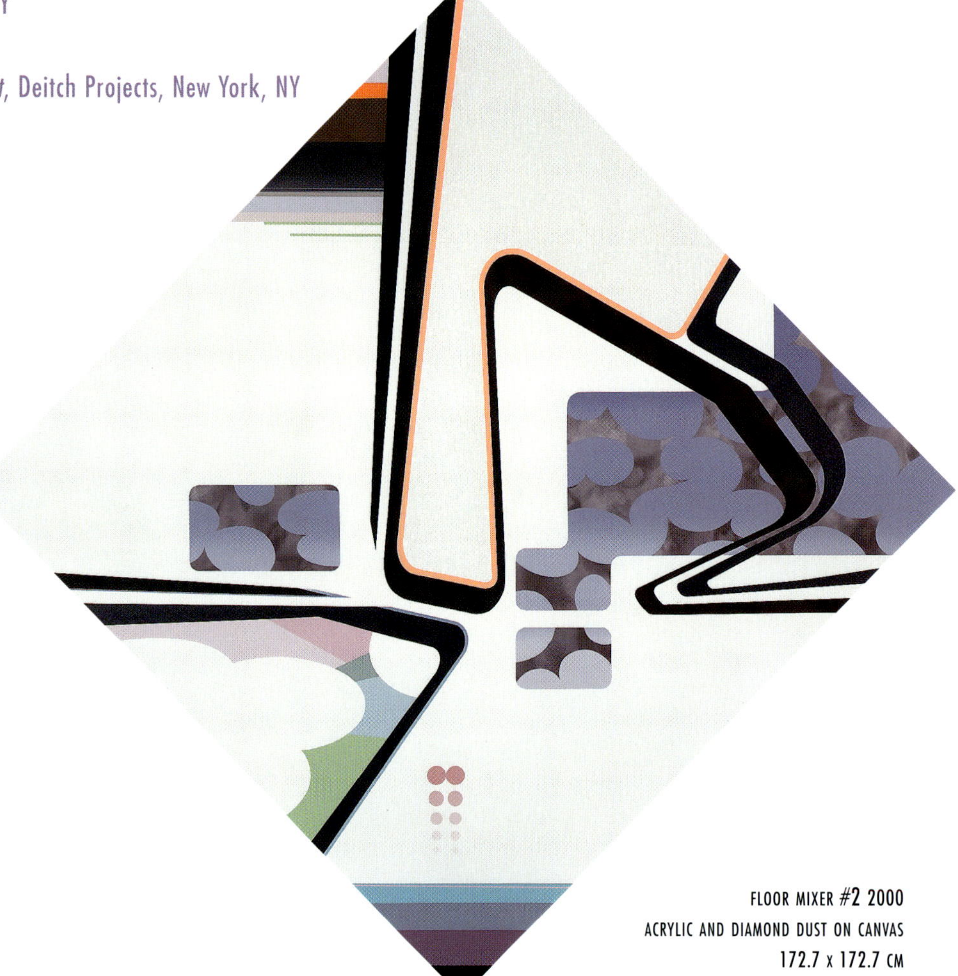

FLOOR MIXER #2 2000
ACRYLIC AND DIAMOND DUST ON CANVAS
172.7 x 172.7 CM
COLLECTION OF DAVID PAGEL & ALISA TAGER

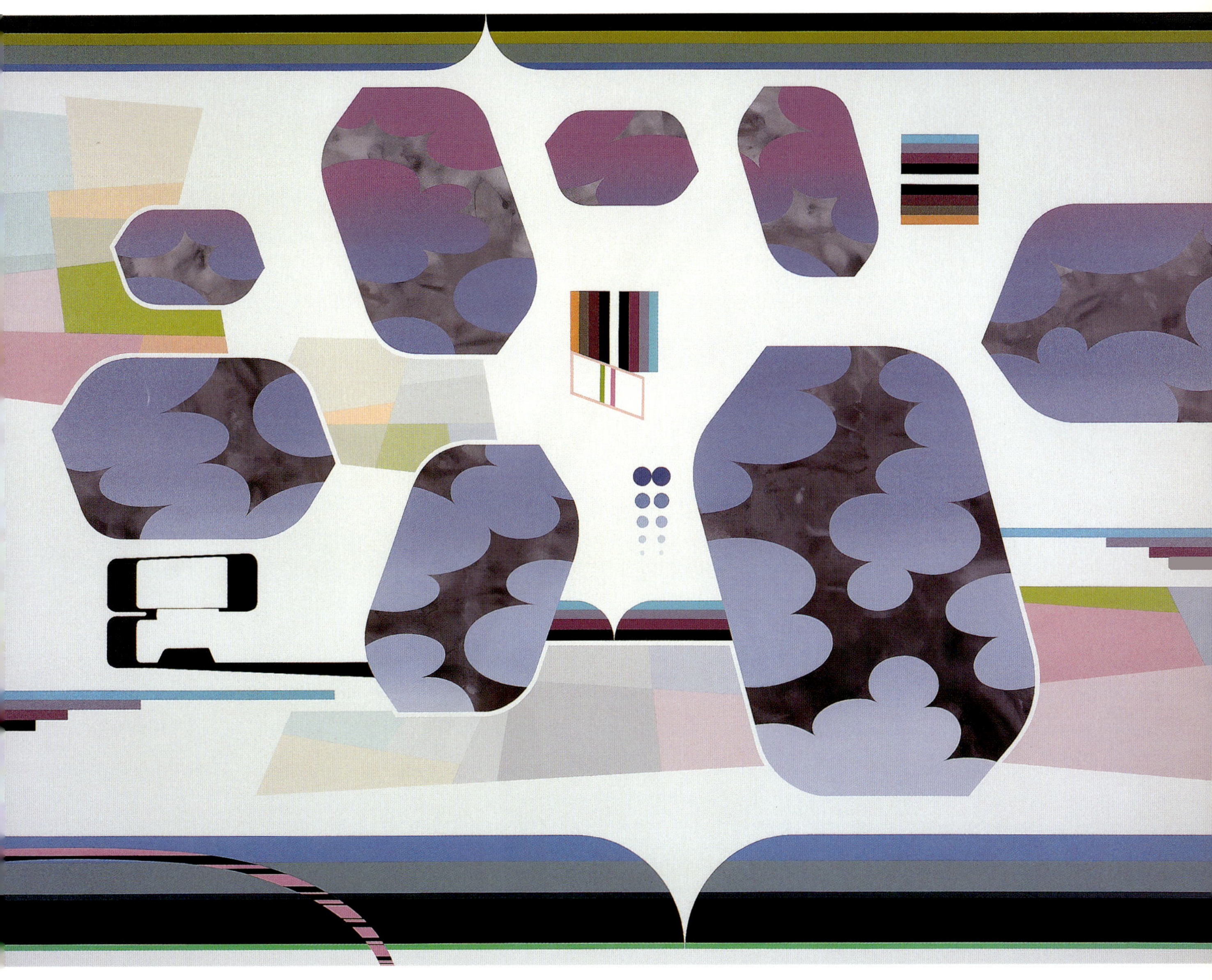

PCH3 2001
ACRYLIC ON CANVAS 127 x 177.8 CM
COURTESY OF THE ARTIST & SHOSHANA WAYNE GALLERY, SANTA MONICA, CA

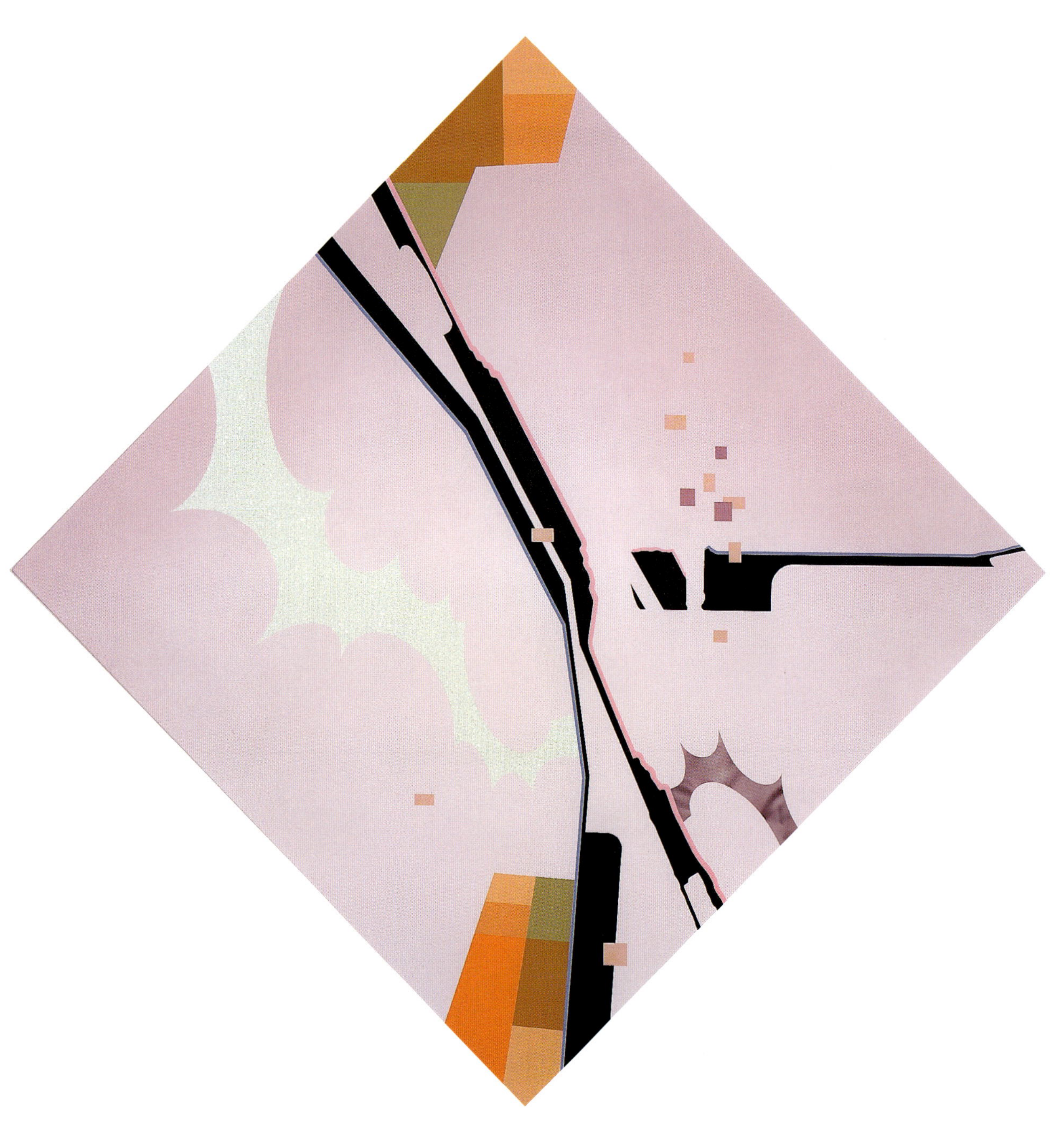

UNTITLED 4.5 2001
ACRYLIC AND DIAMOND DUST ON CANVAS 107.9 x 107.9 CM
COURTESY OF THE ARTIST & SHOSHANA WAYNE GALLERY, SANTA MONICA, CA

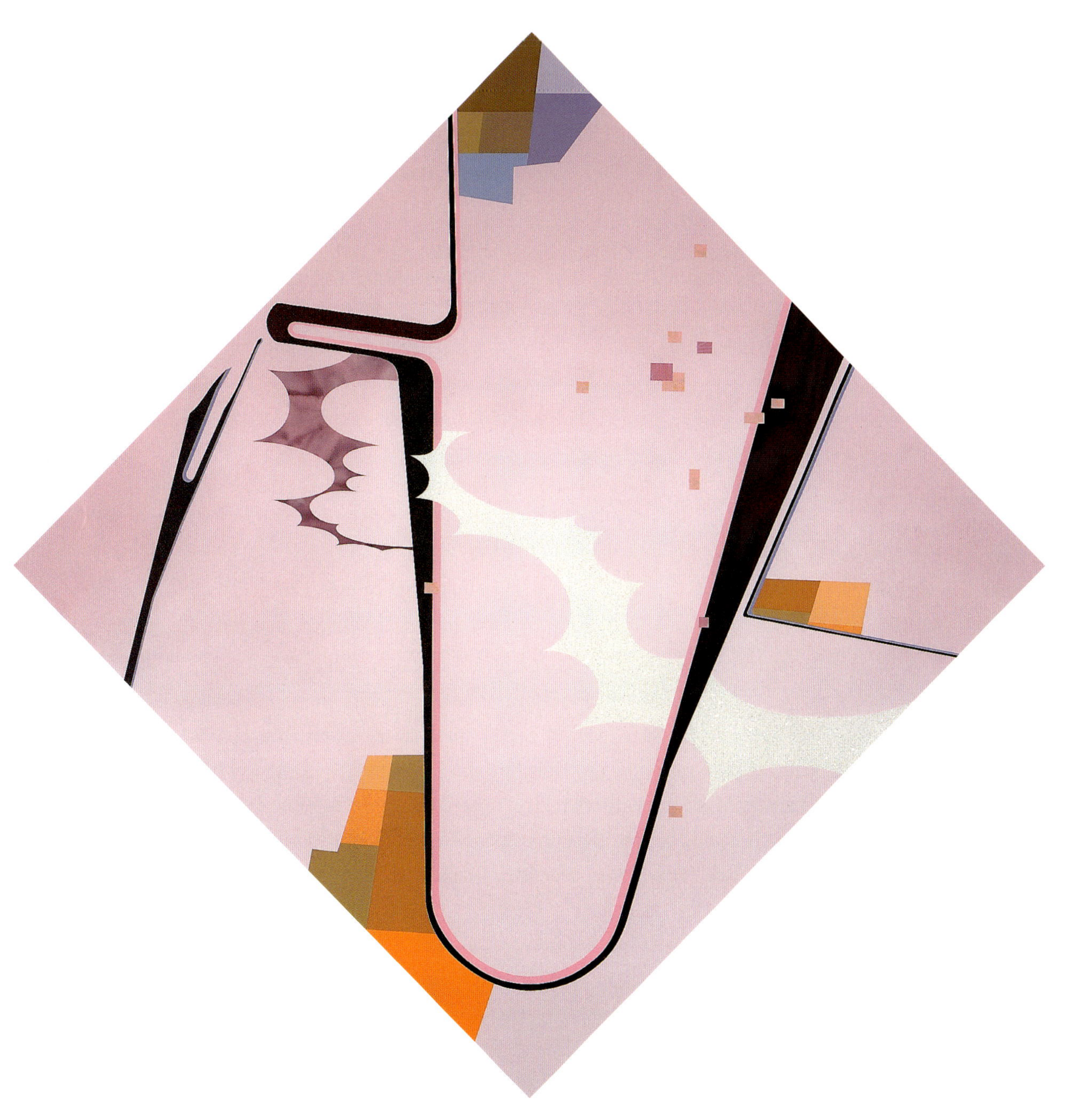

UNTITLED 4.6 2001
ACRYLIC AND DIAMOND DUST ON CANVAS 107.9 x 107.9 CM
COURTESY OF THE ARTIST & SHOSHANA WAYNE GALLERY, SANTA MONICA, CA

Julie Ault, Martin Beck

1957 Born in Boston, MA
Lives in New York, NY

2000
Outdoor Systems, indoor distribution, Neue Gesellschaft für bildende Kunst, Berlin, D (cat.)
Power Up: Sister Corita and Donald Moffett Interlocking, UCLA Hammer Museum, Los Angeles, CA (broch.)
1999
Daydreams & Traffic Jams, for 'Billboard', MASS MOCA, North Adams, MA
1996
Cultural Economies: Histories from the Alternative Arts Movement, Drawing Center, New York, NY
Art is not enough, Shedhalle, Zurich, CH

1963 Born in Bludenz, A
Lives in New York, NY

2001
Televisions, Kunsthalle, Vienna, A
2000
Outdoor Systems, indoor distribution, Neue Gesellschaft für bildende Kunst, Berlin, D (cat.)
1999
Billboard, MASS MOCA, North Adams, MA
1998
There is No Business Like Business, Shedhalle, Zurich, CH
1997
Co-founder of Parasite
storage (displayed), spot, New York, NY

In recent cycles of casino building themed environments modeled after specific cities have been used to entice. Paris, Venice, Rio, New York, Caesar's Rome, ancient Egypt's Luxor among others have provided content and iconography for the design of multi-use casino structures. The prevalent architectural strategy relies on making a composite city from versions of buildings and structures that reference a particular metropolis or place. This allows for the construction of idealized versions of existing cities into clusters of tourism icons and stereotypes.

For example, 'New York, New York' is based upon renditions of facades of recognizable buildings and monuments at 2/3 actual scale collaged together to produce a seamless urban-like envelope. Upon entering, 'the city' continues as a fully climatized indoor urban setting composed of yet more building exteriors and containing the hotel, the casino, a roller coaster, and multiple restaurants and bars. Similar strategies were employed in the planning of Paris, Las Vegas and for The Venetian – the latter being a cluster model of authentically materialized Venetian building replicas at actual scale. This technique of montaging urban fragments has produced models of a new kind of architecture and new kinds of 'cities' – putting assumptions about a building's coherence into question while simultaneously staging the illusion of urban coherence.

Our contribution in 'The Magic Hour' centers on the phenomenon of sanitized urbanism. On a free floating display platform several emblematic components are put into dialogue with one another. They include 'The Making of Luxor,' a videotape which documents the process of designing and building the Luxor casino in Las Vegas; a training video titled 'National Main Street at Work: The Four Point Approach' which promotes the transformation of economically suffering small American towns into retro-grade style displays of a pre-depression urban past; and documentation of a radical urban proposal titled 'No-stop City' from 1970 by the Italian design group Archizoom Associati that proposed the city of the future as a continuous, fully climatized, consumption environment.

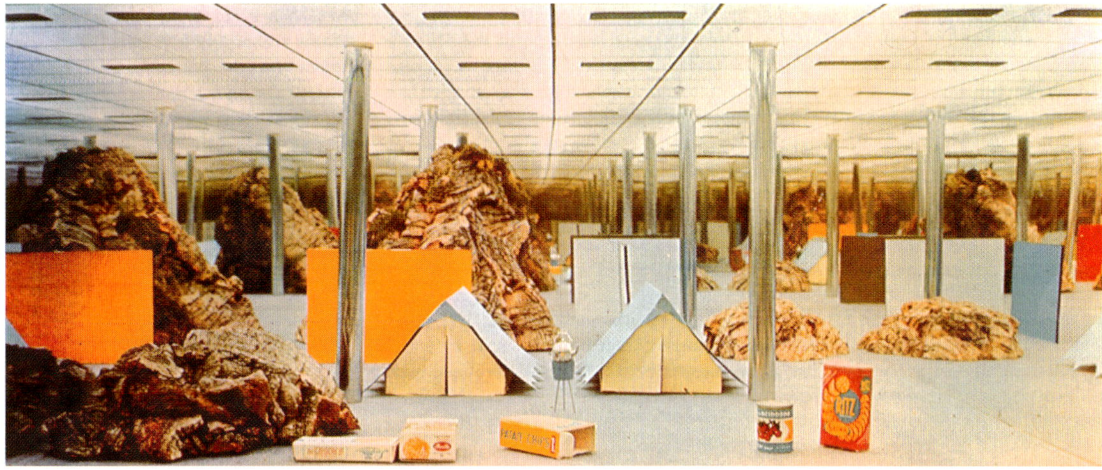

ARCHIZOOM ASSOCIATI, *NO-STOP CITY*, INTERNAL LANDSCAPE, 1970

VIDEOSTILLS FROM *THE MAKING OF LUXOR*, 1994, SCOTT MORRIS PRODUCTIONS, INC., CIRCUS CIRCUS ENTERPRISES

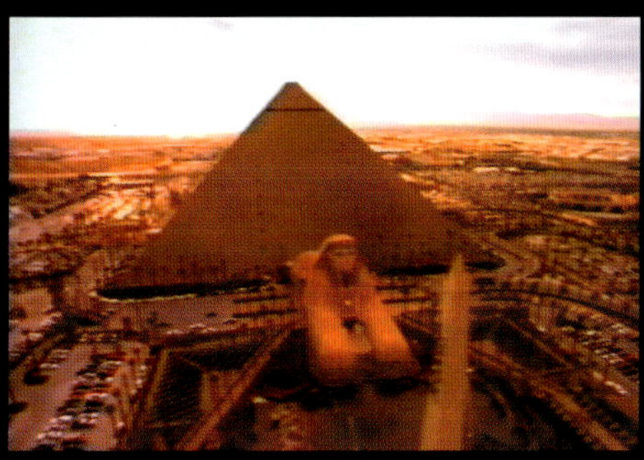

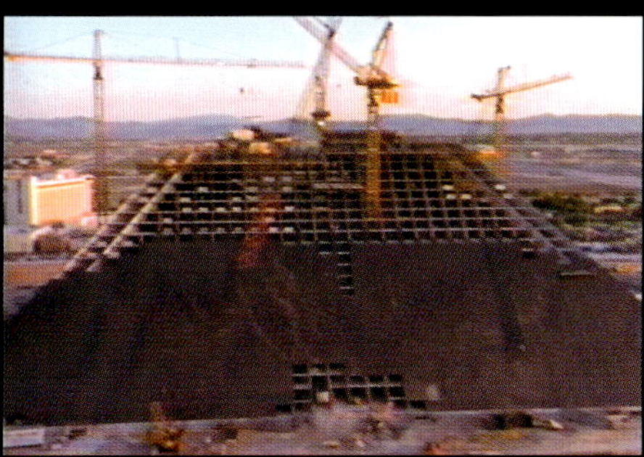

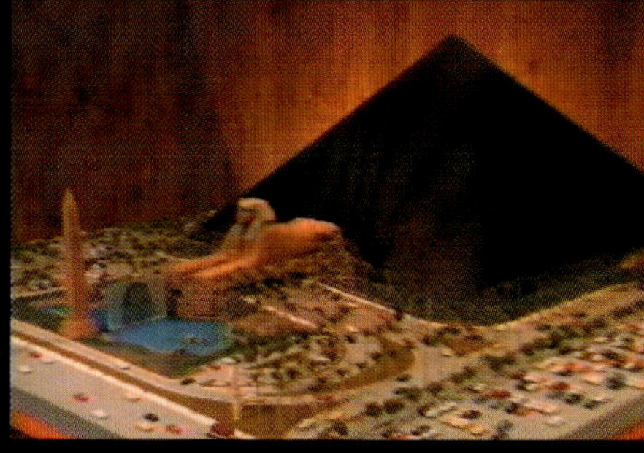

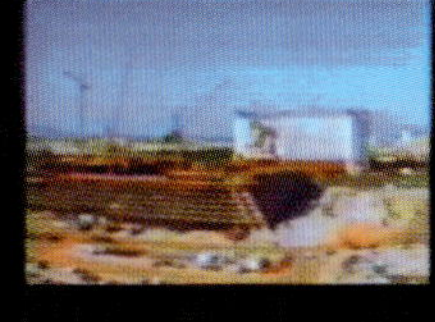

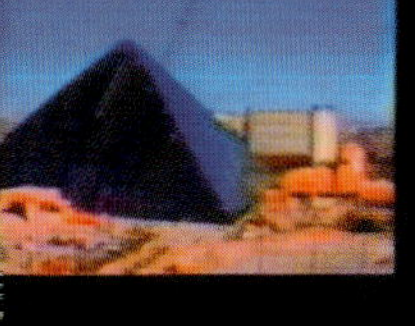

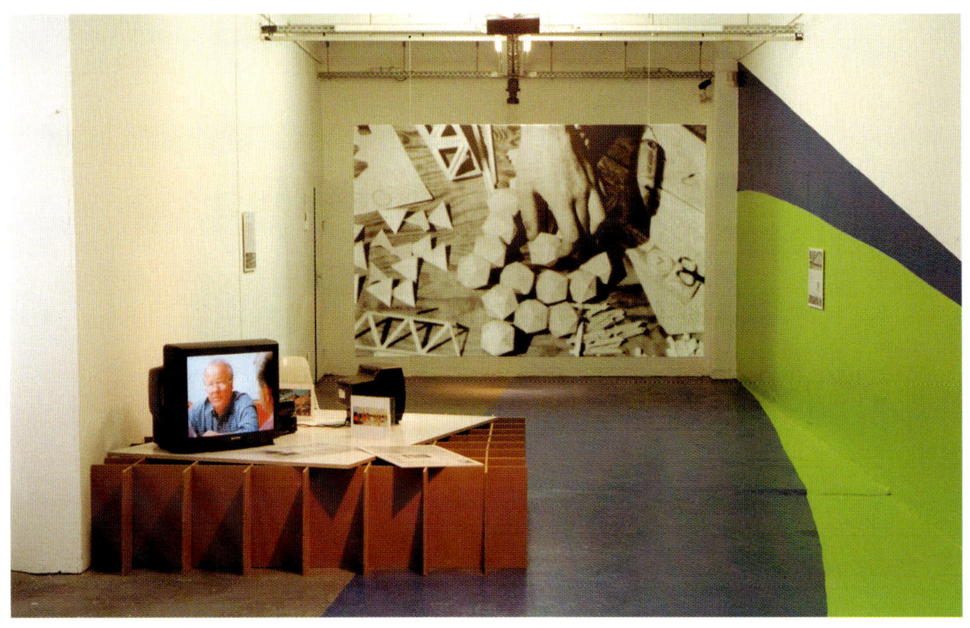

OUTDOOR SYSTEMS, INDOOR DISTRIBUTION 2000
NEUE GESELLSCHAFT FÜR BILDENDE KUNST, BERLIN, 2000, EXHIBITION VIEW OF *MEGASTRUCTURE* ARENA INCLUDING: INDOOR BILLBOARD WITH PHOTOGRAPH OF ARCHIGRAM'S MEGASTRUCTURE CUT-OUT-MODEL, 1970, PHOTO BY REYNER BANHAM / INFORMATION PANELS MEGASTRUCTURE / DISPLAY STRUCTURE MADE FROM HOMASOTE AND FORMICA BOARD / ON MONITOR: *THE MAKING OF LUXOR*, 1994, SCOTT MORRIS PRODUCTIONS, INC., 28 MIN. / INFORMATION PANELS PLEASURE-ZONE ARCHITECTURE / SIGN HOLDER CONTAINING PHOTOGRAPHS OF *NO-STOP-CITY* PROJECT, 1970, ARCHIZOOM.

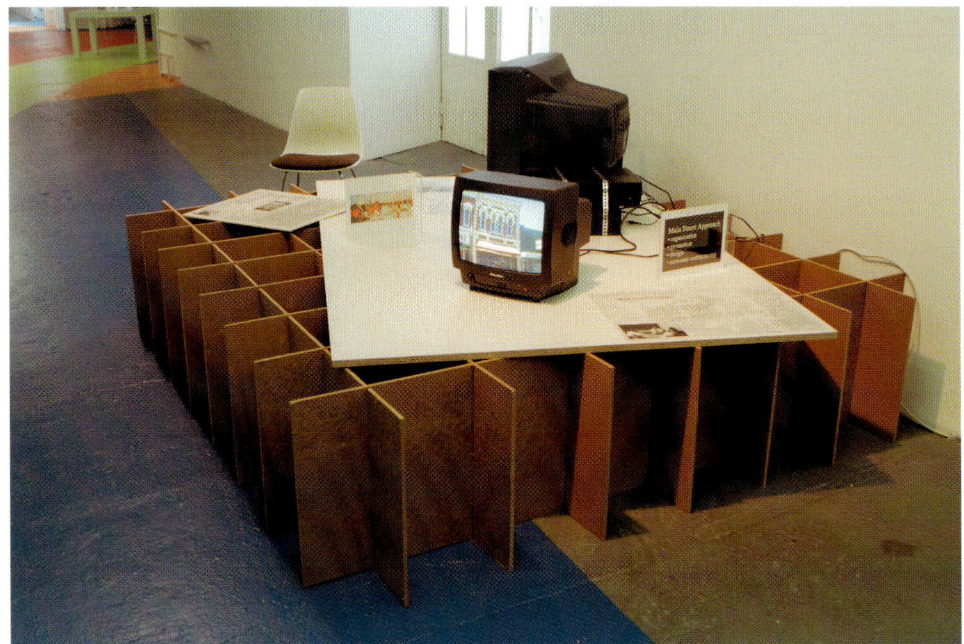

OUTDOOR SYSTEMS, INDOOR DISTRIBUTION, 2000
NEUE GESELLSCHAFT FÜR BILDENDE KUNST, BERLIN, 2000, DETAIL OF *MEGASTRUCTURE* ARENA INCLUDING: ON MONITOR: *NATIONAL MAIN STREET AT WORK: THE FOUR POINT APPROACH*, 1984, THE NATIONAL TRUST FOR HISTORIC PRESERVATION, 20 MIN / INFORMATION PANEL MAIN STREET PROGRAM™ / SIGN HOLDER CONTAINING PHOTOGRAPHS FROM *THE MAIN STREET APPROACH* SLIDE SHOW, 1984.

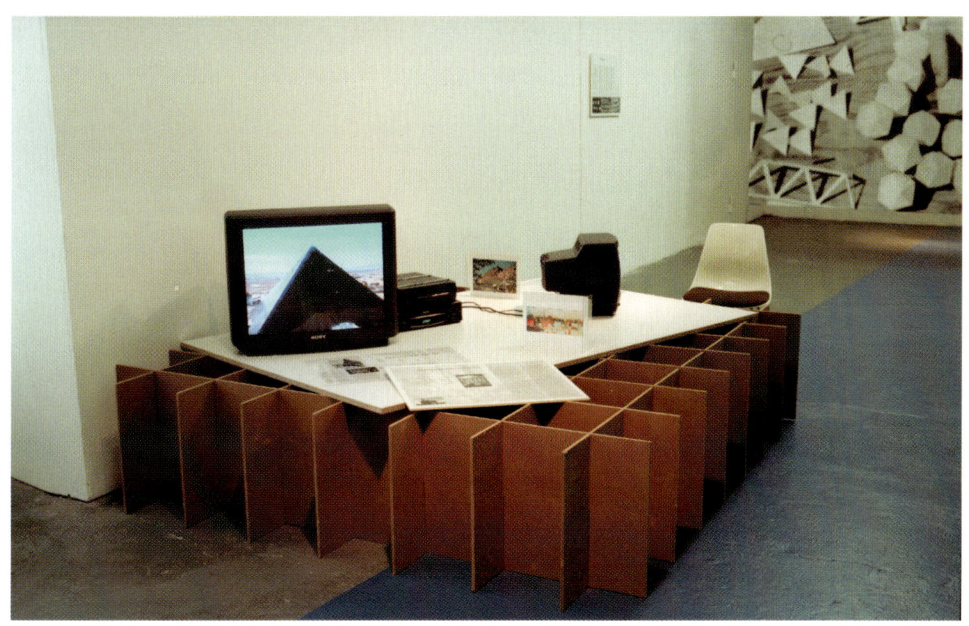

OUTDOOR SYSTEMS, INDOOR DISTRIBUTION 2000
NEUE GESELLSCHAFT FÜR BILDENDE KUNST, BERLIN, 2000, DETAIL OF *MEGASTRUCTURE* ARENA INCLUDING: DISPLAY STRUCTURE MADE FROM HOMASOTE AND FORMICA BOARD / ON MONITOR: *THE MAKING OF LUXOR*, 1994, SCOTT MORRIS PRODUCTIONS, INC., 28 MIN. / INFORMATION PANELS PLEASURE-ZONE ARCHITECTURE / SIGN HOLDER CONTAINING PHOTOGRAPHS OF *NO-STOP-CITY* PROJECT, 1970, ARCHIZOOM.

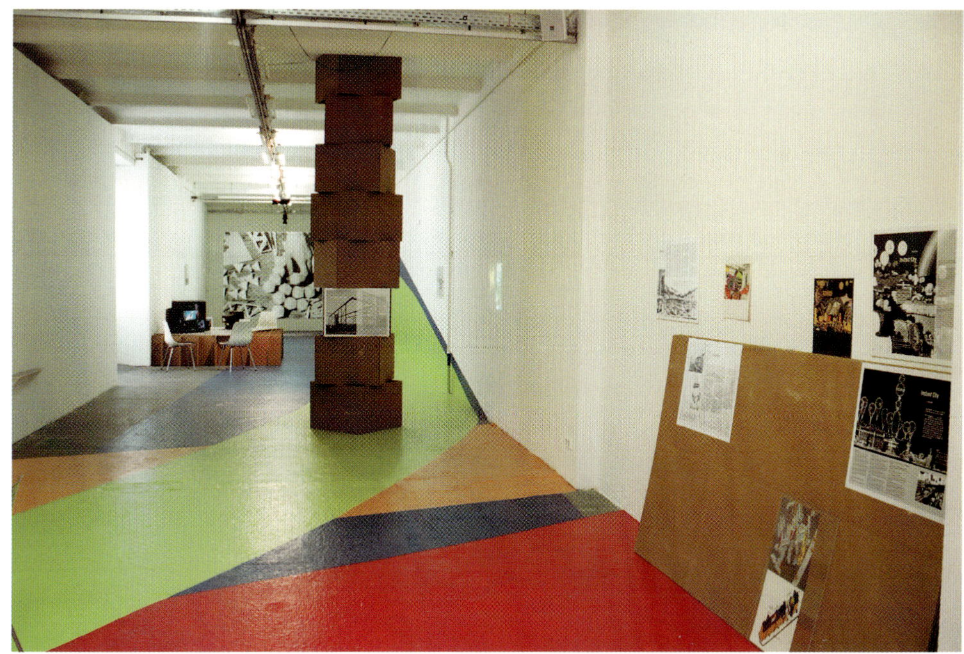

OUTDOOR SYSTEMS, INDOOR DISTRIBUTION 2000
NEUE GESELLSCHAFT FÜR BILDENDE KUNST, BERLIN 2000, EXHIBITION VIEW OF *MODULE* ARENA WITH *FLEXIBILITY* ARENA IN FOREGROUND AND *MEGASTRUCTURE* ARENA IN BACKGROUND. / MODULAR DISPLAY TOWER MADE FROM HOMASOTE INCLUDES: INFORMATION PANEL *CASE STUDY PROGRAM* / PROJECTION OF *HOUSE: AFTER FIVE YEARS OF LIVING*, 1955, CHARLES AND RAY EAMES, 11 MIN., VIDEO TRANSFER FROM 16 MM FILM.

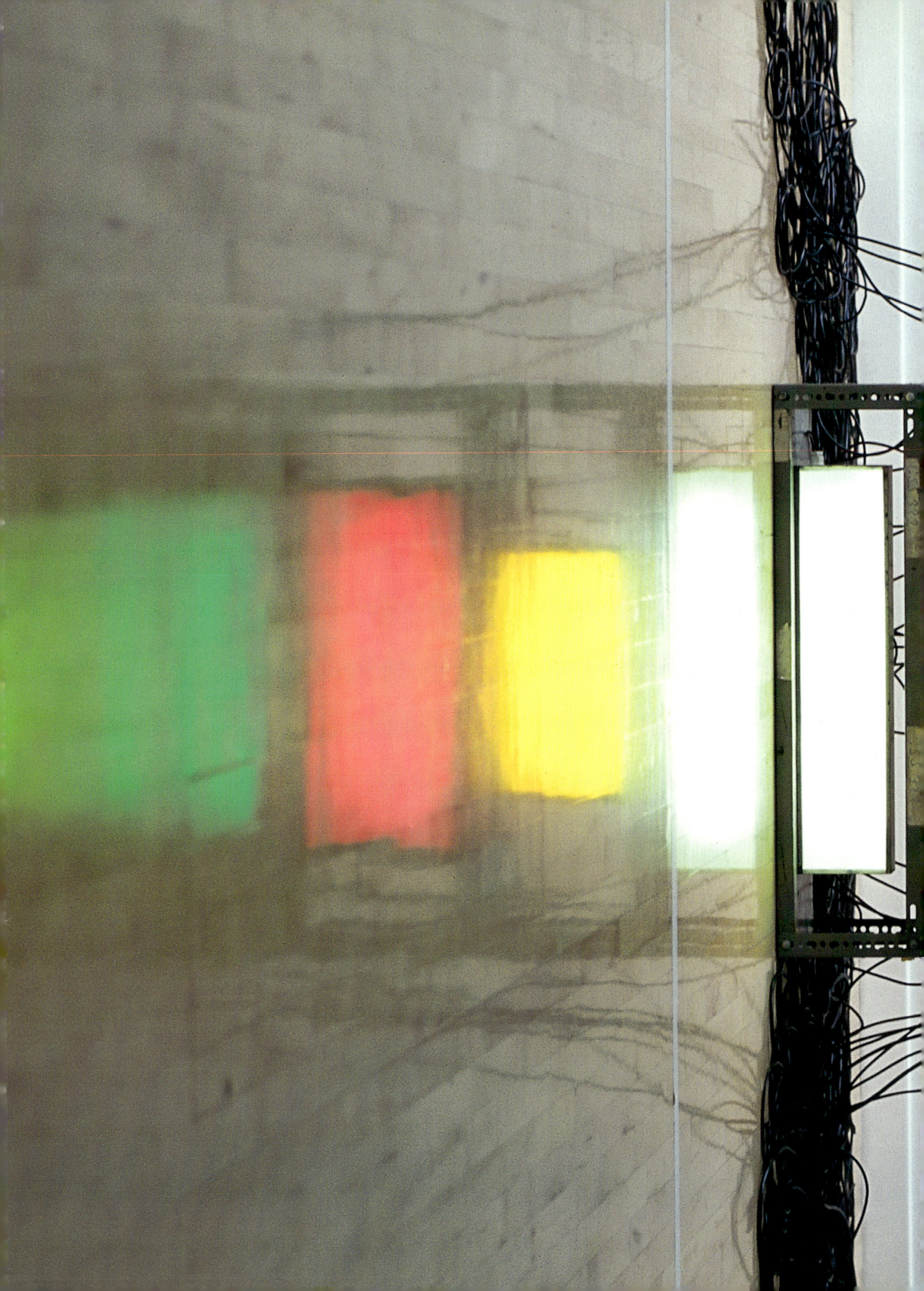

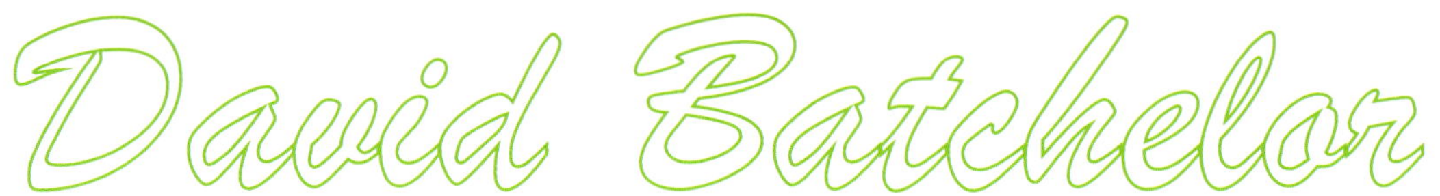

Lives in London, GB

2001

Straight Up, Chapman Fine Art, London, GB

Shiny-Dirty, Habitat, London, GB

Millenium Commission, Norwich Gallery, GB

2000

Apocalypstick, Anthony Wilkinson Gallery, London, GB

British Art Show 5, SNGMA, Edinburgh; City Art Gallery, Southampton; CVA, Cardiff; Ikon Gallery, Birmingham, GB (cat.)

It is, I believe, no exaggeration to say that, in the West, since Antiquity, colour has been systematically marginalized, reviled, diminished and degraded. Generations of philosophers, artists, art historians and cultural theorists of one stripe or another have kept this prejudice alive, warm, fed and groomed. As with all prejudices, its manifest form, its loathing, masks a fear: a fear of contamination and corruption by something that is unknown or appears unknowable. This loathing of colour, this fear of corruption through colour, needs a name: chromophobia.

Chromophobia manifests itself in the many and varied attempts to purge colour from culture, to devalue colour, to diminish its significance, to deny its complexity. More specifically: this purging of colour is usually accomplished in one of two ways. In the first, colour is made out to be the property of some foreign body - usually the feminine, the oriental, the primitive, the infantile, the vulgar, the queer or the pathological. In the second, colour is relegated to the realm of the superficial, the supplementary, the inessential or the cosmetic. In one, colour is regarded as alien and therefore dangerous; in the other, it is perceived merely as a secondary quality of experience, and thus unworthy of serious consideration. Colour is dangerous, or it is trivial, or it is both. (It is typical of prejudices to conflate the sinister and the superficial). Either way, colour is routinely excluded from the higher concerns of the Mind. It is other to the higher values of Western culture. Or perhaps culture is other to the higher values of colour. Or colour is the corruption of culture.

from 'Chromophobia' by David Batchelor, published by Reaktion Books Ltd, London 2000.

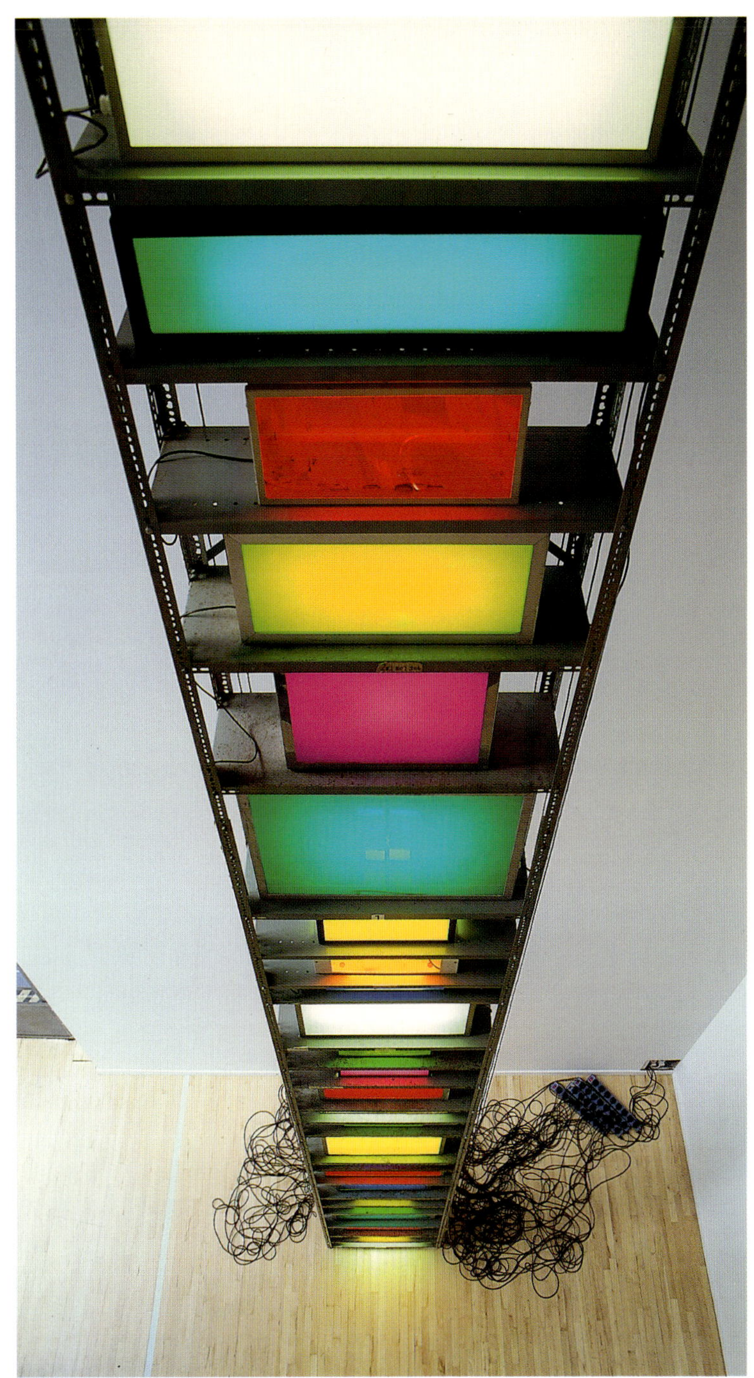

ELECTRIC COLOUR TOWER 6 2001
STEEL SHELVING, LIGHTBOXES, FLUORESCENT LAMPS, ACRYLIC SHEET, CABLE, PLUG BOARDS 626 x 91 x 31 CM
COURTESY: ANTHONY WILKINSON GALLERY, LONDON

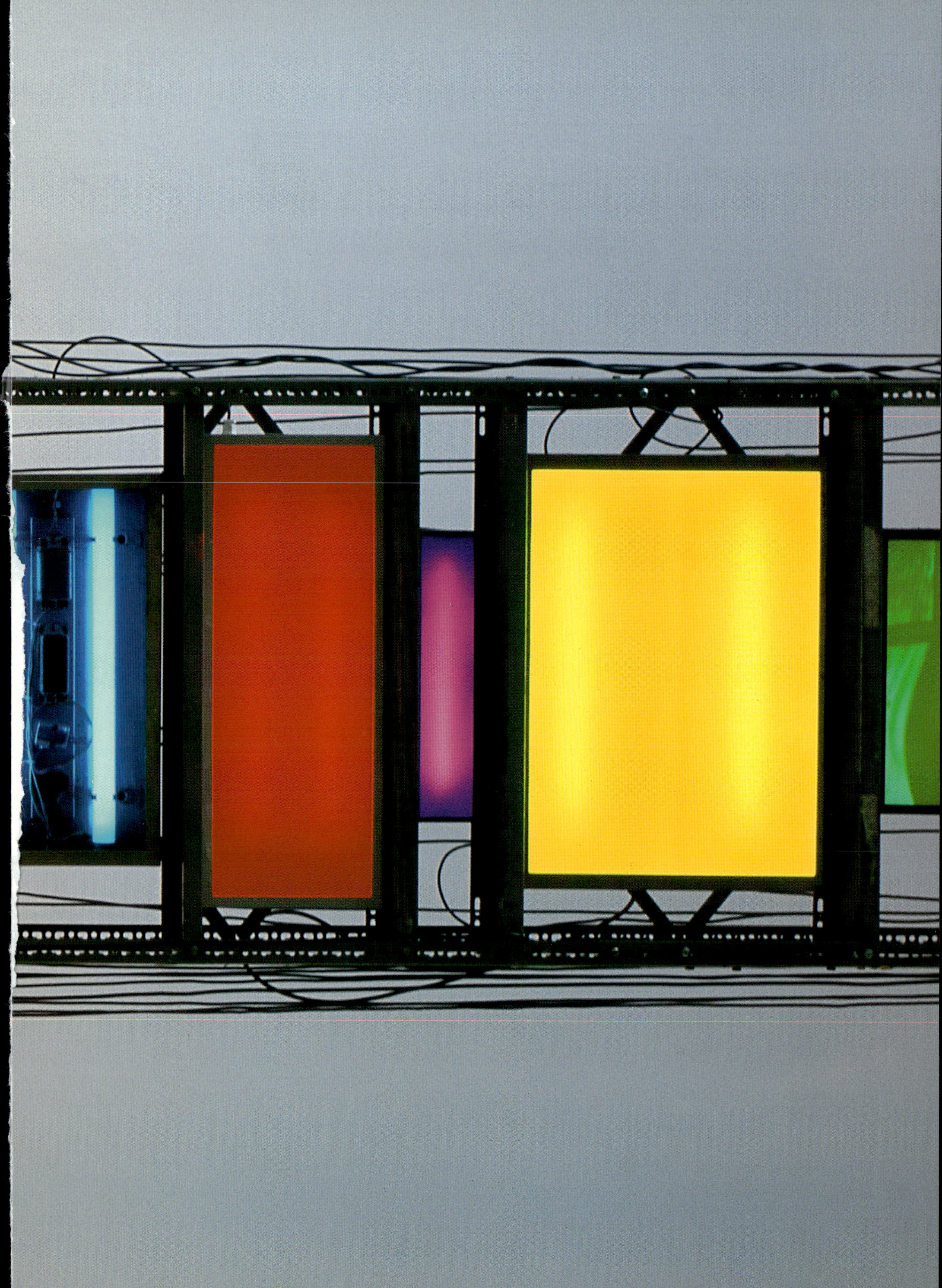

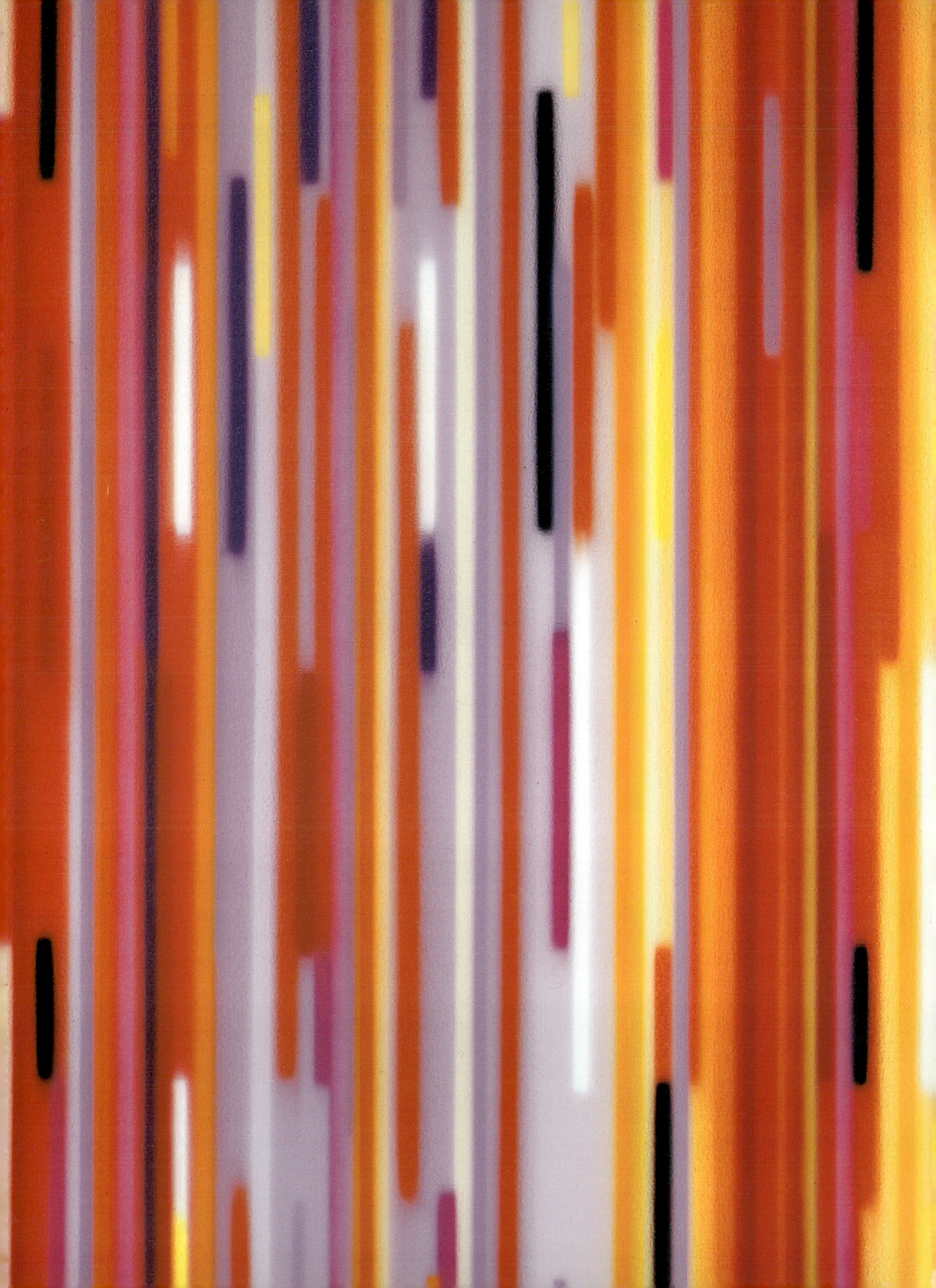

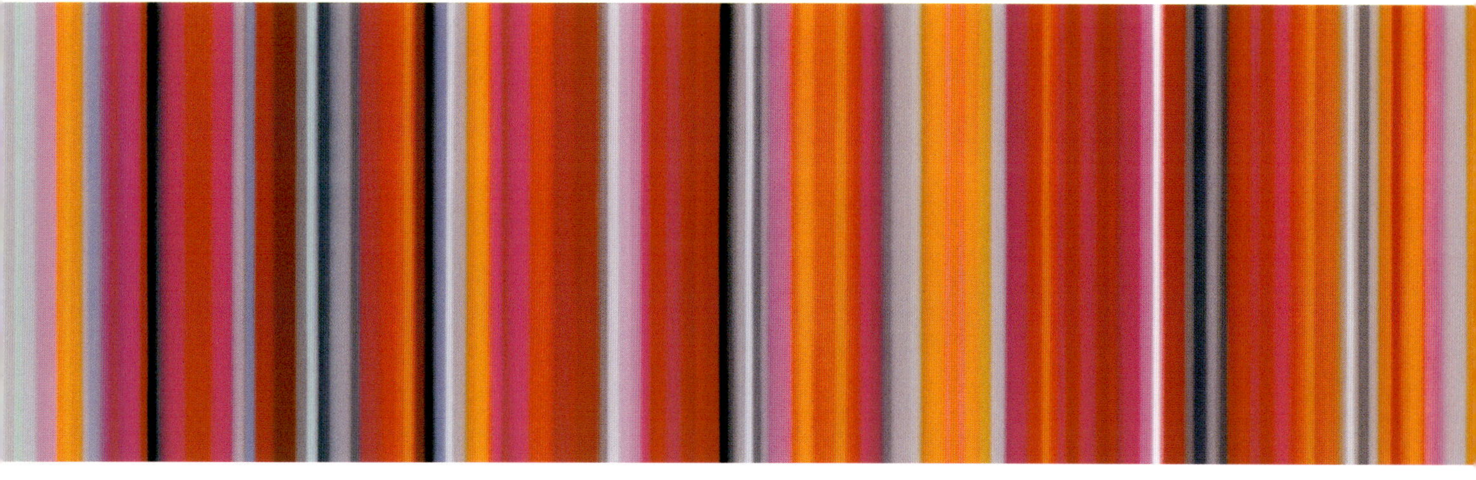

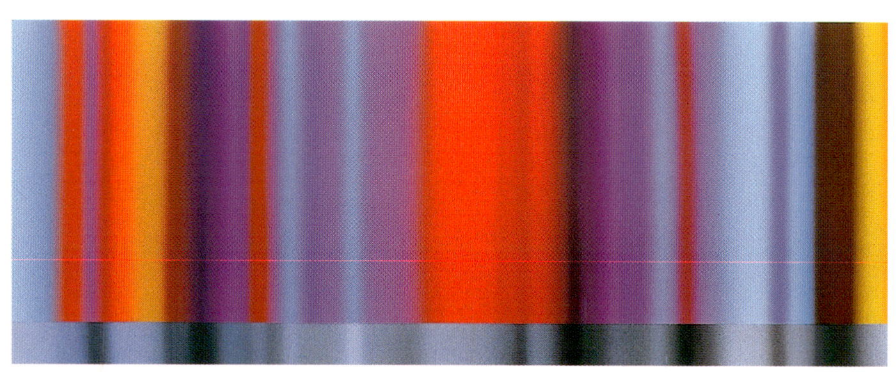

UNTITLED 2001
ACRYLIC ON WOOD PANEL 20.3 x 53.3 CM
COURTESY OF THE ARTIST AND MARK MOORE GALLERY, LOS ANGELES

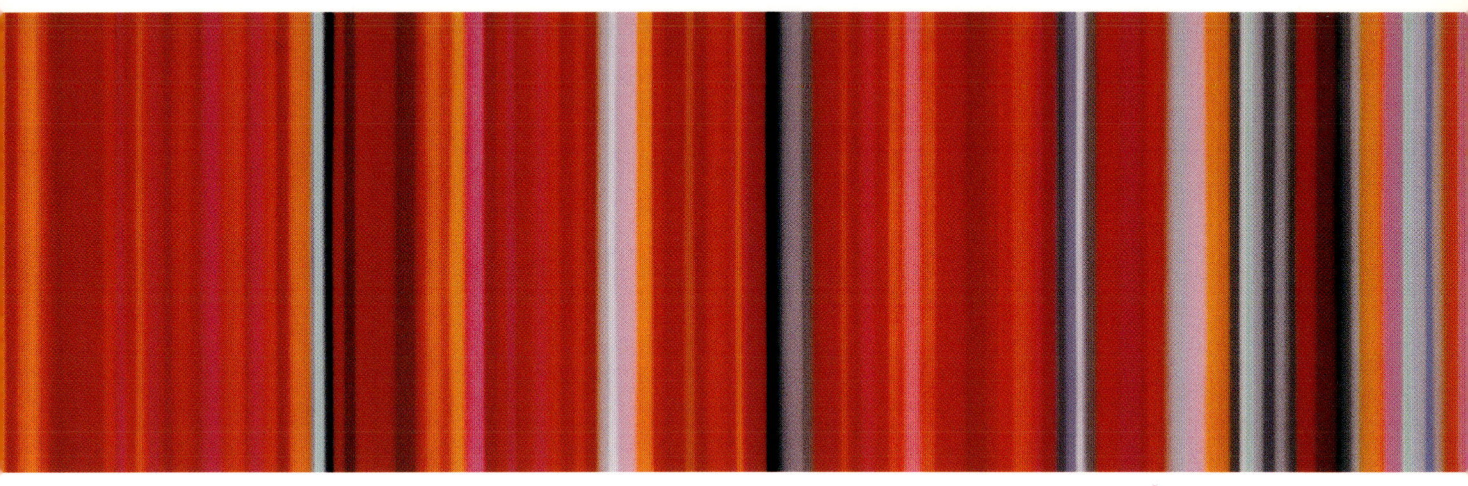

DO IT NOW 2001
ACRYLIC ON CANVAS 53.3 x 365.7 CM
COURTESY OF THE ARTIST AND MARK MOORE GALLERY, LOS ANGELES

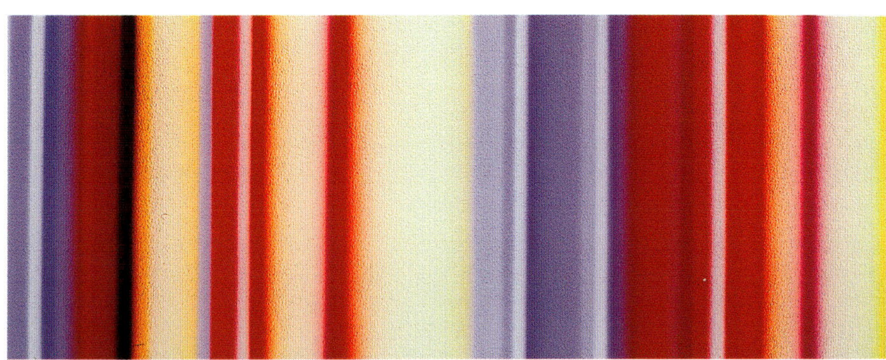

WILD HONEY (STUDY) 2001
ACRYLIC ON CANVAS OVER PANEL 33 x 86.3 CM
COURTESY OF THE ARTIST AND MARK MOORE GALLERY, LOS ANGELES

Jane Callister

1994 M.F.A. University of Nevada, Las Vegas, NV
1996- Assistant Professor, Department of Art Studio, UC, Santa Barbara, CA
Lives in Santa Barbara, CA

2001
Jane Callister, Frumkin/Duval, Santa Monica, CA
The Dreams Stuff is Made of, Frankfurt Art Fair, D
pornglossdope, Southfirst art, Brooklyn, New York, NY
2000
Jane Callister, Tiffany Szilage Gallery, St. Petersburg, FL
Velvet, Andrea Swartz Gallery, San Francisco, CA

INTROSPECTIVE, EXTROVERT #1, 2, 3 1999
ACYRLIC, FAUXKING, VELVET FLECK ON PANEL 60.9 x 45.7 CM
COURTESY OF THE ARTIST AND SHOSHANA WAYNE GALLERY, SANTA MONICA, CA
PHOTO: ANTHONY CUNHA

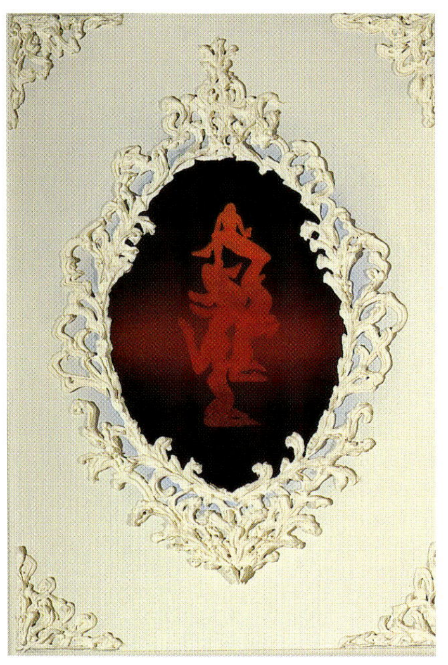

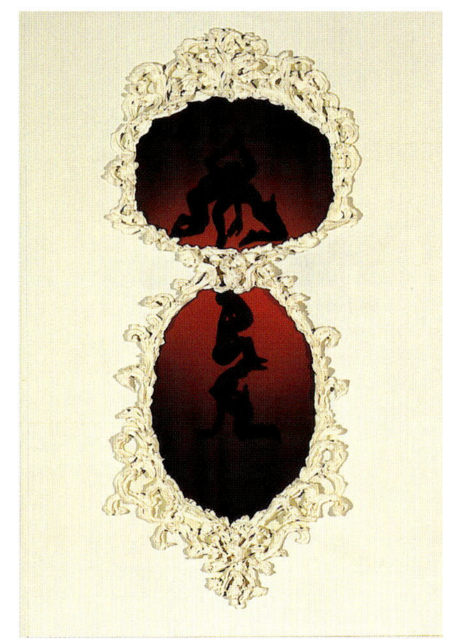

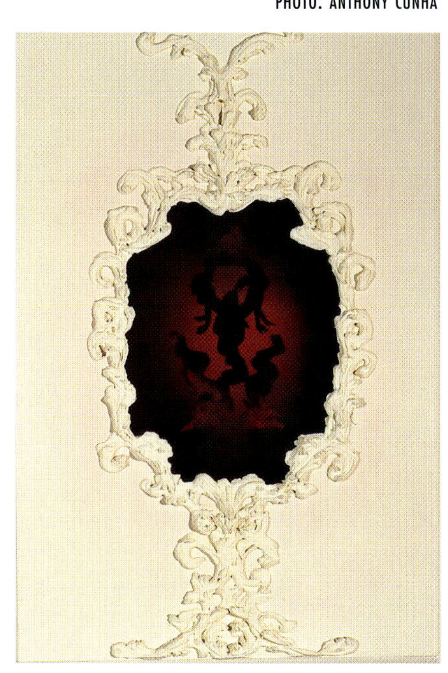

The whole city floats on a sleek *frisson* of anxiety and promise that those of us addicted to such distraction must otherwise induce by motion or medication.

'A Home in the Neon', from 'Air Guitar' by Dave Hickey, Distributed Art Publishers, New York 1997

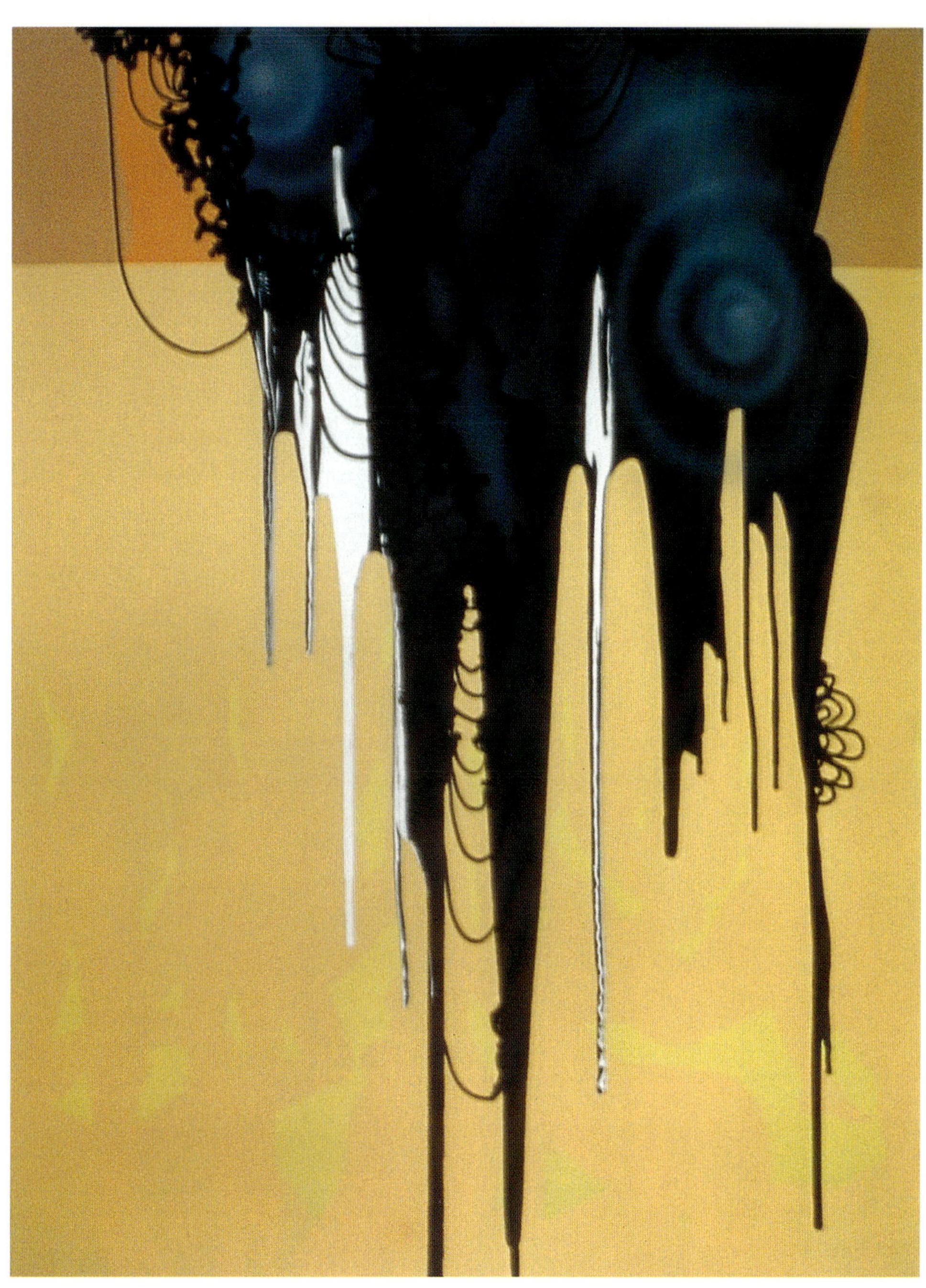

SONIC DRIP 2001
ACRYLIC ON CANVAS 76.2 x 60.9 CM
COURTESY OF SHOSHANA WAYNE GALLERY, SANTA MONICA, CA

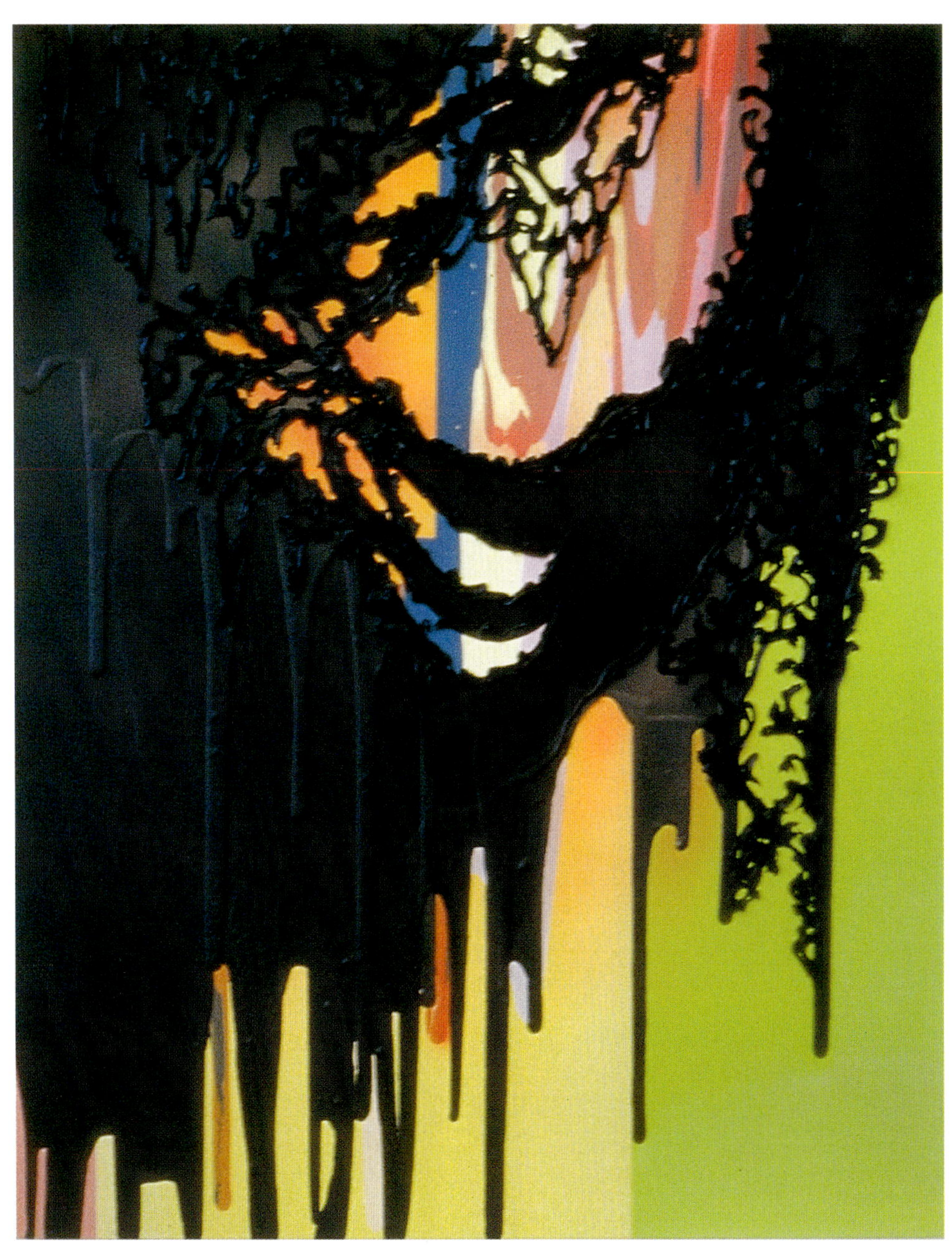

COSMIC LINGERIE 2000
ACRYLIC ON CANVAS 76.2 x 60.9 CM
COURTESY OF SHOSHANA WAYNE GALLERY, SANTA MONICA, CA

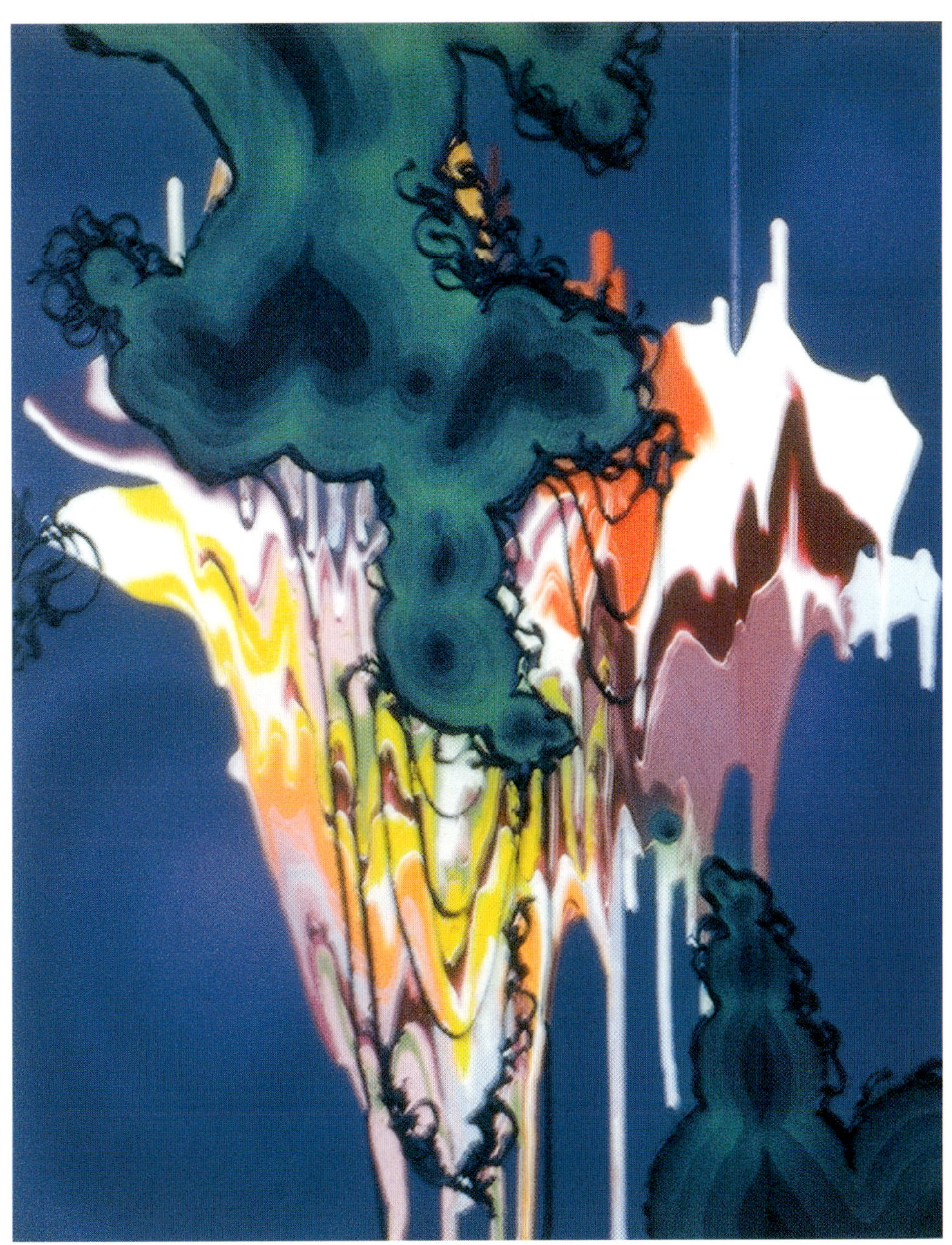

GREEN CHAOS 2001
ACRYLIC ON CANVAS 76.2 x 60.9 CM
COURTESY OF SHOSHANA WAYNE GALLERY, SANTA MONICA, CA

Karen Carson

1943 Born in Corvallis, OR
1966 B.A. University of Oregon, OR
1971 M.F.A. University of California, Los Angeles, CA
1994 Artist in Residence, University of Nevada, Las Vegas, NV
Lives in Los Angeles and Idaho

2001
Karen Carson, Rosamund Felsen Gallery, Santa Monica, CA
2000
12 Divas, Molly Barnes Gallery, Santa Monica, CA
1999
Radical Past: Art and Music in Pasadena, 1960-74, Norton Simon Museum, Armory Center for the Arts, Arts Center College of Design, Pasadena, CA
1998
Pop Abstraction, Museum of American Art of the Pennsylvania Academy of Fine Arts, Philadelphia, PA
1997
Karen Carson, Bill Maynes Gallery, New York, NY

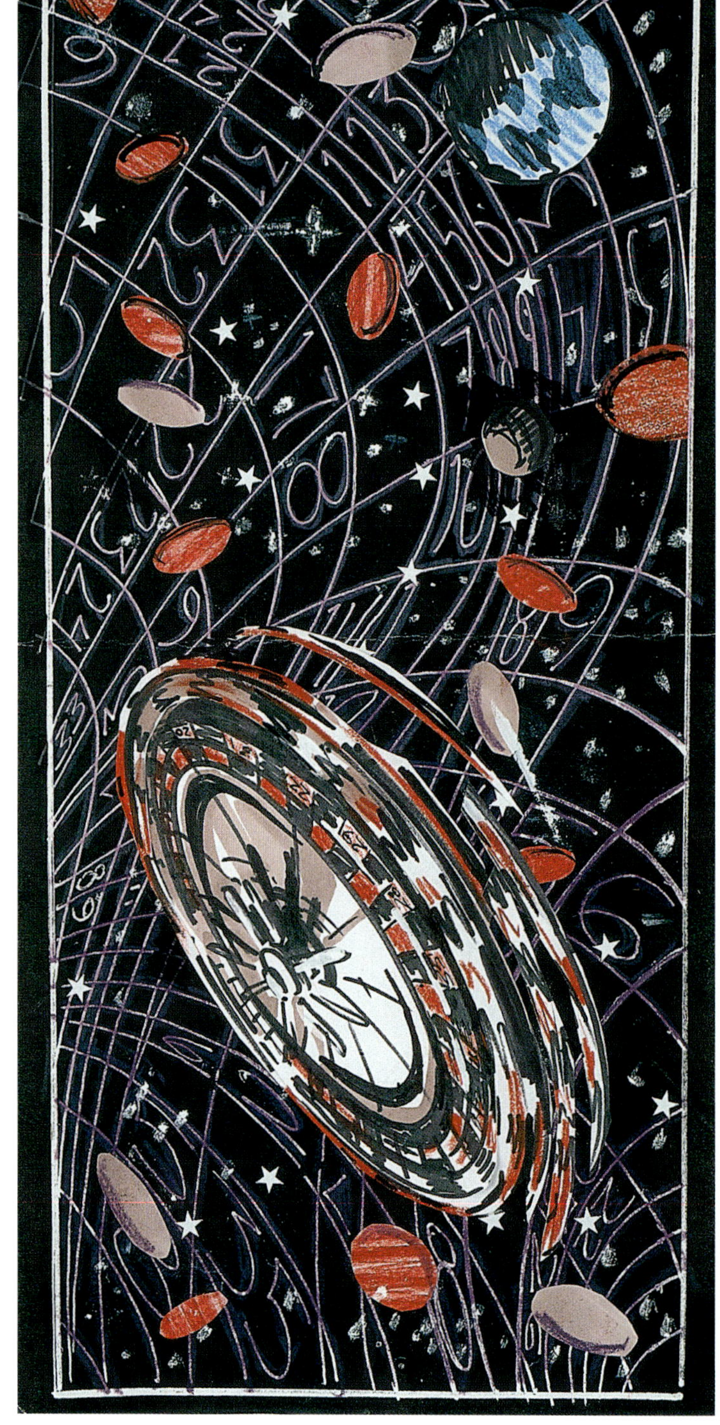

STUDY FOR COSMIC ROULETTE 2001
PAPER AND PHOTOCOPY COLLAGE AND PENCIL ON PAPER
33.6 X 17.1 CM
COURTESY OF THE ARTIST AND ROSAMUND FELSEN GALLERY, SANTA MONICA, CA

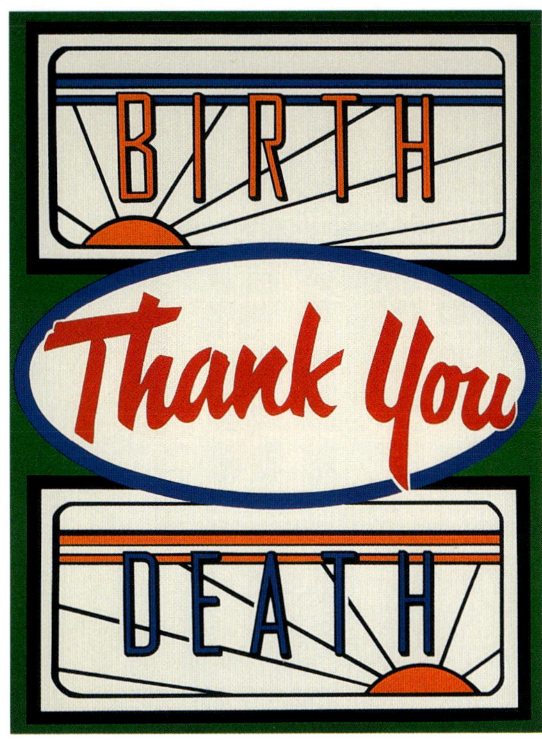

THANK YOU 1994
SILKSCREEN ON PAPER (EDITION OF 15) 83.8 x 66 CM
COURTESY OF THE ARTIST AND ROSAMUND FELSEN GALLERY, SANTA MONICA, CA
PHOTO: DOUGLAS M. PARKER STUDIO

MIND, BODY AND SOUL 1994
SILKSCREEN ON PAPER (EDITION OF 15) 83.8 x 66 CM
COURTESY OF THE ARTIST AND ROSAMUND FELSEN GALLERY, SANTA MONICA, CA
PHOTO: DOUGLAS M. PARKER STUDIO

I grew up in a home in which decorum, restraint and fear were permanent house guests. No matter how much fun we had, somehow it had to stop soon!

The antithesis of Lutheran moderation materialized for me in the glowing form of Las Vegas where I spent three months teaching at University of Nevada at Las Vegas in 1994.

I am only a mild sinner, and I enjoy calm. A trip to Vegas promised an enticing adventure to a place where excess is the norm.

At the time I was repairing from a long valium habit and my nervous system was 'ga ga' from its new freedom. I was literally vibrating from the impact of all the lights, noise and traffic.

As a shield, I intended to put my dabbling in Zen to use, and I needed a place to sit. I was unable to find anything but a dusty little native plant botanical garden adjoining a parking lot.

Strangely enough it was in the casinos, with the ding, ding, ding of the slots, the thump of coins dropping karmic rewards, that I found a place I could focus, live in the moment, and feel universal camaraderie with fellow travelers. There was no past and no future.

The calm was not induced by the gambling itself. It was the strange stoppage of time, the repetitive sound, the spatial disorganization, and constant twilight that made for a world between worlds, a stress-free cosmic plane.

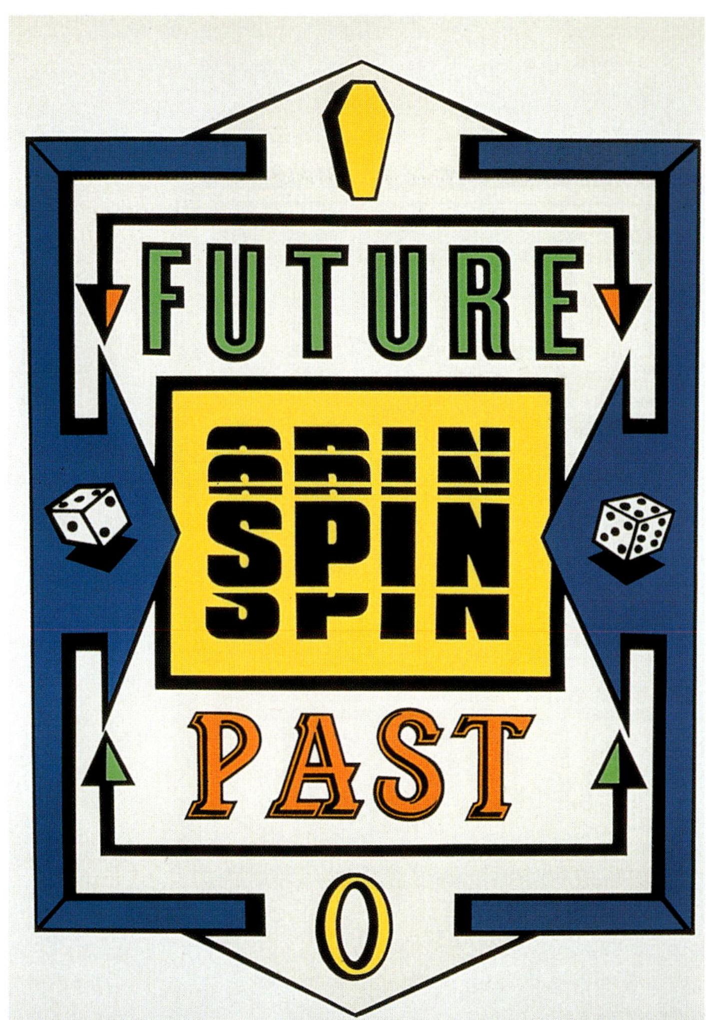

SPIN 1994
SILKSCREEN ON PAPER (EDITION OF 15) 83.8 x 66 CM
COURTESY OF THE ARTIST AND ROSAMUND FELSEN GALLERY, SANTA MONICA, CA
PHOTO: DOUGLAS M. PARKER STUDIO

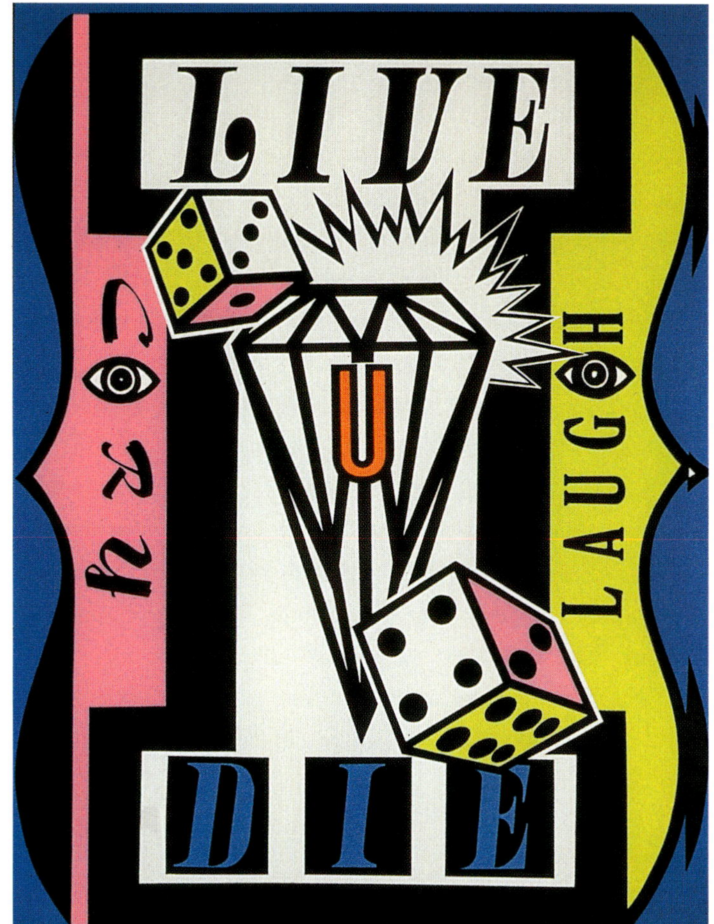

LIVE, DIE 1994
SILKSCREEN ON PAPER (EDITION OF 15) 83.8 x 66 CM
COURTESY OF THE ARTIST AND ROSAMUND FELSEN GALLERY, SANTA MONICA, CA
PHOTO: DOUGLAS M. PARKER STUDIO

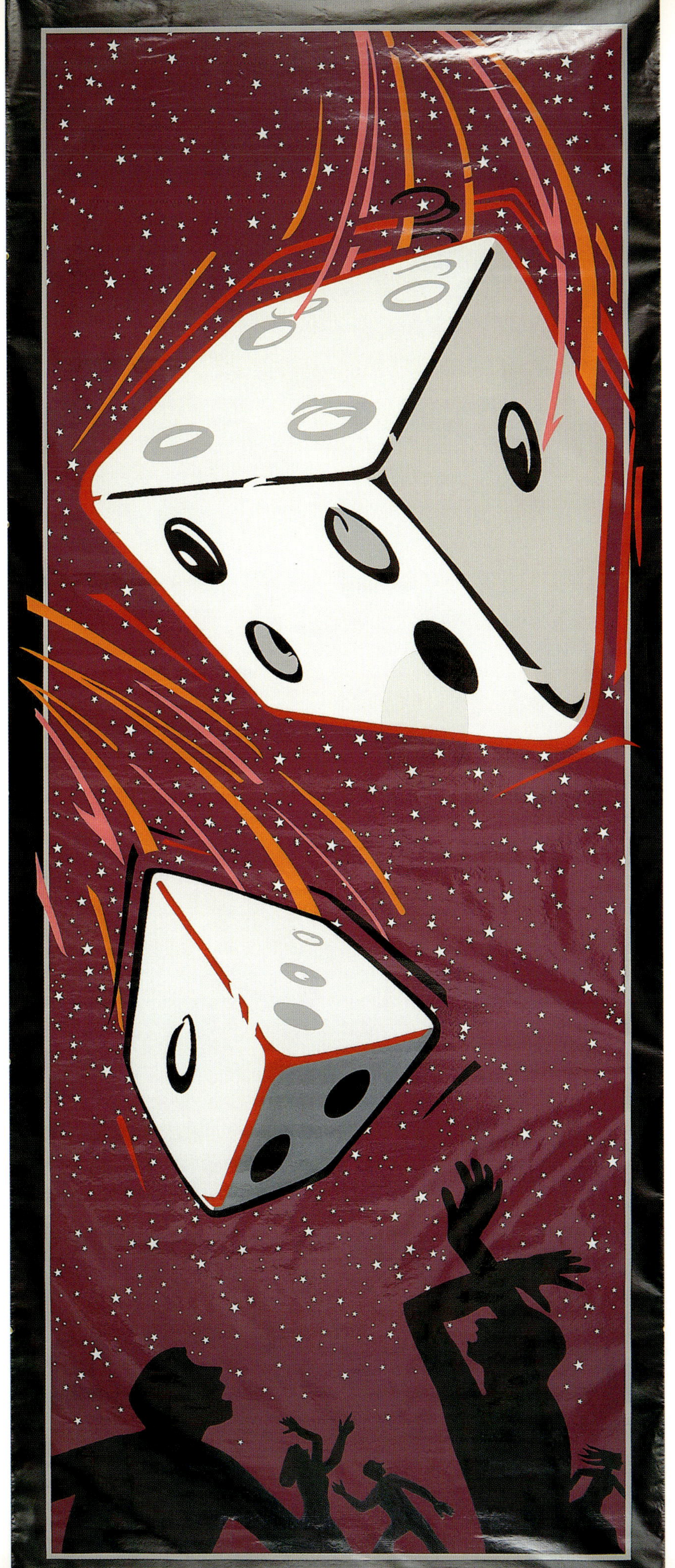

COSMIC DICE 2001
ENAMEL ON VINYL
457.2 x 182.8 CM
COURTESY OF THE ARTIST AND
ROSAMUND FELSEN GALLERY, SANTA
MONICA, CA
PHOTO: ANTHONY CUNHA

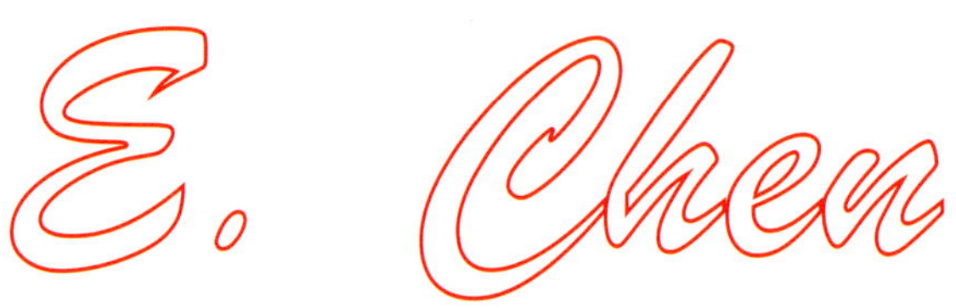

1966 Born in Taiwan
1988 B.A. Fu-Jen Catholic University, Taiwan
1993 M.F.A. University of California, Los Angeles, CA
1996 M.A. Architecture, University of California, Berkeley, CA
1993 E Design was founded
Lives in Los Angeles, CA

2000
E. Chen, Richard Telles Fine Art, Los Angeles, CA
1999
E. Chen, Richard Telles Fine Art, Los Angeles, CA
New Romance, Post, Los Angeles, CA
1998
Titanica, Richard Telles Fine Art, Los Angeles, CA

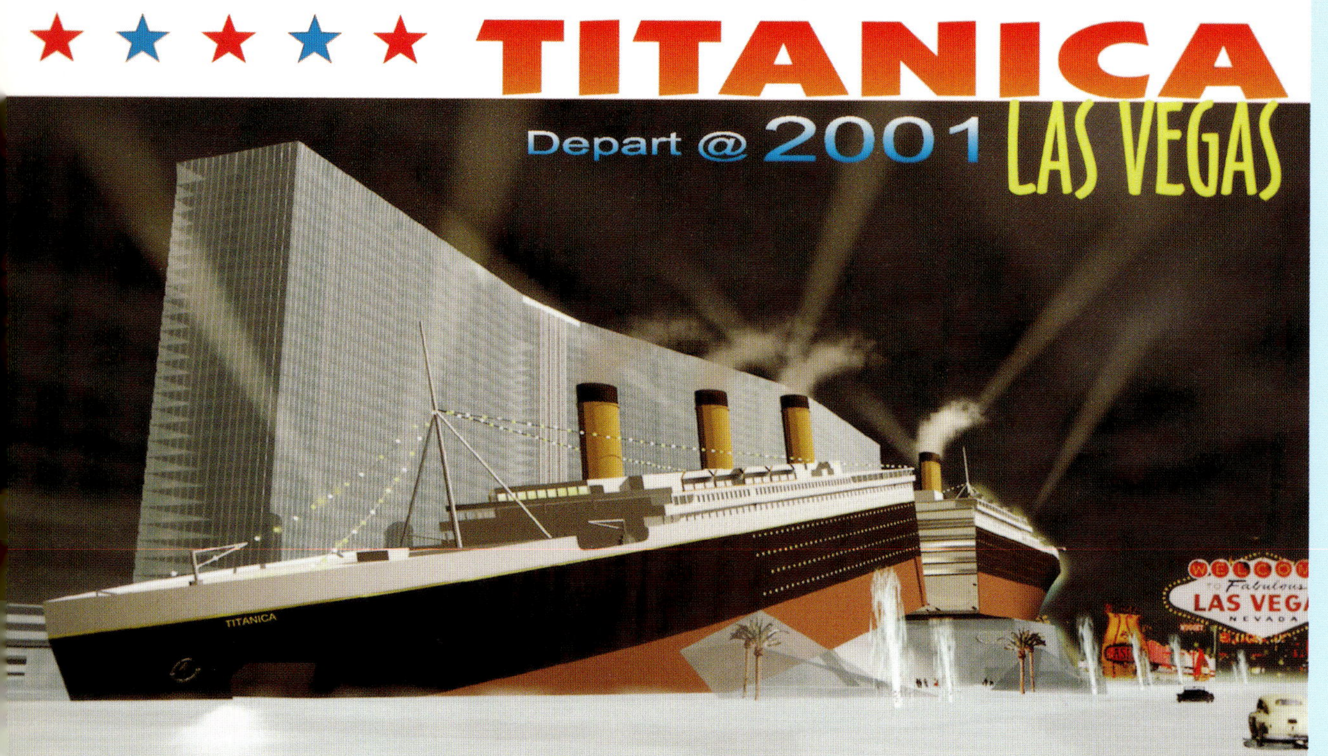

E DESIGN IS PROUD TO ANNOUNCE THE LAUNCHING OF A REVOLUTIONARY NEW PROJECT: TITANICA LAS VEGAS, IN LAS VEGAS, NEVADA. TITANICA LAS VEGAS WILL BE THE ULTIMATE ENTERTAINMENT AND HOLIDAY DESTINATION, INCLUDING A FIVE STAR HOTEL, 4 FLOORS OF GAMING, UNDER WATER WORLD, NORSE LAND AND VIKING VILLAGE, RESTAURANTS, RETAIL AND MUCH MORE.

PROGRAM

TITANICA LAS VEGAS WILL FEATURE 4 FULL FLOORS OF GAMING, TOTALING OVER 180,000 SQUARE FEET. DESIGNED WITH THE SAME TURN OF THE CENTURY OPULENCE AS ITS NAMESAKE, TITANICA LAS VEGAS WILL OFFER THE SOPHISTICATION OF THE GREAT CRUISE LINERS WITH FULL MODERN AMENITIES. AT 35 STORIES, THE FIVE STAR HOTEL AT THE TITANICA LAS VEGAS, IN THE IMAGE OF AN ICEBERG, WILL HOST OVER 4,000 ROOMS, INCLUDING EXECUTIVE, LUXURY AND PRESIDENTIAL SUITES. THE HOTEL AT THE TITANICA LAS VEGAS WILL BE THE ULTIMATE OASIS IN THE HOT NEVADA DESERT. GUESTS WILL BOARD LIFEBOATS IN UNDER WATER WORLD TO VIEW THE RE-CREATED WRECKAGE OF THE TITANIC, AN INTERACTIVE TITANIC MUSEUM, AS WELL AS A FULL OCEANIC AQUARIUM. NORSE LAND AND VIKING VILLAGE WILL OFFER THEMED ENTERTAINMENT AND FUN FOR THE WHOLE FAMILY. KIDS AND THEIR PARENTS WILL EXPLORE THE FAR NORTH BY TRAVELING ON VIKING SHIPS THROUGH ICEBERGS, FJORDS AND ICE CAVES. THE MULTI-LEVEL RETAIL PORTION OF TITANICA LAS VEGAS WILL HOUSE PURVEYORS OF THE HIGHEST END LUXURY GOODS, A MULTIPLEX THEATER, AS WELL AS FULL HEALTH AND BEAUTY SPAS. THE RESTAURANTS OF TITANICA LAS VEGAS WILL FEATURE CUISINE FROM AROUND THE WORLD WITH AN ARRAY OF INTERNATIONALLY RENOWNED CHEFS.

THEME AND IMAGE

TITANICA LAS VEGAS WILL EMBODY ALL OF THE OPULENCE OF EARLY TWENTIETH CENTURY. THIS OPULENCE AND GRANDEUR WILL BE REFLECTED IN THE INTERIOR FINISHES AND ARCHITECTURAL DETAILING, AS WELL AS IN THE CASINO'S GRAPHICS AND SIGNAGE, AND EMPLOYEES' UNIFORMS. THE HOTEL AT TITANICA LAS VEGAS WILL EMBODY A FUTURISTIC THEME. THIS WILL COMPLEMENT TITANICA LAS VEGAS, AS THE ORIGINAL SHIP, WITH ITS STREAM LINED MODERNISM, WAS AT THE CUTTING EDGE OF TECHNOLOGY FOR ITS TIME. SIMILARLY, THE ICEBERG HOTEL WILL BE AT THE CUTTING EDGE OF ARCHITECTURAL TECHNOLOGY. THE 30 STORY HIGH GLASS CURTAIN WALL WILL BE THE INTERFACE BETWEEN THE SCORCHING HEAT OF THE NEVADA DESERT AND THE COOL INTERIORS OF THE GUESTROOMS. USING RECENT ADVANCES IN GLASS TECHNOLOGY, THE HOTEL AT THE TITANICA LAS VEGAS WILL NEGOTIATE THE EXTREMES IN TEMPERATURE, AND LEAD DESIGN IN THIS FIELD AT THE NEXT TURN OF CENTURY.

SITE REQUIREMENTS AND DIMENSIONS

TITANICA LAS VEGAS SEEKS TO REMAIN TRUE TO THE SPIRIT OF ITS NAMESAKE. A LARGE PART OF THE ORIGINAL GLORY WAS THE SHIP'S MAGNITUDE. AS SUCH, THE TITANICA LAS VEGAS WILL REMAIN FAITHFUL WITH THE FOLLOWING DIMENSIONS: LENGTH: 882 FEET / WIDTH: 92 FEET / DEPTH: 97 FEET. THESE ARE JUST THE DIMENSIONS FOR THE CASINO ELEMENT OF THE RECONSTRUCTED SHIP. THE OTHER ELEMENTS OF THE PROJECT, INCLUDING SITE, PARKING, HOTEL, AND ASSOCIATED RETAIL AND ENTERTAINMENT, COMBINED WITH TITANICA LAS VEGAS, WILL REQUIRE A SITE OF ROUGHLY 570,000 SQUARE FEET AT GRADE. TITANICA LAS VEGAS WILL RISE TO 12 STORIES ABOVE GRADE. THE 4,500 ROOMS HOTEL WILL RISE 35 FLOORS ABOVE GRADE.

ABOUT E DESIGN

E DESIGN WAS FOUNDED IN 1993 AND IS BASED IN SAN FRANCISCO, CALIFORNIA, WITH A BRANCH OFFICE IN LOS ANGELES. TITANICA LAS VEGAS REPRESENTS E DESIGN'S CONTINUING EXPLORATION OF THE LINKS BETWEEN VISUAL CULTURE AND ARCHITECTURE. IT IS OUR BELIEF THAT ARCHITECTS MUST ACTIVELY ENGAGE ISSUES OF BROAD PUBLIC INTEREST IN ORDER TO INITIATE PUBLIC DIALOGUE ABOUT ISSUES OF ART AND ARCHITECTURE.

PRELIMINARY COST ESTIMATES

2 BILLION DOLLARS

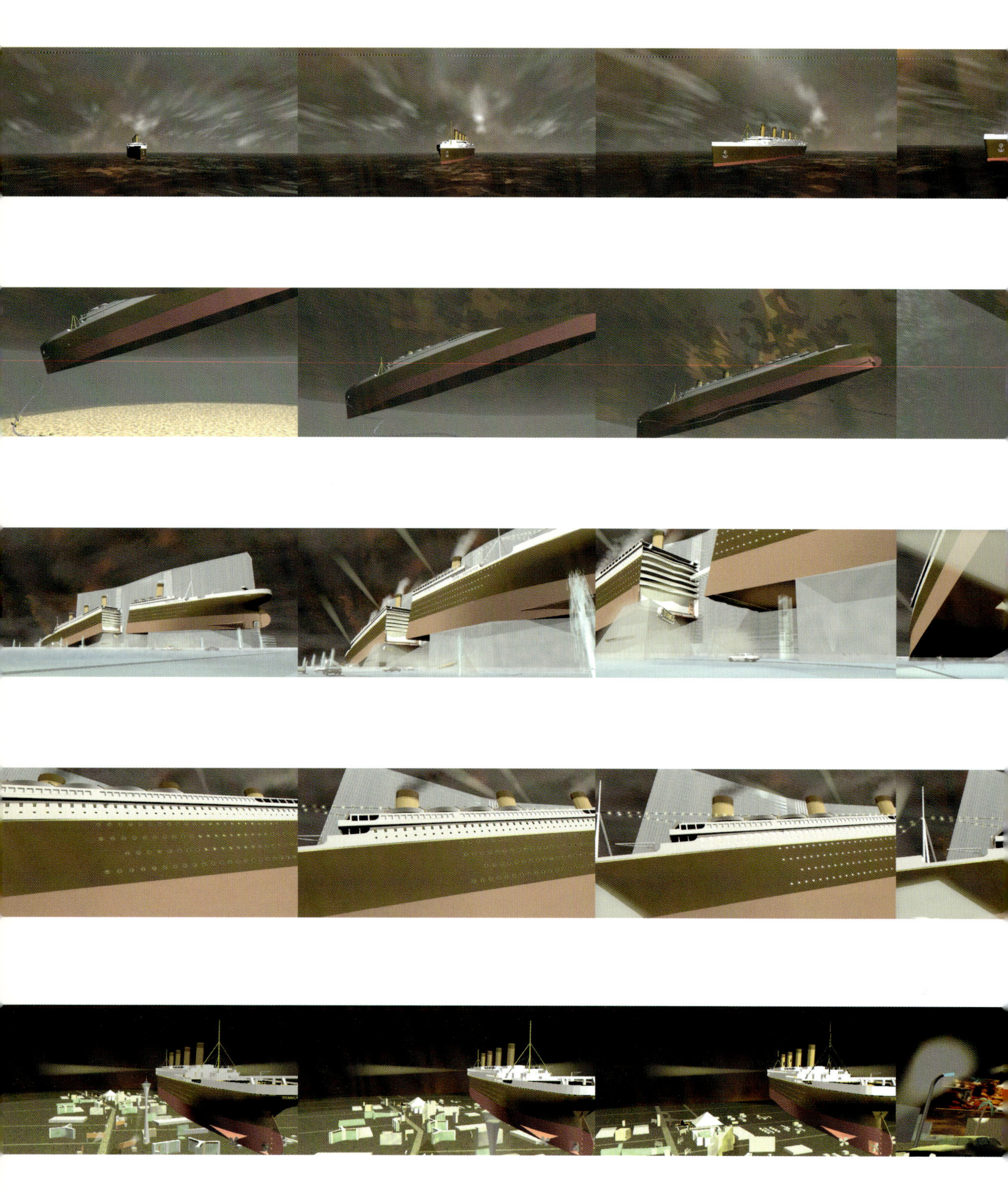

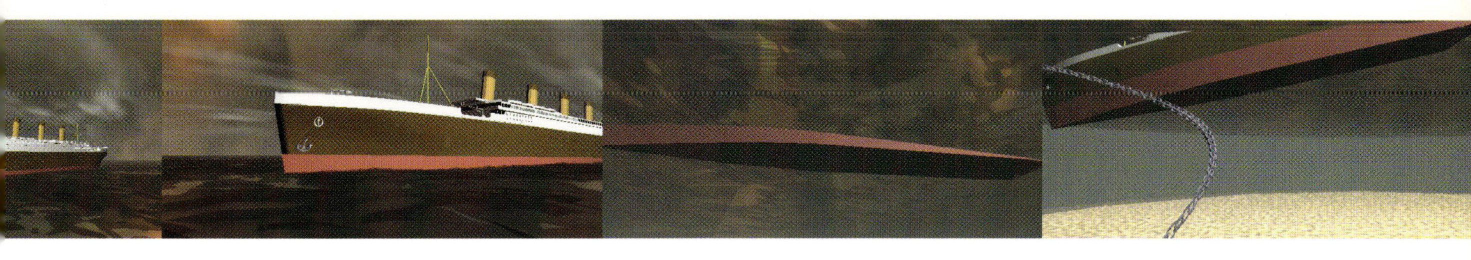

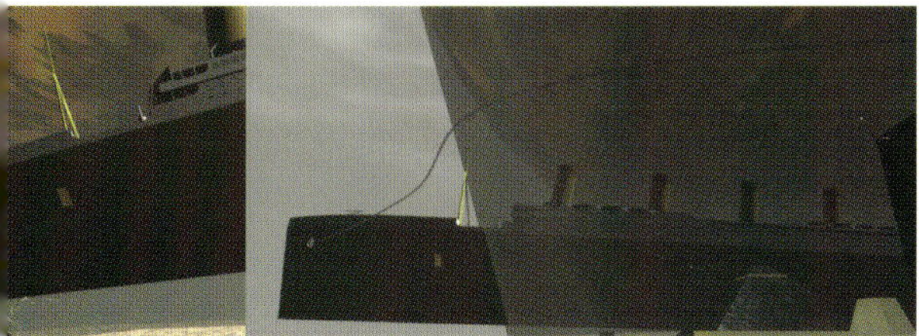

TITANICA LAS VEGAS 2001
MIXED MEDIA
FOR MORE INFORMATION CONTACT
E DESIGN@WWW.TITANICA.COM
COURTESY OF THE ARTIST AND RICHARD TELLES FINE ART, LOS ANGELES

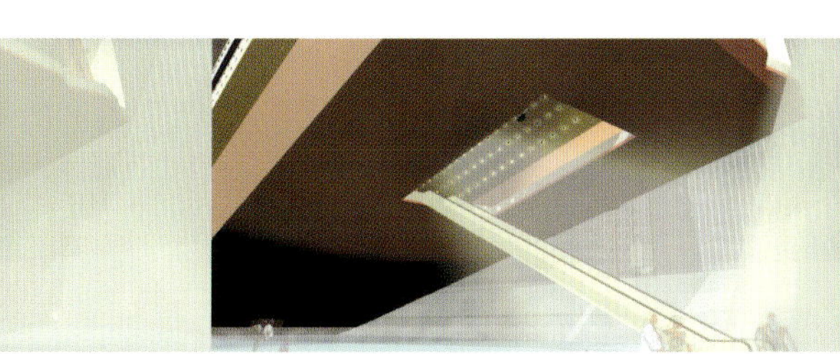

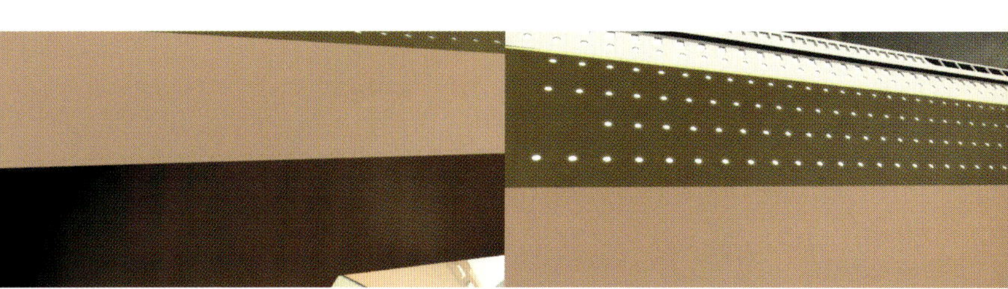

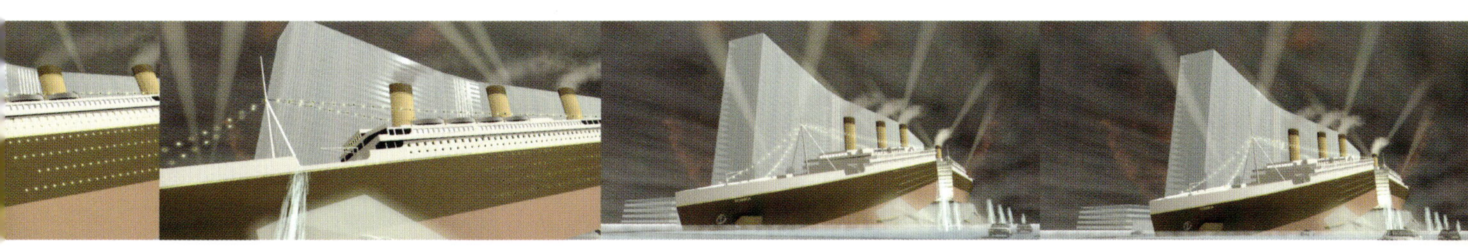

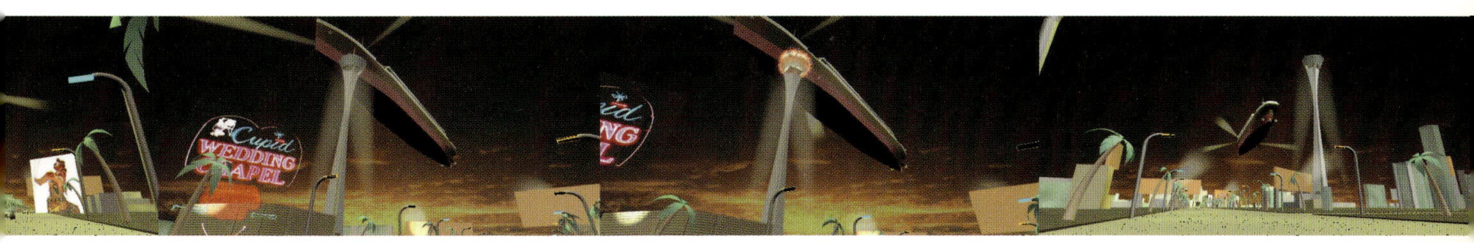

News Reader: *There's yet another Titanic project in the works, only this one belongs to Las Vegas. Here's the plan: build a life-size disintegrating ocean-liner parked in front of a giant phoney iceberg, and then put it on the Vegas Strip. Scott Rock's report has more. (music)*

Scott Rock (reporter): *The rusting hollow of the Titanic lies silently on the ocean floor as a monument to the tragedy, but it may soon be raised in a very different neighbourhood (music): Sin City.*

Alex Cox (E Design designer): We are best at doing the extreme.

Scott Rock: *Extreme, indeed. Alex Cox is part of a team of designers who plan to build an exact replica of the Titanic ship right on the Vegas Strip. The hotel, called Titanica, will be broken in two parts and located in front of a massive iceberg-shaped complex. The entire ship may even move, to mimick the sinking.*

Alex Cox: It would be pinned, basically, at the end here. This section of the ship will be rotated up and down.

Scott Rock: *Cox and his colleagues at E Design in Berkeley, California, said they came up with the idea before Jim Cameron's movie hit big. They discarded some less compelling designs.*

Alex Cox: This posed much more of a serious engineering challenge.

Scott Rock: *But now development is on the fast track and they are in the process of securing two billion dollars in financing.*

Jennifer Will (E Design designer): The main three floors for gaming are located here.

Scott Rock: *Jennifer Will said the gaming rooms would be decorated in a sumptuous period style, as would the 400 suites aboard the ship, but the 4000 rooms in the neighbouring hotel would be slick and modernistic. They are planning a penguin and polar bear display, a subterranean complex with museum and water ride, and a live action show on the deck.*

Jennifer Will: Our live action show will fully recreate original events like the descent of the lifeboats with actors and actresses in Imperial dress.

Scott Rock: *Las Vegas has never been known for its reserve. Aren't these designers concerned about exploiting the tragedy?*

Jennifer Will: It is more a monument to romance and to the heroism of people who were involved in the Titanic. It's sort of like a celebration of their lives, instead of tramping on them.

News Reader: *But passengers won't be boarding the Titanic anytime soon. E Design expects construction to begin in 2001.*

TV interview with Mark Ford from 'EXTRA' TV news show, CBS. Airing date: Pacific Time, Aug. 9, 1998

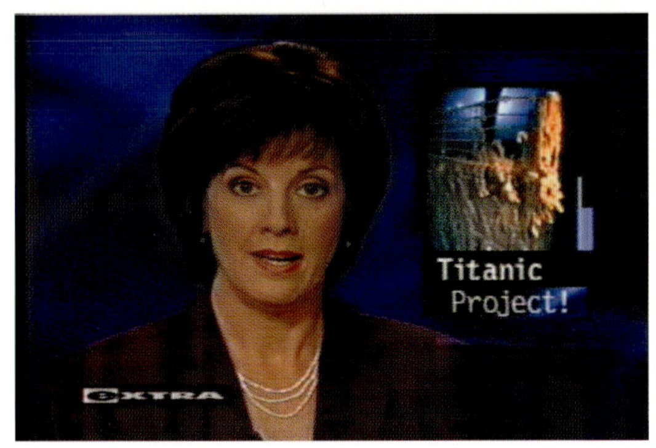
Titanic
Project!
EXTRA

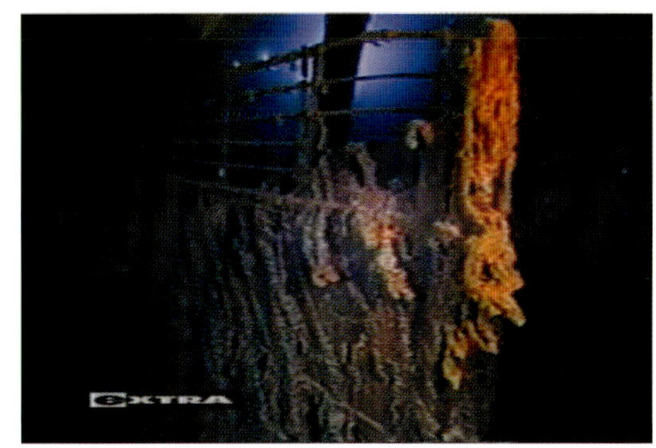
EXTRA

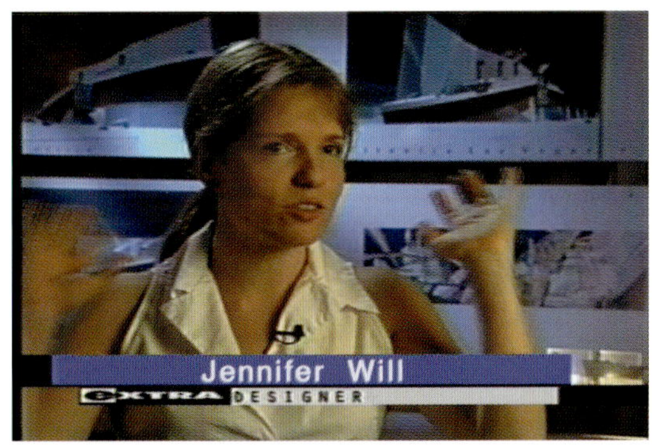
Jennifer Will
EXTRA DESIGNER

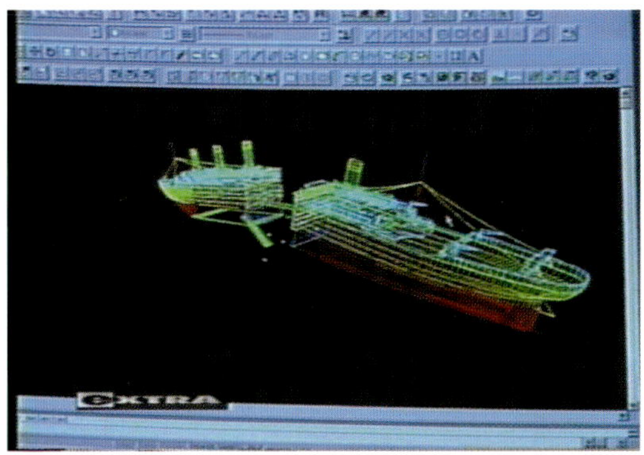
EXTRA

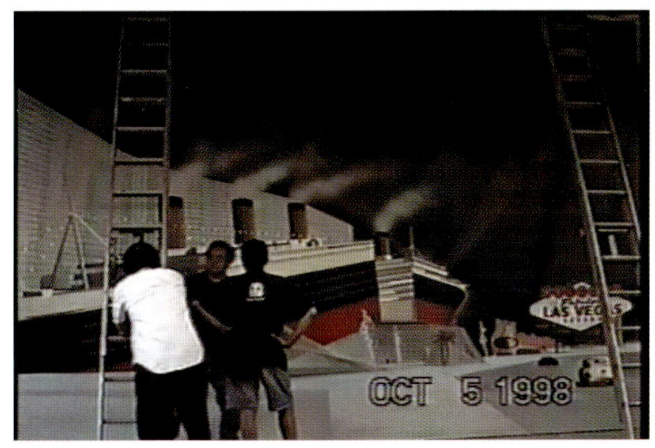
LAS VEGAS
OCT 5 1998

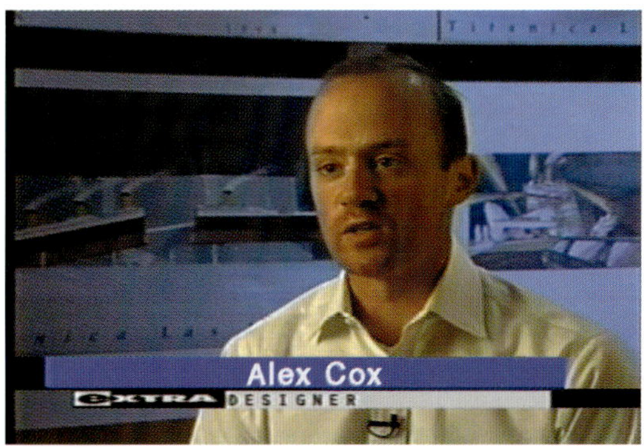
Alex Cox
EXTRA DESIGNER

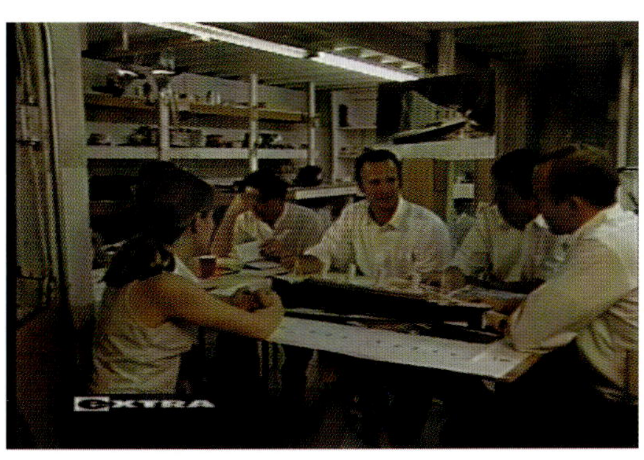
EXTRA

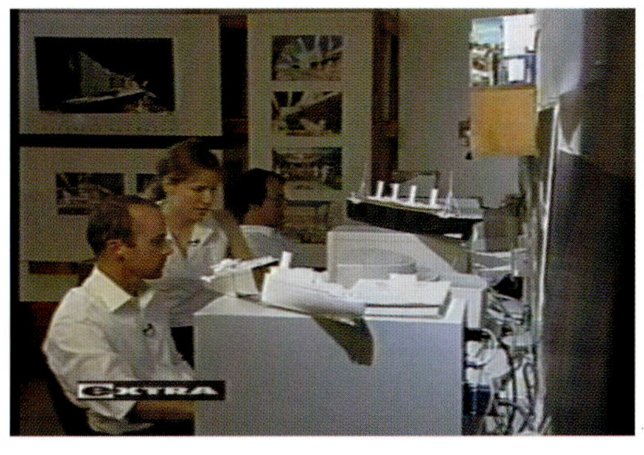
EXTRA

Marcel Duchamp

1887 Born near Blainville, F
1968 Died in Neuilly-sur-Seine, F

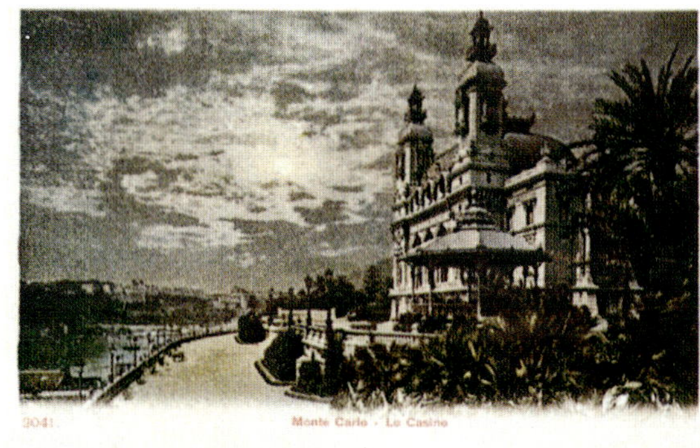

MOONLIGHT ON THE CASINO OF MONTE CARLO

EXTRAIT DES STATUTS

Art. 1er. — La Société a pour objet :

1° L'exploitation de la Roulette de Monte-Carlo dans les conditions ci-après.

2° L'exploitation du Trente et quarante et autres mines de la Côte d'Azur sur délibération du Conseil d'Administration.

Art. 2. — Le rendement annuel est basé sur un système à montante, éprouvé sur cent mille boules, propriété exclusive du Conseil d'Administration.

L'application du système aux chances simples permet de servir un dividende de 20 %.

Art. 3. — La Société pourra, sur délibération de l'Assemblée générale, rembourser tout ou partie des obligations au plus un mois après la date de la décision.

Art. 4. — Le paiement des coupons aura lieu le 1er Mars de chaque année ou par semestre, au gré des actionnaires.

OBLIGATIONS POUR LA ROULETTE DE MONTE CARLO, PARIS 1924
OFFSETDRUCK 31.4 x 19.6 CM (EDITION OF 30)
COURTESY OF NEUE GALERIE GRAZ

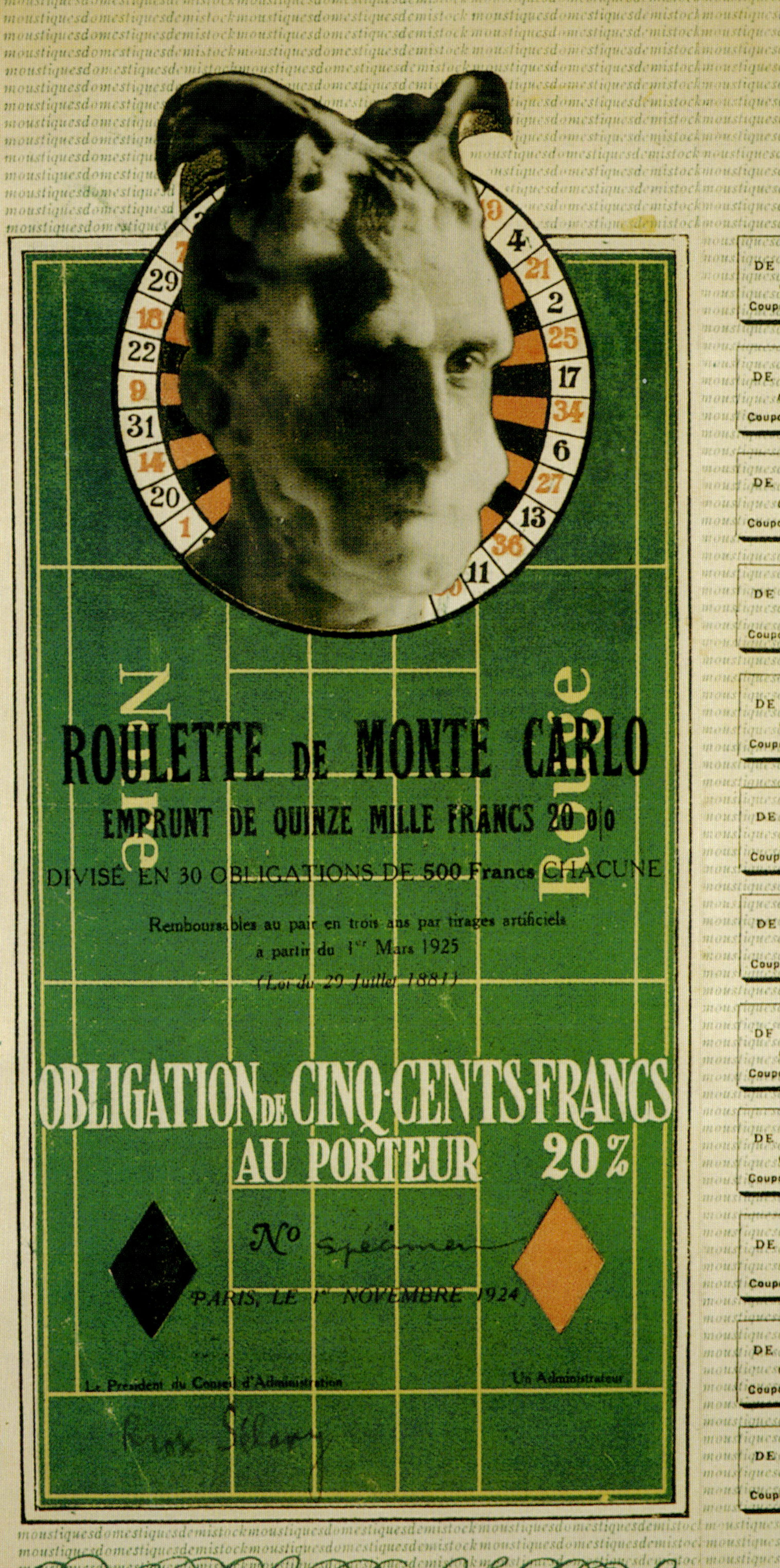
moustiquesdomestiquesdemistock
Noire
Rouge
ROULETTE DE MONTE CARLO
EMPRUNT DE QUINZE MILLE FRANCS 20 o|o
DIVISÉ EN 30 OBLIGATIONS DE 500 Francs CHACUNE
Remboursables au pair en trois ans par tirages artificiels
à partir du 1er Mars 1925
(Loi du 29 Juillet 1881)
OBLIGATION DE CINQ-CENTS-FRANCS
AU PORTEUR 20%
No
PARIS, LE 1er NOVEMBRE 1924
Le Président du Conseil d'Administration
Un Administrateur
ROULETTE
DE MONTE-CARLO
OBLIGATION N°
Coupon d'intérêt de 25 frs

Jane Hilton

1962 Born in Beaconsfield, Bucks, GB
1981-84 B.A. Music and Visual Art, Lancaster University, GB
1984-88 Photographer's Assistant
Lives in London, GB

2000
A Positive View, The Truman Brewery, London, GB
Crush, Hoax Gallery, London, GB
1999
Hoax, Hoax Gallery, London, GB
Primavera Fotographica, Faro, P
1998
The Whole Year Inn, The Agency Contemporary Art, London, GB

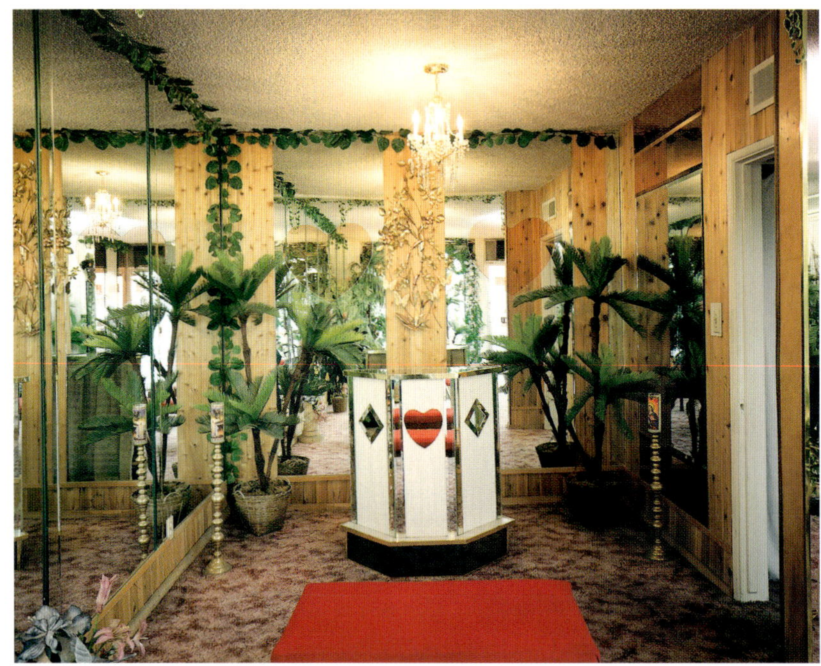

THE HITCHING POST 1998
C-TYPE PRINT 29.2 x 38.1 CM, FRAMED 60.9 x 50.8 CM
COURTESY OF THE ARTIST

Chapel Ministers, Las Vegas
transcribed from the video by Jane Hilton:

I've married a quarter of a million of people. The most weddings I ever did in a twenty-four hour period was on a Saturday 14 February – I did 188 weddings. I didn't have time to sit down and have something to eat, I didn't get a wink of sleep, and I did it in a single building where they have four chapels – I just went from room to room to room. I found out just recently from the Recorders' office – they contacted me – that I did the three millionth wedding in Clark County (from 1909 to just this year). We do more weddings than any city in the world. This year we will probably do 125,000 weddings in Las Vegas.

Reverend James B. Terrell

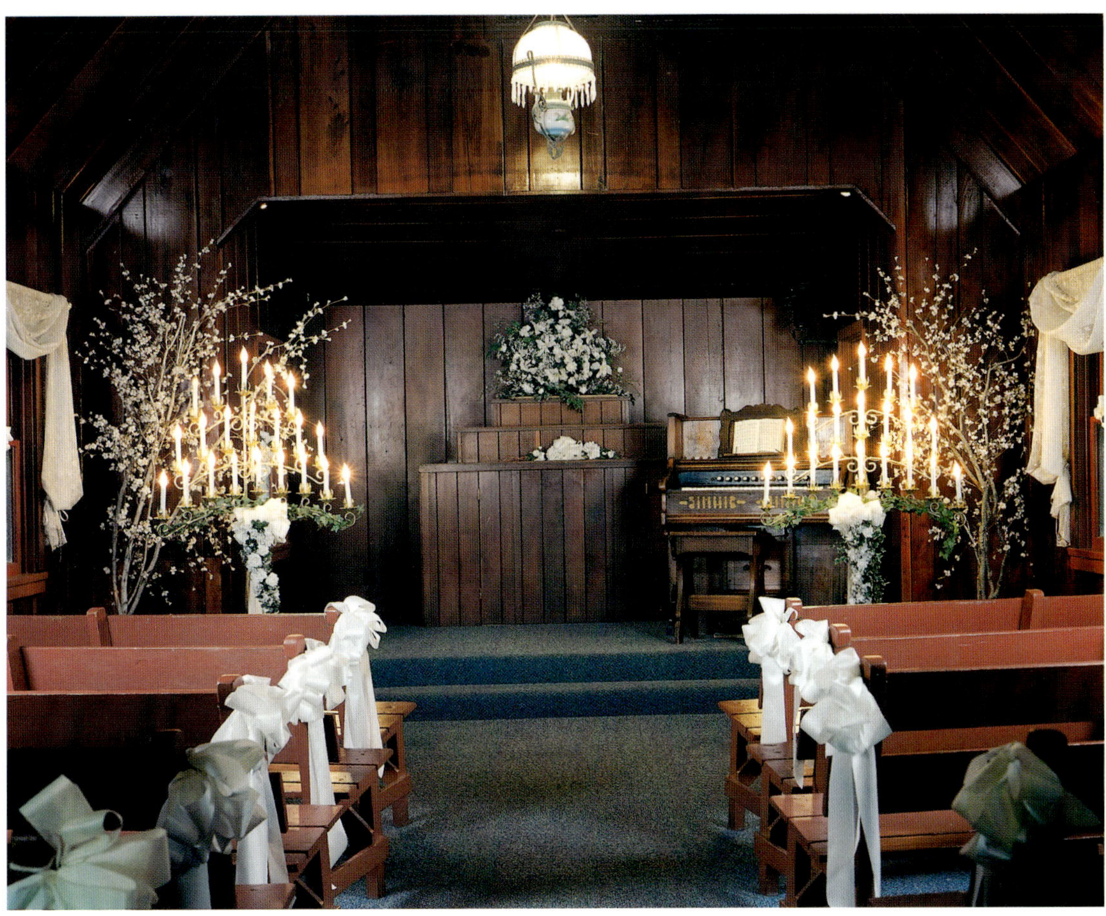

THE LITTLE CHURCH OF THE WEST 1998
C-TYPE PRINT 29.2 x 38.1 CM, FRAMED 60.9 x 50.8 CM
COURTESY OF THE ARTIST

I was called down to the chapel one evening, at around eight. There were four people there – the groom, best man, bride and bridesmaid. The bride had on a little bitty string bikini – I mean nothing but a string on the bottom – and on top she just had two little bits of paper, about so big, glued to the end of her breast, and she had a veil that must have been thirty feet long. And he had on a little bitty pair of under shorts – and, pardon the expression, but he looked like he had a potato stuck in there – and a big tall top hat. And when I saw them I just circled around them and went to the back and picked up the phone and called the lady working behind the desk at front and said "I'm not doing that wedding with them dressed like that. I'm not lowering myself to their standards." I have never seen someone as furious as that bride was. She was demanding that I do their wedding. So I said "Ma'am, I'm not doing your wedding unless you go and get dressed."... They took the coat from the best man and a shawl or something from the bridesmaid, wrapped it around themselves and went in and got married. Now a couple of weeks later we got sent a clipping from them from the newspaper. They had gone home and put on that tacky mess they had on and told the newspaper that's how they got married, got photographed and sent us the clipping.

Reverend James B. Terrell

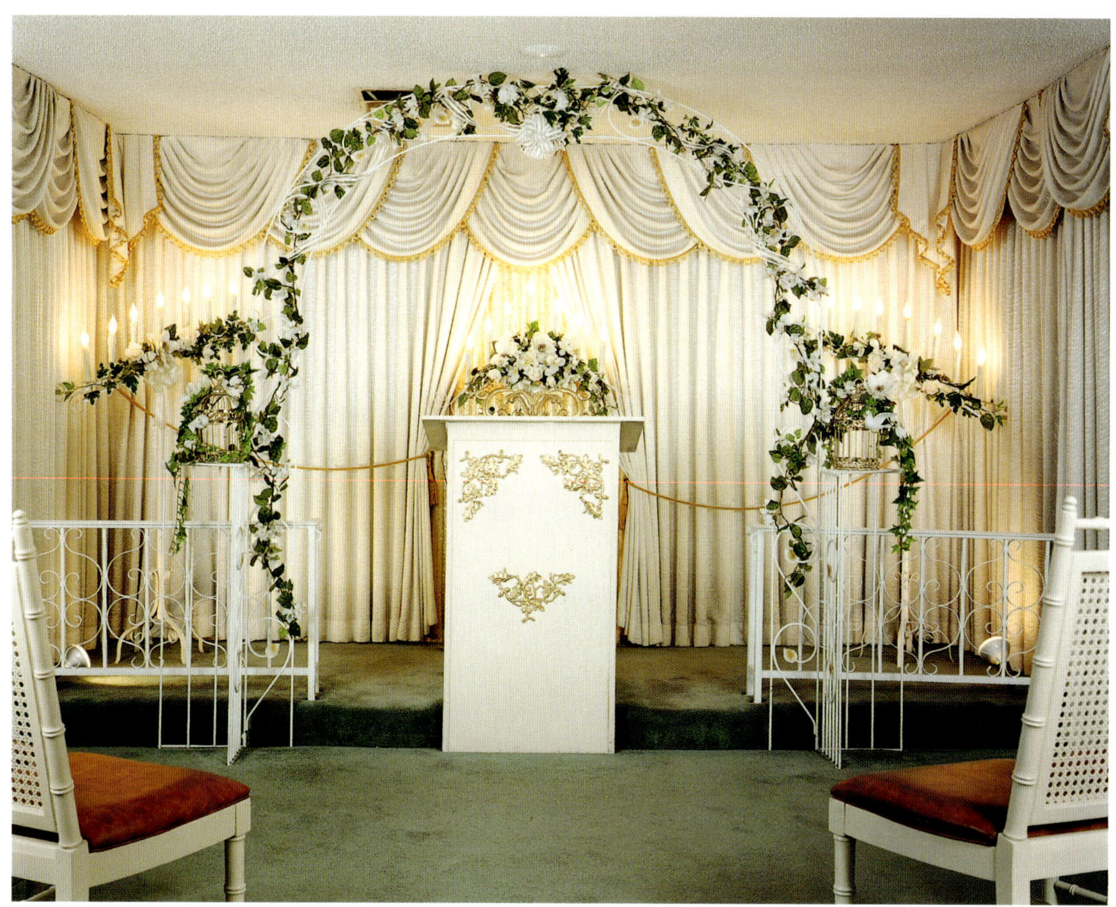

CHAPEL OF THE BELLS 1998
C-TYPE PRINT 29.2 x 38.1 CM, FRAMED 60.9 x 50.8 CM
COURTESY OF THE ARTIST

I did a wedding, I walked out of the chapel, and as I'm going down the hallway I stepped into a little office – about five by four feet – to call another chapel to see if they needed me before I go home. I heard the people coming out of the chapel and they were very loud. There were nine women and two men. The groom and his best man probably weighed no more than 110 pounds, and the nine women started at about 250 pounds each and went up from there. The bride and the mother are leading everyone down the hallway and all of them are just loud except for the two men – they were very quiet. The bride and mother looked at me in that office, jumped through the door, and just started hitting and beating on me. The other seven women now came right in behind them, all them, just working me over. The two men were trying to get in the chapel to stop what was going on. They couldn't get in since they were so much smaller than the women. When it was finally over the police arrested them in their hotel. They could never get a reason out of them why they did what they did. They literally blacked my eye, they cut my cheek, they cut my hand. They were a wild bunch!

Reverend James B. Terrell

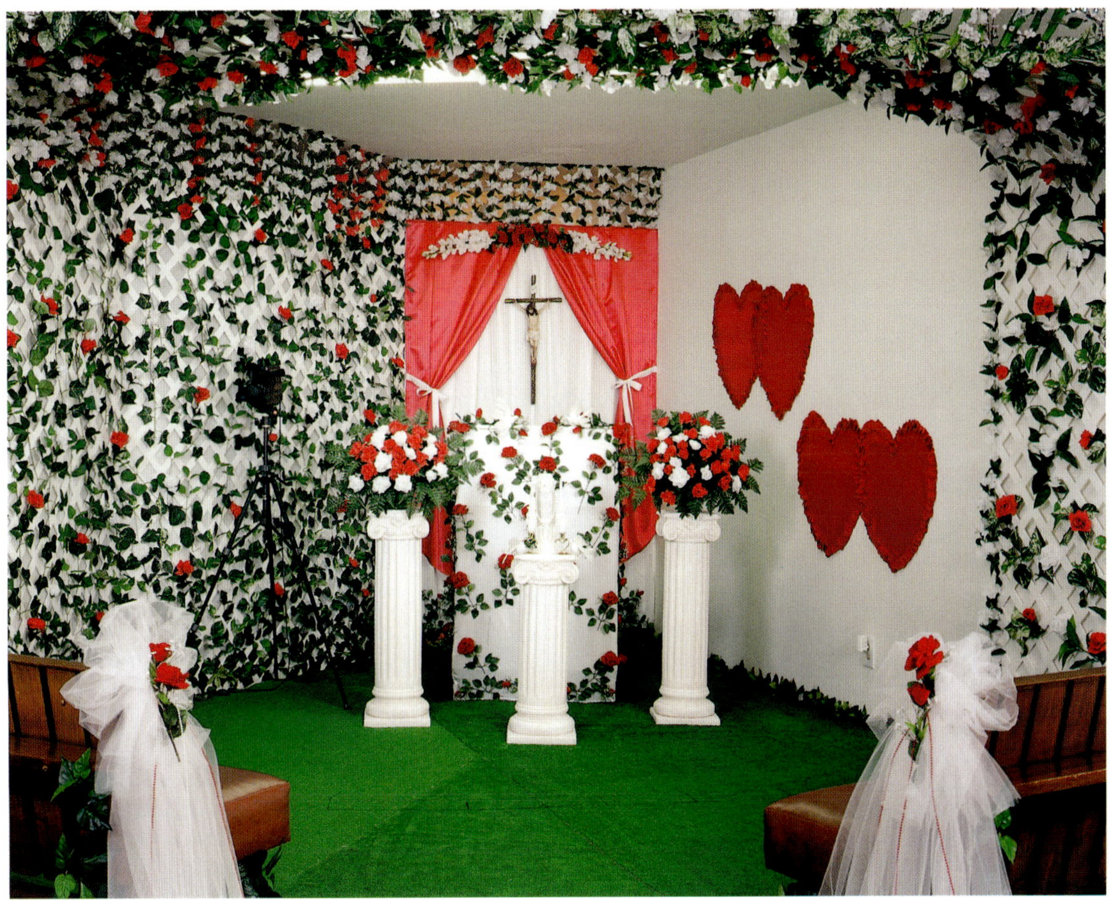

SWEETHEARTS CHAPEL 1998
C-TYPE PRINT 29.2 x 38.1 CM, FRAMED 60.9 x 50.8 CM
COURTESY OF THE ARTIST

Then we have the children come in. I adore the children. If I see a child with a couple and I know they have a child out of wedlock, I've even baptised the child after the marriage. I'll do the marriage and then I'll do a baptism. Well, often these children, they have children, and then they decide they want to get married – maybe they've lived together four, five, six, seven years, sometimes longer. People come in from Mexico often like that. And the children are so cute standing there, and I want to make them part of the ceremony, so I'll find out whose child it is. If it's her child before the marriage I'll say to him "will you accept this child into the ceremony and make him part of the family?", and then I'll say to the child "will you accept him into your family"? It's so nice – the little child looks up and says he will. I think it unifies the family. I had one person who was in a re-marriage and she asked me if I would ask the groom if he would love, honour and make part of the family her dog. I have had the strangest requests you can imagine. But sometimes you just have to be very serious and just listen because people are being serious when they ask for these things. Then I found out afterwards that he absolutely hated that dog. Can you believe it?

Reverend Marlys Sand

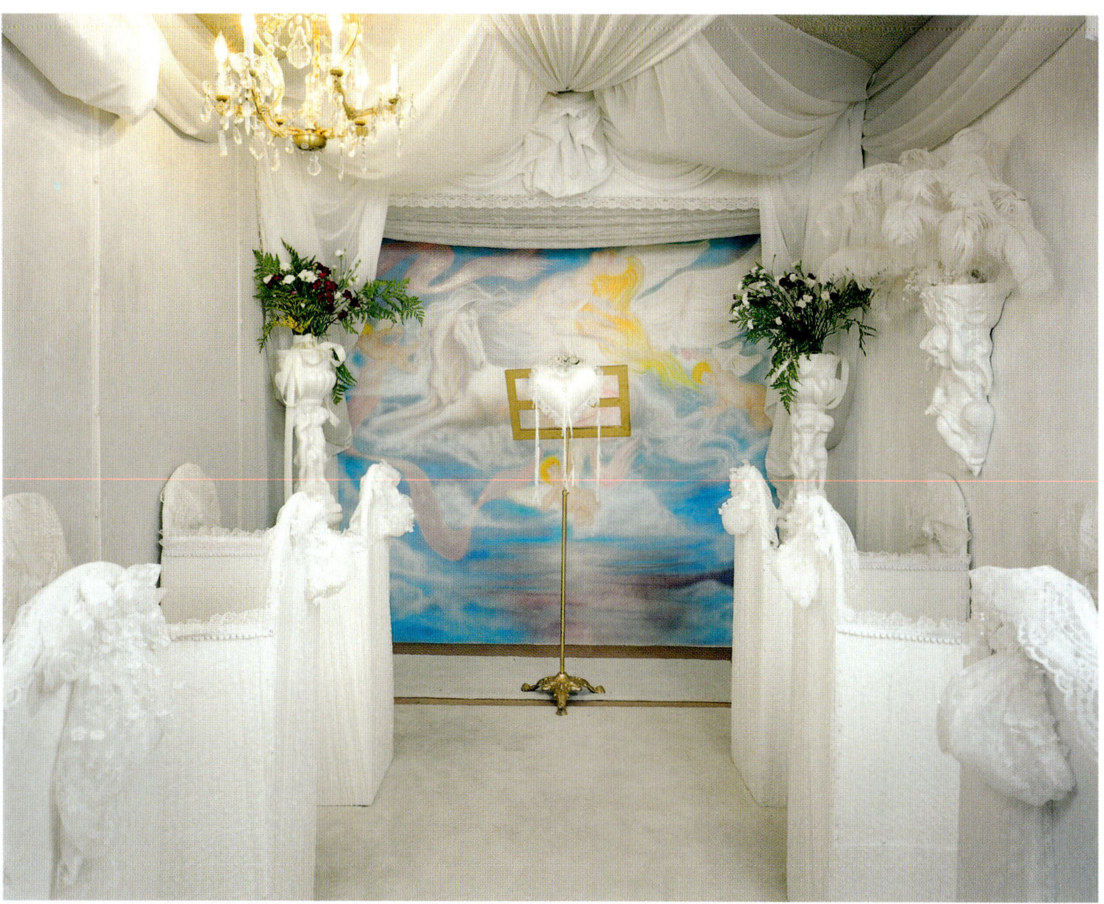

THE ANGEL CHAPEL, DIVINE MADNESS FANTASY WEDDING CHAPEL 1998
C-TYPE PRINT 29.2 x 38.1 CM, FRAMED 60.9 x 50.8 CM
COURTESY OF THE ARTIST

Then I have some that want to sing to the groom ... As I said "face each other – look lovingly into each others'' eyes", she said "now stop there, because I want to sing to him". And all of a sudden a tape came on and she sang three verses to the groom. It's very unusual. She didn't sing too bad – she certainly wasn't a professional – but she sang some love song that she had found that she wanted to sing to him. Cute.

Reverend Marlys Sand

Sometimes if you go in and you see the couple you have to be very careful not to say "are you going to give her away at the altar", because it may not be the father, it may be the groom. So we have to be very cautious. I've caught myself a few times. I've even had it with a woman and a very young man and I think it may be the mother, and it's not. So I don't say anything until they say who is the groom and who is the bride.

Reverend Marlys Sand

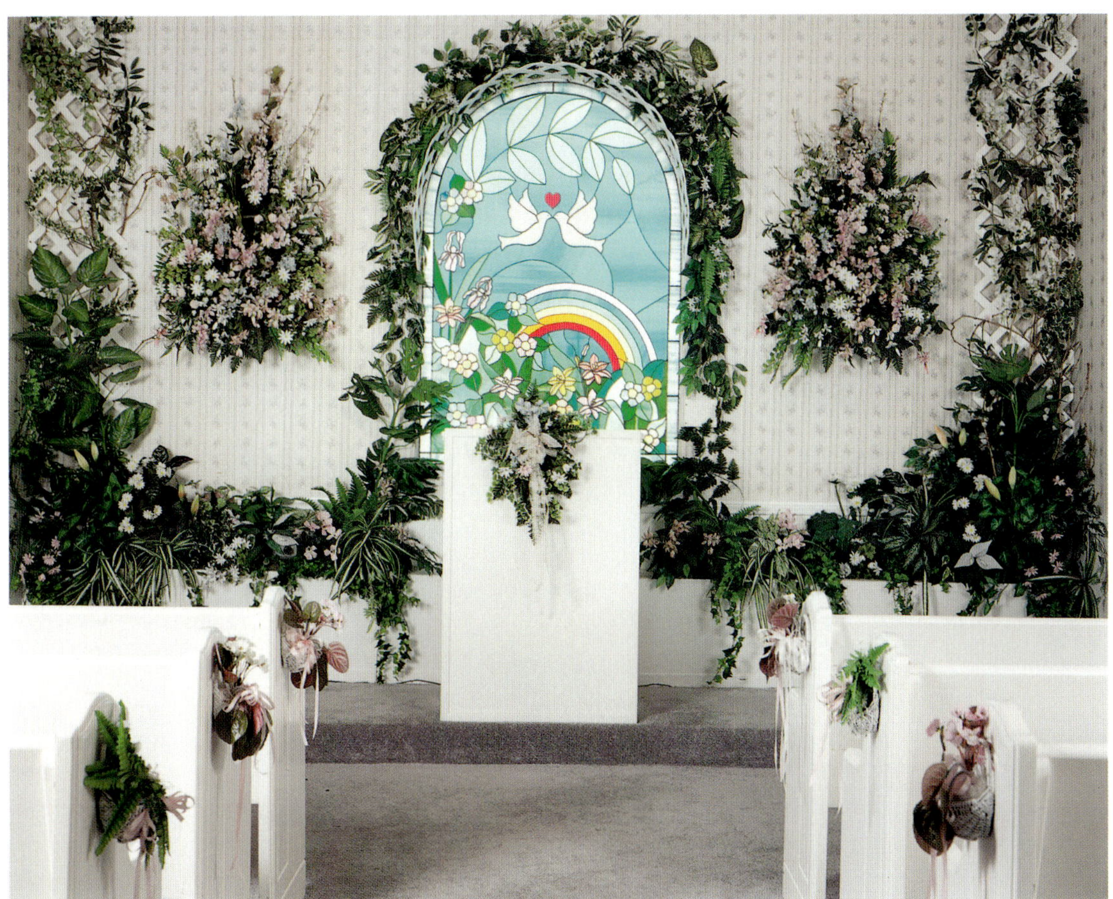

THE CHAPEL OF LOVE 1998
C-TYPE PRINT 29.2 x 38.1 CM, FRAMED 60.9 x 50.8 CM
COURTESY OF THE ARTIST

We have a new wedding that I don't think you know about called 'Love in a Limo'. What it is is that they pick them up from the airport or the hotel, and take them to the spot where they want to get married – and they have champagne and roses – and if they want to get married in the limo they can, and then they can go right back to the airport and get on their plane. But generally we'll step out in front of a beautiful waterfall or a hotel they like. It's all handled from the minute they step off the plane – we even get their license for them. It's an incredible service because it makes it awfully easy for them, and yet they have a lovely time. We're very accommodating. Well, this is Las Vegas, we've got to remember that.

Reverend Marlys Sand

Jim Isermann

1955 Born in Kenosha, WI
1977 B.F.A. University of Wisconsin, Milwaukee, WI
1980 M.F.A. California Institute of the Arts, Valencia, CA
Lives in Palm Springs, CA

2001
Jim Isermann, Richard Telles Fine Art, Los Angeles, CA
Jim Isermann, Feature, New York, NY
Beau Monde: Toward a Redeemed Cosmopolitanism, Site Santa Fe, Fourth International Biennial Exhibition, Santa Fe, NM (cat.)
2000
Jim Isermann, The RISD Museum, Procidence, RI
Made in California: NOW, L.A. County Museum of Art, Los Angeles, CA

UNTITLED (0200) 2000
CONTRAVISION™
INSTALLATION: USF
COURTESY OF THE ARTIST AND RICHARD TELLES FINE ART, LOS ANGELES

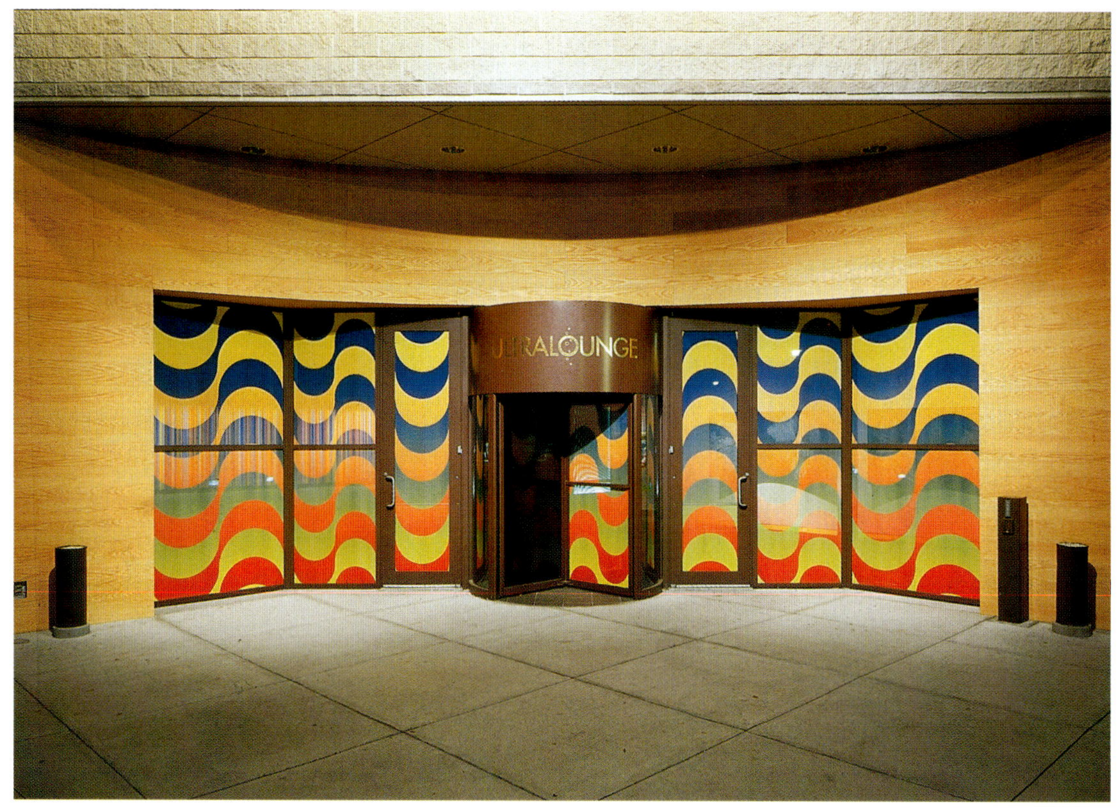

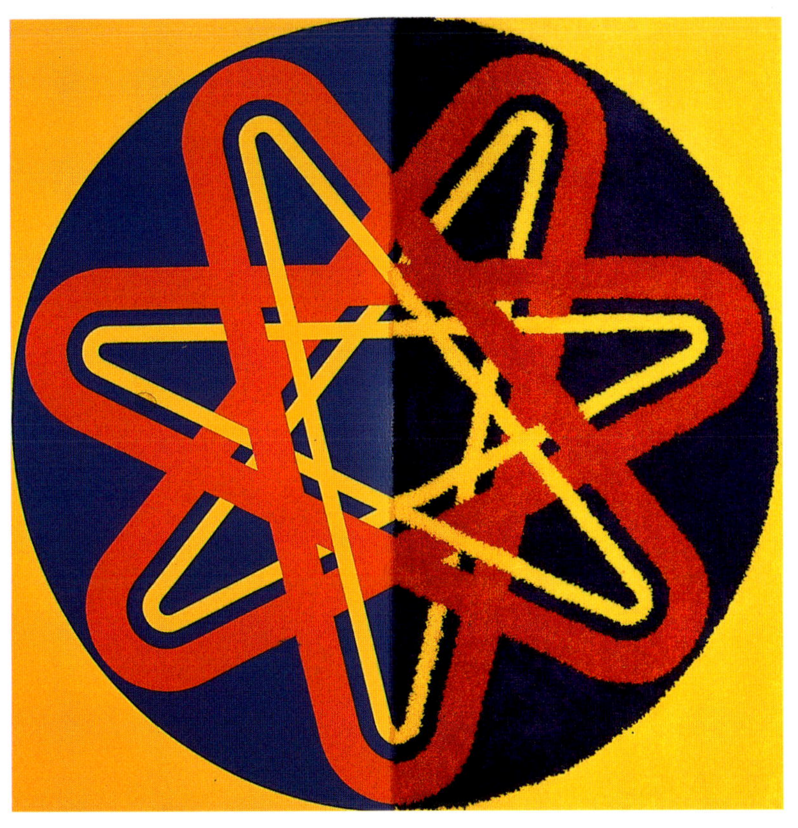

UNTITLED (1388) 1988
ENAMEL PAINT AND ACRYLIC SHAG
243.8 x 243.8 x 5 CM
COURTESY OF THE ARTIST AND RICHARD TELLES
FINE ART, LOS ANGELES

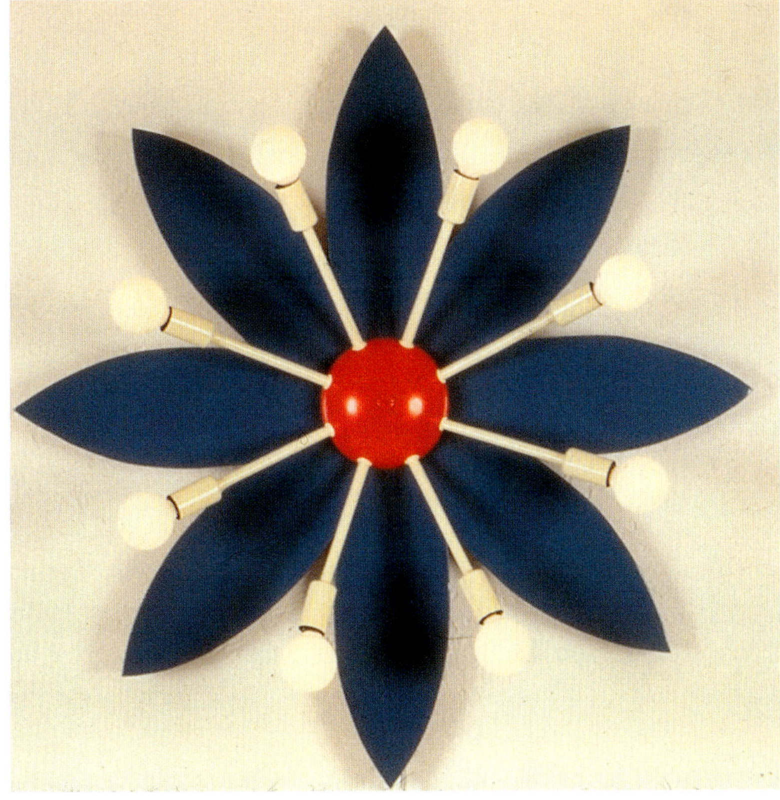

FLOWER LITE 1983
MIXED MEDIA 73.6 x 73.6 x 17.7 CM
COURTESY OF THE ARTIST AND RICHARD TELLES
FINE ART, LOS ANGELES

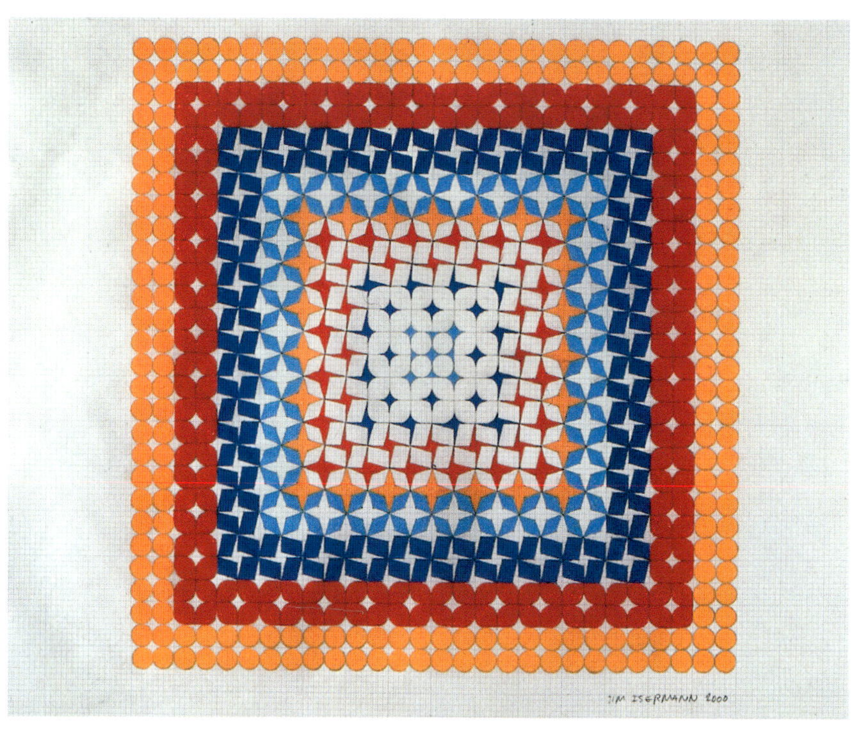

UNTITLED 2000
COLOR PENCIL ON PAPER 43.1 x 55.8 CM
COURTESY OF THE ARTIST AND RICHARD TELLES FINE ART, LOS ANGELES

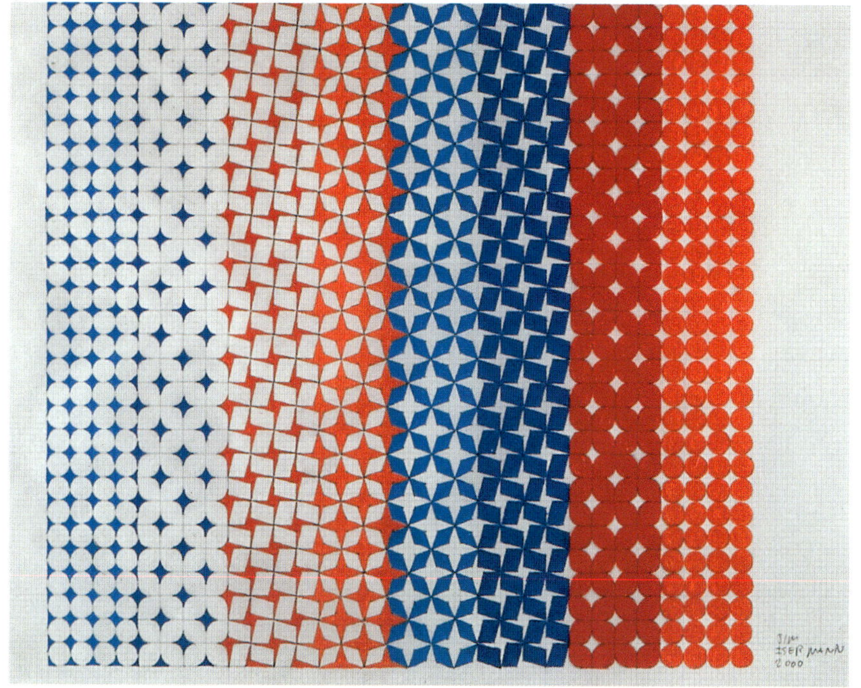

UNTITLED 2000
COLOR PENCIL ON PAPER 43.1 x 55.8 CM
COURTESY OF THE ARTIST AND RICHARD TELLES FINE ART, LOS ANGELES

LOGIC RULES 2000-01
MUSEUM OF ART, RISD,
PROVIDENCE
COURTESY OF THE
ARTIST AND RICHARD
TELLES FINE ART,
LOS ANGELES

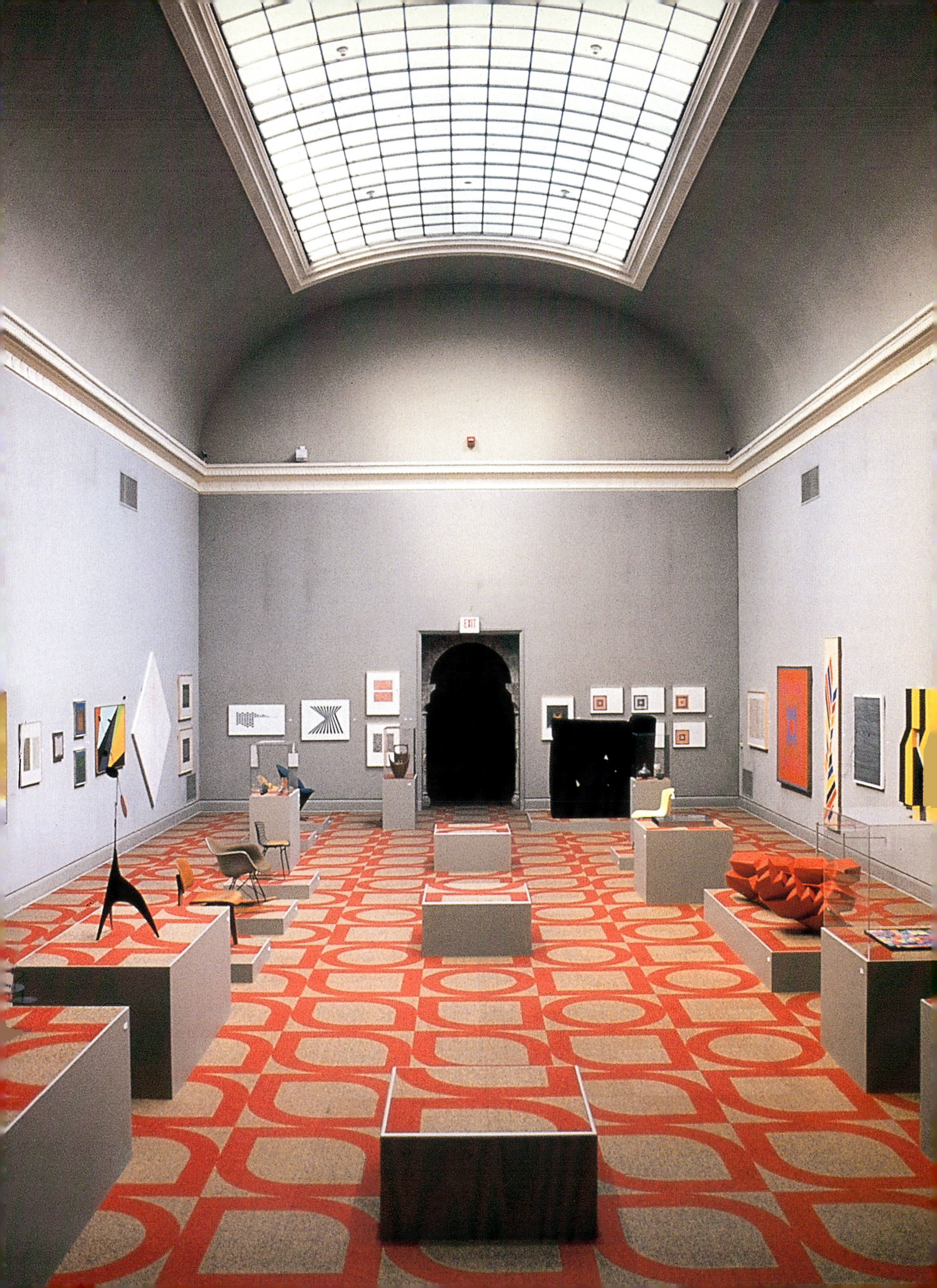
EXIT

Rem Koolhaas

1944 Born in Rotterdam, NL
Educated at the Architectural Association School in London from 1968 until 1972, he produced the 'Berlin Wall as Architecture' (1970) and 'Exodus, or the Voluntary Prisoners of Architecture' (1972). In 1972 he received a Harkness Fellowship for research in the United States, studied at Cornell University and then became visiting Fellow at the Institute for Architecture and Urban Studies in New York. While in New York, he wrote 'Delirious New York,' a retroactive Manifesto for Manhattan, which was published in 1978.
In 1975 Rem Koolhaas founded the Office for Metropolitan Architecture (OMA) with Elia and Zoe Zenghelis and Madelon Vriesendorp in London and has been involved in building and urban planning projects ever since.
In 1995, he published together with graphic designer Bruce Mau 'SMLXL,' a book that documents the work of OMA and Koolhaas' interest in contemporary society, building and urban development.
Since 1995 he is professor of architecture and urban design at Harvard University. He conducts design research into a focused investigation of current urban-architectural conditions in various parts of the world. Currently he is involved in thesis advising through the ongoing 'Project on the City.' The projects include a study of five cities in the 'Pearl River Delta;' 'Shopping,' an analysis of the role of retail consumption in the contemporary city and recently a study on 'Lagos,' Nigeria.
The work of the office has won several international awards, including the Pritzker Architecture Prize 2000, and was the subject of a retrospective exhibition held at the Museum of Modern Art, New York in 1995: 'Rem Koolhaas and the Place of Public Architecture'.

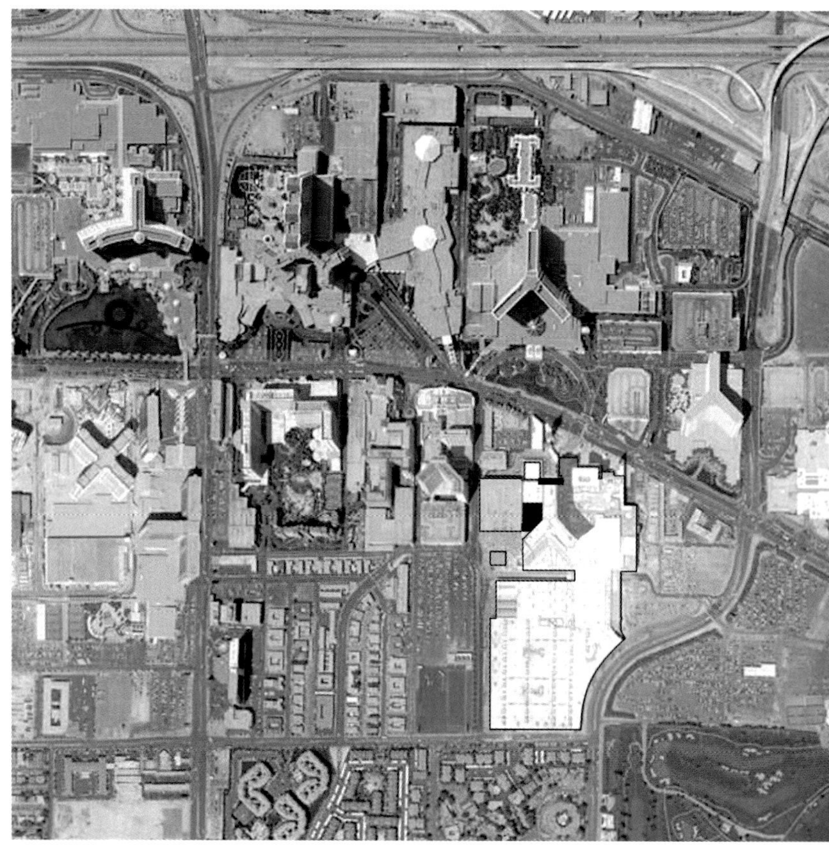

AIRIAL OF THE VENETIAN RESORT COMPLEX, LAS VEGAS
COPYRIGHT OMA 2000

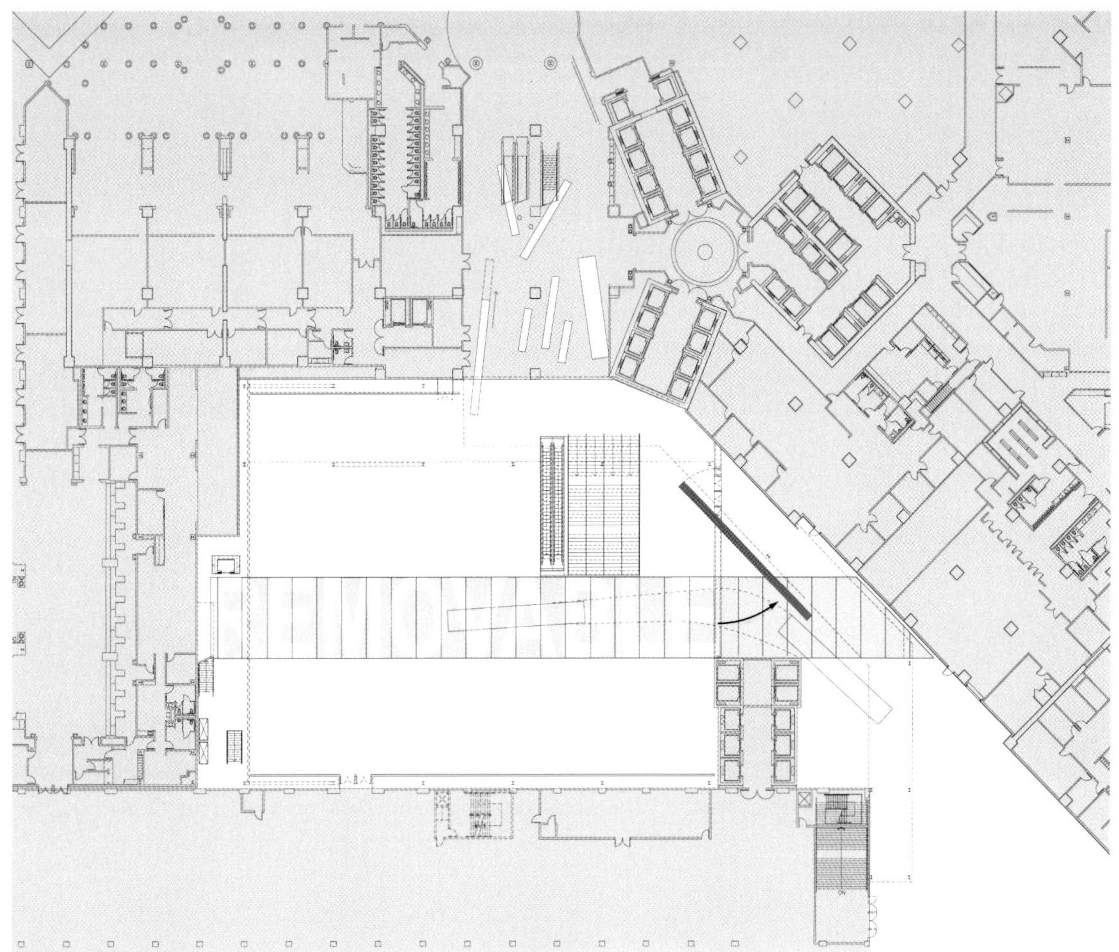

PLAN OF THE EXHIBITION HALL OF GUGGENHEIM LAS VEGAS WITH THE FLEXIBLE FLOOR

The Las Vegas co-operation between the Hermitage and the Guggenheim is one of the first concrete projects to result from a larger, long-term collaboration agreement between the State Hermitage Museum in St. Petersburg, Russia, and the Solomon R. Guggenheim Foundation in New York that was signed and announced June 2000 in St. Petersburg.

Guggenheim Las Vegas and the Hermitage-Guggenheim Museum, two contrasting exhibition spaces designed by Rem Koolhaas within The Venetian Resort complex in Las Vegas, will be opened on October 7, 2001.

The Guggenheim Las Vegas is a massive free-standing exhibition hall, built between the casino and the parking structure of The Venetian. It will be accessive through the hotel lobby only; the only exterior wall is a huge mega-door, that can be opened to bring in large art works. The exhibition space, whose 70-foot ceiling gives the main room a hangar-like feeling, features a massive skylight, a functioning industrial crane, and additional lower level galleries. The floor of the ground level is flexible and may be opened to reveal a trench that drops down to lower-level galleries and spans the length of the exhibition space.

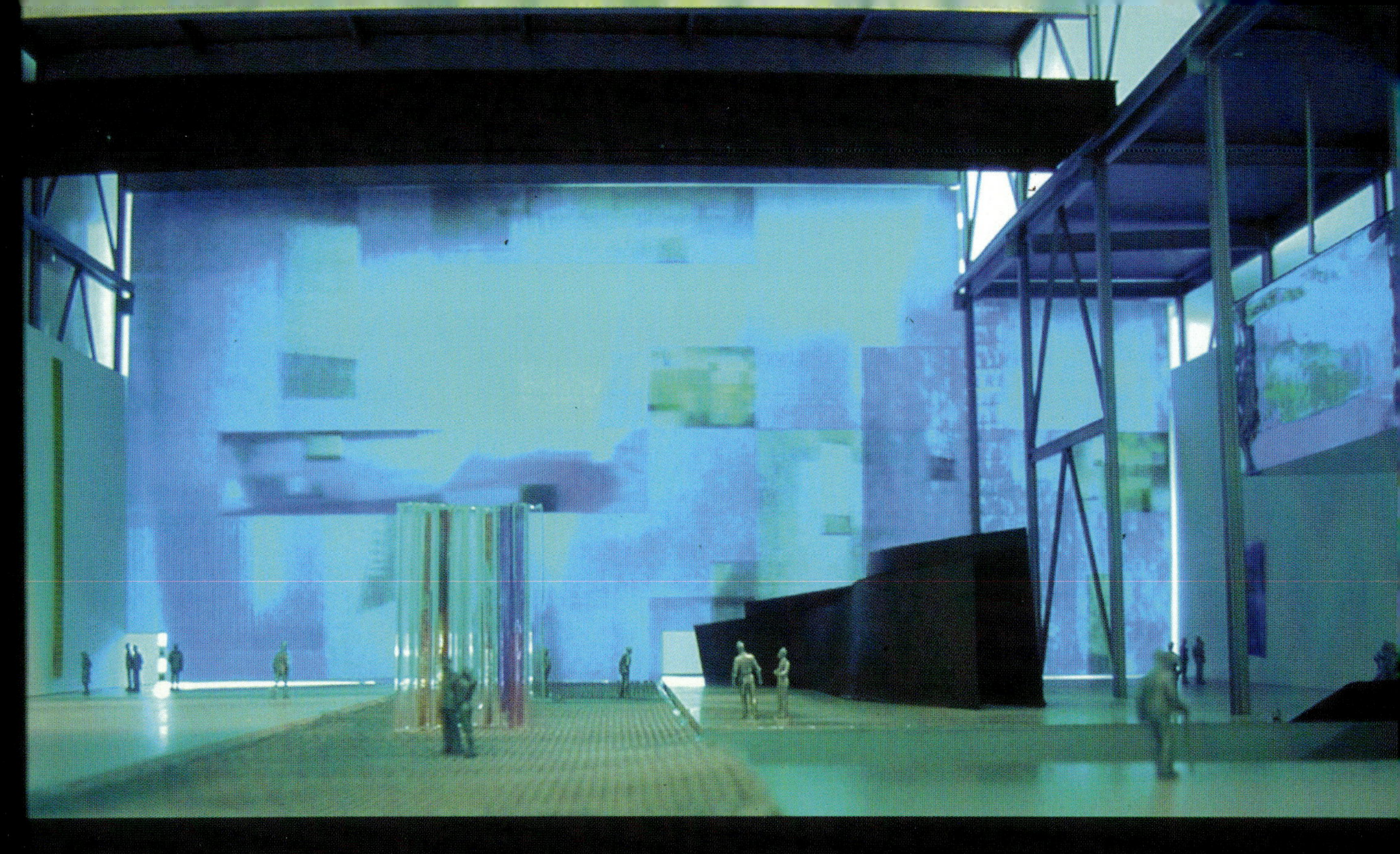

INTERIOR VIEWS OF THE EXHIBITION HALL OF GUGGENHEIM LAS VEGAS

As Thomas Krens, Director of the Solomon R. Guggenheim Foundation, explained, "the rationale for the Guggenheim Las Vegas is complex. I remember being captured almost thirty years ago by Robert Venturi's argument – presented in his compact but landmark book, 'Learning From Las Vegas' about the derivative authenticity of Las Vegas 'vernacular' architecture. Although I could have scarcely imagined working with Las Vegas as a site even one year ago – since my very first visit to the city took place only at the beginning of this year – the fascination of the place is undeniable. When Sheldon Adelson and Rob Goldstein first approached us about bringing 'The Art of the Motorcycle' exhibition to Las Vegas, it still did not seem likely that the Guggenheim could be there until we began talking about architecture. Sheldon's and Rob's willingness to consider a permanent new building – and an ambitious architectural statement – and their agreement that Rem Koolhaas would be the architect, created the possibility for the Guggenheim to engage the image of Las Vegas head on and come up with a creative solution that would add substantially to the character of Las Vegas on the one hand, as it maintained the dignity of a traditional cultural institution on the other. From a purely museological standpoint, it is our plan to build a space of an absolutely unique character and capacity.

The Guggenheim Las Vegas has been designed as an exhibition space – not as a museum with a permanent collection. Our challenge was to design a building that had the aesthetic and practical capability to do things that

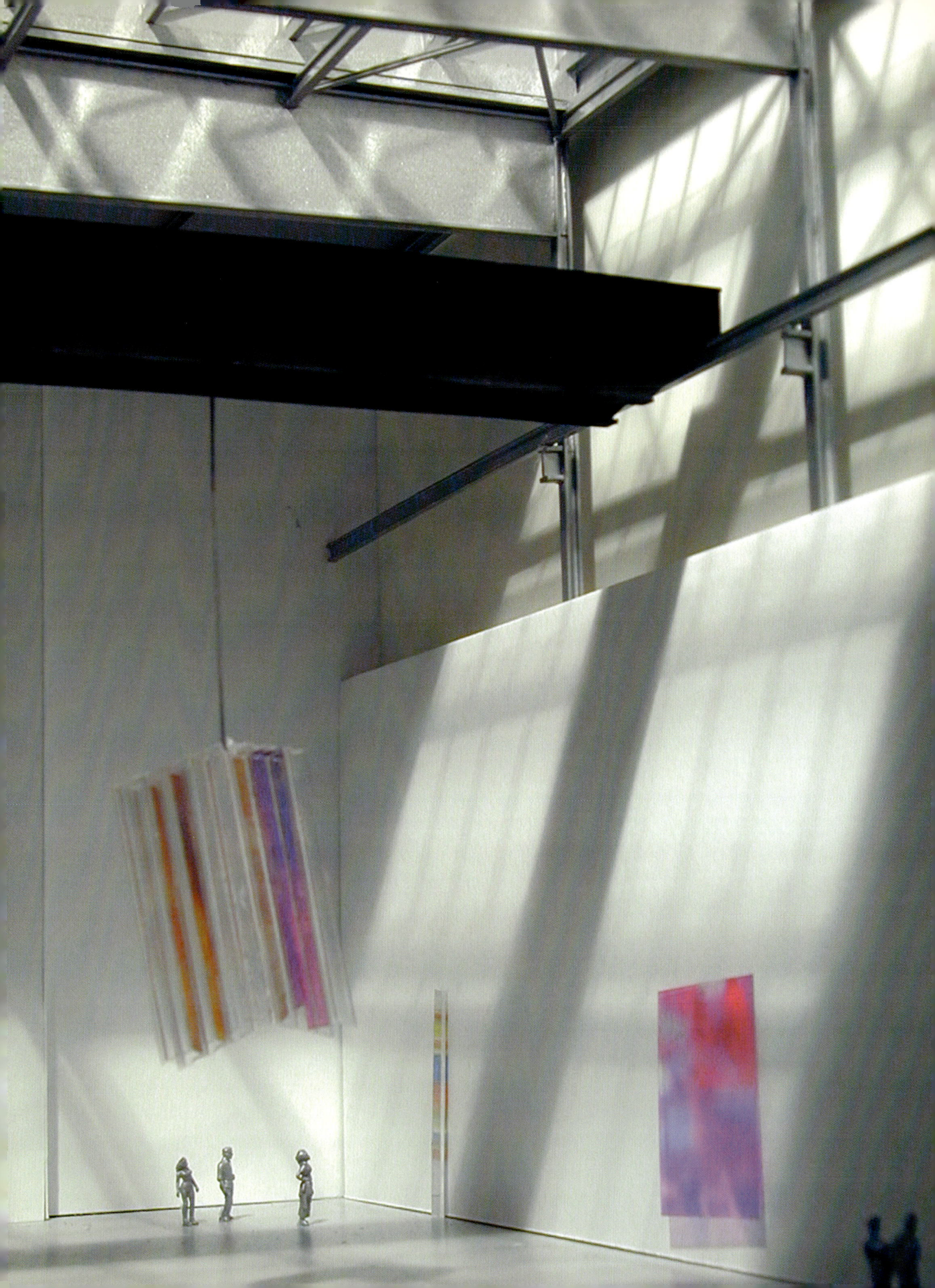

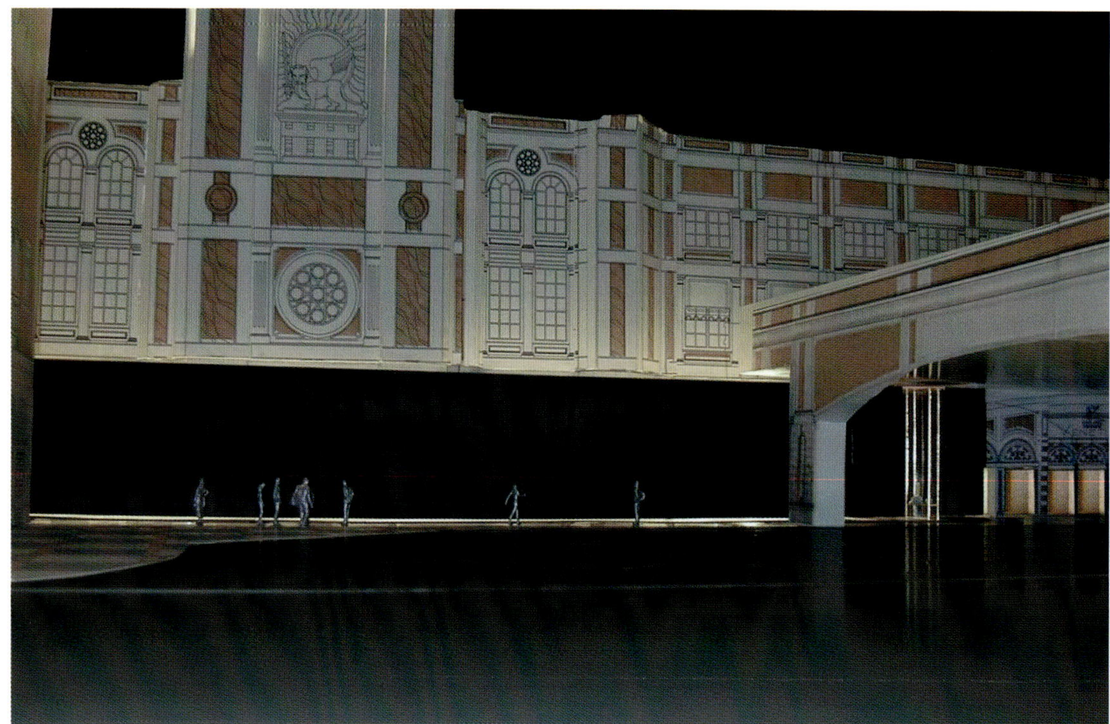

THE 'JEWELBOX', HERMITAGE-GUGGENHEIM, AT NIGHT, IN THE BACK THE FACADE OF THE VENETIAN LAS VEGAS

were not possible in any other museum or exhibition space in the world. The Guggenheim Las Vegas will be able to accommodate exhibitions ranging from 'The Art of the Motorcycle' to a retrospective of massive Richard Serra sculpture, from design, fashion, and architecture exhibitions to comprehensive presentations of multi-media, video, and high-technology based art. The one quality that exhibitions of this kind require is a scale, practicality and elasticity of space that is absolutely unique, in fact impossible to find in any museum that I know of. That was the challenge for Rem Koolhaas, and the result – in my opinion – is extraordinary."

'The Art of the Motorcycle,' the Guggenheim's exhibition that explores motorcycle design and technology, designed by architect Frank O'Gehry, will inaugurate the Guggenheim Las Vegas.

The Hermitage-Guggenheim Las Vegas is a joint effort between the two art institutions. It will present art works from the two collections. The first exhibition will show 'Masterpieces and Master Collectors: Impressionist and Early Modern Paintings from the Hermitage and Guggenheim Museums'.

The museum is, by contrast to Guggenheim Las Vegas, an intimate, 'jewelbox'-like space, embedded into the facade of the Venetian, which will present masterworks in a very special, contemporary setting. Its walls are constructed of Cor-Ten steel, a material associated with the large-scale sculptures of artists as Richard Serra – it has never before been used in this way in a museum gallery.

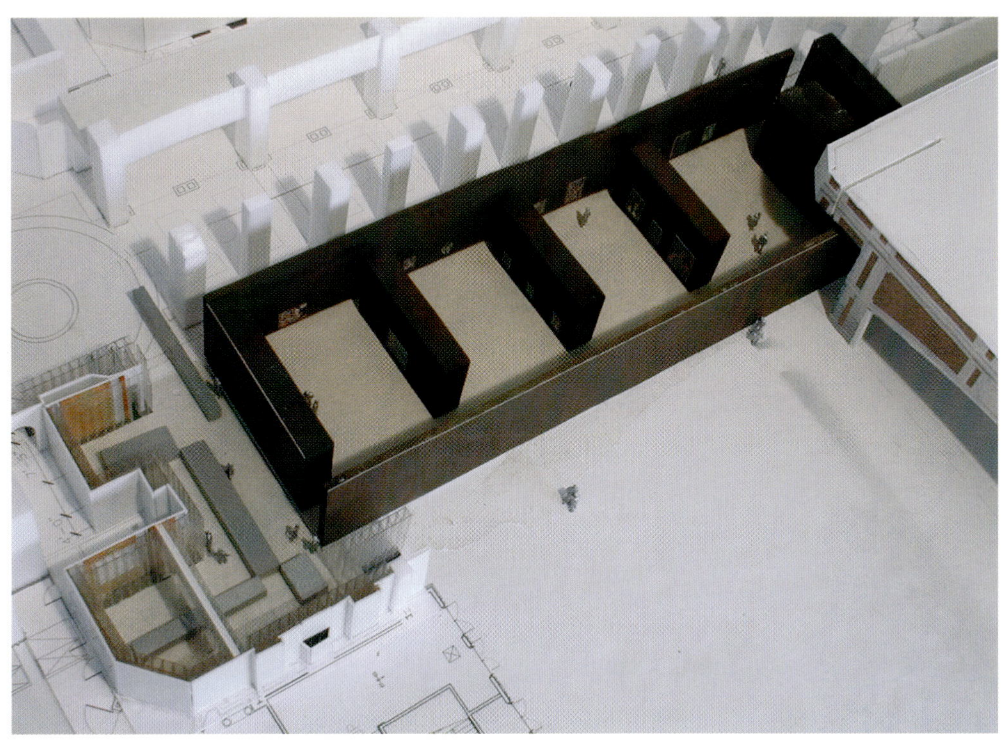

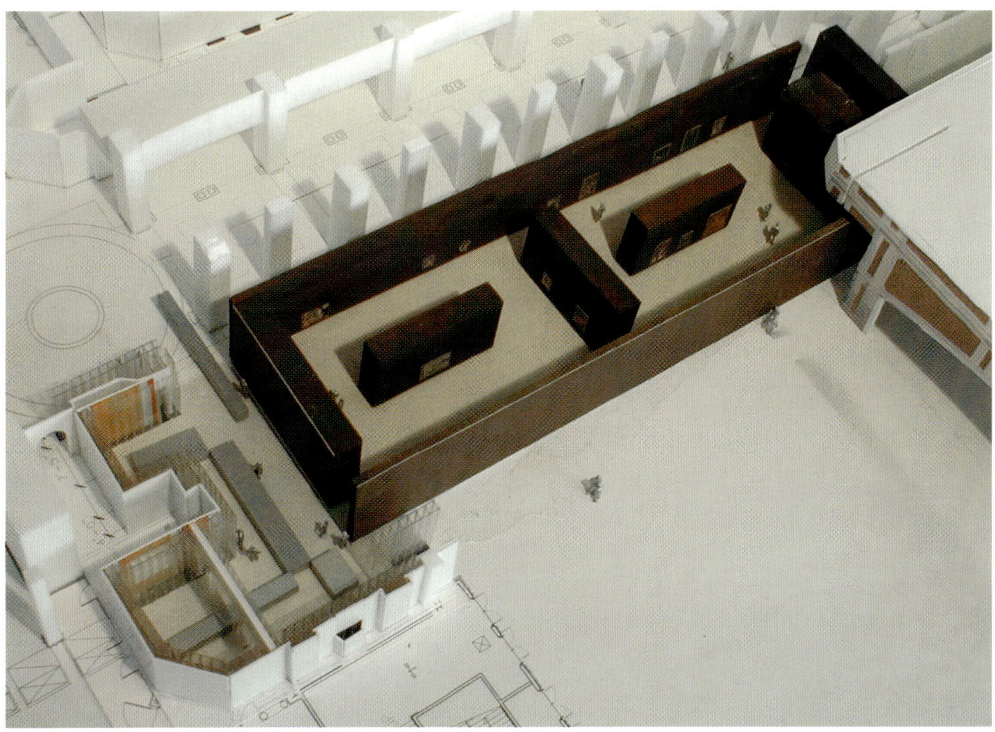

MODELS OF THE 'JEWELBOX', HERMITAGE-GUGGENHEIM LAS VEGAS

Liberace:

A Tribute to Mr. Showmanship
curated by Jeffrey Vallance
Liberace Museum, Las Vegas 1995
featuring Philip Argent, Mark Brandvik, Jane Callister, Doug Harvey, Wayne Littlejohn and Jim Shaw

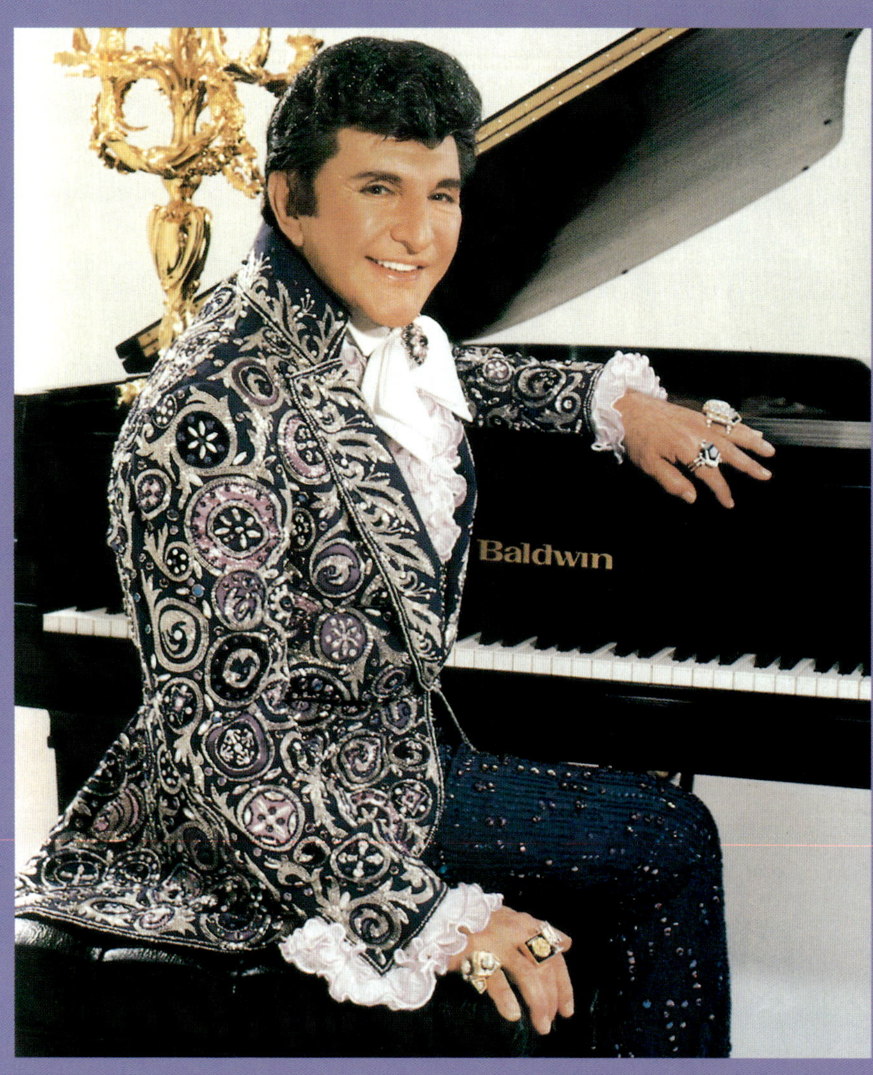

LIBERACE IN FRONT OF HIS PIANO

The LIBERACE Museum

A Visual Tribute to Mr. Showmanship Exhibition

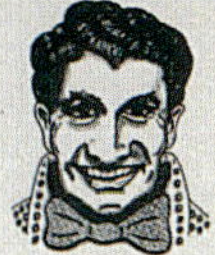

← Famed Pianist

Painting by Vallance at the Liberace Museum installed in between Liberace's pianos, chandeliers and bejeweled costumes.

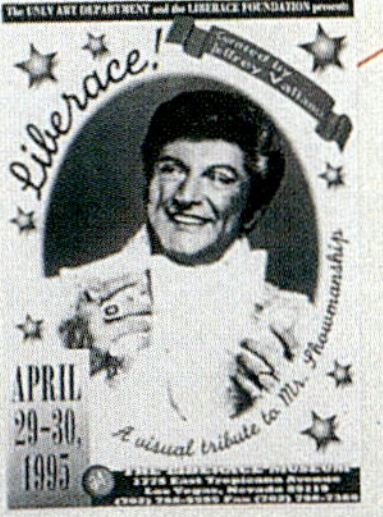

acrylic and glitter on canvas

LIBERACE IN FULL GLORY
(Detail of Installation)

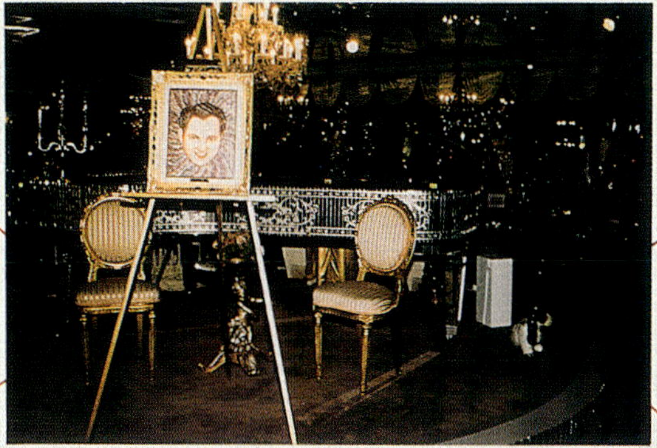

Installation at the Liberace Museum in Las Vegas

The Liberace museum is completely crammed with his glittering outfits, custom cars, rare pianos, dazzling rings and loads of little stuffed poodles. There was hardly any place to put the art, so it had to go in between the existing displays, making it almost impossible to tell the art from the Liberace artifacts.

Invitation to Liberace Museum

Liberace!
APRIL 29-30, 1995
A visual tribute to Mr. Showmanship

LA WEEKLY
March 27–April 2, 98
MR. SHOWMANSHIP'S JEWELS

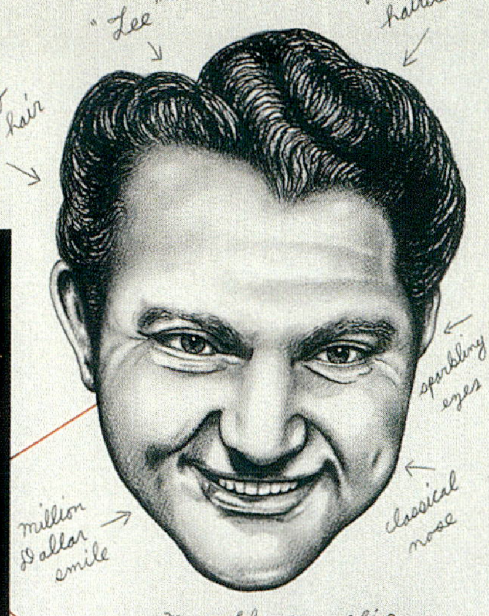

"Lee"
gorgeous hairdo
finely coiffed hair
sparkling eyes
classical nose
million Dollar smile

Mr. Showmanship

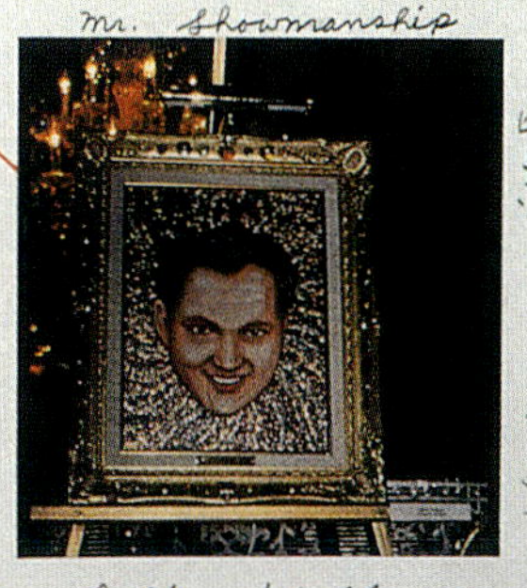

Vortex of Glitter

1998 LAS VEGAS Jeffrey Vallance

THE LIBERACE MUSEUM - A VISUAL TRIBUTE TO MR. SHOWMANSHIP EXHIBITION 1998
PENCIL, PEN AND COLLAGE ON PAPER 55.8 x 76.2 CM
COURTESY OF THE ARTIST AND LEHMANN MAUPIN, NEW YORK

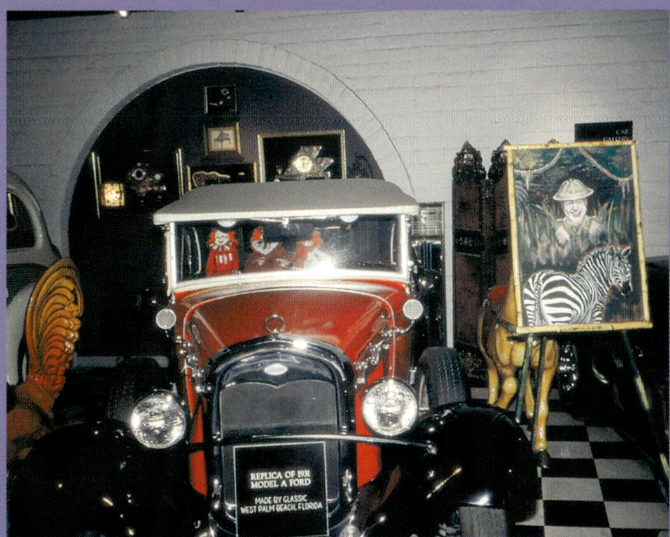

MARK BRANDVIK
LIBERACE ON SAFARI 1995
INSTALLATION VIEW, 'THE LIBERACE TRIBUTE EXHIBITION' AT THE LIBERACE MUSEUM, LAS VEGAS 1995
COURTESY OF THE ARTIST

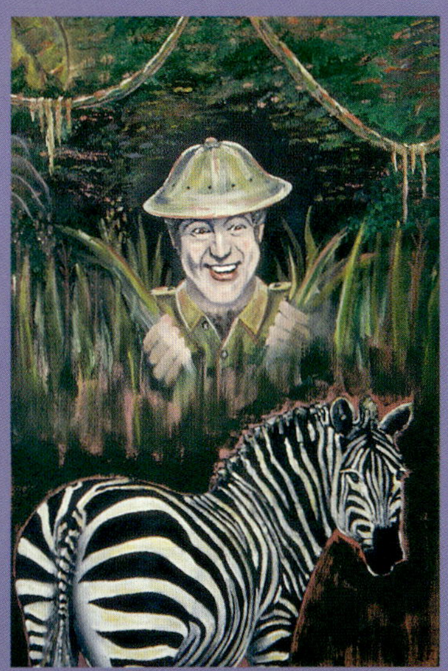

LIBERACE ON SAFARI 1995
ACRYLIC AND OIL ON CANVAS WITH BAMBOO
55.8 x 78.7 CM
COURTESY OF THE ARTIST

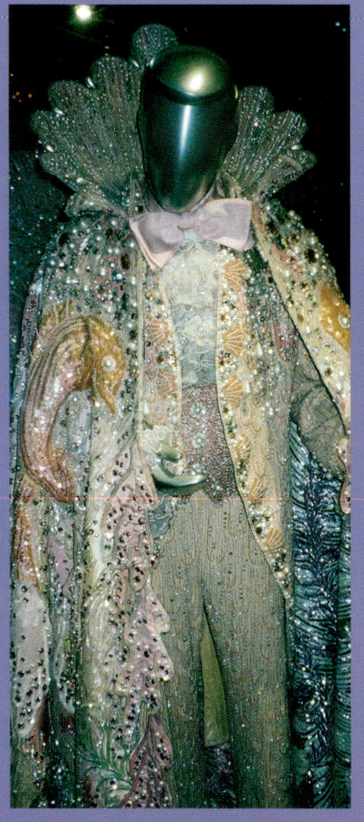

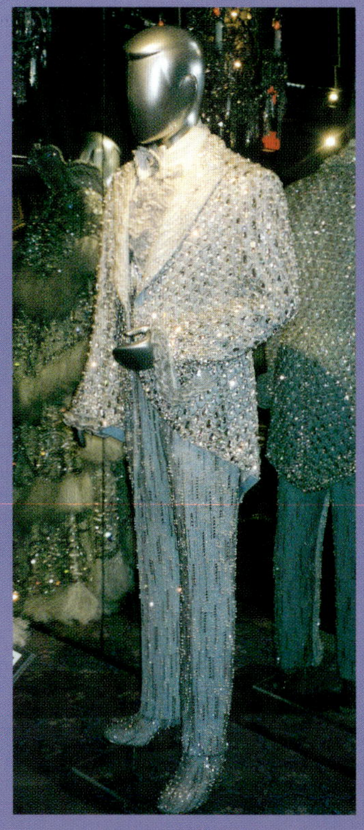

TWO OF LIBERACE'S COSTUMES IN THE LIBERACE MUSEUM AT LAS VEGAS, PHOTOS BY ALEX FARQUHARSON

WAYNE S. LITTLEJOHN
TINKLING ON THE IVORIES (LIBERACE MUSEUM INSTALLATION) 1995
CAST GYPSUM, WOOD, GLASS, OIL, PRINT MEDIUM
86.3 x 137.1 x 30.4 CM

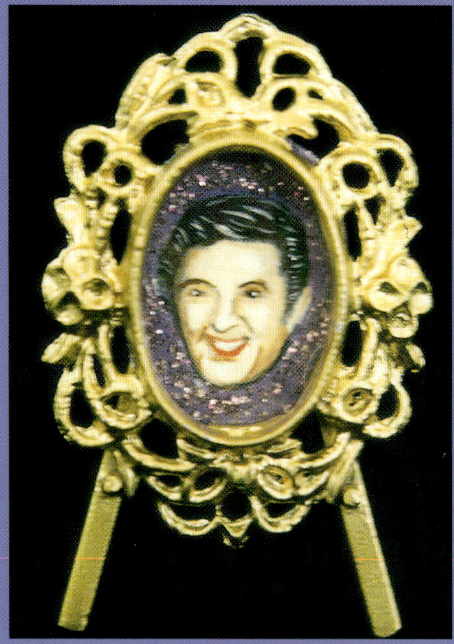

JEFFREY VALLANCE
WORLD'S SMALLEST LIBERACE PAINTING 1995
5.8 x 2.5 CM, DOME 19.5 x 13.9 x 11.4 CM
COURTESY OF THE ARTIST AND ROSAMUND FELSEN GALLERY, SANTA MONICA, CA

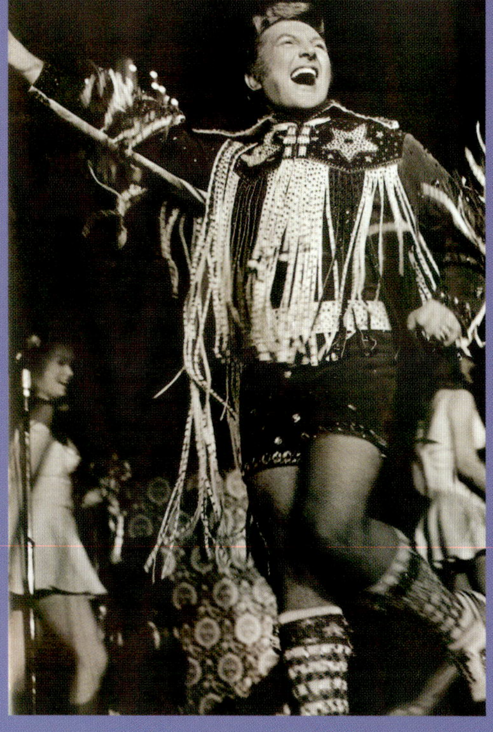

"WEARING THE JOKE COSTUME THAT WAS WRITTEN INTO THE CONTRACT"

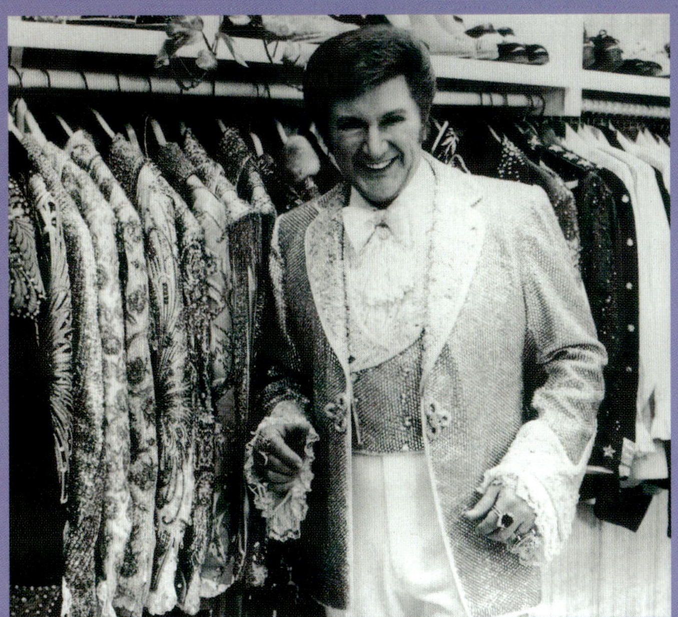

"AS YOU CAN SEE, I REALLY DO SUPPORT THE AUSTRIAN RHINESTONE BUSINESS"

DOUG HARVEY
SPECTOGRAPHIC PORTRAIT OF LIBERACE PAINTED IN THE MANNER OF THE GEOMETRIC ABSTRACTIONISTS 1995
ACRYLIC, OIL, ENAMEL, GLITTER ON PANEL
73.6 x 96.5 CM
COURTESY OF THE ARTIST

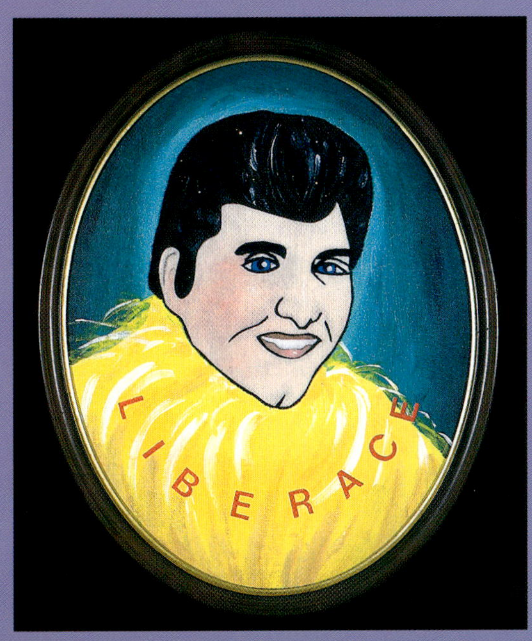

JAMES GOBEL
LIBERACE 1996-2001
ACRYLIC, FELT, YARN, GLITTER ON BOARD 50.8 x 40.6 CM
COURTESY OF KRAVETS/WEHBY GALLERY, NEW YORK

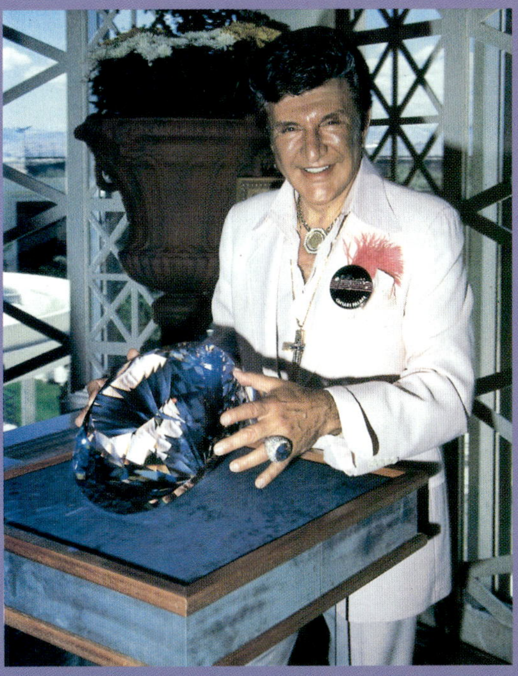

"THE BIGGEST RHINESTONE IN THE WORLD, MADE BY SWAROVSKI, AUSTRIA. THEY BROKE THE MOLD AFTER CASTING IT."

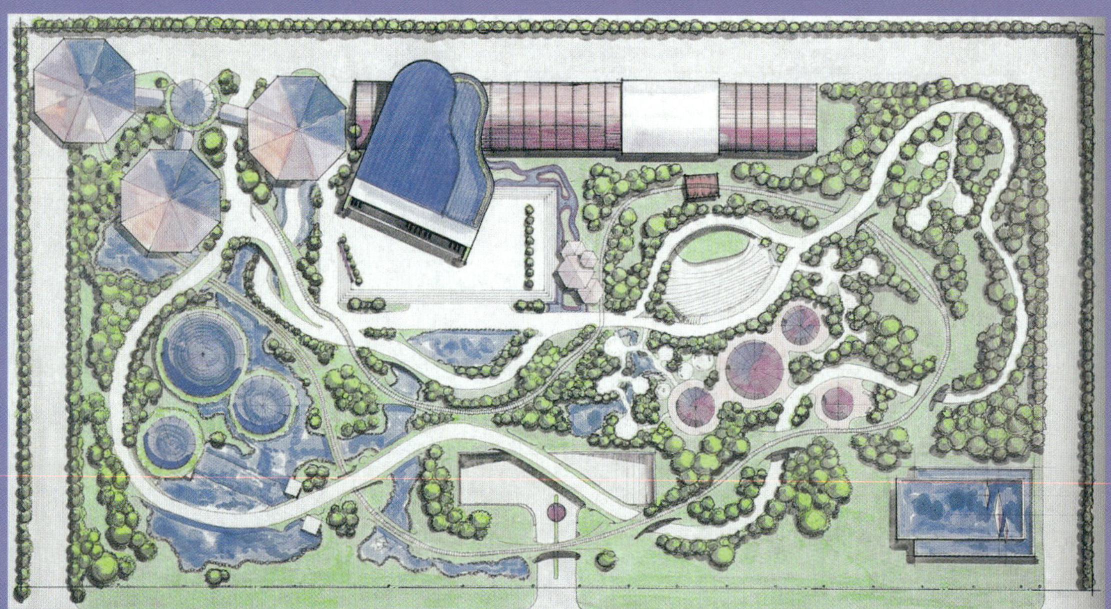

"The Liberace park is going to be a complex set in an exquisitely landscaped park, complete with reflection pools and fountains that keep time to music – "The Dancing Waters" with which I've been associated. There'll be no automobiles in the park, except the antique cars in the museum. The parking area will be screened off by artificially created hills, and shuttle buses will bring people from it to the complex. The park will also have several elegant shops (Rodeo Drive, eat your heart out) in a beautiful mall. They'll sell all of the things with which I'm associated, from fabulous fur creations by my furrier, to custom-designed jewelry, to crystal creations from the rhinestone factory in Austria. There will be outlets for all of the products we're beginning to license under the Liberace name: like designer clothes, cosmetics, and fragrances. An office-condominium complex, privately owned and overlooking the park, will be built of glass and steel in the shape of (what else?) diamonds. The park will be built on land adjacent to my Tivoli Gardens Restaurant. For those who don't want to have a full meal at the restaurant, the park will be studded with a series of attractive gazebos serving desserts, special pizzas, and other ethnic snacks. The one thing they won't be is your typical fast-food operation. They'll be managded by my people from the Tivoli Gardens, with the same high standards of elegance and service. Beauty and elegance will be the keynotes of the entire complex. If I didn't think we could achieve that, I wouldn't even embark on such a mammoth undertaking. Why, even the airlines are planning to reroute their approaches to the airport so they can point out Liberace Park as one of the highlights of Las Vegas."

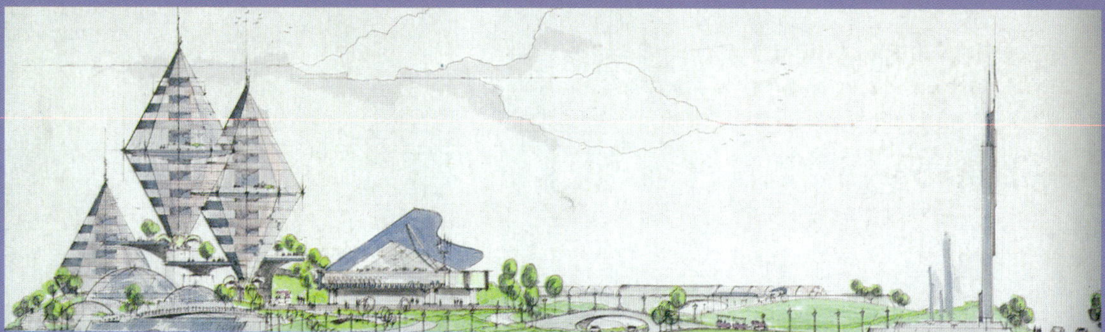

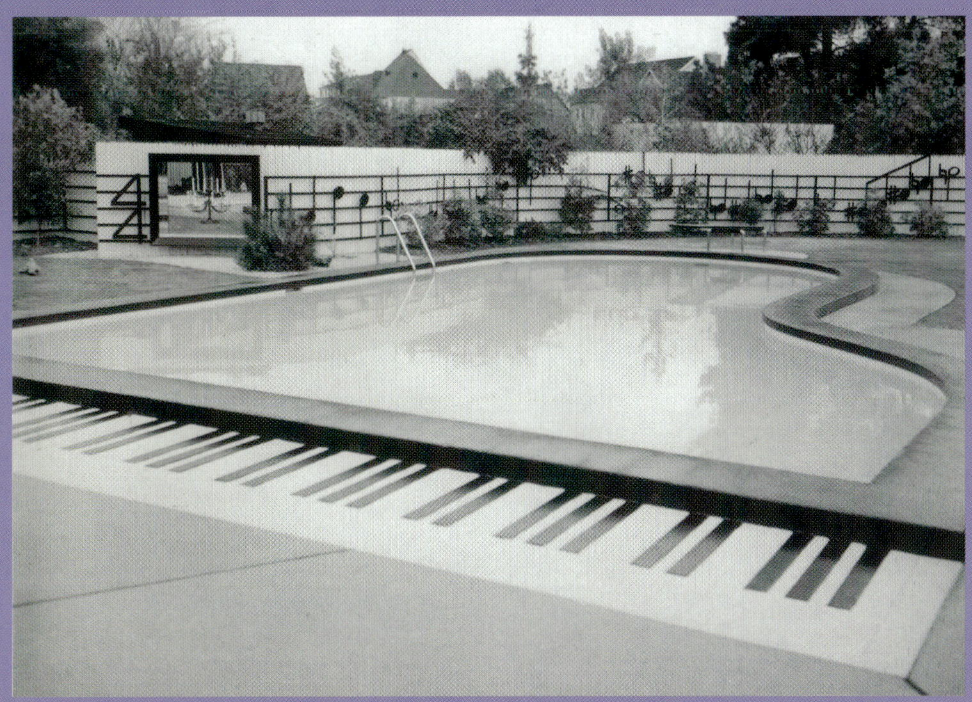

"THE FAMOUS PIANO POOL IN MY FIRST LOS ANGELES HOME"

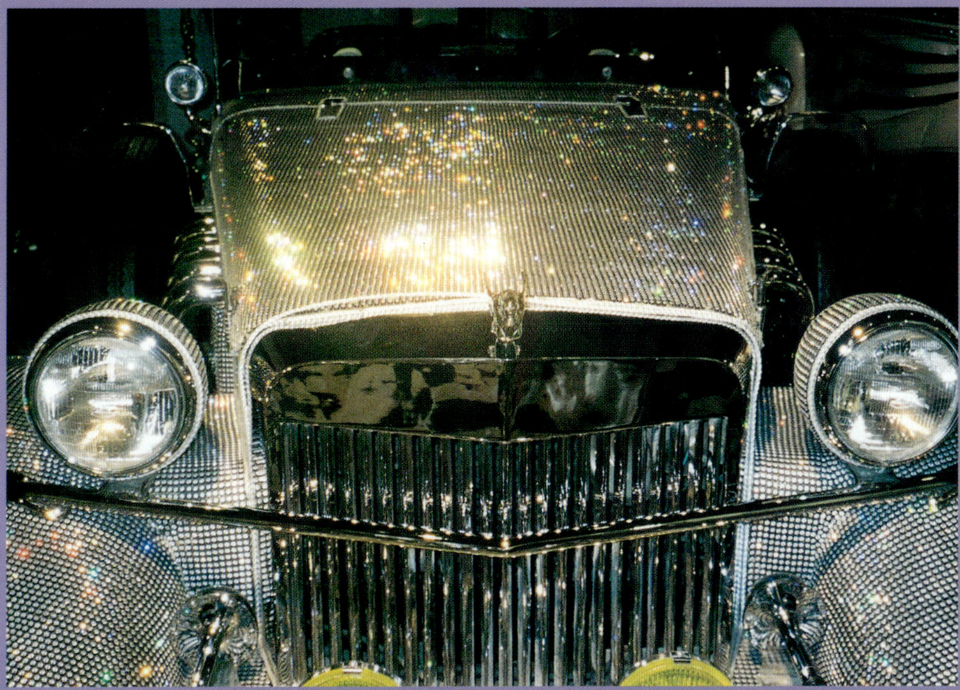

ONE OF LIBERACE'S CARS IN THE LIBERACE MUSEUM AT LAS VEGAS, PHOTO BY ALEX FARQUHARSON

All images, quotes and captions, if not indicated otherwise, from: 'The Wonderful Private World of LIBERACE' by Liberace, Harper & Row, Publishers, New York 1986

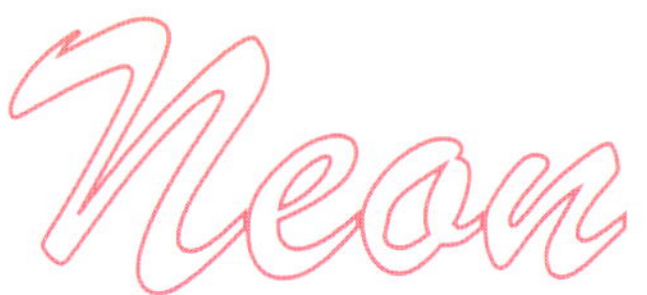

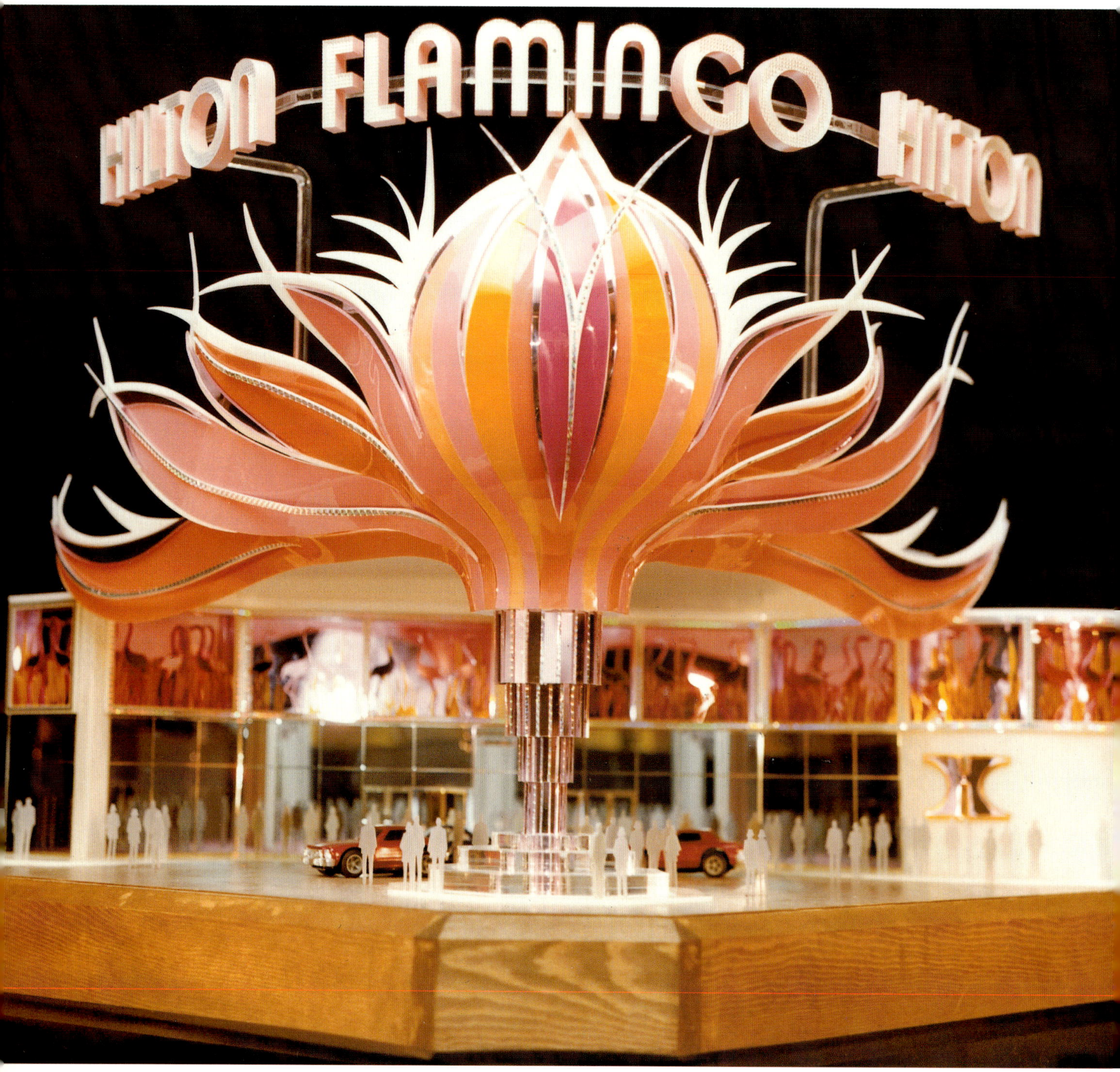

FLAMINGO-HILTON HOTEL-CASINO-MODEL OF PORTE-COCHÈRE SIGNWORK, DESIGNED BY RAUL RODRIGUEZ FOR HEATH & CO., (LOS ANGELES), 1976. THIS SIGNWORK IS STILL IN USE. PHOTO BY CHARLES F. BARNARD

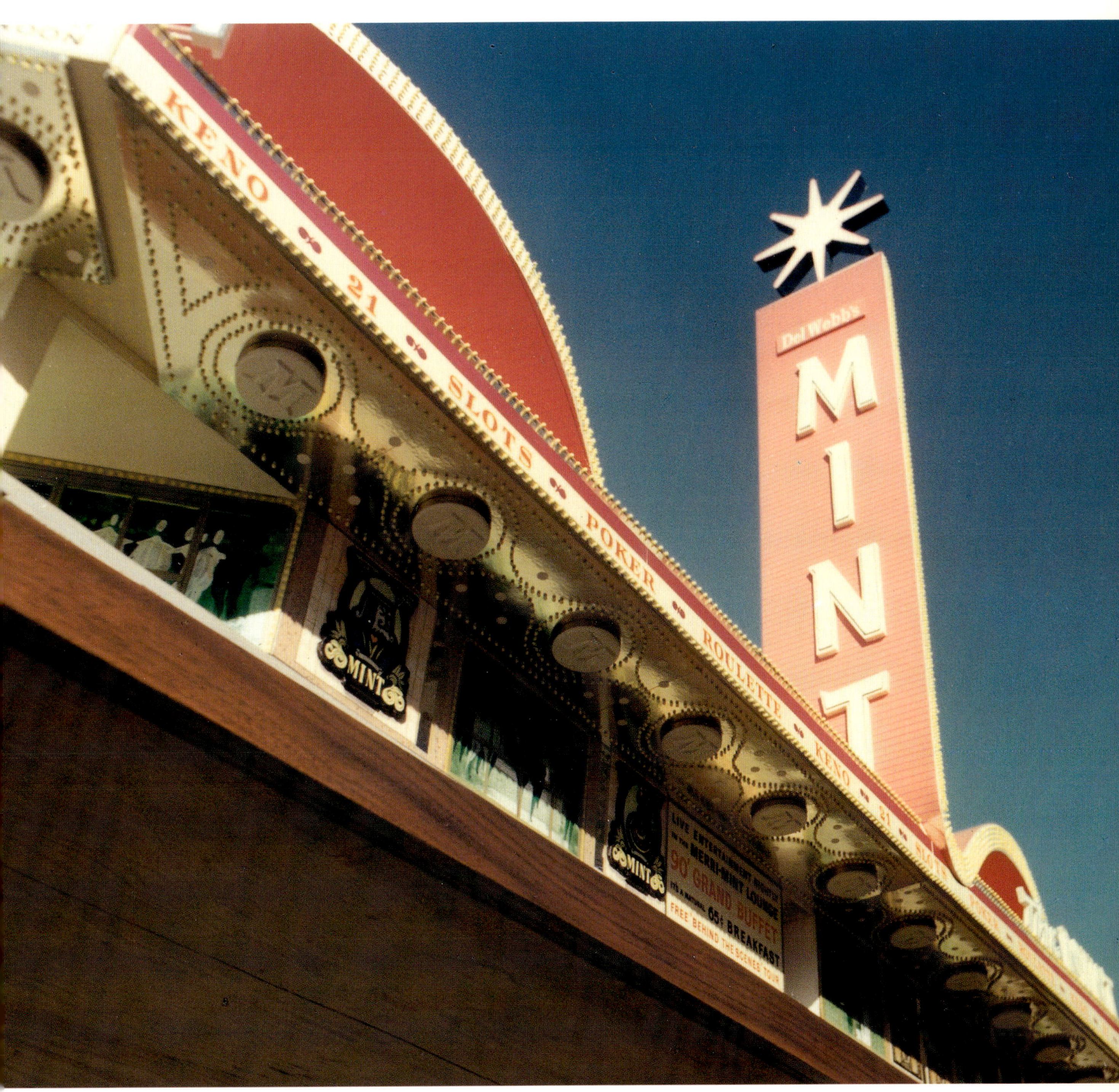

MINT HOTEL-CASINO-MODEL OF 1970'S REMODELING PROJECT BY AD ART ELECTRIC SIGN CO., INC. (STOCKTON, CA). PROJECT INCLUDED NEW FASCIA AND SOFFITT WORK AND NEW SIDEWALK-LEVEL GRAPHICS, ALL INTEGRATED WITH EXISTING SIGNWORK. MINT WAS DEMOLISHED IN THE LATE 1980S WHEN PROPERTY WAS ACQUIRED BY THE ADJACENT HORSESHOE CLUB. PHOTO BY CHARLES F. BARNARD

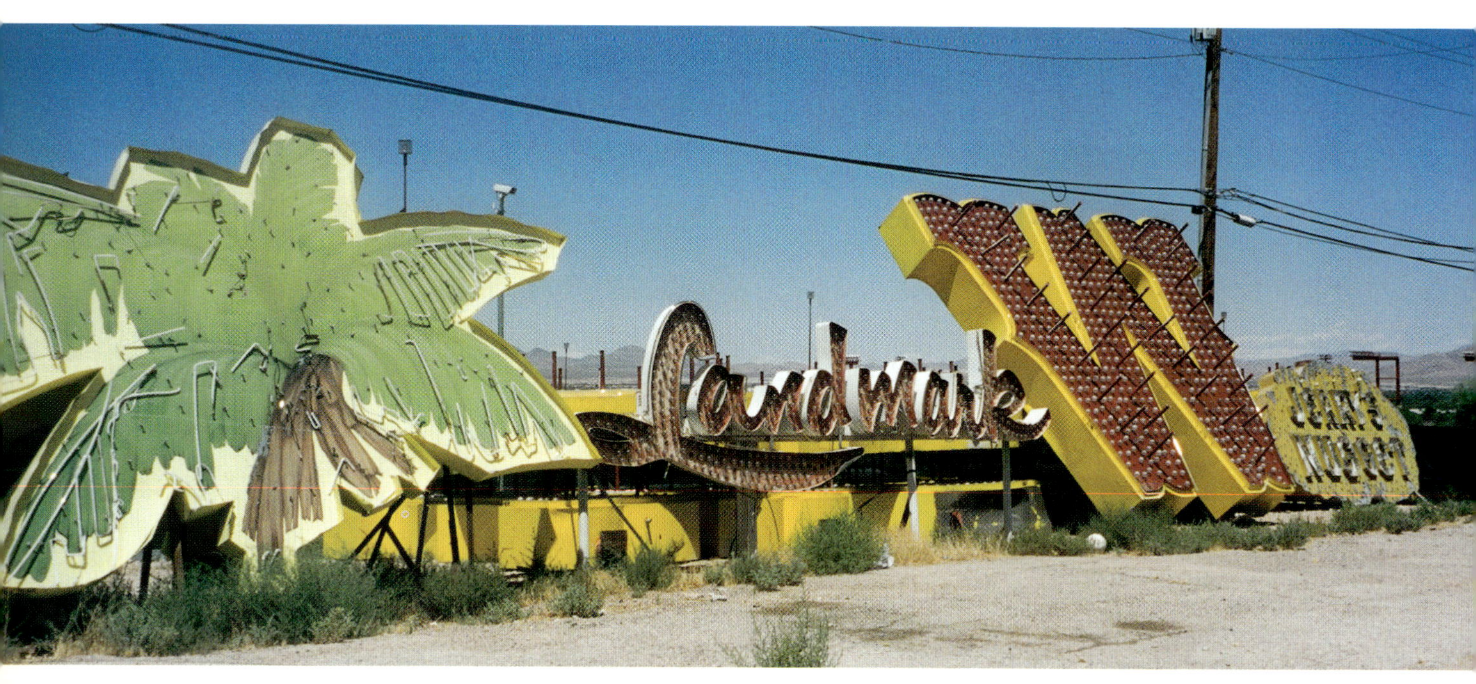

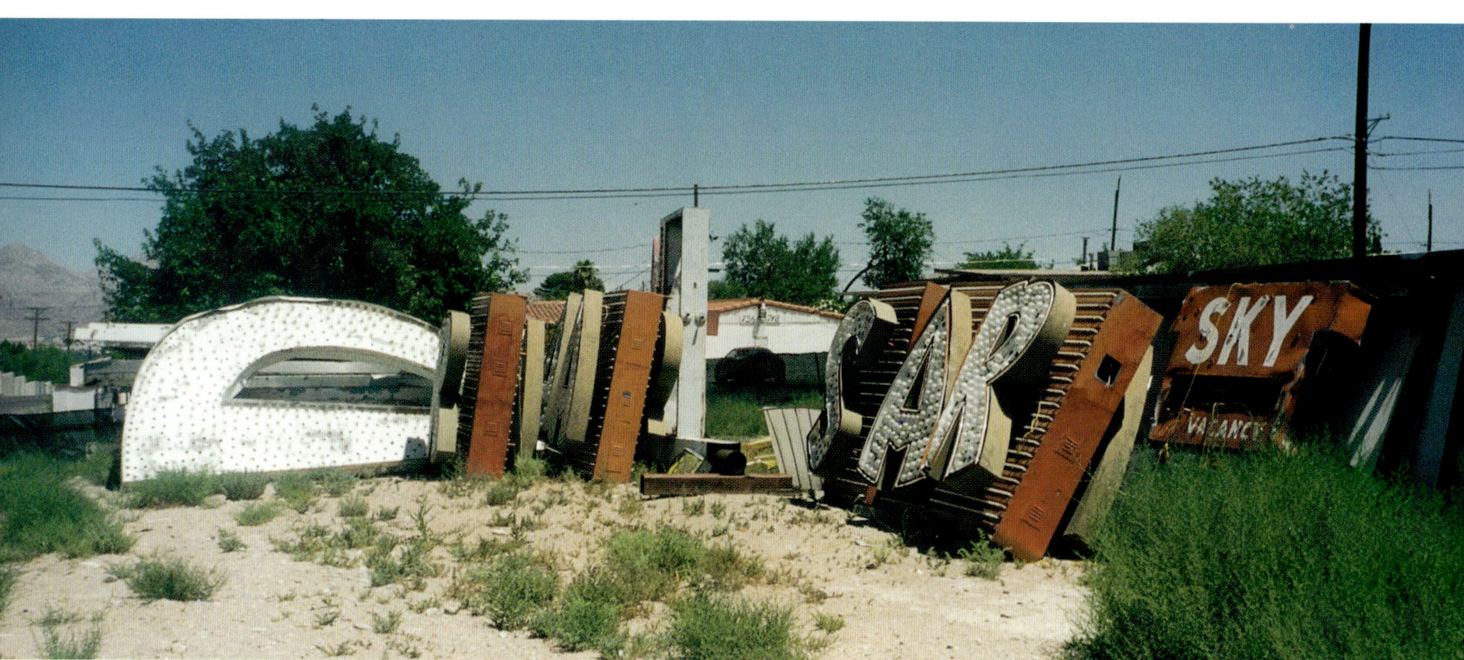

NEON MUSEUM'S BONEYARD, PHOTOS BY ALEX FARQUHARSON

'VEGAS VICKIE', ANIMATED NEON SIGN FOR THE GLITTER GULCH CASINO, LAS VEGAS. THIS RENDERING (1981) WAS BY CHARLES F. BARNARD. SIGN WAS MANUFACTURED AND INSTALLED BY AD ART ELECTRIC SIGN CO., INC. (STOCKTON, CA). STILL IN USE TODAY, IT HAS BECOME ONE OF LAS VEGAS'S MOST FAMILIAR ICONS. PHOTO BY CHARLES F. BARNARD

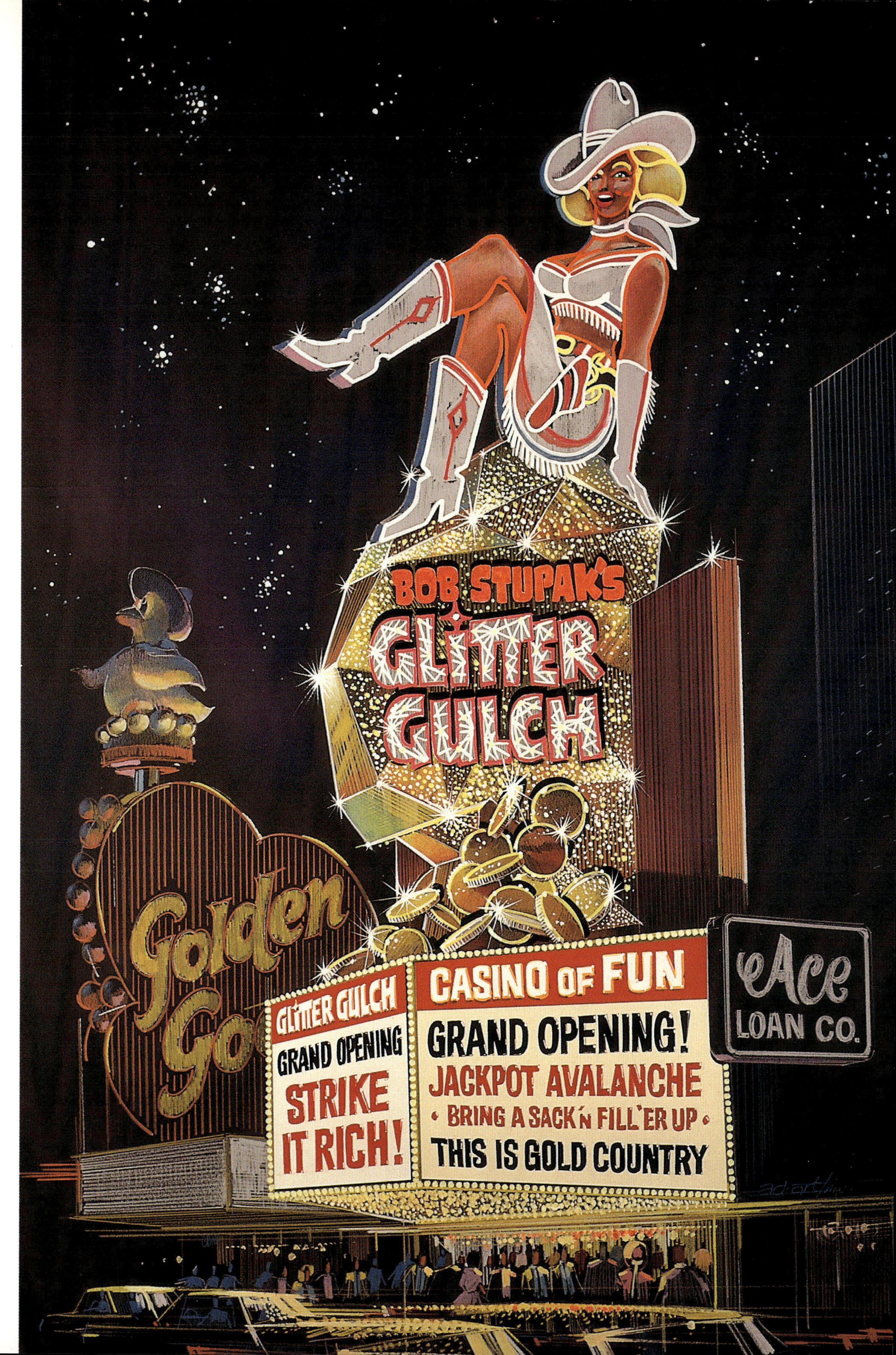
BOB STUPAK'S
GLITTER
GULCH
Golden
Go
GLITTER GULCH
GRAND OPENING
STRIKE
IT RICH!
CASINO OF FUN
GRAND OPENING!
JACKPOT AVALANCHE
• BRING A SACK'N FILL'ER UP •
THIS IS GOLD COUNTRY
Ace
LOAN CO.

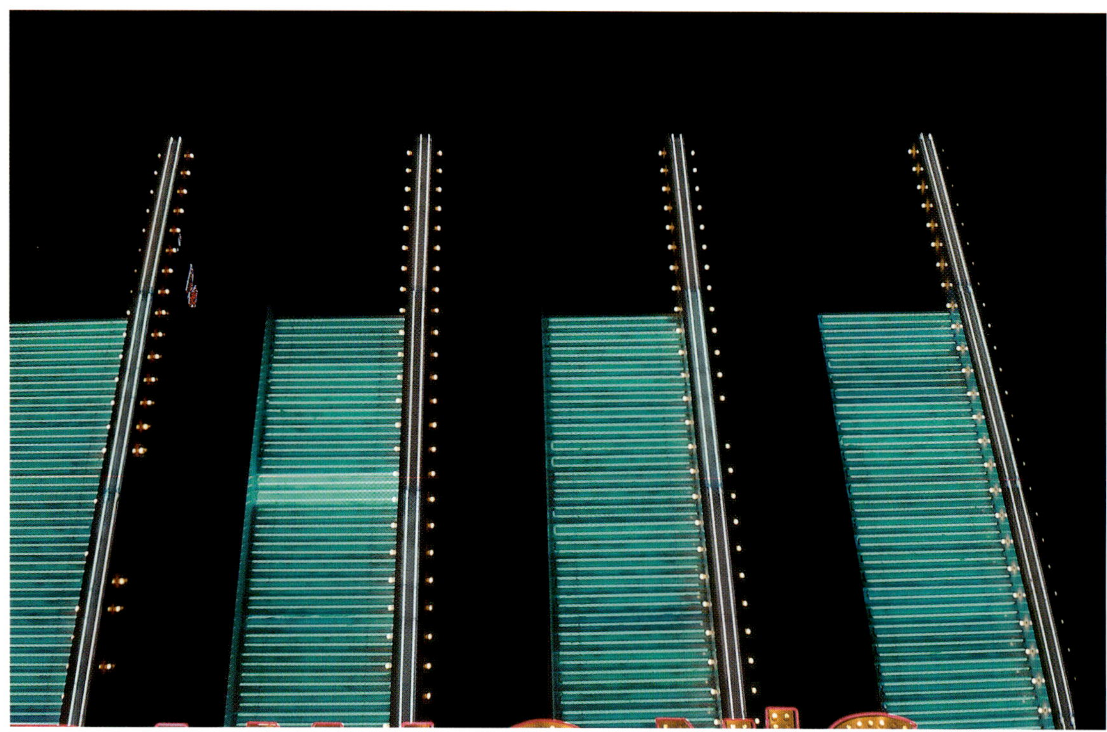

BINION'S HORSESHOE, PHOTO BY ROLF RICKE

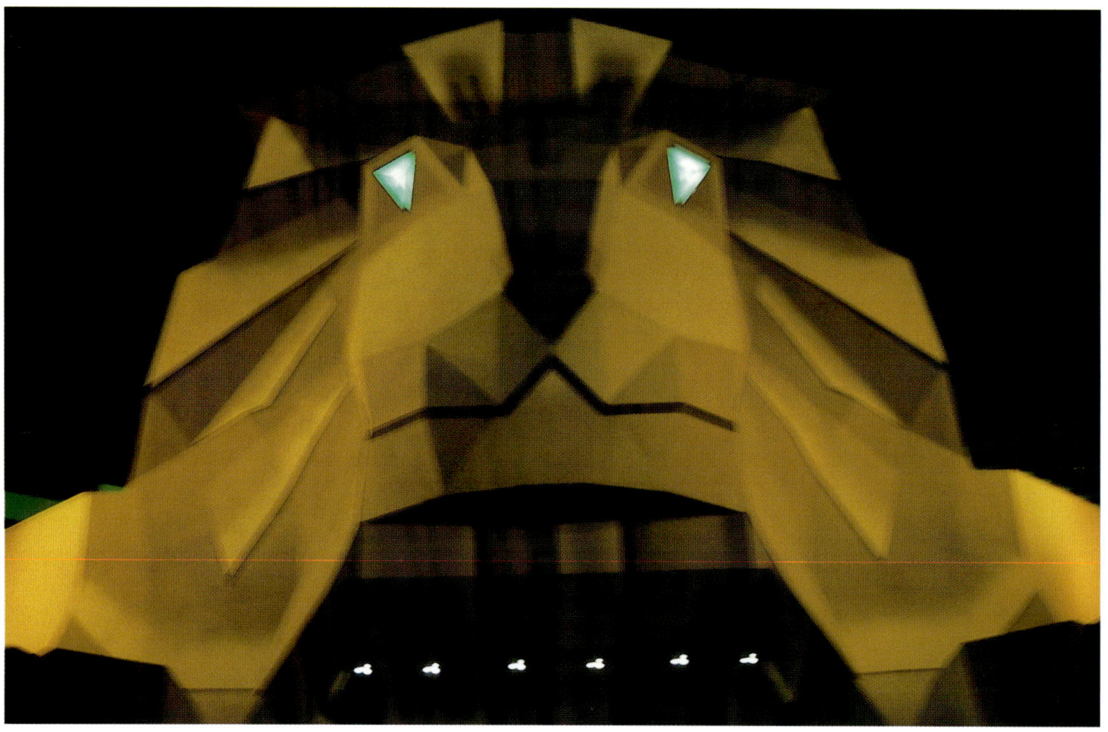

THE MGM LION ABOVE THE ENTRANCE OF THE MGM GRAND HOTEL, IN THE MID-1990S REMOVED, PHOTO BY ROLF RICKE

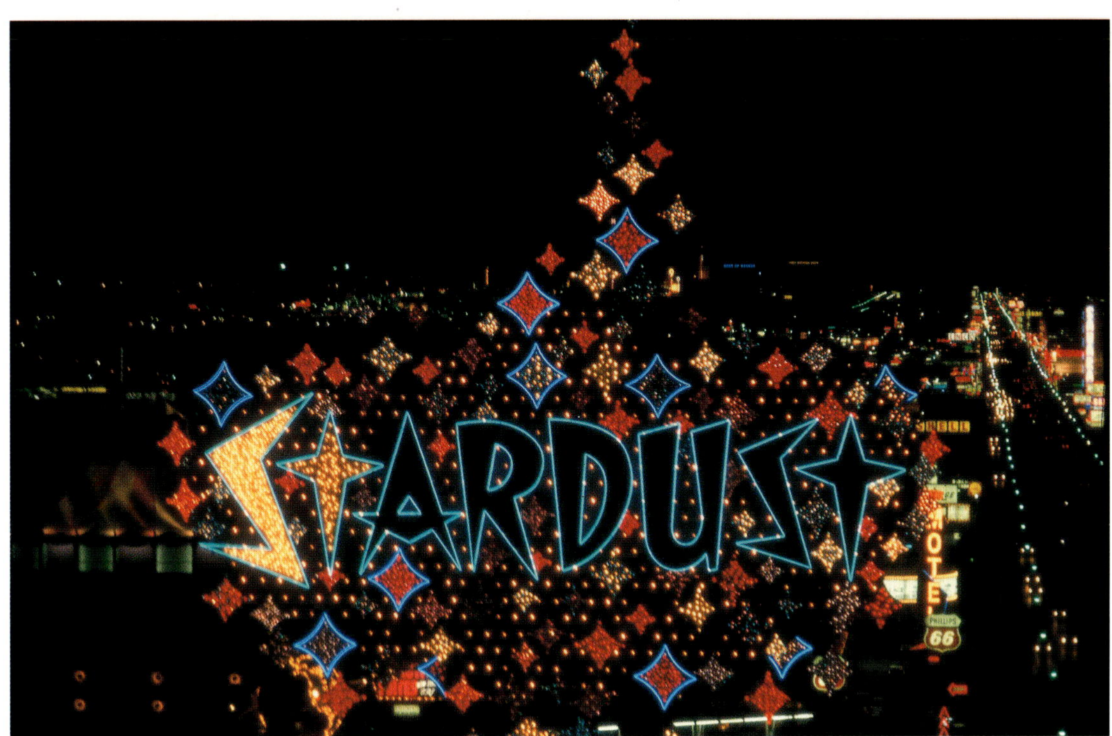

STARDUST SIGN, PHOTO BY VENTURI, SCOTT BROWN & ASSOCIATES

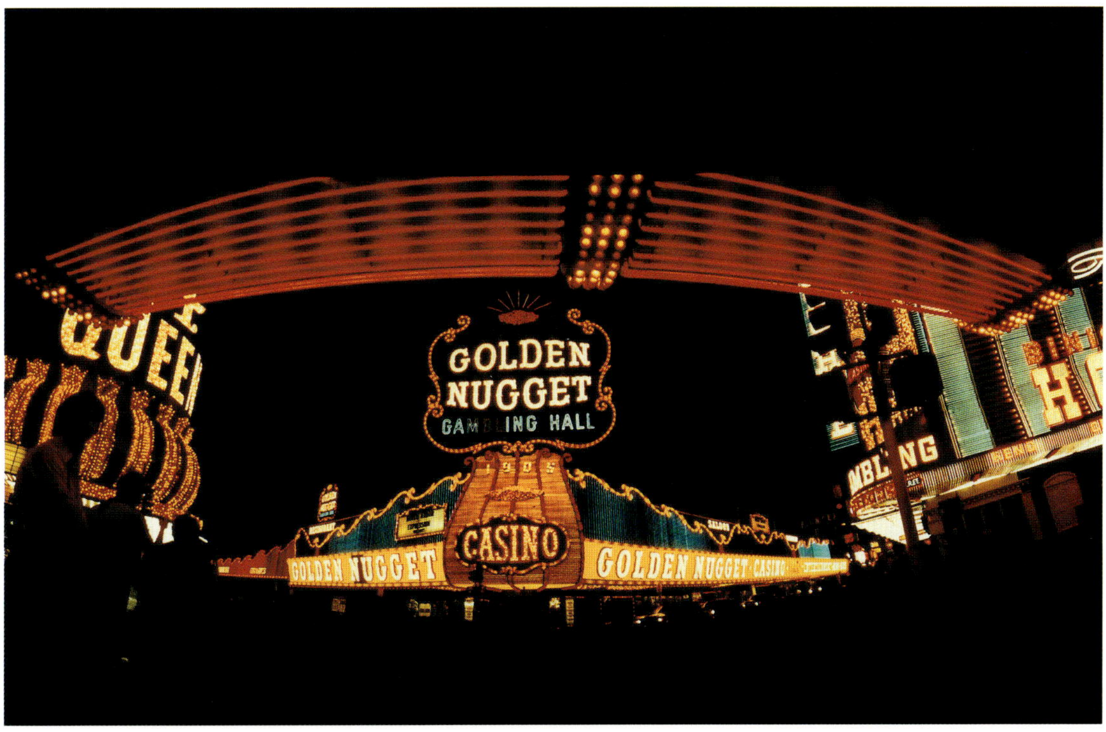

THE GOLDEN NUGGET CASINO, PHOTO BY VENTURI, SCOTT BROWN & ASSOCIATES (STEVEN IZENOUR)

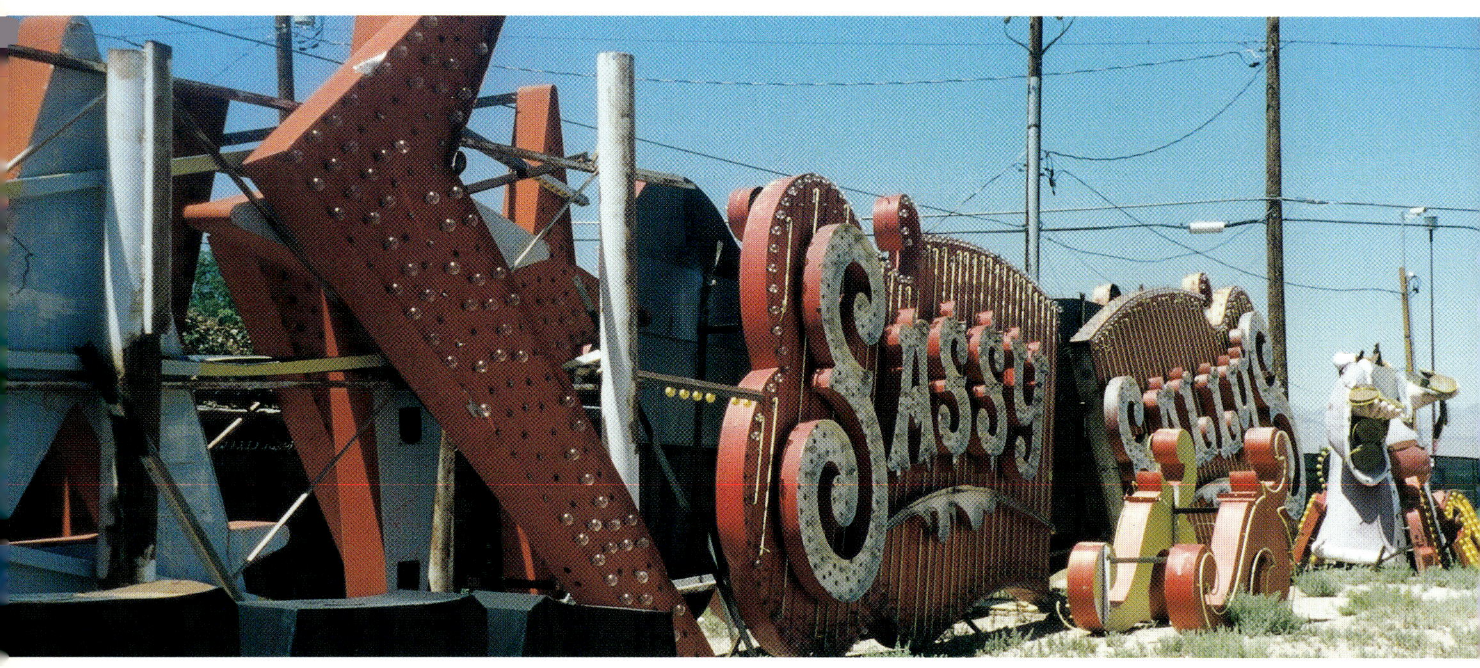

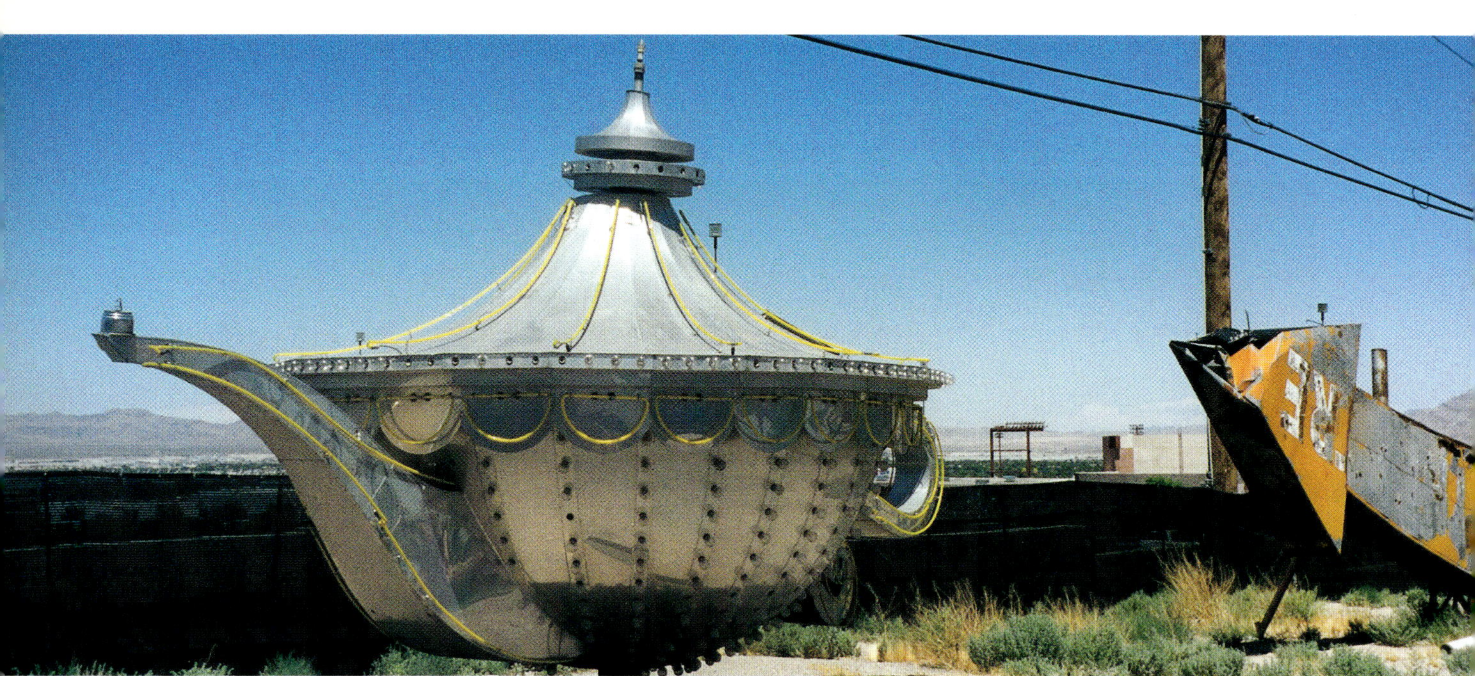

NEON MUSEUM'S BONEYARD, PHOTOS BY ALEX FARQUHARSON

STARDUST PYLON SIGN RENDERING (1966) BY CHARLES F. BARNARD. SIGN WAS MANUFACTURED AND INSTALLED BY AD ART ELECTRIC SIGN COMPANY, INC., (STOCKTON, CA). FOR MANY YEARS THIS SIGN WAS LISTED IN THE GUINNESS BOOK OF WORLD RECORDS AS THE WORLD'S TALLEST ELECTRIC SIGN – AND IS STILL IN USE AT THE STARDUST HOTEL IN LAS VEGAS. PHOTO BY CHARLES F. BARNARD

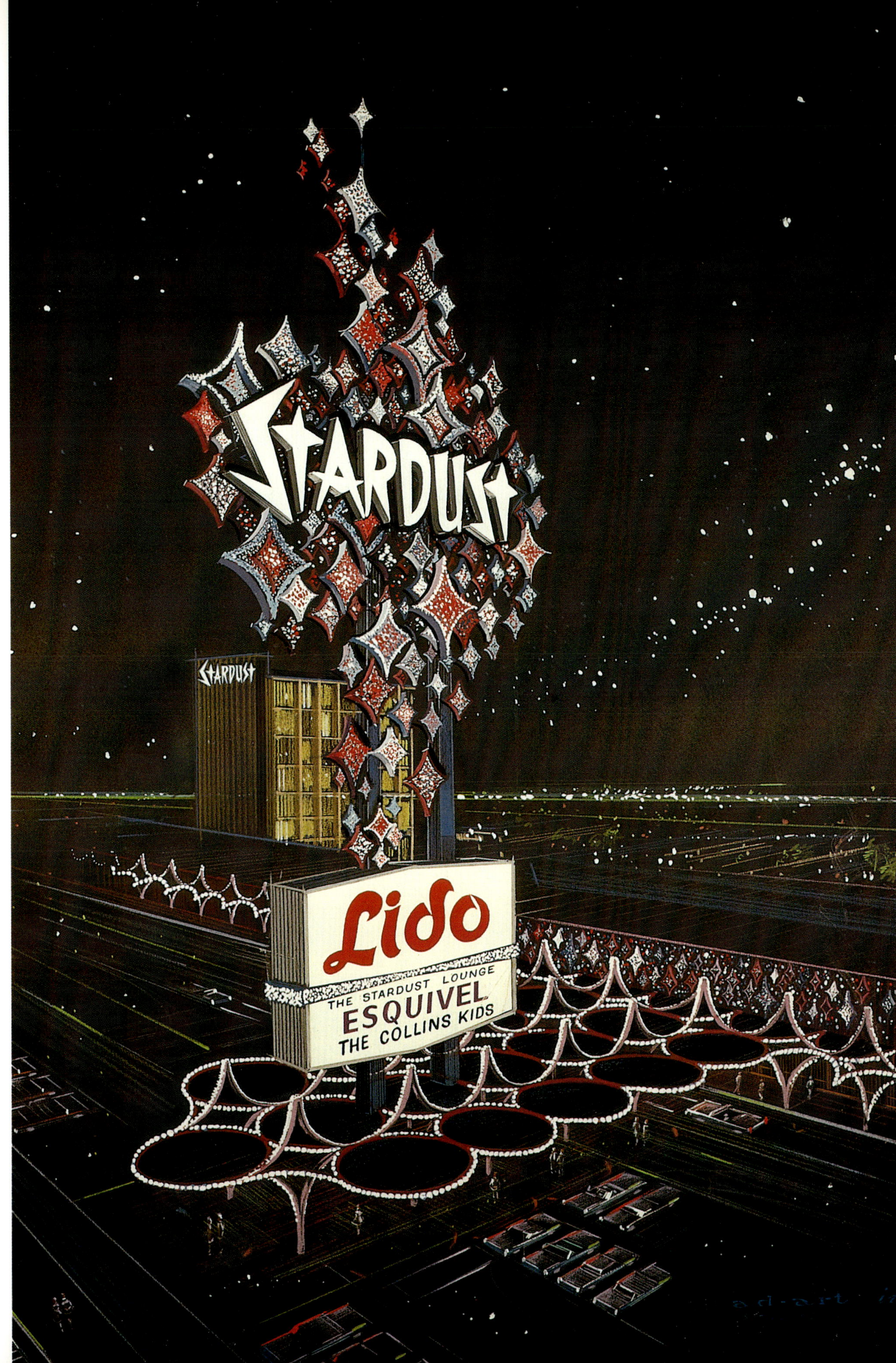
STARDUST
STARDUST
Lido
THE STARDUST LOUNGE
ESQUIVEL
THE COLLINS KIDS

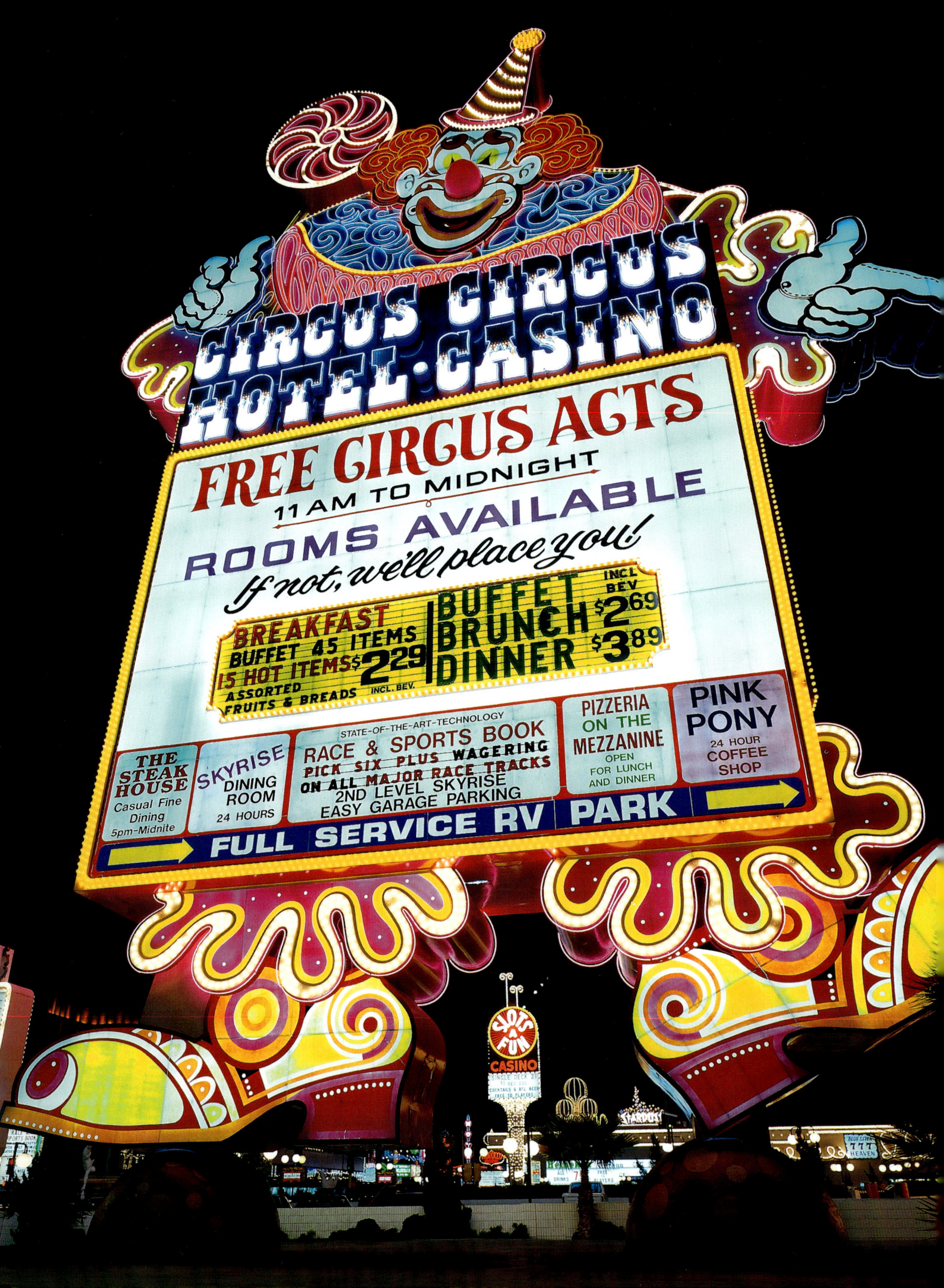
CIRCUS CIRCUS
HOTEL·CASINO
FREE CIRCUS ACTS
11 AM TO MIDNIGHT
ROOMS AVAILABLE
If not, we'll place you!
BREAKFAST
BUFFET 45 ITEMS
15 HOT ITEMS $2.29
ASSORTED
FRUITS & BREADS INCL. BEV.
BUFFET
BRUNCH $2.69
DINNER $3.89
INCL BEV
THE STEAK HOUSE
Casual Fine Dining
5pm-Midnite
SKYRISE
DINING ROOM
24 HOURS
STATE-OF-THE-ART-TECHNOLOGY
RACE & SPORTS BOOK
PICK SIX PLUS WAGERING
ON ALL MAJOR RACE TRACKS
SKYRISE
2ND LEVEL SKYRISE
EASY GARAGE PARKING
PIZZERIA
ON THE
MEZZANINE
OPEN
FOR LUNCH
AND DINNER
PINK
PONY
24 HOUR
COFFEE
SHOP
FULL SERVICE RV PARK
SLOTS A FUN
CASINO

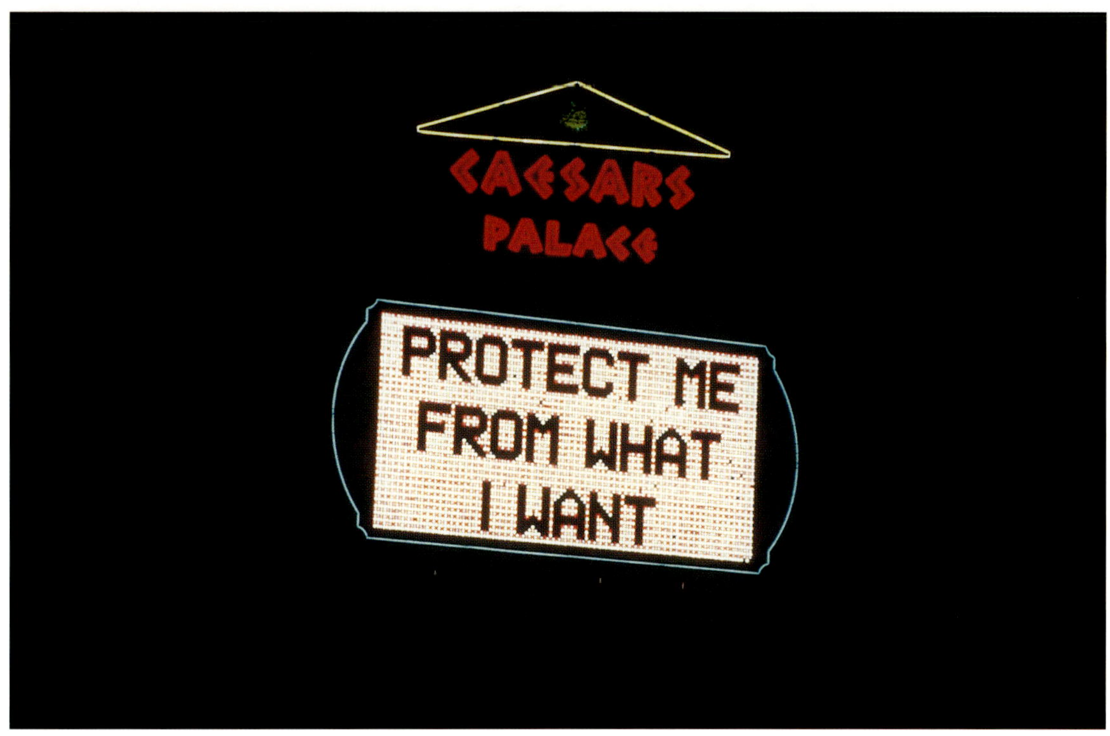

JENNY HOLZER
PROTECT ME FROM WHAT I WANT (CAESARS PALACE. LAS VEGAS, NEVADA), FROM THE SERIES 'TRUISMS' 1977-79
COURTESY OF NEVADA INSTITUTE OF CONTEMPORARY ART

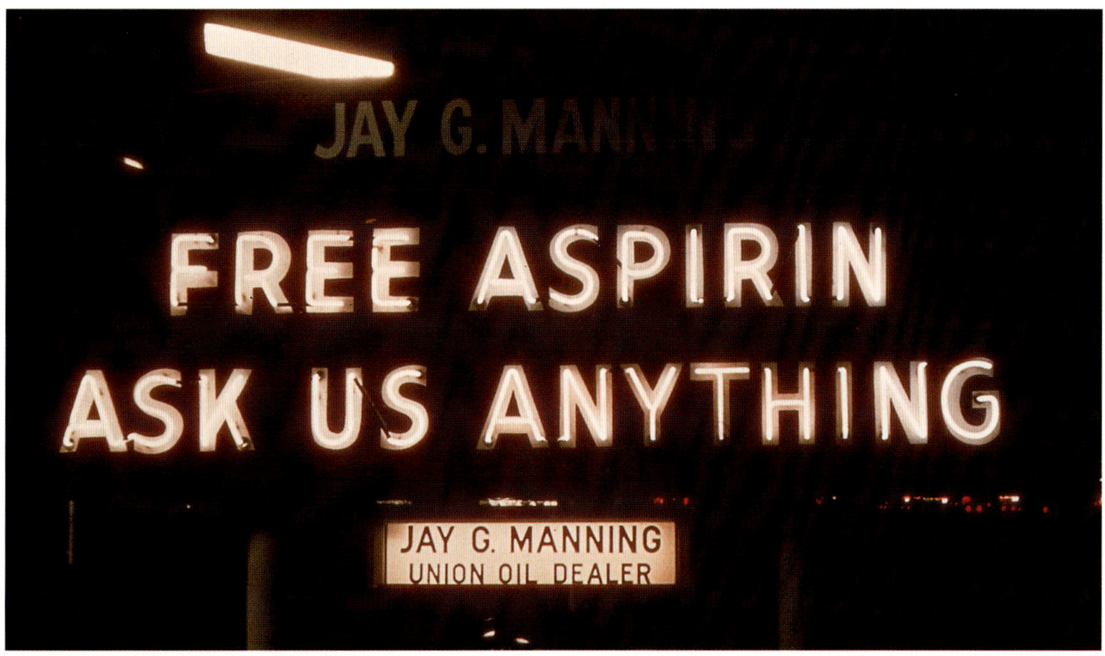

PHOTO BY VENTURI, SCOTT BROWN & ASSOCIATES

THE CIRCUS CIRCUS SIGN, PHOTO BY VENTURI, SCOTT BROWN & ASSOCIATES

Silke Otto-Knapp

1970 Born
1992-97 Degree in Cultural Studies, University of Hildesheim, D
1995-96 M.A. Fine Arts, Chelsea College of Art and Design, London, GB
Since 1995 Member of gallery committee at Cubitt, one of the few remaining artist-run studios and gallery spaces in London
Lives in London, GB

2001/02
Get out of Here – exhibition on the subject of going away, Zacheta, Warsaw, PL
2000
Silke Otto-Knapp, Galerie Karin Guenther, Hamburg, D
songs sung by men from the point of view of a woman, Platform, London, GB
1999
limit-less, Galerie Krinzinger, Vienna, A
Where do you want to go today...?, Cubitt, London, GB

I drove up Bonanza Road, which leads from downtown, climbs several hundred feet, and dead-ends at the foot of Sunrise Mountain with a commanding view of the whole valley. This used to be a popular lover's lane – until the Mormons build their spired temple at the end of the road. At night the temple watches over the valley like a bemused guardian angel. The lights of the valley appear as in a galaxy. Downtown and the Strip glow as a thick centre, with great arms of starry lights spinning outward from it. Like a spindle at its center rises Las Vegas's latest addition, the Strathosphere Tower. At 135 stories, it's the tallest thing west of Mississippi. There's a roller coaster on top.
I was reminded of the competing theories on the fate of the Universe: expansion to the point of oblivion, eventual collapse under its own weight, or a delicate balance resulting in permanent equilibrium. Las Vegas faces a similar set of possibilities. And for the city of the Next Big Thing, how that plays out will be the biggest thing of all.

William R. Newcott, 'Believing Las Vegas', National Geographic, December 1996, p. 81.

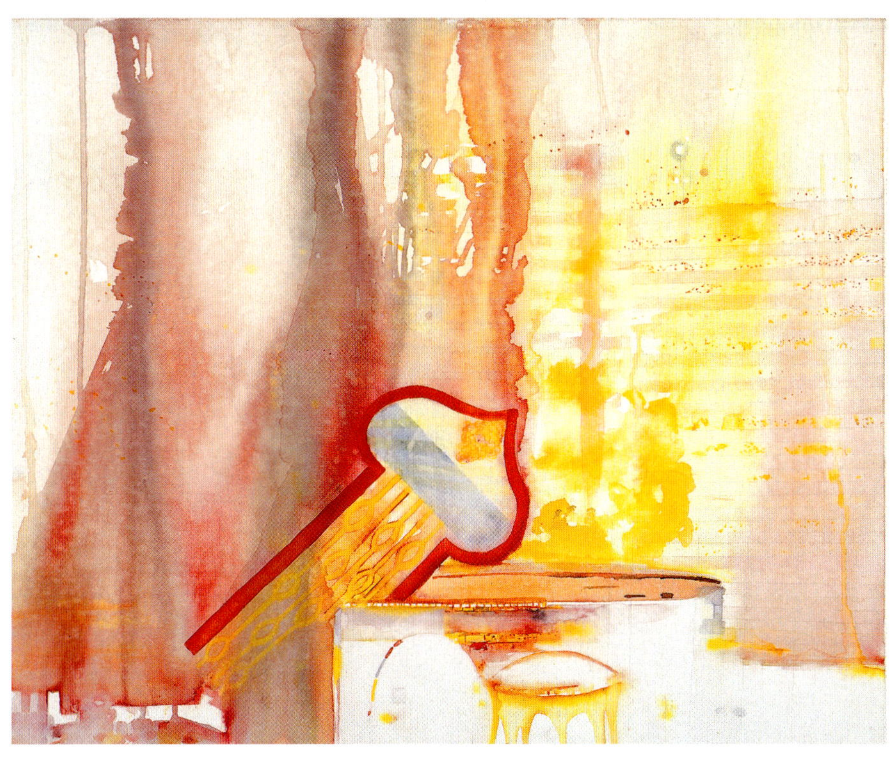

EXPLOSION 2000
WATER COLOUR ON CANVAS 65 x 81 CM
COURTESY: HELABA LANDESBANK HESSEN,
GIROZENTRALE, FRANKFURT AM MAIN
PHOTO: WOLFGANG GÜNZEL

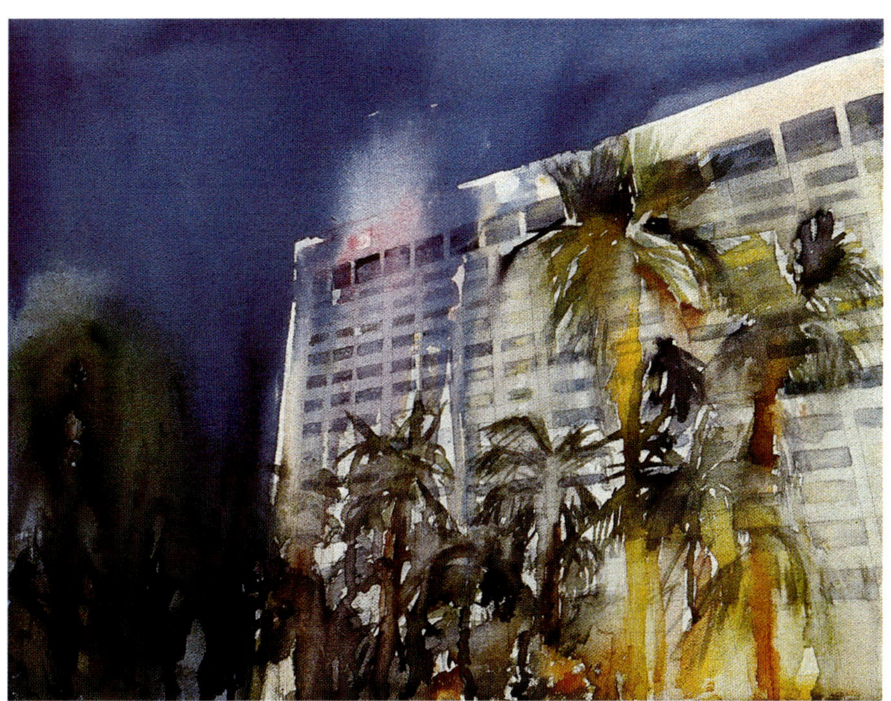

FLAMINGO (THE MAGIC HOUR) 2001
WATER COLOUR ON CANVAS 30 x 38 CM
COURTESY: HELABA LANDESBANK HESSEN,
GIROZENTRALE, FRANKFURT AM MAIN
PHOTO: WOLFGANG GÜNZEL

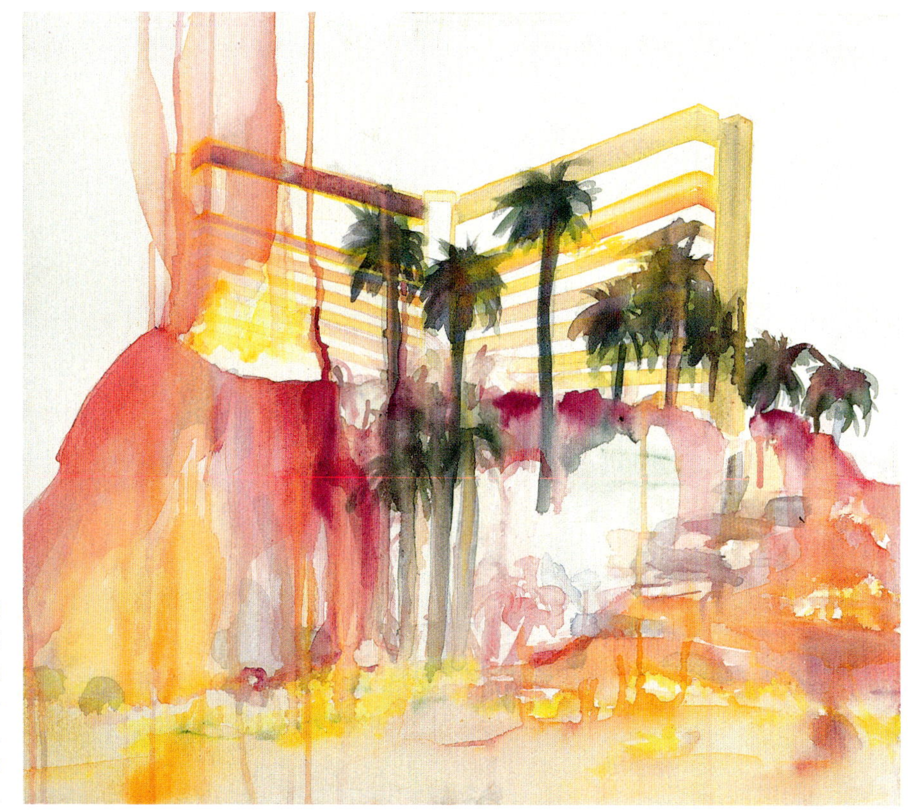

FIREFALL 2000
WATER COLOUR ON CANVAS
50 x 60 CM
COURTESY: HELABA LANDES-BANK HESSEN, GIROZENTRALE, FRANKFURT AM MAIN
PHOTO: WOLFGANG GÜNZEL

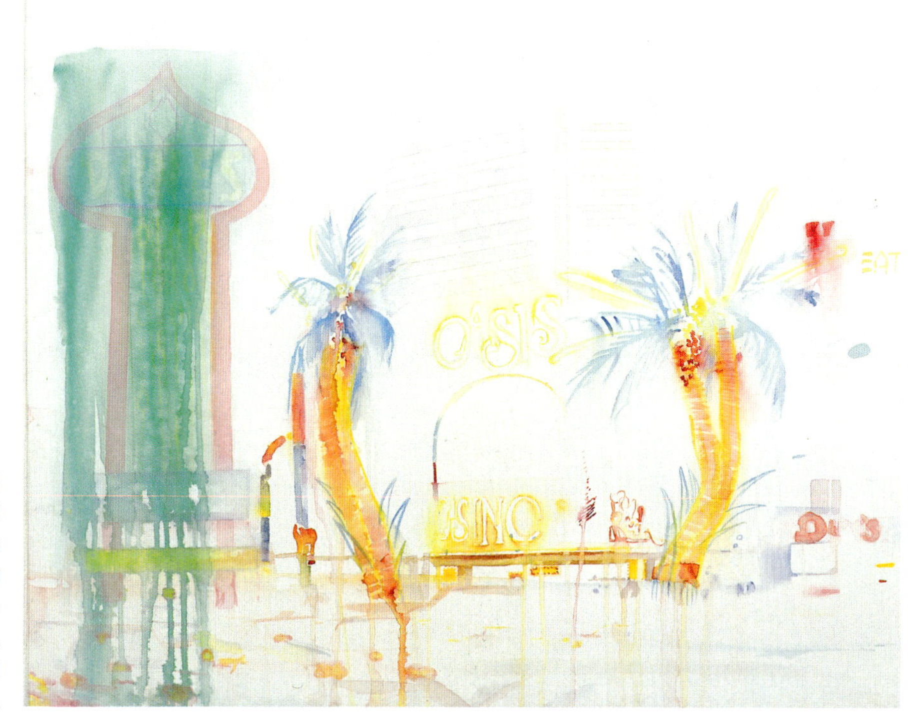

THE DUNES (BLUE PALMTREES) 2000
WATER COLOUR ON CANVAS
65 x 81 CM
COURTESY: HELABA LANDES-BANK HESSEN, GIROZENTRALE, FRANKFURT AM MAIN
PHOTO: WOLFGANG GÜNZEL

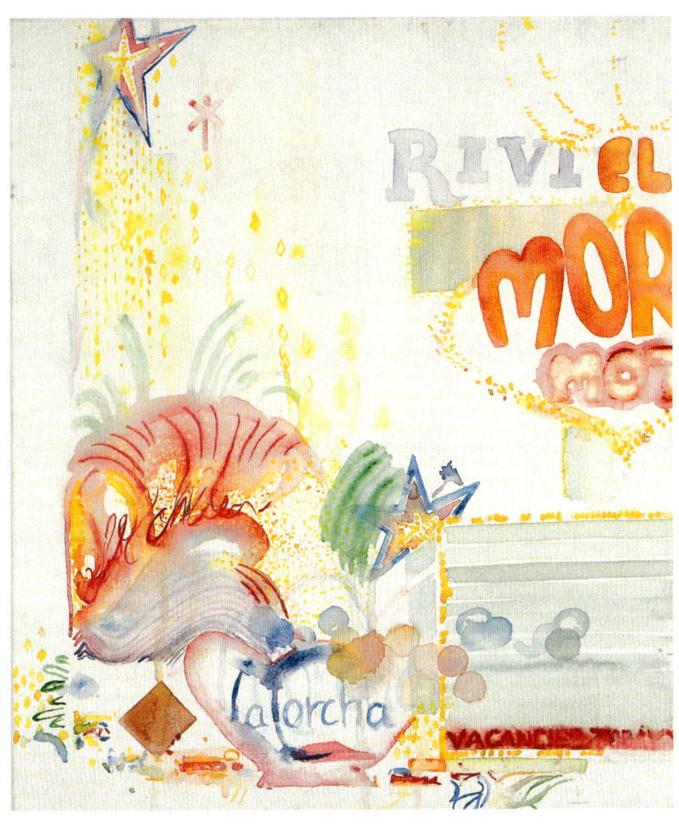

RIVIERA 2000
WATER COLOUR ON CANVAS 46 x 38 CM
COURTESY: HELABA LANDESBANK HESSEN, GIROZENTRALE, FRANKFURT AM MAIN
PHOTO: WOLFGANG GÜNZEL

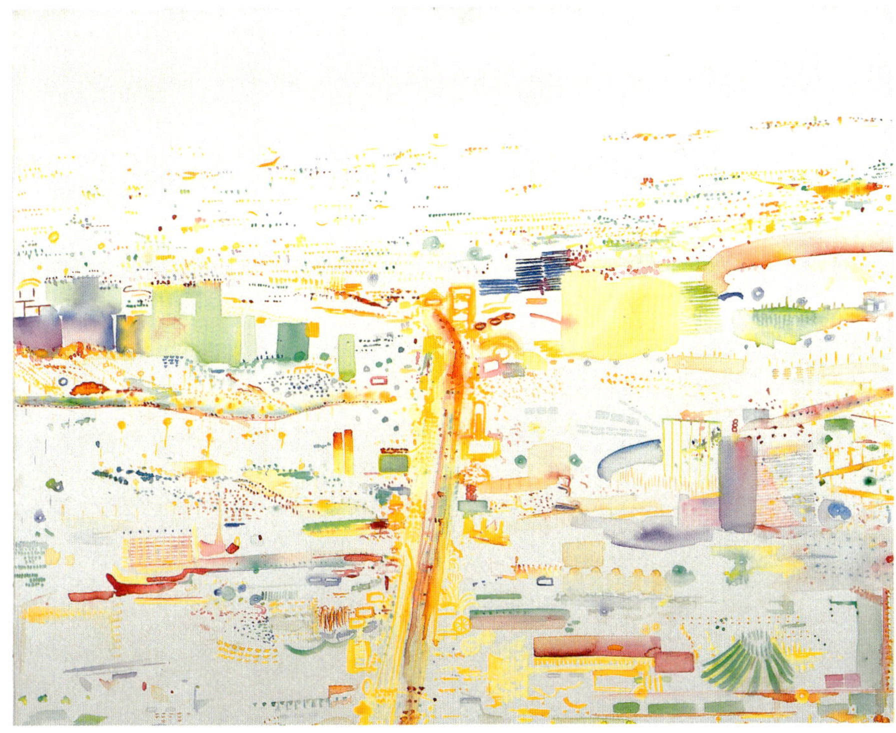

STRIP 2000
WATER COLOUR ON CANVAS
65 x 81 CM
COURTESY: HELABA LANDESBANK HESSEN, GIROZENTRALE, FRANKFURT AM MAIN
PHOTO: WOLFGANG GÜNZEL

Raymond Pettibon

1957 Born in Tucson, AZ
1977 B.A. UCLA, Los Angeles, CA
Lives in Hermosa Beach, Los Angeles, CA

2001
Raymond Pettibon, Whitechapel Art Gallery, London, GB
The Books 1978-2001, David Zwirner, New York, NY
2000
Raymond Pettibon, Sadie Coles, London, GB
Made in California, Los Angeles County Museum of Art, CA
The American Century: Art and Culture 1950-2000,
Whitney Museum of American Art, New York, NY (cat.)

AT LEAST I GOT TO SEE VEGAS 1983
PEN AND INK ON PAPER 30.4 x 22.8 CM
COLLECTION OF SHAUN CALEY REGEN, LOS ANGELES

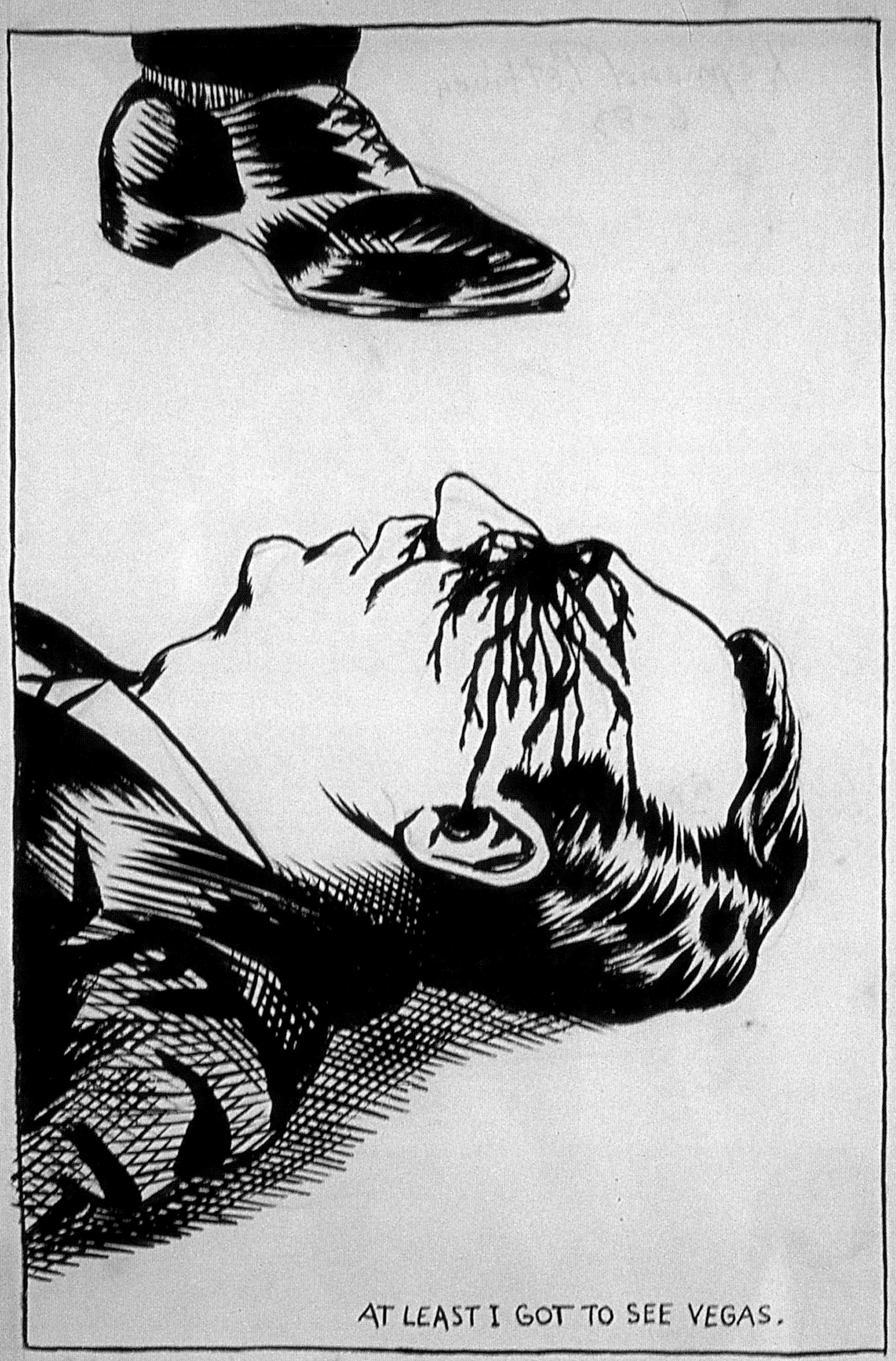
AT LEAST I GOT TO SEE VEGAS.

Jack Pierson

1960 Born in Plymouth, MA
Lives in New York and Provincetown, MA

2001
Jack Pierson, Regen Projects, Los Angeles, CA
2000
Jack Pierson, Chaim & Read Gallery, New York, NY
The American Century: Art and Culture 1950-2000,
Whitney Museum of American Art, New York, NY (cat.)
1997
Jack Pierson, Frankfurter Kunstverein, Frankfurt, D
1996
Defining the Nineties, Museum of Contemporary Art,
Miami, FL

THE GOLD SUIT 1997
C-PRINT 101.6 x 76.2 CM (EDITION OF 10)
COURTESY OF THE ARTIST AND CHEIM & READ GALLERY, NEW YORK

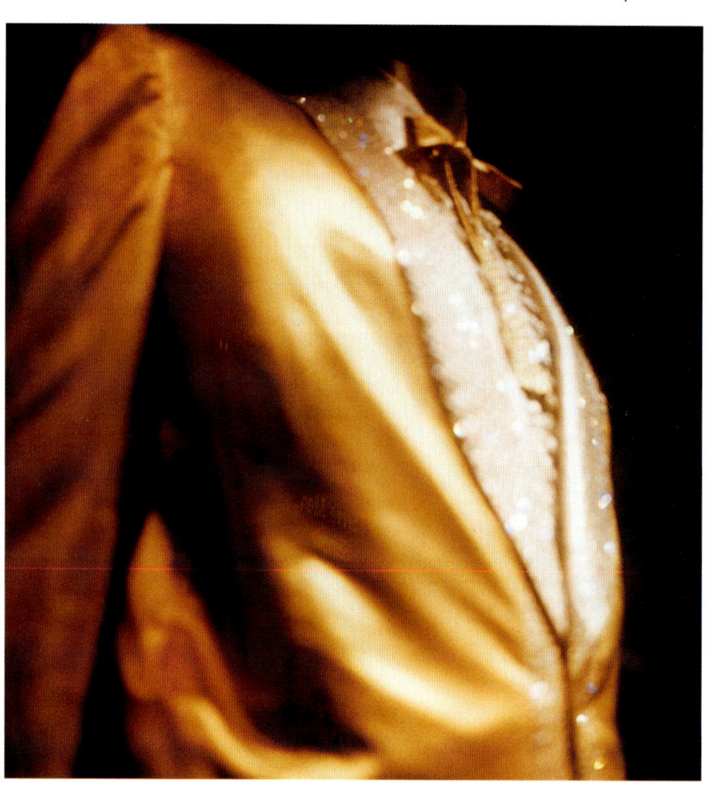

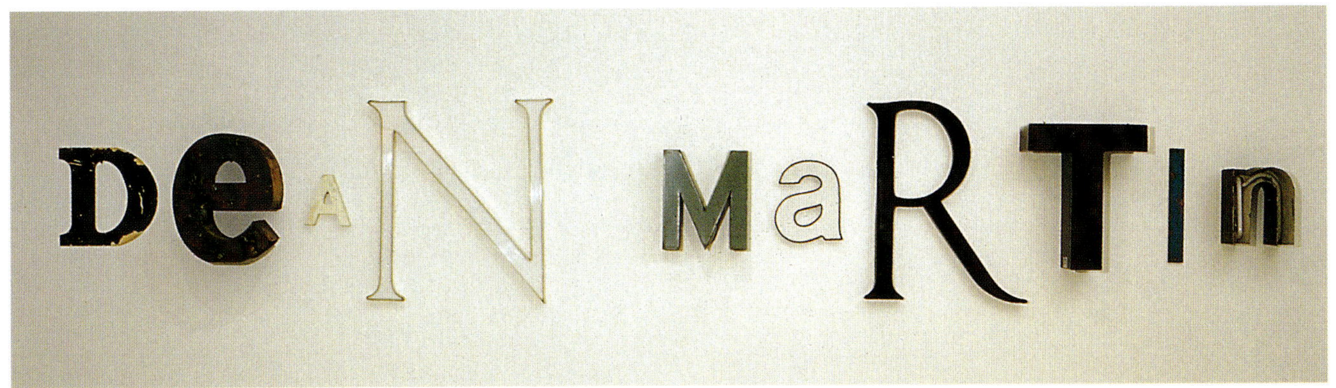

DEAN MARTIN 1996
SIGN LETTERING, DIMENSIONS VARIABLE (63.5 X 64.1 CM)
JP 153
COURTESY OF DEAN VALENTINE AND AMY ADELSON, LOS ANGELES

TROUBADOUR 1997
C-PRINT 101.6 X 76.2 CM (EDITION OF 10)
COURTESY OF THE ARTIST AND CHEIM & READ GALLERY, NEW YORK

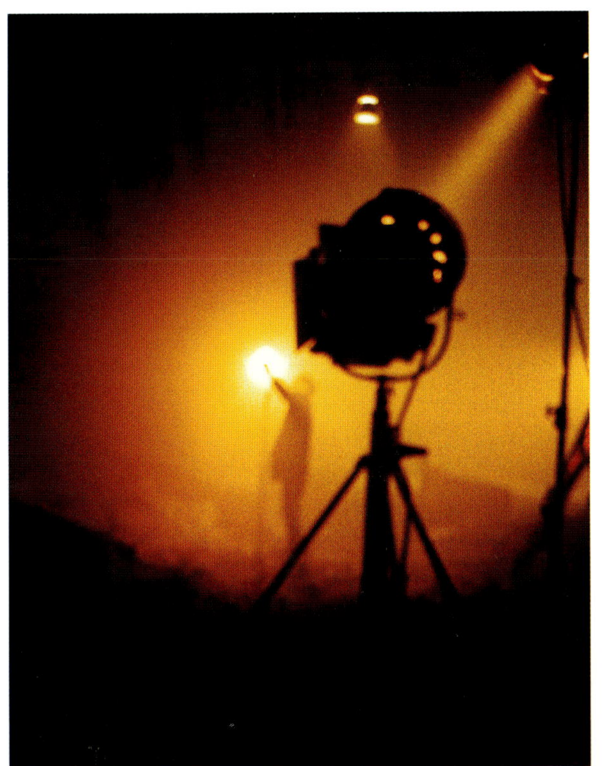

MISSY, 19TH STREET 1998
C-PRINT 101.6 X 76.2 CM (EDITION OF 10)
COURTESY OF THE ARTIST AND CHEIM & READ GALLERY, NEW YORK

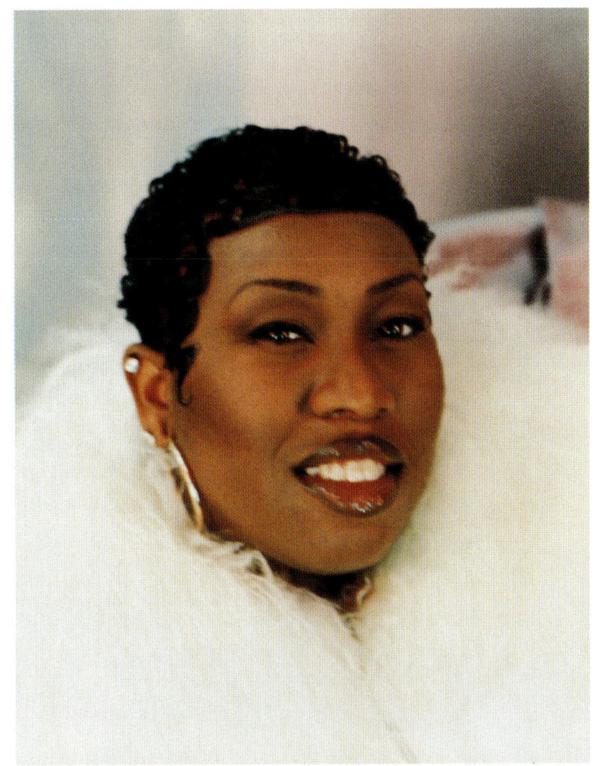

RED STRIP 1998
C-PRINT 76.2 x 101.6 CM (EDITION OF 10)
COURTESY OF THE ARTIST AND CHEIM & READ GALLERY, NEW YORK

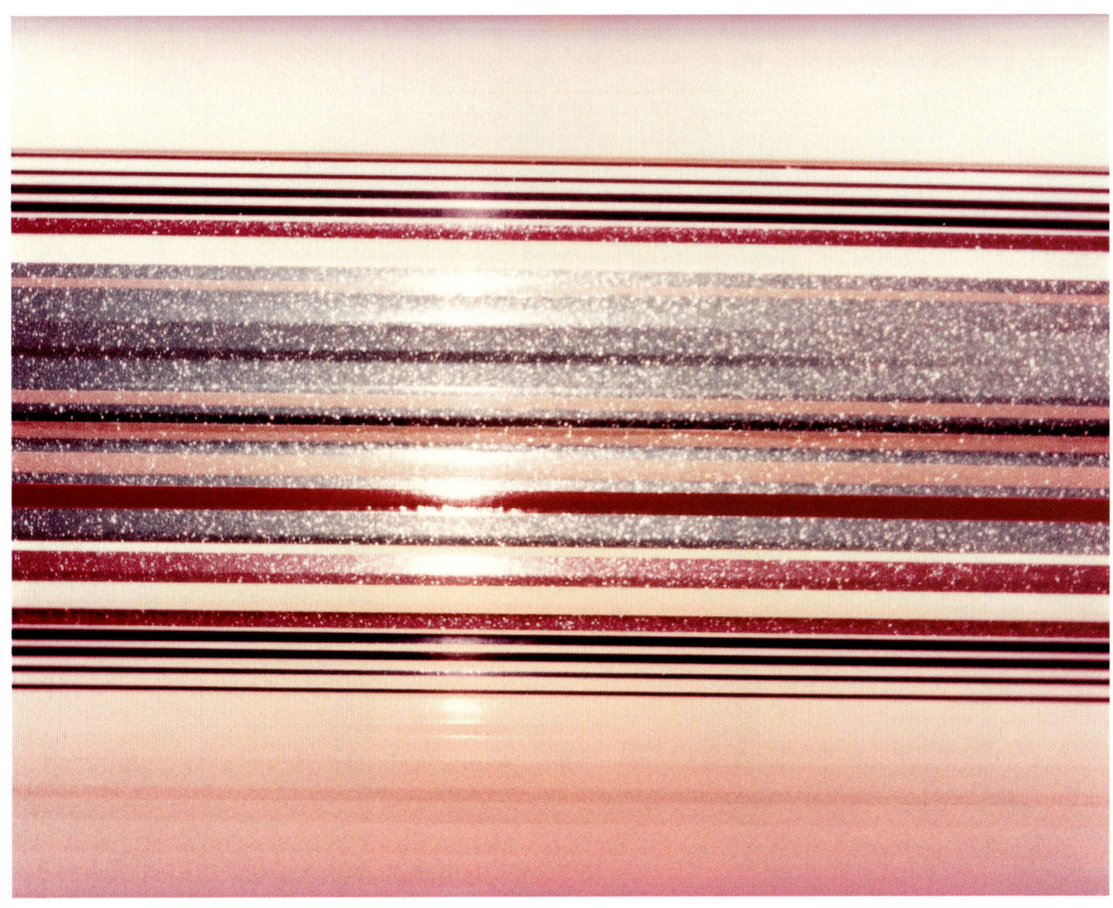

STRIPED ONE 1998
C-PRINT 101.6 x 76.2 CM (EDITION OF 10)
COURTESY OF THE ARTIST AND CHEIM & READ GALLERY, NEW YORK

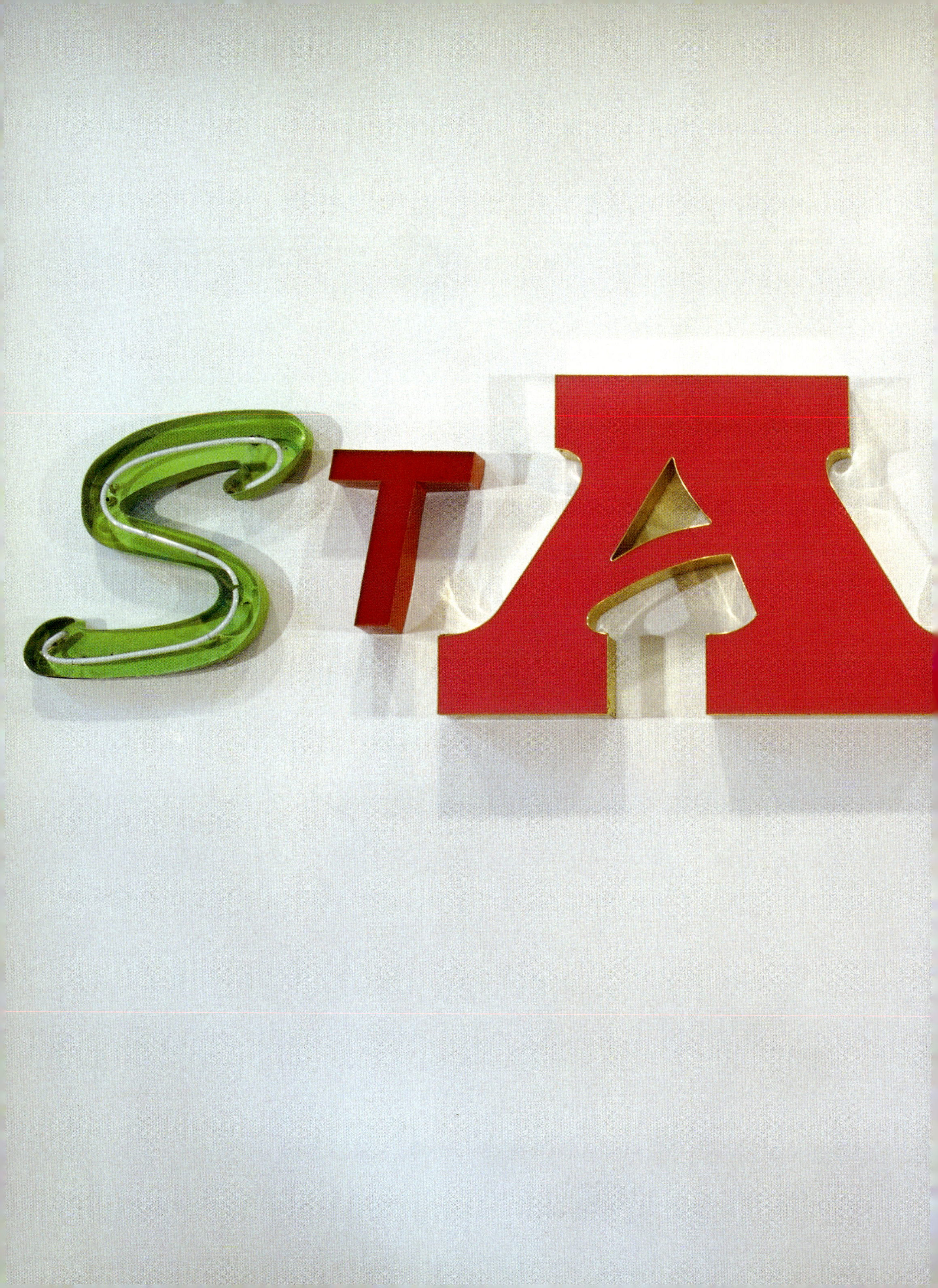

STA

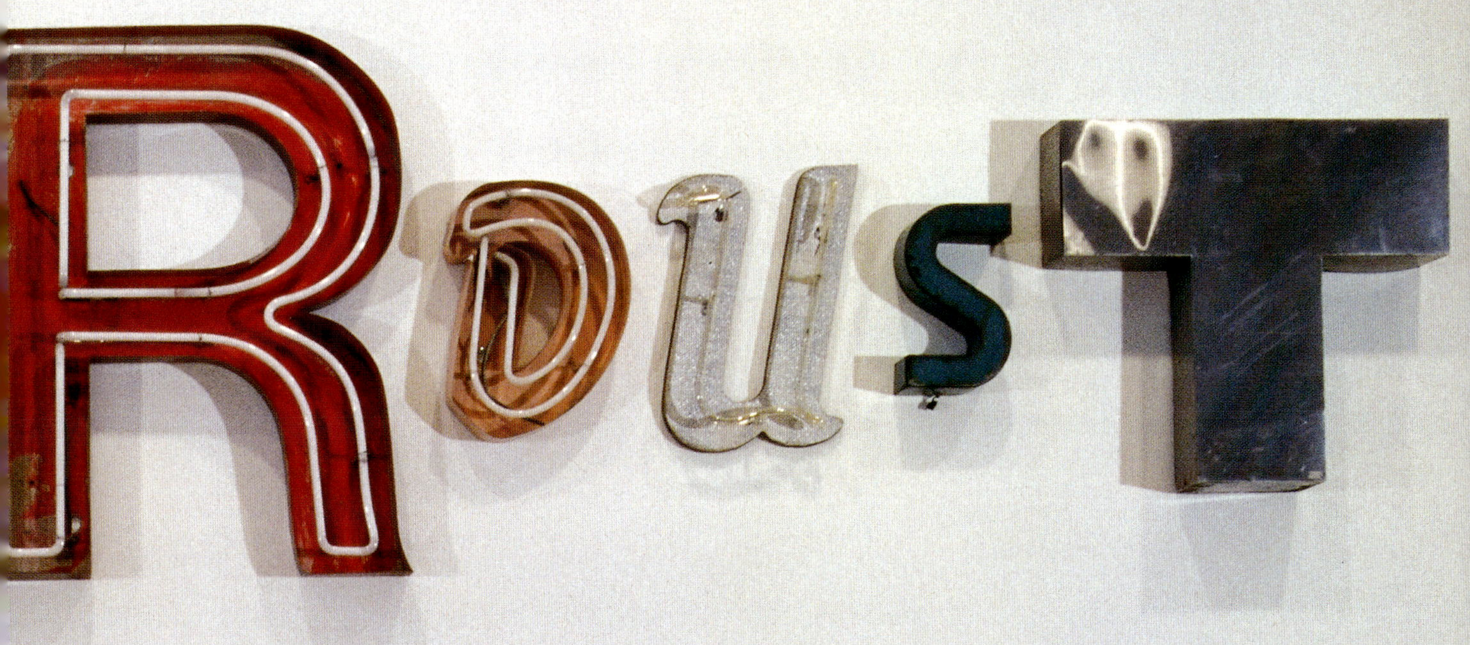

STARDUST 1995
FOUND SIGN LETTERING: METAL, PLASTIC, NEON TUBING, DIMENIONS VARIABLE
COLLECTION OF ENRON CORPORATION
COURTESY: TEXAS GALLERY, HOUSTON
PHOTO: RICK GARDNER, HOUSTON

David Reed

1946 Born in San Diego, CA
1966 Skowhegan School of Painting and Sculpture, Skowhegan, ME
1967 New York Studio School, New York, NY
1968 B.A. Reed College, Portland, OR
Lives in New York, NY

2001
David Reed. You look good in blue, Kunstverein St. Gallen Kunstmuseum, St. Gallen, CH; traveled to Kunstverein Hannover, D (cat.)
1999
David Reed, Max Protetch Gallery, New York, NY
1998
David Reed Paintings: Motion Pictures, Museum of Contemporary Art, San Diego, CA; traveled to the Wexner Center for the Arts, The Ohio State University, Columbus, OH; the Rose Art Museum, Brandeis University, Waltham, MA; to P.S.1 Contemporary Art Center, Long Island City, New York, NY (cat.)
1997
David Reed, Galerie Rolf Ricke, Cologne, D
David Reed, Patricia Faure Gallery, Los Angeles, CA
1996
David Reed, Donna Beam Fine Art Gallery, University of Nevada, Las Vegas, NV

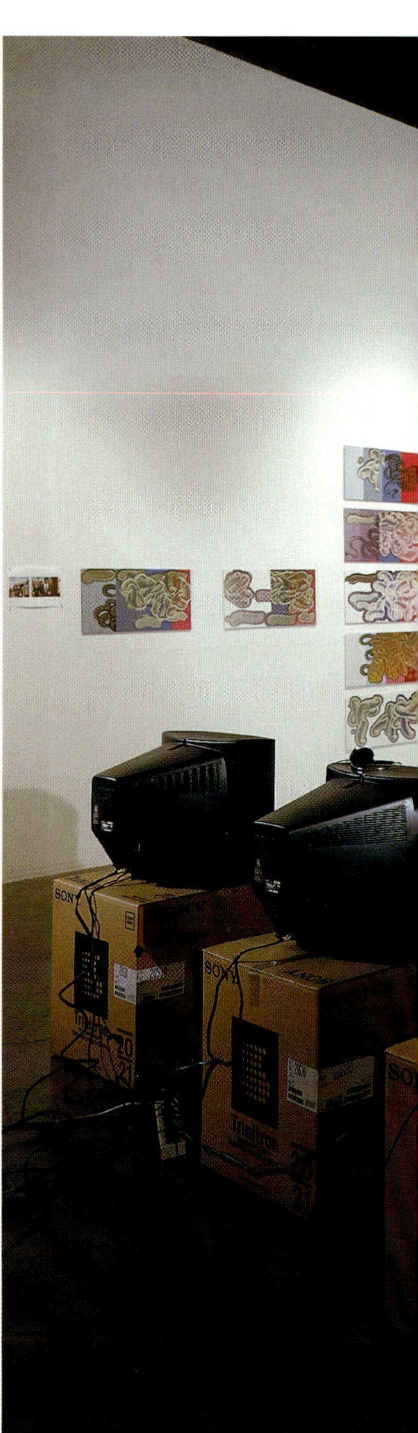

LAS VEGAS PIECE, INSTALLATION VIEW, PATRICIA FAURE GALLERY 1997
COURTESY OF PATRICIA FAURE GALLERY, SANTA MONICA, CA

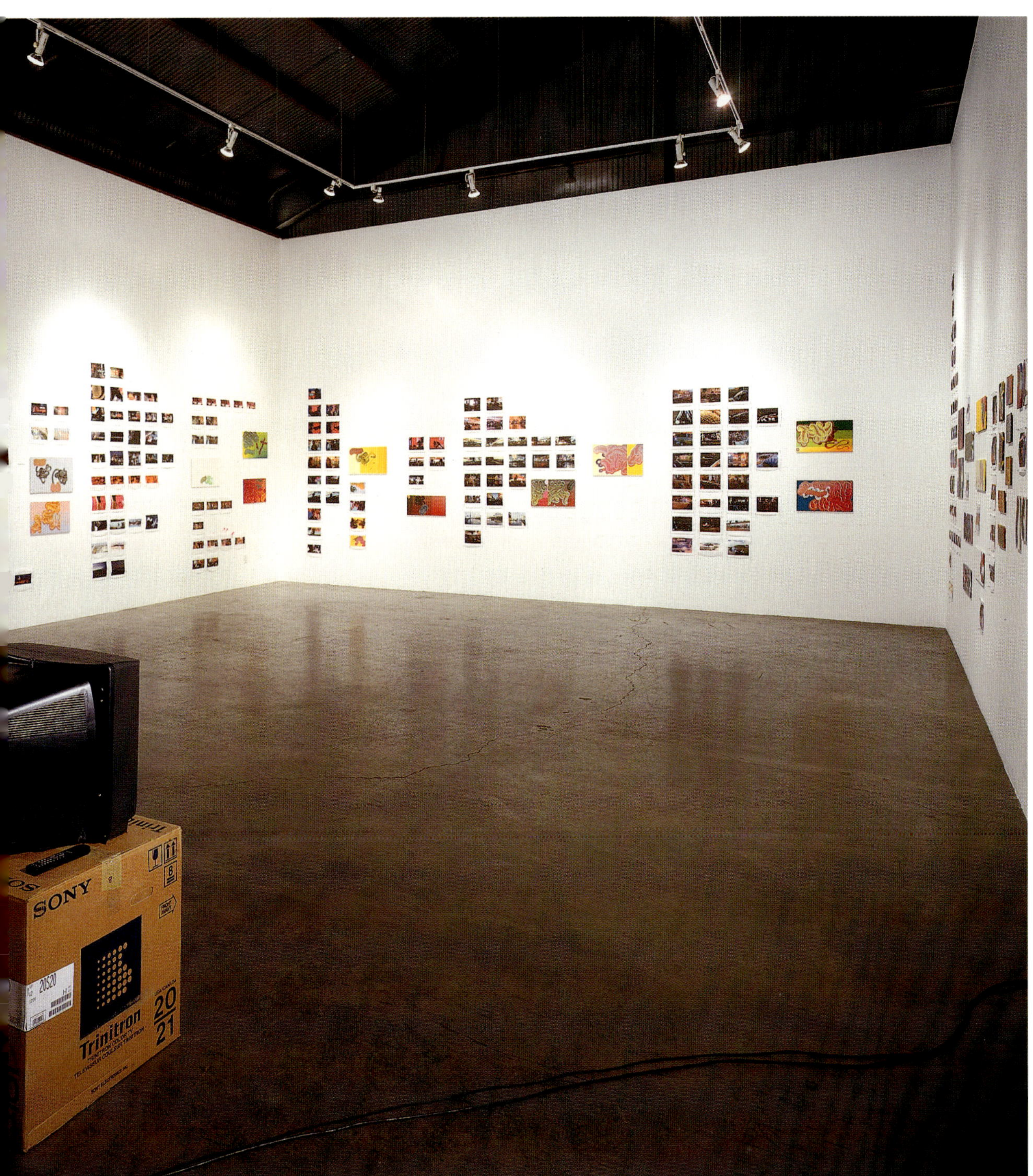
SONY
20S20
20
21
Trinitron

KILL ME AGAIN
METRO GOLDWYN MAYER 1989

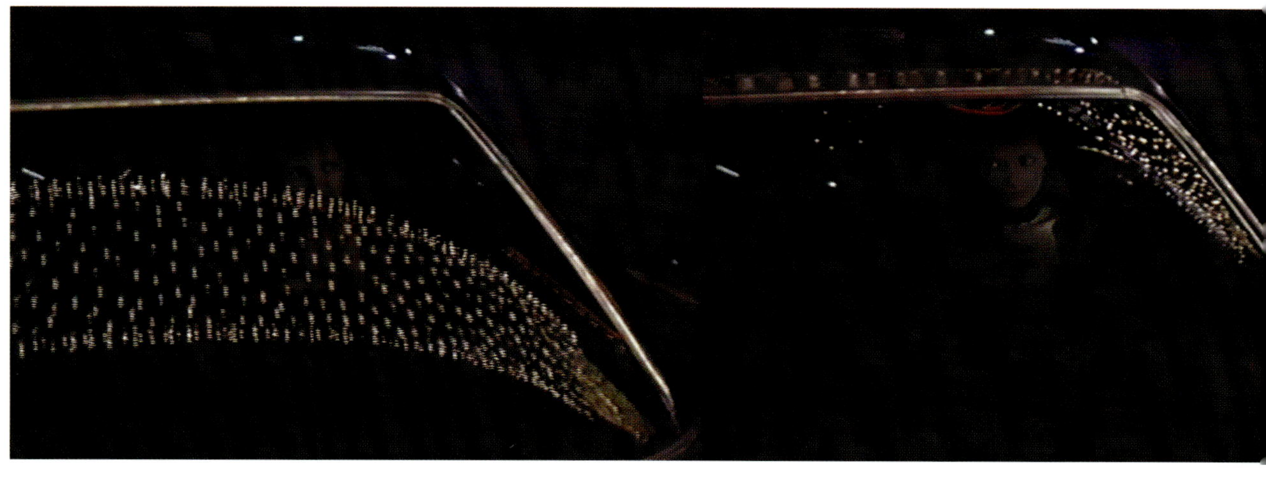

In Las Vegas, I love to walk on the Strip. I first came to the desert in 1967 to paint the landscape: searching for mystical visions. Inside the tree I was painting, I saw a smaller tree, and then another inside that, and then yet another, going on to infinity. Dark bushes glowed on the side of a desolate hill. The tree by the shack where I lived, I imagined, was covered with fruit like the Tree of Good and Evil and, as I continued to paint, it burst into flames like the Tree of Knowledge. But on the Strip there's no need to search, the neon signs, turning matter to color, are enormous visionary apparitions built for everyone to see. And there's none of the desert's former isolation. It's easy to talk to other visitors in the porte-cochere while waiting for the valet to get my car. The guy in the tuxedo asks if I've seen any shows. A tourist in a bright shirt and shorts suggests 'O' by Cirque de Soleil. Equals, they talk of gambling. Who's going to have a lucky night?

(#356) #15 1996
OIL AND ALKYD ON SOLID GROUND 21.5 x 70.8 CM
PRIVATE COLLECTION, ZURICH

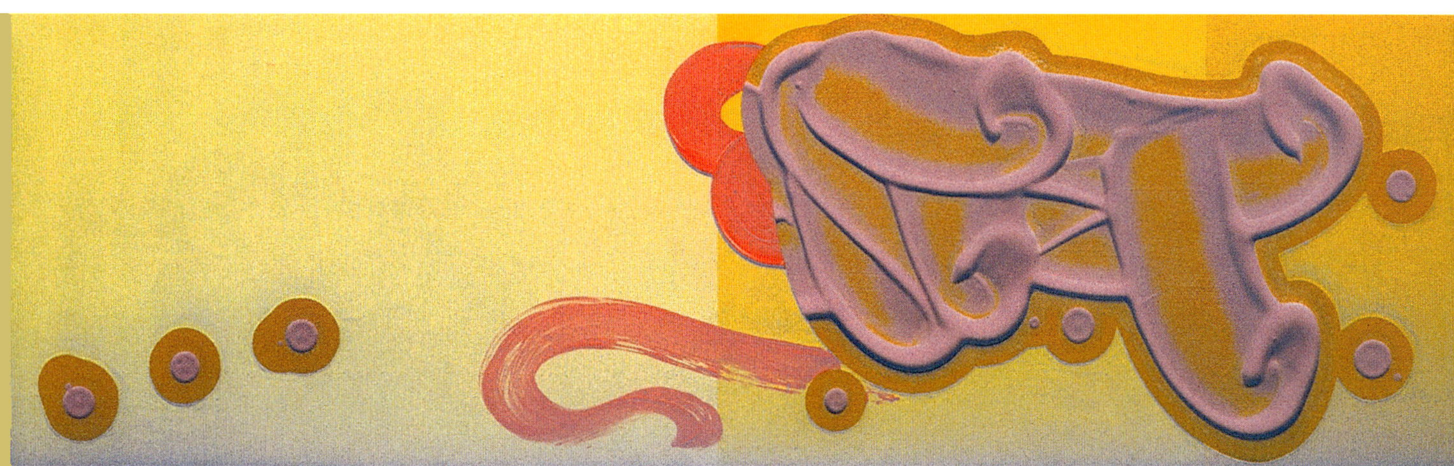

Walking along the Strip at dusk, the man-made and natural colors can't be told apart. The pinks, mauves, turquoises and powder-blues of the sunset often seem more garish, more exotic, than the neon signs and artificial lights. In the desert I painted such sunsets, trying to be aware of myself on the surface of the Earth and even feel myself revolving with the Earth until I reached the zone of transition between the light and dark sides of the planet. At that moment, when the sun was just disappearing around the edge of the planet, I tried to capture the light; the light that had crossed over the horizon and was bent by the atmosphere; sunlight that had come to me across the greatest possible distance. Overexcited, my hands were often covered with paint and colored light as I looked for the last flashes of green extending in great bands over the dome of the darkening sky. I see, on the Strip, that my hands are covered with similar hues and I feel that I'm not walking, but swimming through endlessly changing color.

DIAMONDS ARE FOREVER
UNITED ARTISTS 1971

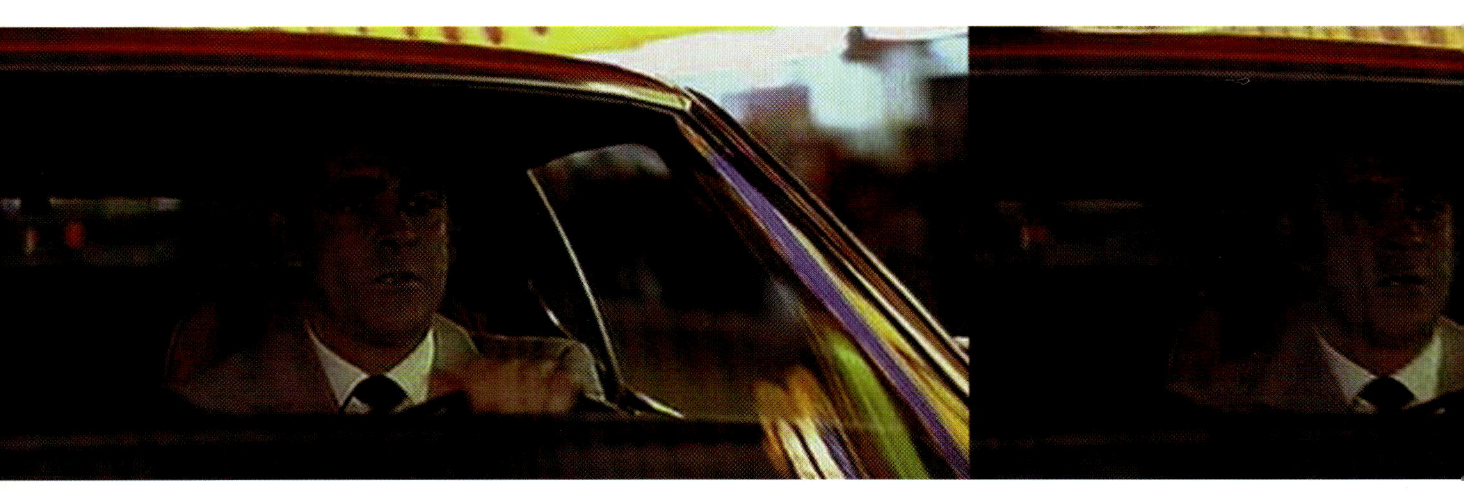

Driving through the desert to find a place to paint, I was fascinated with the mirages of pooled water just ahead on the blacktop highway. Watching the pools vanish as my car approached, I enjoyed that confusion between what was real and what wasn't. When driving in the desert, the distances are so huge, one has time to see movement and illusion interact. Illusion is part of the psychology of the desert. Before filming exterior scenes in Las Vegas the streets and sidewalks are usually hosed down with water. Called the 'wash down,' this increases reflections on the ground. There are seldom thunderstorms in Las Vegas and this trick is very wasteful, but one doesn't notice the artifice in a movie. The reflections on the street seem so natural. In a movie, the 'wash down' causes a kind of reverse mirage. One doesn't see what is there. Then, this reverse mirage causes a technological mirage. I'm sure that when I walk on the Strip I see more reflections, perhaps when they aren't there, because of what I've seen in movies.

(#356) #23 1996-97
OIL AND ALKYD ON SOLID GROUND 21.5 x 70.8 CM
COLLECTION LINDA YEANEY, LOS ANGELES
COURTESY OF PATRICIA FAURE GALLERY, SANTA MONICA

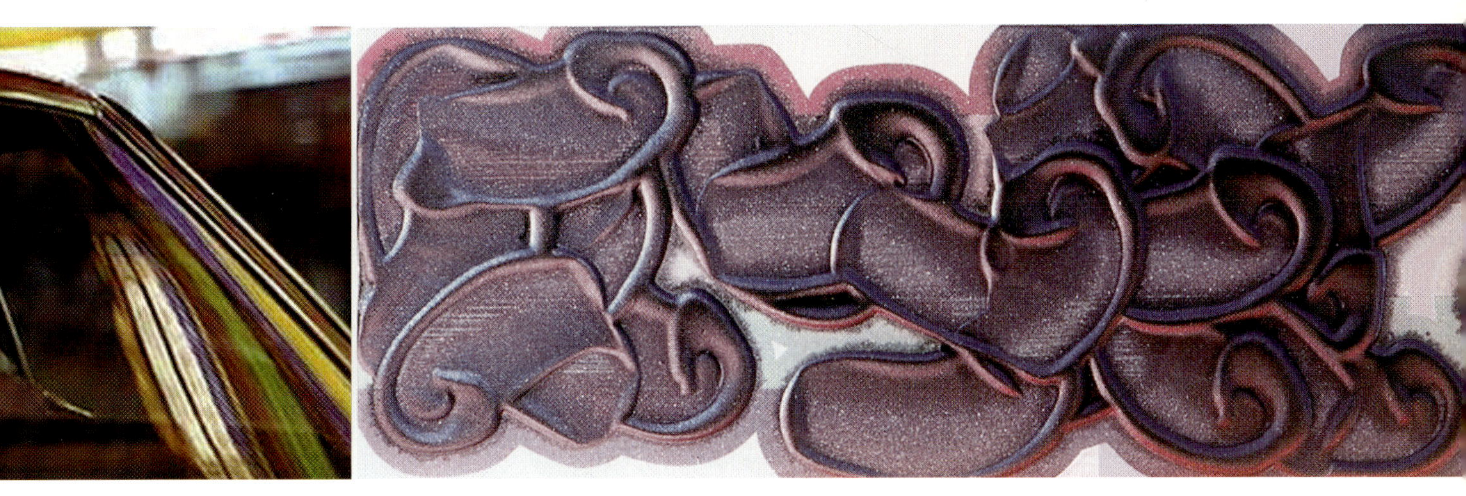

I often imagine one of the limousines in Liberace's museum, the one covered with mirrored mosaic tiles, speeding down the Strip at dusk or streaking along a desert highway blasted by the midday sun, flashing the lights and color of the environment all around. Who is that inside driving? I can't quite see. Is the car empty? Am I inside?

(#356) #10-2 1996
OIL AND ALKYD ON SOLID GROUND 21.5 x 70.8 CM
BEVERLY AND STANLEY ERDREICH, BIRMINGHAM, AL

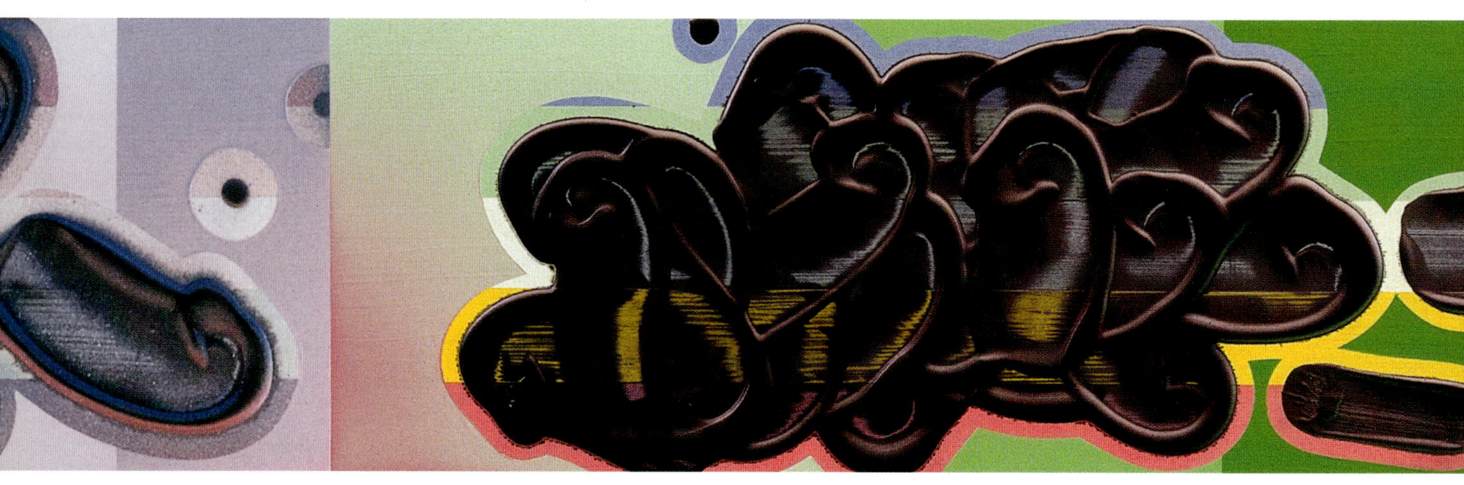

In Las Vegas movies there are always scenes, looking in through the windshield, of the lead characters driving. The emotions on their faces are visible behind the glass which is alive with moving reflected lights. These scenes show us that character itself can change in such a place. The mysticism of the desert erodes individual psychology – and in Las Vegas individual psychology is secondary to illusion. The whole interiors of some porte-cocheres are lined with mirrors causing infinite reflections. Reflecting surfaces are everywhere. It's impossible to tell where certain reflections are coming from. Where did that color come from? Who can tell. Sometimes, churning through these colors, I think that I've lost the boundaries of my body and no longer know who I am. "There really is something beautiful about all of these lights," one detective says to another in 'Crime Story,' Michael Mann's TV series, "It's dangerous," says the other, "makes you change your rhythm." Is this what happened to pilgrims coming to Rome and going from bright daylight into dark churches lit with candles, filled with incense and music?

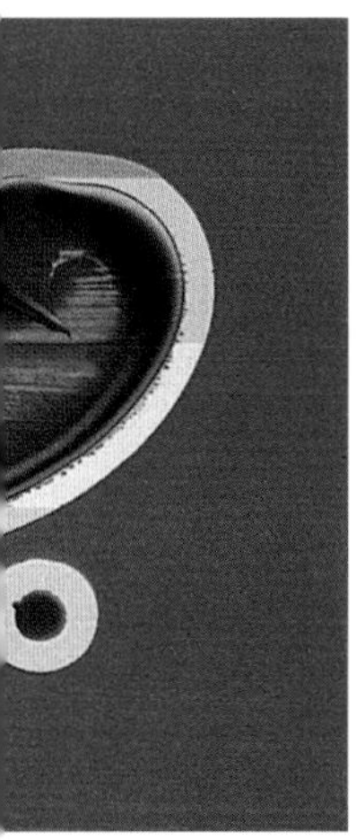

In John Ford's movie Fort Apache, Henry Fonda plays a new commanding officer from the East. When warned about the Apaches, he says that he was not impressed by the Indians he saw from the stagecoach on his way to the fort. John Wayne, the Westerner, knows that what's important in the desert is what's unknown, what can't be seen. And he knows that you'd better understand this or you're in for trouble. "If you saw them," Wayne says to Fonda, "they weren't Apaches."

Victoria Reynolds

1962 Born in Tyler, TX
1990 B.F.A. University of Oklahoma, Norman, OK
1993 M.F.A. University of Nevada, Las Vegas, NV
Lives in Las Vegas, NV

2001
Blodig och Genomstekt, Galleri Ahnlund, Umeå, S
Diabolical Beauty, Contemporary Arts Forum, Santa Barbara, CA
The Life You Save may Be Your Own, 31 Grand, New York, NY
2000
Bienvenido: The Living Desert, Living Desert, Las Vegas, NV
1999
Sins of the Flesh, Angstrom Gallery, Dallas, TX

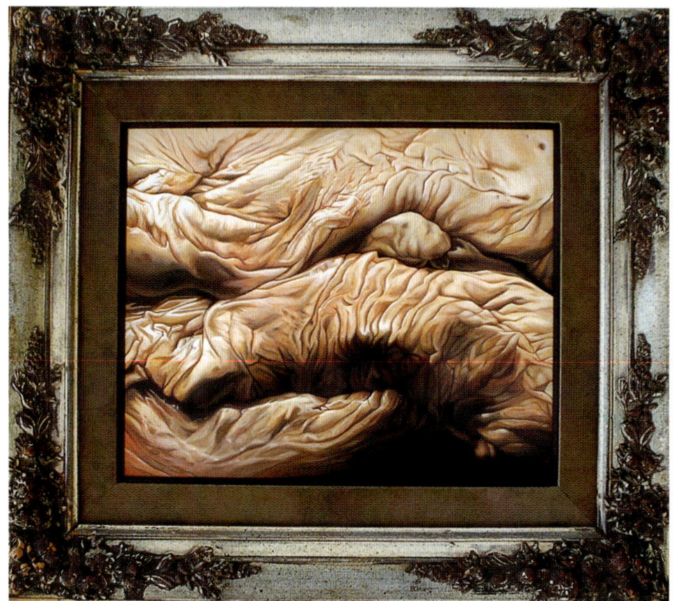

EYE OF THE BUNG 1999
OIL ON PANEL, FRAMED
67.6 x 78.1 CM
COURTESY OF THE ARTIST

Choose the right video poker machine and you'll never have to work again. And at certain casinos, valets, cocktail waitresses, and showgirls can live extremely high on the hog. White Cadillacs abound in the UNLV parking lot, and many students of mine wore tight little black skirts with spike heels. A desperate sense of greed and hedonism abides in the heart of every nickel slot player, red light district customer, and low-life asking you for gas money at the 7-11 to get his wife and kids back home.

Vegas is a red meat town offering tempting morsels for every palate. The Golden Steer steakhouse, sumptuously decorated like a brothel in ornate flocked wallpaper, displays a pair of John Wayne's guns and an original oil by Norman Rockwell of cowboy actor Walter Brennan. The late Benny Binion of Binion's Horseshoe Casino served meat at his steakhouse direct from his own ranch. After midnight the steaks are wonderfully cheap. The Circus Circus steakhouse is art critic Dave Hickey's favorite. Caesars Palace remains the classic house of indulgence, with buff Roman centurions and a chubby gray automaton of Bacchus toasting the awed masses. The Venetian Casino displays a bombastic reproduction of Tintoretto's Apotheosis of Venice and has recently installed a branch of the Guggenheim. And less than an hour out of town, small hot trailers cluster behind Nevada's brothels' gated

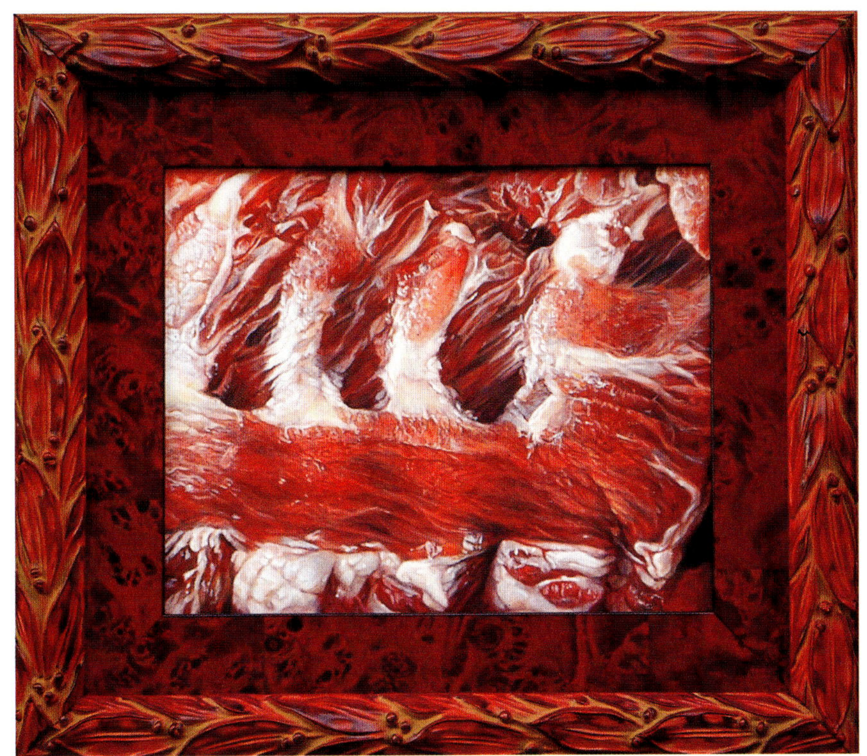

RIBS FOR EVE 1999
OIL ON PANEL, FRAMED
33 x 38.1 CM
COLLECTION OF LINDSEY NOBEL

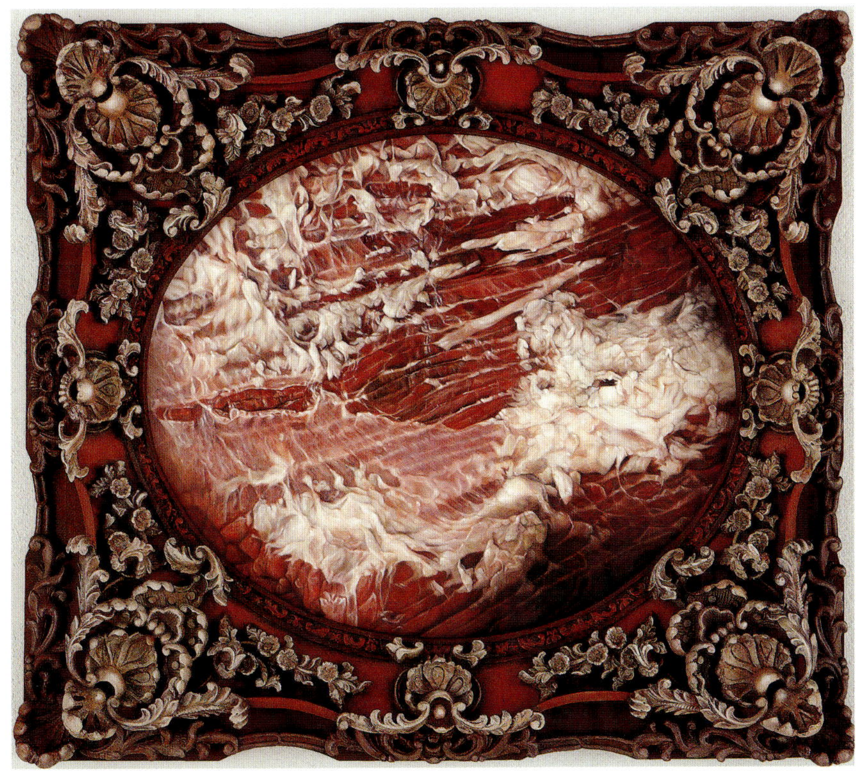

FOR THE CARNAL IN DANTE'S HELL
1999
OIL ON PANEL, FRAMED
71.1 x 81.2 CM
COURTESY OF THE ARTIST

entrances. In the night, red brothel lights continually spin, lonely beacons in the desiccated wasteland. One of the brothel's lobbies I looked into had a mini-mall aesthetic, with plastic furniture and a lone case of dusty souvenirs. The room was spare and almost antiseptic.

My studio was located at 'The Living Desert,' a run-down apartment complex situated among desolate, baked stretches of sand, close to prostitutes' quarters and urine-soaked alleyways across the street from the UNLV campus. It was named after the Walt Disney movie of the same title. On its origins, some say that it was built as a detox center for the early Vegas entertainers. Others claim that the bunker-style apartments were built by the Atomic Energy Commission to house workers when they were testing the Bomb. Most Vegas residents claim that the city's ground is still radioactive, which would account for the overabundance of cancerous growths there. A third theory is that 'The Living Desert' was one of Las Vegas first luxury hotels. Like Area 51, no architectural plans or waterworks have been filed with the city, and the street 'Living Desert' does not appear on any maps. The apartments' components have been cannibalized from various implosions of old Vegas hotels. Most recently, all the doors have been replaced with those of the old Hacienda.

In their heyday, these apartments are said to have housed such notables as Elvis and Debbie Reynolds. More recently, artists such as Jim Shaw, the Reverend and Missus Ethan Acres, Jeffrey Vallance and myself had our studios there. The apartments also shelter a host of disabled veterans, retirees, illegals, artists, and psychiatric patients unable to afford the more prestigious residences of Las Vegas.

'The Living Desert' has a colorful history. One summer all the roofs were removed in the heart of Vegas' monsoon season and dozens of apartments were flooded. The water streamed down in my apartment. I rushed around, throwing scraps of plastic over my Meat Paintings. The apartment complex gained recognition in three subsequent features in the local TV news. During the roof work, one of the Mexican workmen fell into an apartment below, directly into bed with an elderly Catholic woman who, in World War II, provided shelter for Jews in Holland. Another frequent occurrence for a majority of the residents was the continuous explosion and overflow of water heaters inside the apartments. Achilles, the Reverend and Missus Acres' large black lab, suffered alone through one of these explosions. When they returned and opened the front door, clouds of steam billowed out, and their drenched dog, stomach to the ground, crept forward miserably. Across the street, a crew of six Mexican men, often perching on their old pickup truck in the sweltering parking lot, were known for their vocal appreciation of the female form. While catcalling to one female neighbor, they suddenly got their windshield bashed in with a baseball bat. Whenever I photographed meat outside in daylight, curious neighbors clustered around, asking questions, offering suggestions, or telling me their woes: 'My son-in-law stole $100,000 out of my bank account!' Throughout the neighborhood, a favorite pastime is leaning in doorways drinking a beer, detaining friends at the mailboxes, or watching the occasional ambulance roll down the street.

Located outside under the apartments' bathrooms are access holes to plumbing, which provide shelter for stray cats competing with the large dark cockroaches who nest and swarm there. (Inside the humans' bathrooms above, the soft mewling of newborn kittens is often heard coming up through the bathtub drain.) Many meats featured in the Vegas Meat Paintings, after a thorough roasting in the oven, were placed outside for the cats. The more bold and popular stray cats have feasted on cotto salami with peppercorns, smoked ham, prosciutto, hot head cheese, pimento loaf, beef bottom round, brisket, skirt steak, trimmed and garnished tri-tip, pork uterus, beef pizzles, goat fat, honeycomb beef tripe, and Bible tripe, but they drew the line at the pork bungs.

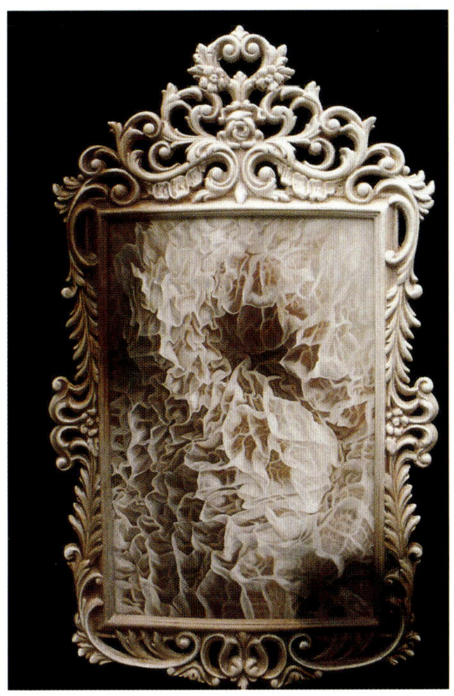

TRIPE ON THE S-CURVE 1998
OIL ON PANEL, FRAMED 73.6 x 44.4 CM
COLLECTION OF LIBBY LUMPKIN

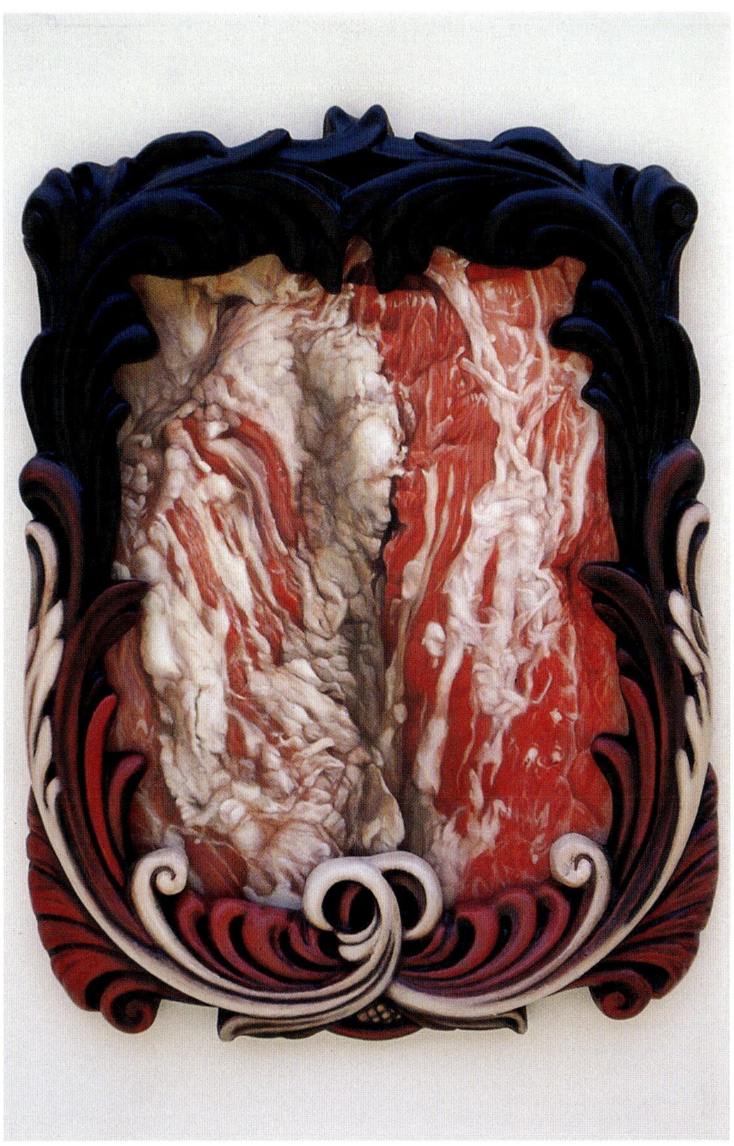

CARNAL DECOR 1997
OIL ON PANEL, FRAMED 36.8 x 28.5 CM
PRIVATE COLLECTION

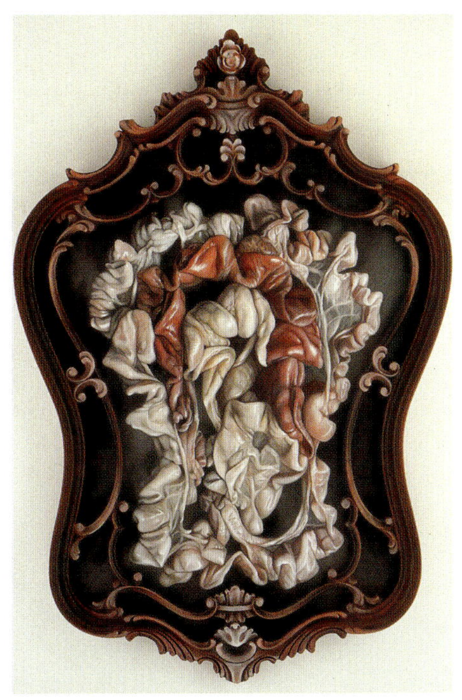

BEAUTIFUL UTERAL GARLANDS 1999
OIL ON PANEL, FRAMED 88.9 x 61.5 CM
COURTESY OF THE ARTIST

Jim Shaw

1952 Born in Midland, MI
1974 B.F.A. University of Michigan, Ann Arbor, MI
1978 M.F.A. Cal Arts, Los Angeles, CA
Lives in Los Angeles, CA

2001
Dreamt of Drawings, Emily Tsingou Gallery, London, GB
2000
Thrift Store Paintings, ICA, London, GB
1999
Jim Shaw, Galerie Praz-Delavallade, Paris, F; Metro Pictures, New York, NY
1998
Jim Shaw: Träume, Frankfurter Kunstverein, Frankfurt, D
1997
Performance Anxiety, MCA, Chicago, IL; MCA, San Diego, CA

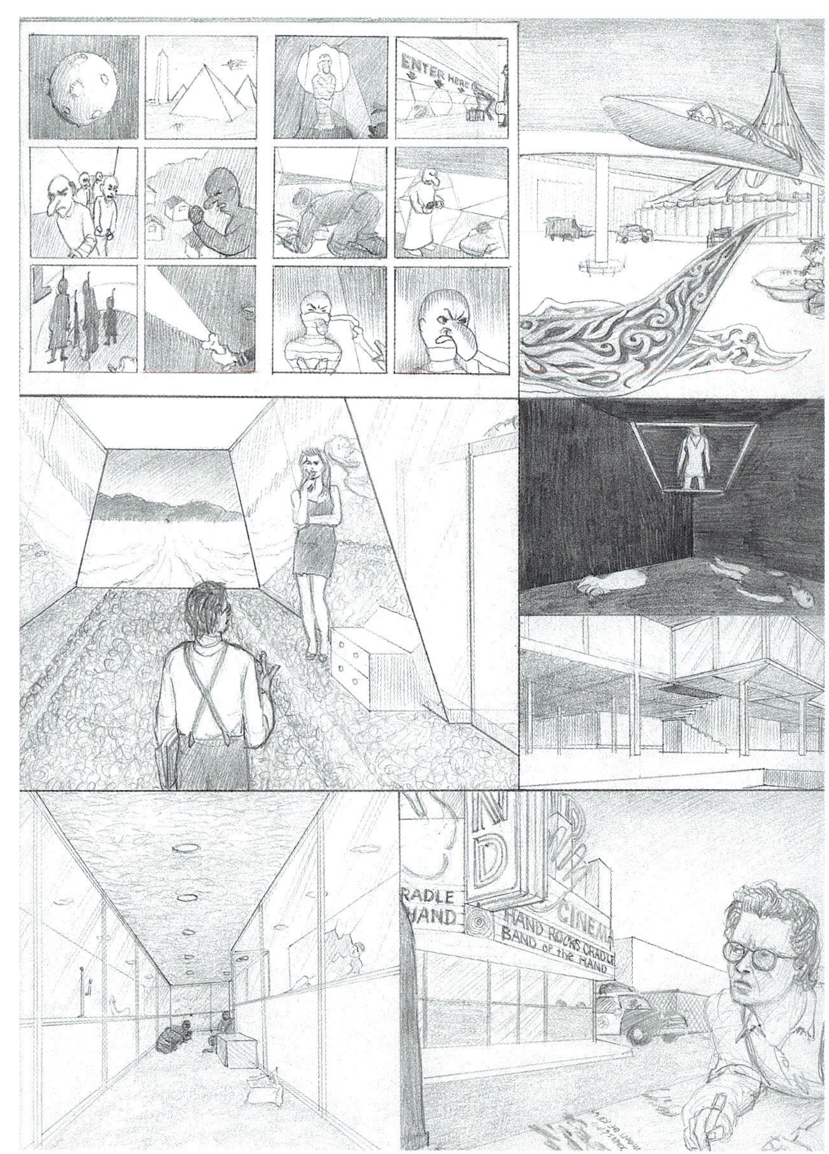

DREAM DRAWING (I WAS IN THE PARKING LOT OF A CROSS BETWEEN MELODYLAND AND CIRCUS CIRCUS) 1995
PENCIL ON PAPER, 30.4 x 22.8 CM
COURTESY OF THE ARTIST AND PATRICK PAINTER GALLERY, LOS ANGELES

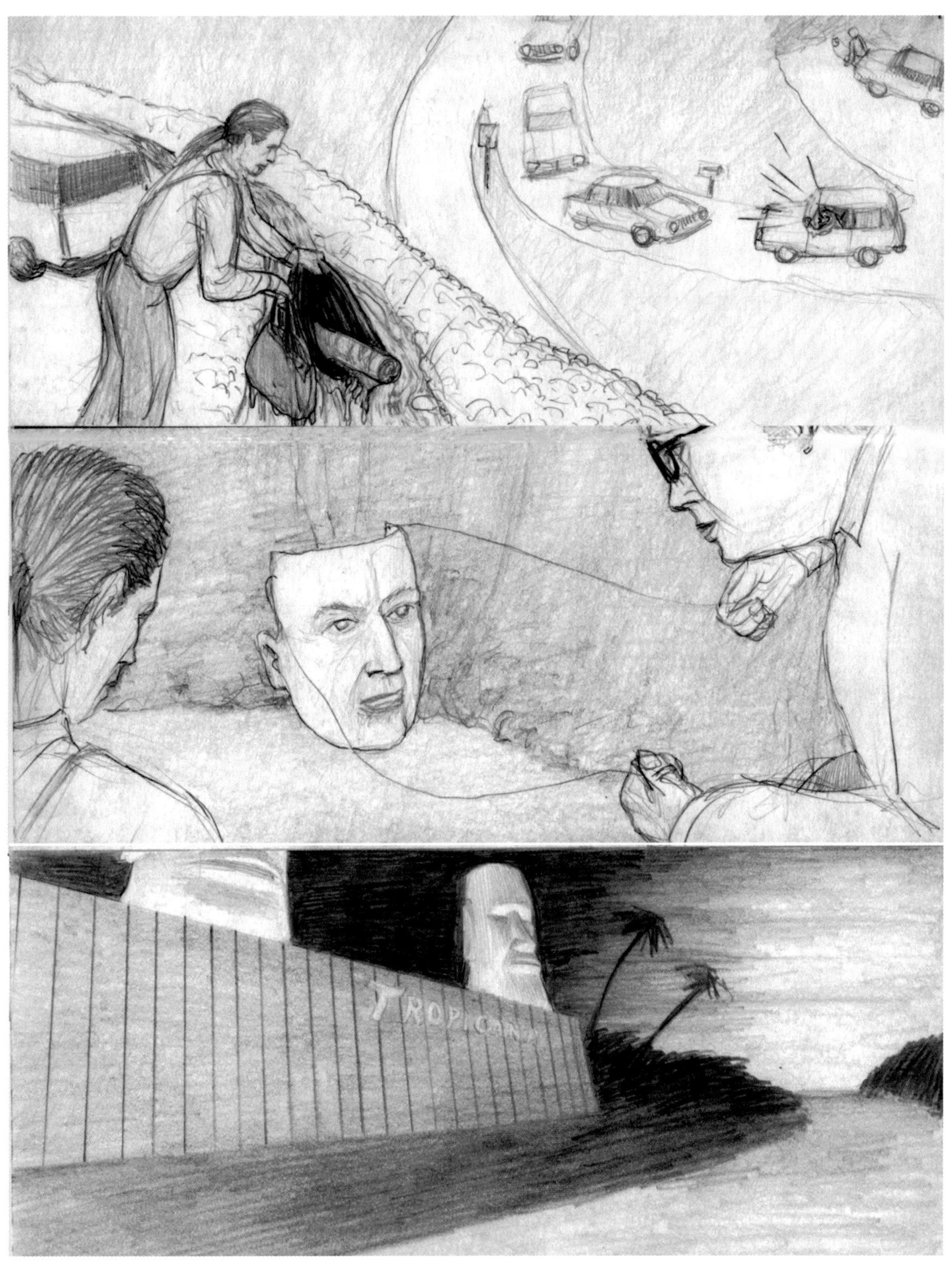

DREAM DRAWING (I AWAKE NEAR A SMALL MOUNTAIN STREAM, HAVING SLEPT IN THE CAR) 1993
PENCIL ON PAPER, 30.4 x 22.8 CM
COURTESY OF THE ARTIST AND PATRICK PAINTER GALLERY, LOS ANGELES

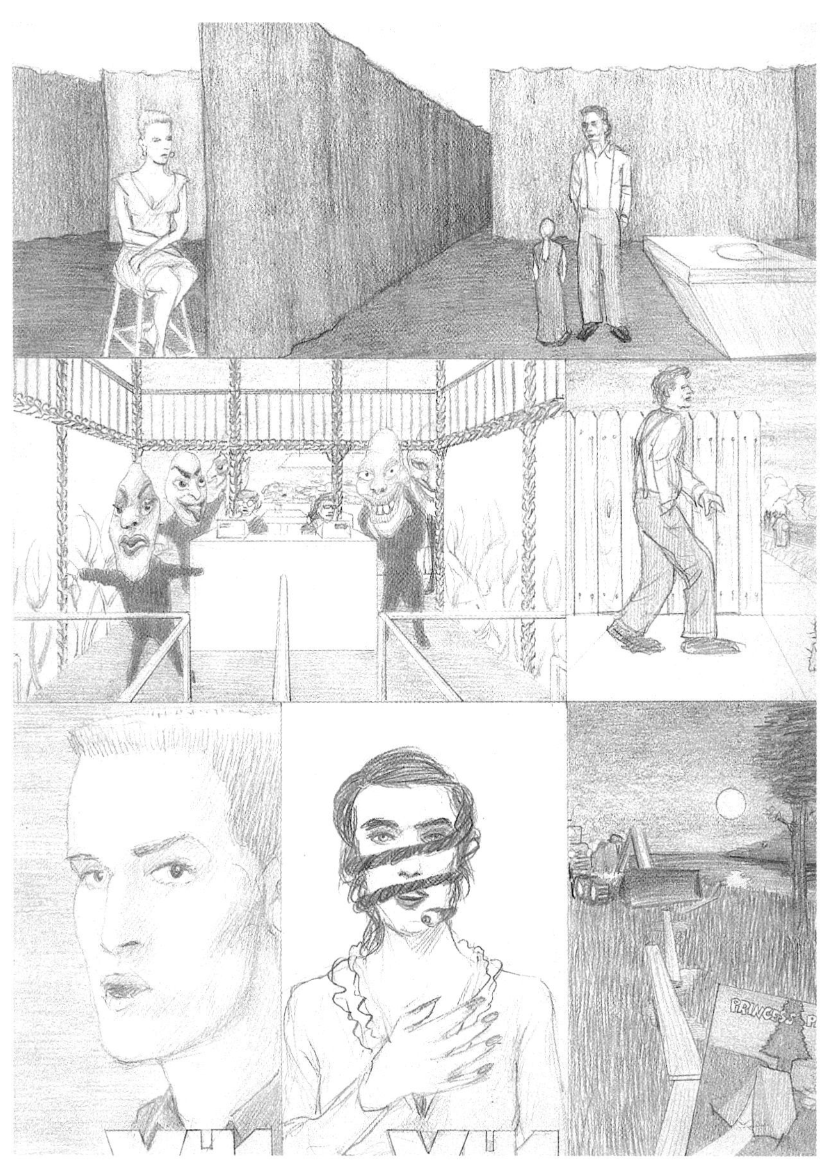

DREAM DRAWING (IN AN INDUSTRIAL SPACE IN LAS VEGAS SUBDIVIDED BY CURTAINS OF CREPE...) 1995
PENCIL ON PAPER, 30.4 x 22.8 CM
COURTESY OF THE ARTIST AND PATRICK PAINTER GALLERY, LOS ANGELES

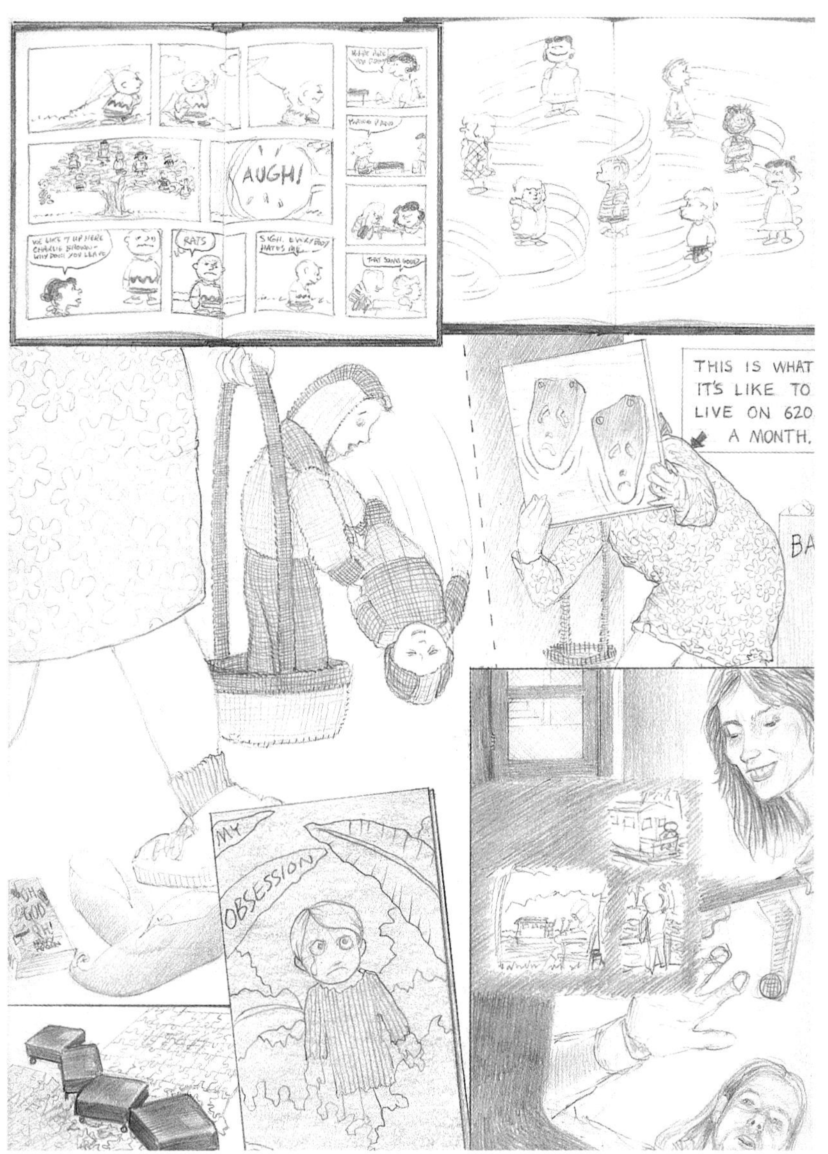

DREAM DRAWING (I WAS TRYING TO FIGURE OUT WHICH PIECES TO DO FOR THIS SHOW) 1995
PENCIL ON PAPER, 30.4 x 22.8 CM
COURTESY OF THE ARTIST AND PATRICK PAINTER GALLERY, LOS ANGELES

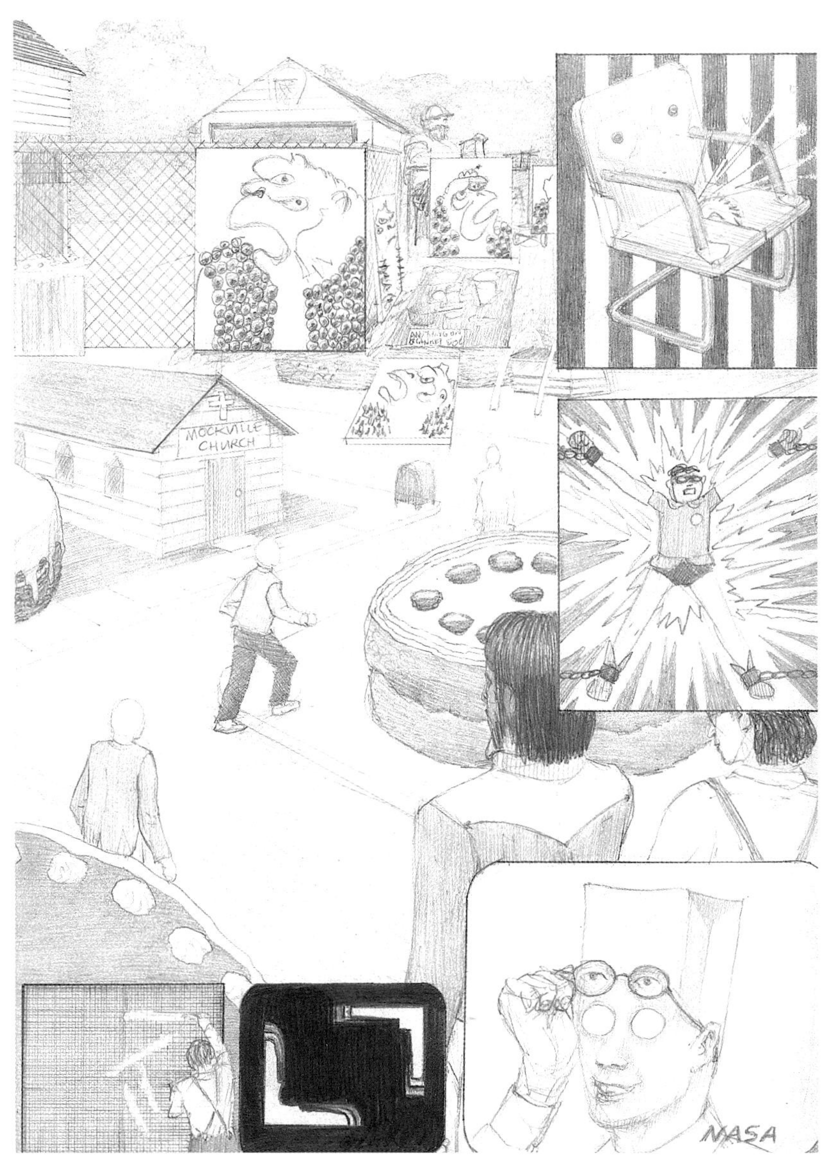

DREAM DRAWING (MARNIE & I WERE DRIVING THRU A POOR PART OF MIDLAND & SAW A RESTAURANT) 1996
PENCIL ON PAPER, 30.4 x 22.8 CM
COURTESY OF THE ARTIST AND PATRICK PAINTER GALLERY, LOS ANGELES

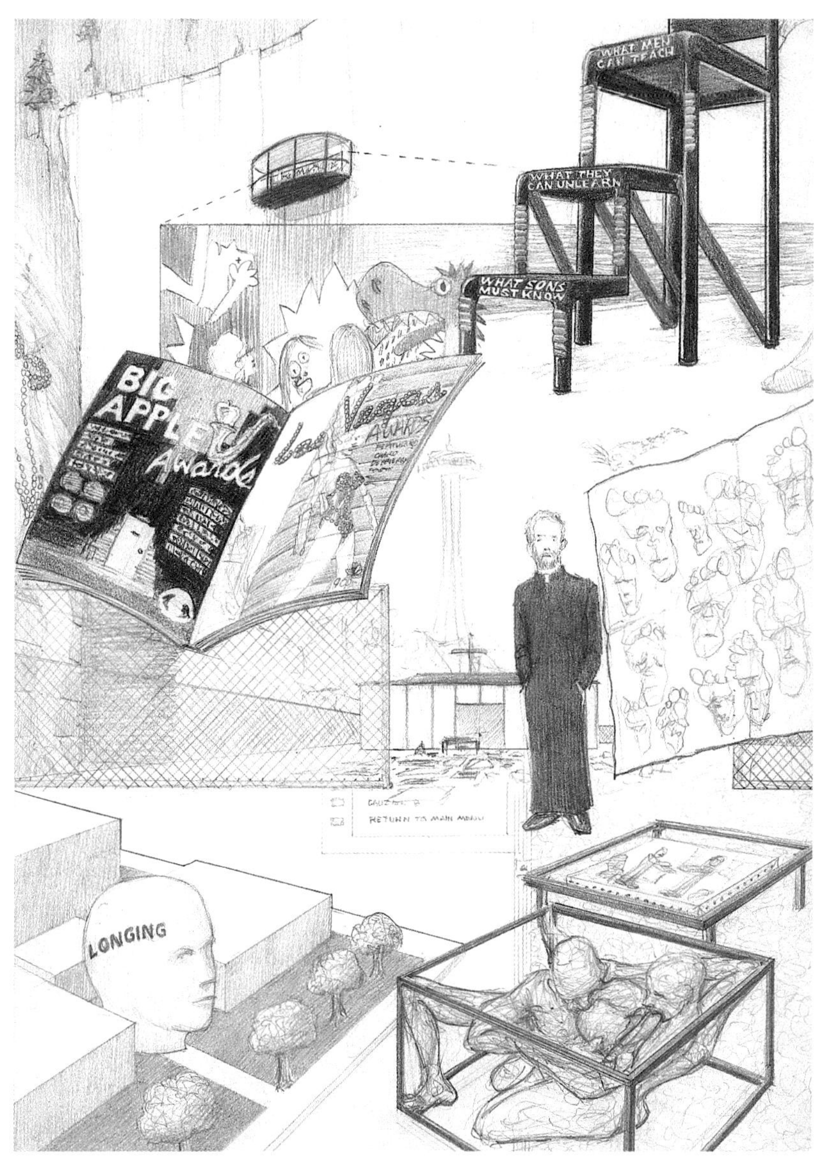

DREAM DRAWING (AT THE BASE OF A LARGE WESTERN RIVER WAS A DAM WITH A BUILDING IN ITS CENTER) 1996
PENCIL ON PAPER, 30.4 x 22.8 CM
COURTESY OF THE ARTIST AND PATRICK PAINTER GALLERY, LOS ANGELES

Bridget Smith

1966 Born in England, GB
1988 B.A. Goldsmith's College, London, GB
1995 M.A. Goldsmith's College, London, GB
2000 Tate Tokyo Residency, JP
Lives in London, GB

2000
Bridget Smith, Frith Street Gallery, London, GB
Bridget Smith, Galerie Barbara Thumm, Berlin, D
Because a Fire was in my Head, South London Gallery, London, GB
Real Places, Westfälischer Kunstverein, Münster, D
1999
Blue Suburban Skies, Photographers Gallery, London, GB

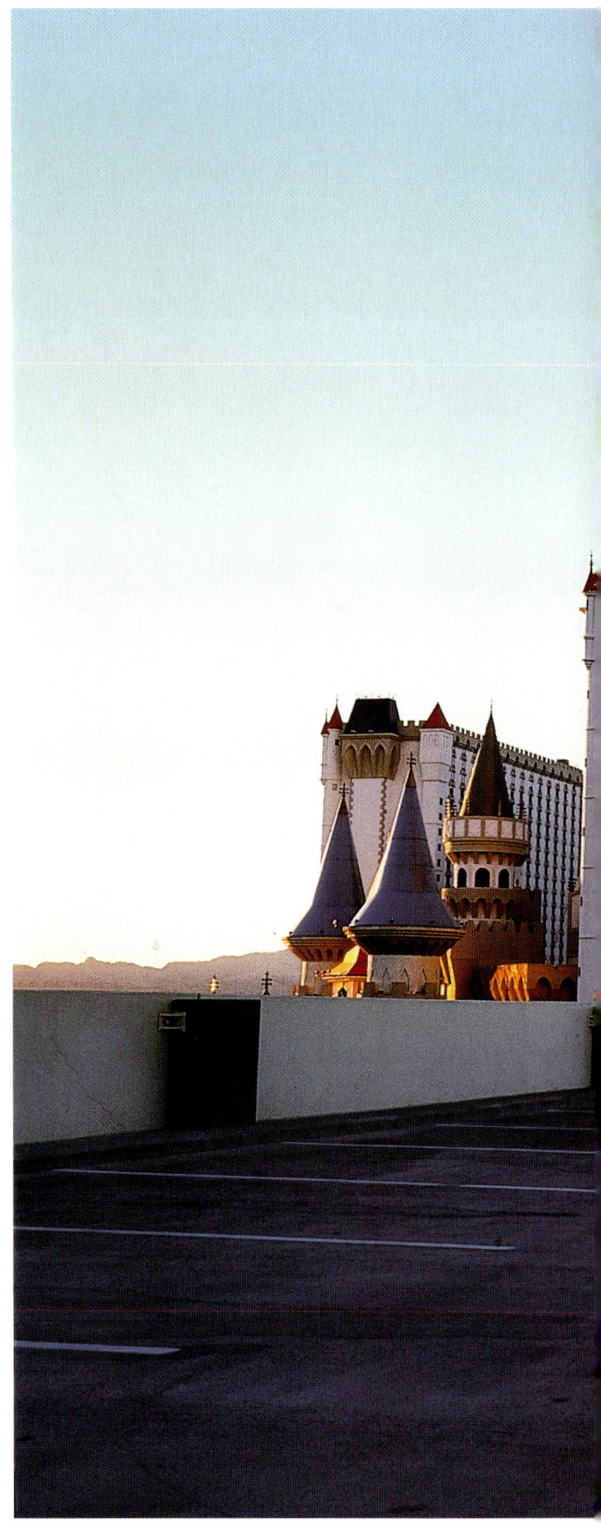

EXCALIBUR (DAWN) 1999
C-PRINT MOUNTED ON ALUMINIUM 119.5 x 162.5 CM
COURTESY OF FRITH STREET GALLERY, LONDON

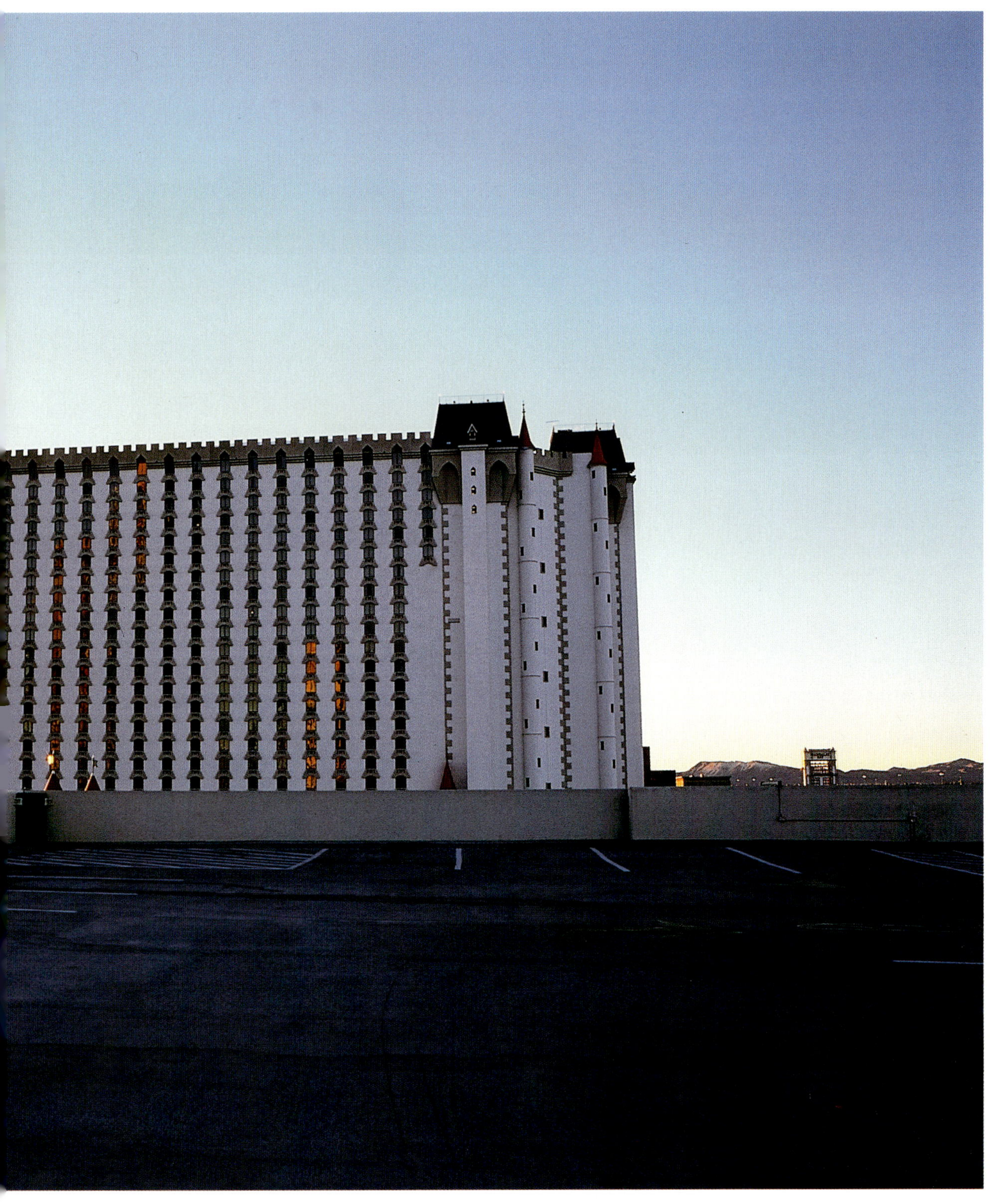

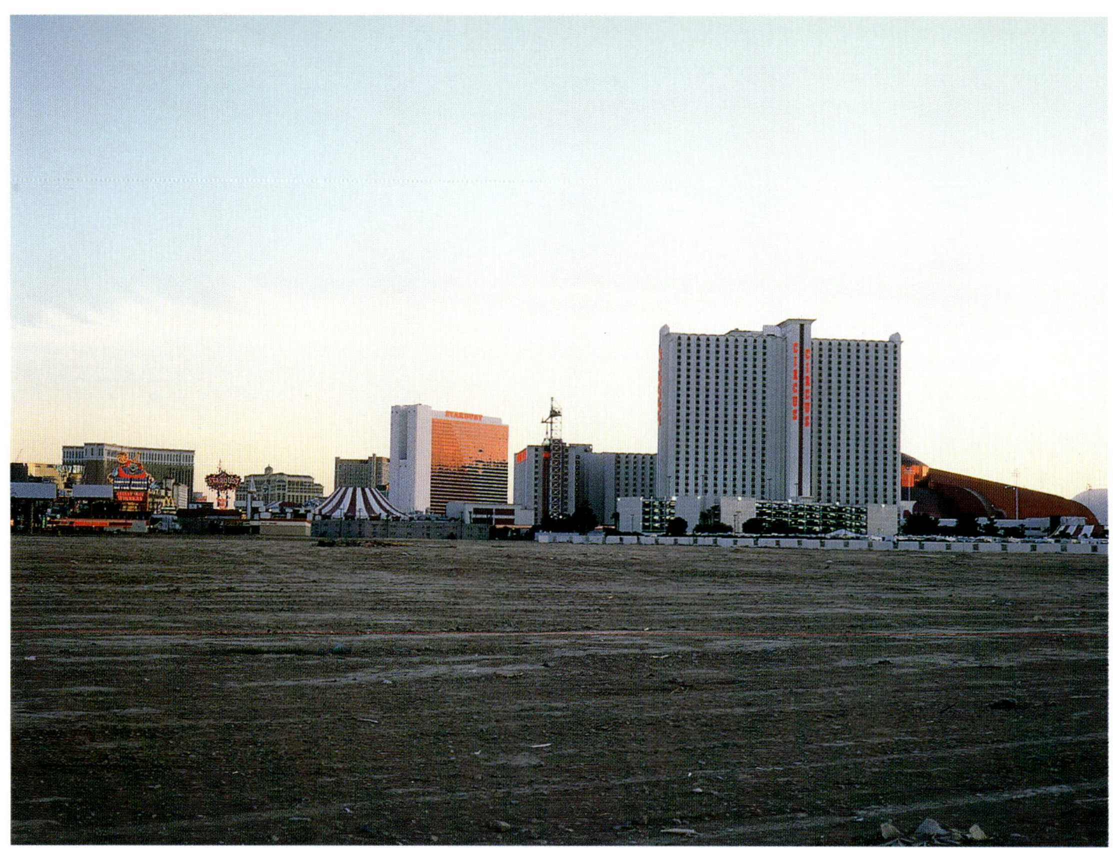

CIRCUS CIRCUS (SIDE VIEW) 1999
C-PRINT MOUNTED ON ALUMINIUM 119.5 x 162.5 CM
COURTESY OF FRITH STREET GALLERY, LONDON

MONTE CARLO, LAS VEGAS 1996
C-PRINT MOUNTED ON ALUMINIUM 119.5 x 162.5 CM
COURTESY OF FRITH STREET GALLERY, LONDON

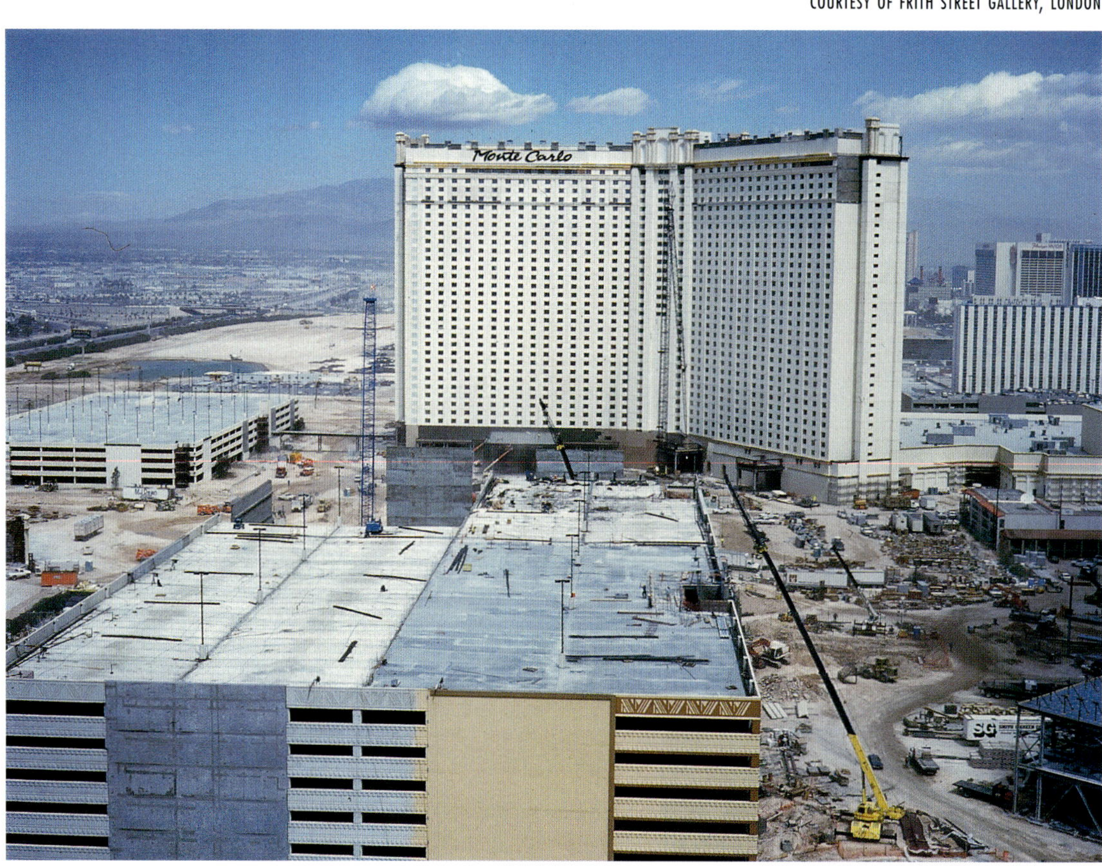

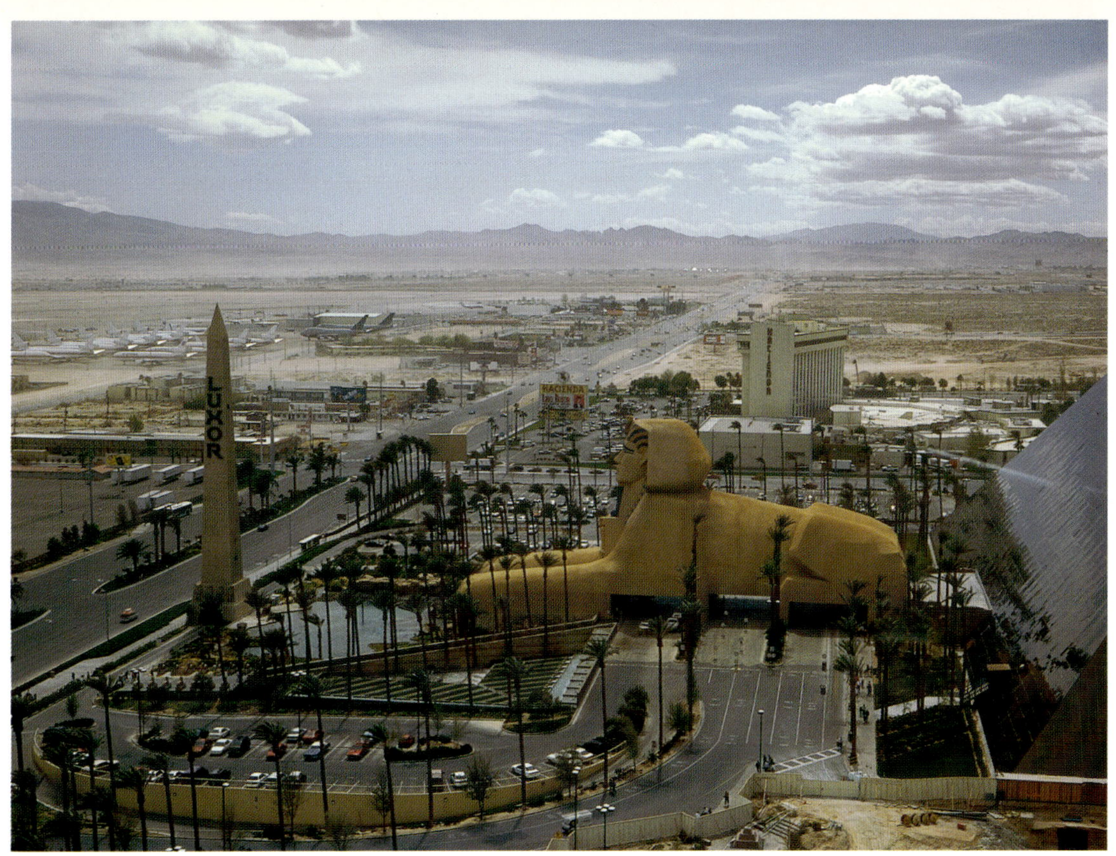

LUXOR, LAS VEGAS 1996
C-PRINT MOUNTED ON ALUMINIUM 119.5 x 162.5 CM
COURTESY OF FRITH STREET GALLERY, LONDON

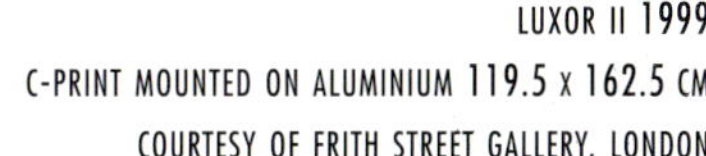
LUXOR II 1999
C-PRINT MOUNTED ON ALUMINIUM 119.5 x 162.5 CM
COURTESY OF FRITH STREET GALLERY, LONDON

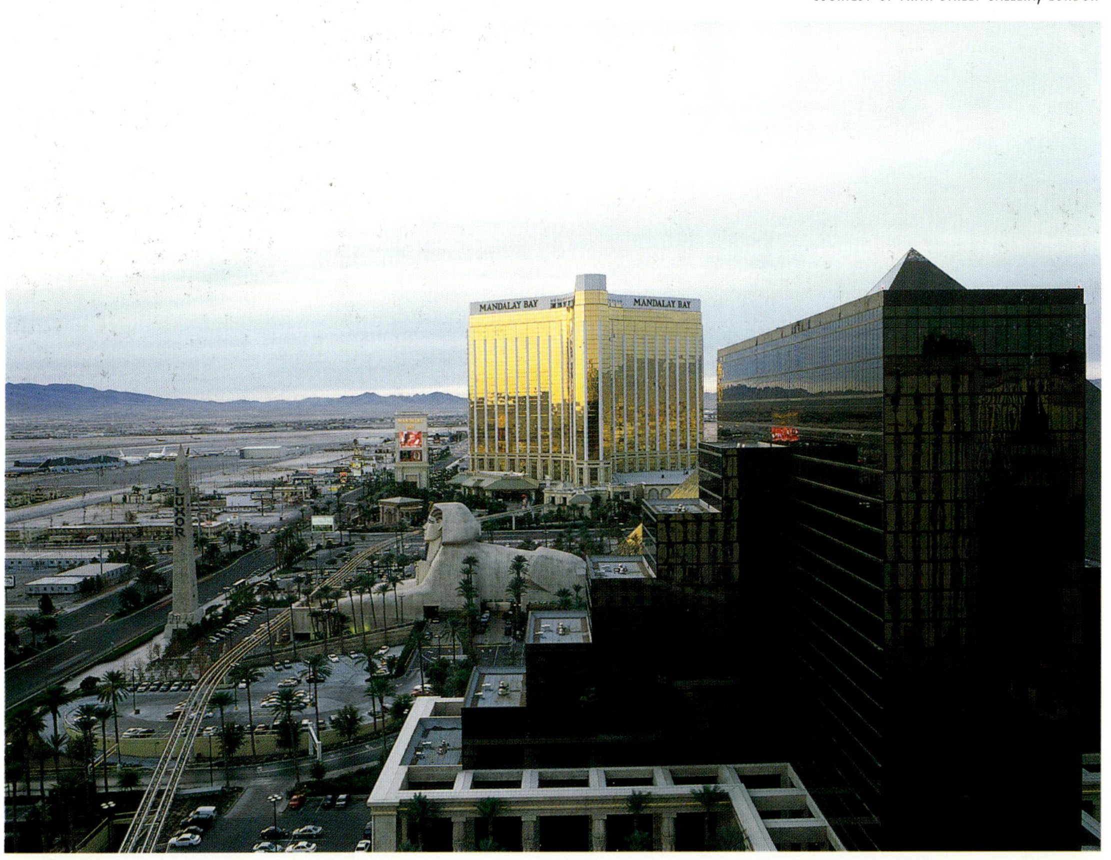

Jeffrey Vallance

1955 Born in Torrance, CA
1981 M.F.A. The Otis Art Institute of the Parsons School of Design, Los Angeles, CA
Lives in Las Vegas, NV and Umea, Vasterbotten County (Lapland), S

2001
The Virgin, The Poet and the President, Lehmann Maupin, New York, NY
2000
inSITE 2000, San Diego, CA/Tijuana, Mexico
1999
Anomalies, Rosamund Felsen Gallery, Los Angeles, CA
Paranormal Diagrams: Heretical Theories, Art Institute of Boston, MA
Jeffrey Vallance: Culture Mix, Musée d'Art de la Ville de Paris, F

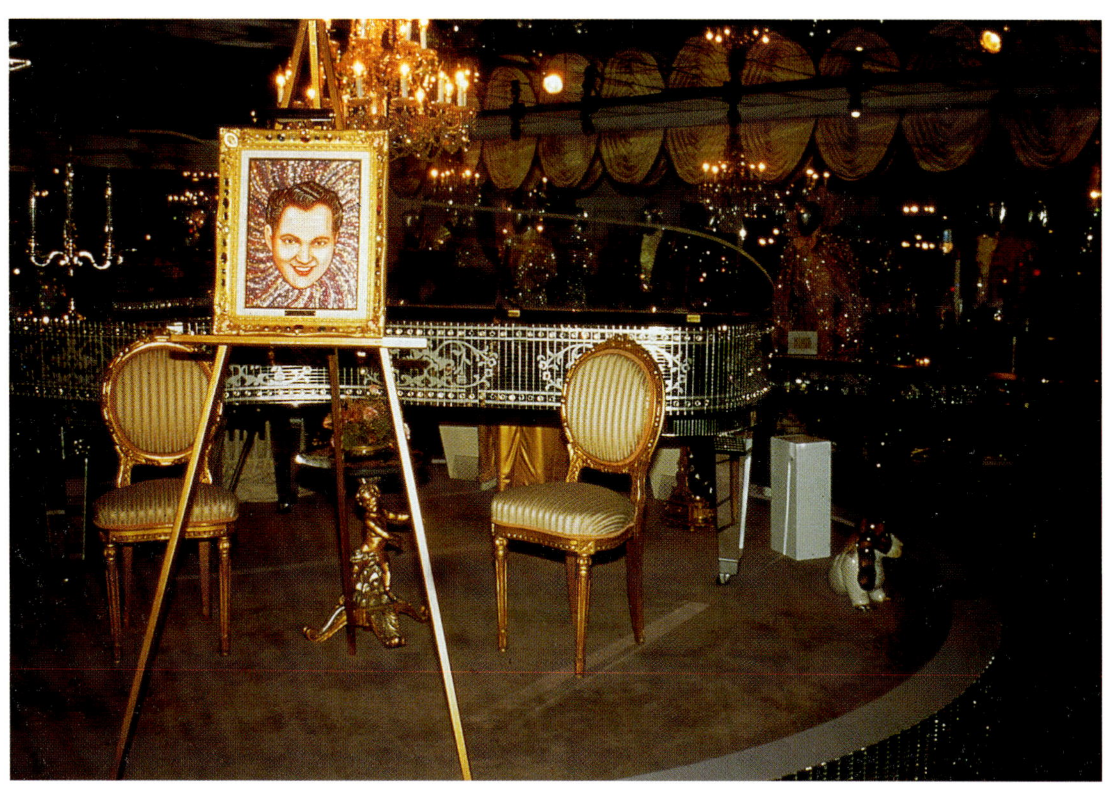

LIBERACE IN FULL GLORY 1995
INSTALLATION VIEW, 'LIBERACE TRIBUTE EXHIBITION', THE LIBERACE MUSEUM, LAS VEGAS
COURTESY OF THE ARTIST AND ROSAMUND FELSEN GALLERY, SANTA MONICA, CA

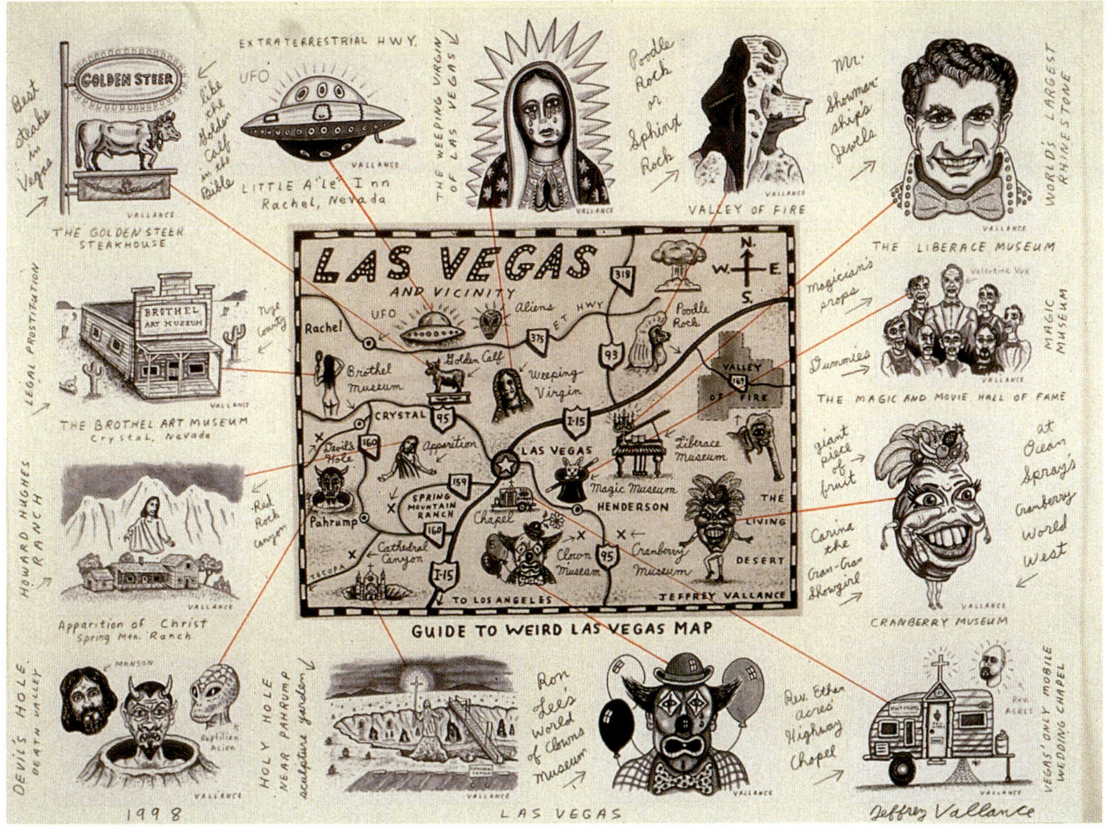

GUIDE TO WEIRD LAS VEGAS MAP 1998
PENCIL, PEN AND COLLAGE ON PAPER 55.8 x 76.2 CM
COURTESY OF THE ARTIST AND LEHMANN MAUPIN, NEW YORK

CLOWN OASIS - AN EXHIBITION OF WORKS BY ARTISTS AND CLOWNS AT RON LEE'S WORLD OF CLOWNS LAS VEGAS, NEVADA 1998
PENCIL, PEN AND COLLAGE ON PAPER 55.8 x 76.2 CM
COURTESY OF THE ARTIST AND LEHMANN MAUPIN, NEW YORK

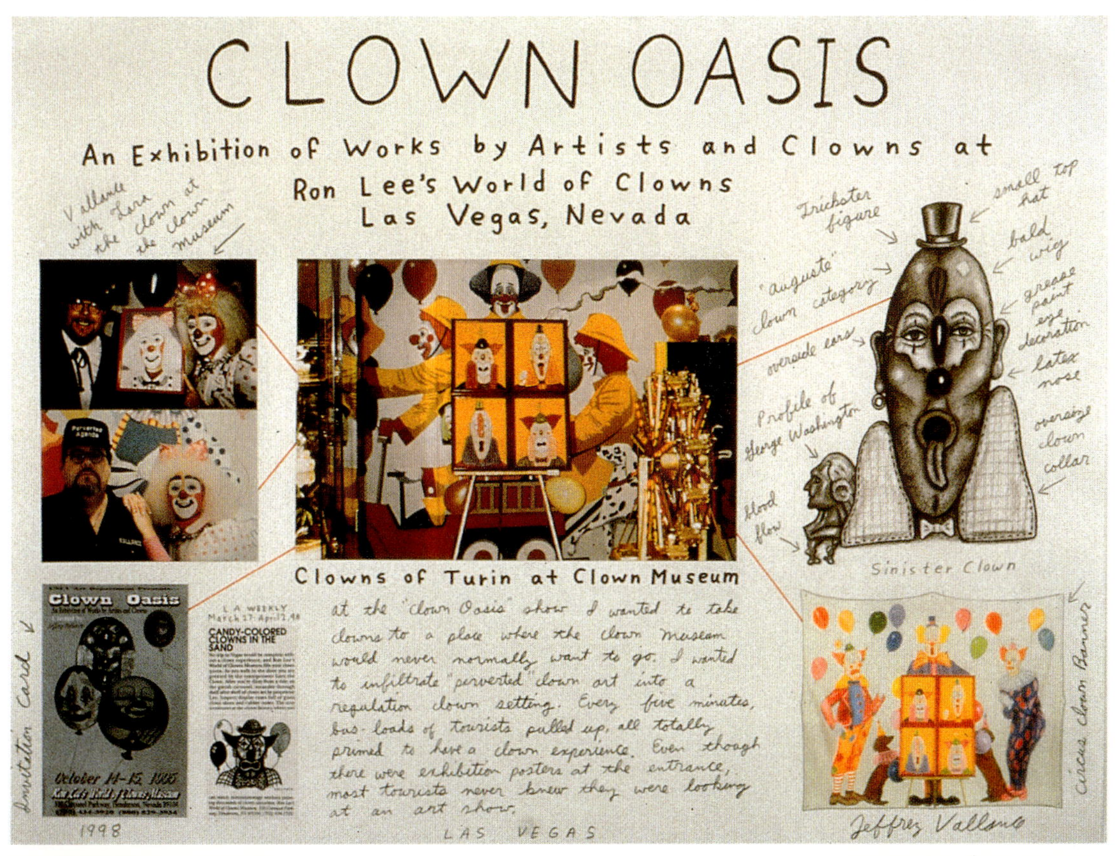

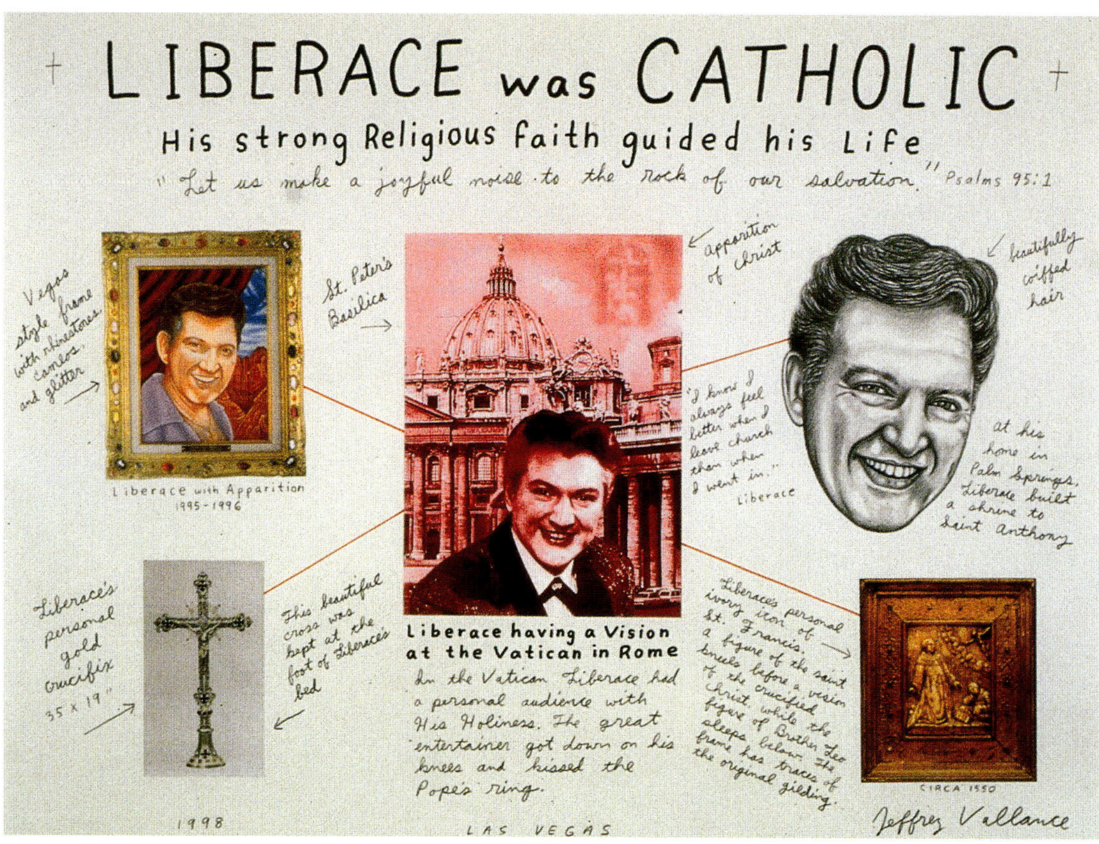

LIBERACE WAS CATHOLIC - HIS STRONG RELIGIOUS FAITH GUIDED HIS LIFE 1998
PENCIL, PEN AND COLLAGE ON PAPER 55.8 x 76.2 CM
COURTESY OF THE ARTIST AND LEHMANN MAUPIN, NEW YORK

ELVIS SWEATCLOTH 1998
PENCIL, PEN AND COLLAGE ON PAPER 55.8 x 76.2 CM
COURTESY OF THE ARTIST AND LEHMANN MAUPIN, NEW YORK

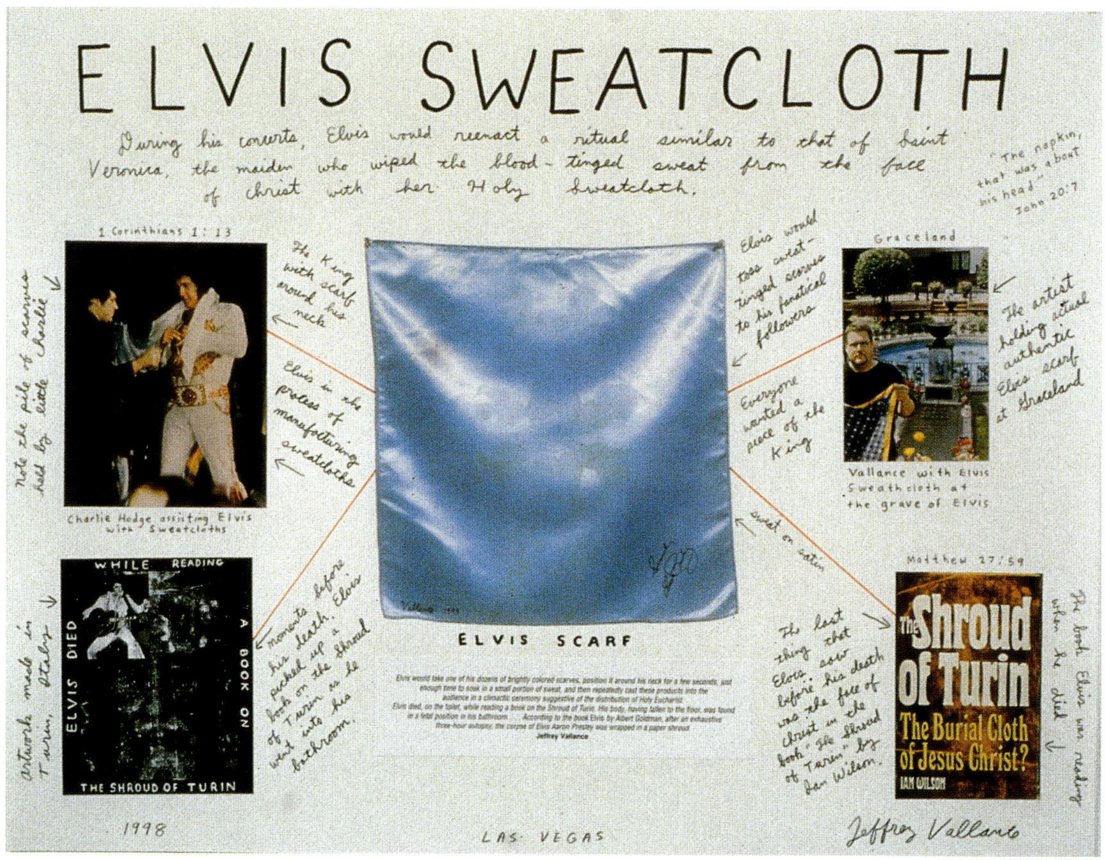

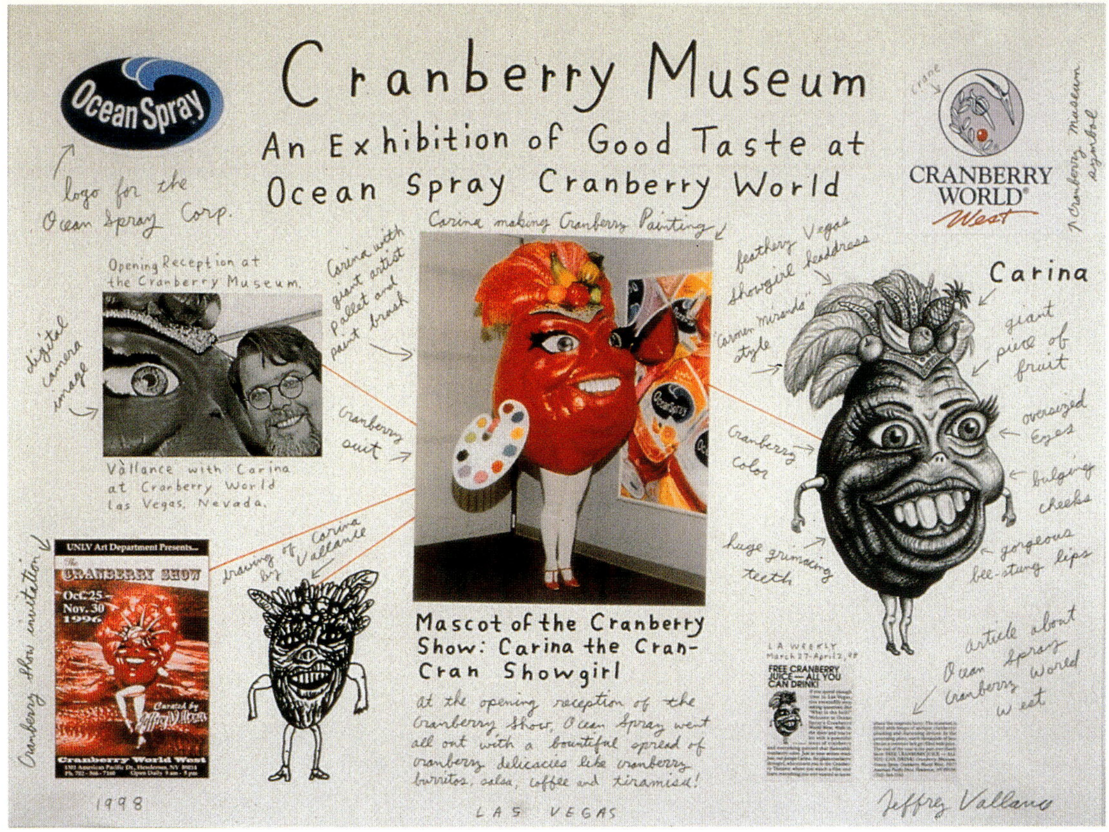

CRANBERRY MUSEUM - AN EXHIBITION OF GOOD TASTE AT OCEAN SPRAY CRANBERRY WORLD 1998
PENCIL, PEN AND COLLAGE ON PAPER 55.8 x 76.2 CM
COURTESY OF THE ARTIST AND LEHMANN MAUPIN, NEW YORK

VEGAS APOCALYPSE: CRUCIFIXION 1998
PENCIL ON PAPER 45.7 x 60.3 CM
COURTESY OF THE ARTIST AND ROSAMUND FELSEN GALLERY, SANTA MONICA, CA

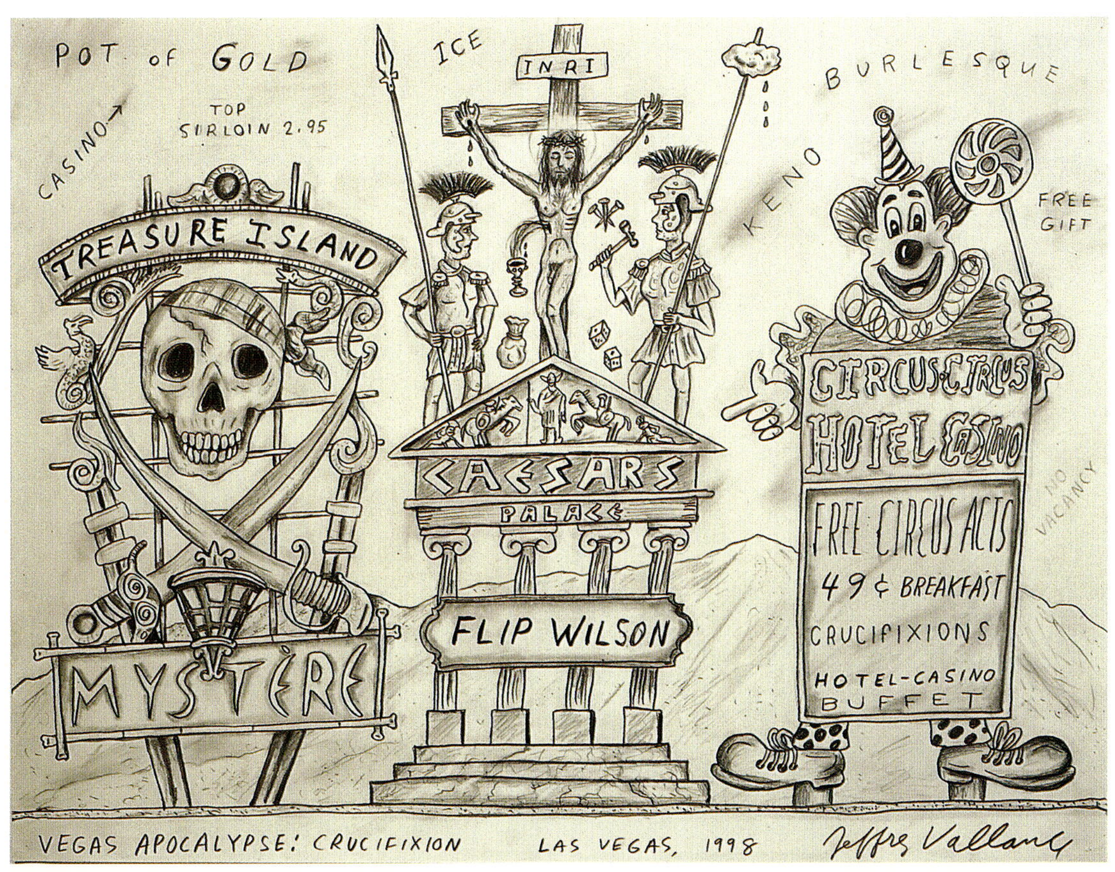

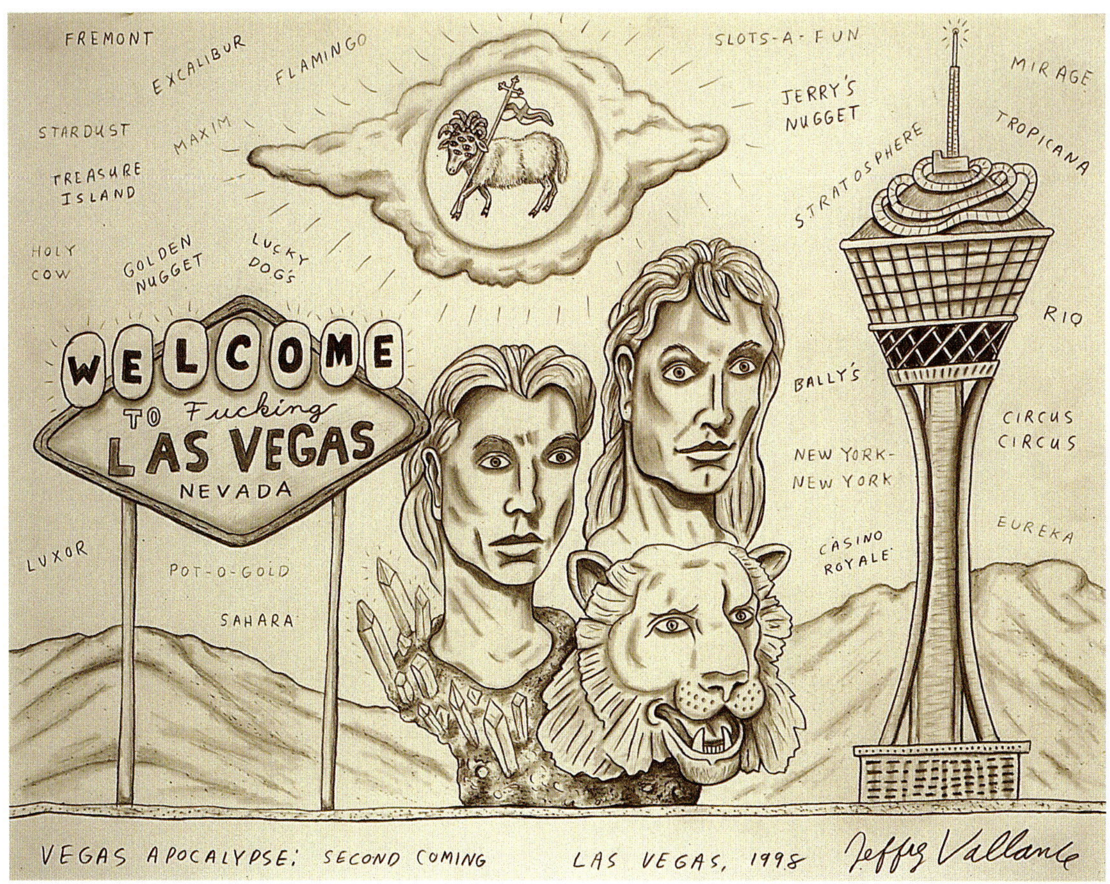

VEGAS APOCALYPSE: SECOND COMING 1998
PENCIL ON PAPER 45.7 x 60.3 CM
COLLECTION JAMES HINDERER AND DAWN SAARI
COURTESY OF THE ARTIST AND ROSAMUND FELSEN GALLERY, SANTA MONICA, CA

VEGAS APOCALYPSE: BEAST/SHOWGIRL 1998
PENCIL ON PAPER 45.7 x 60.3 CM
COURTESY OF ROSAMUND FELSEN GALLERY, SANTA MONICA, CA

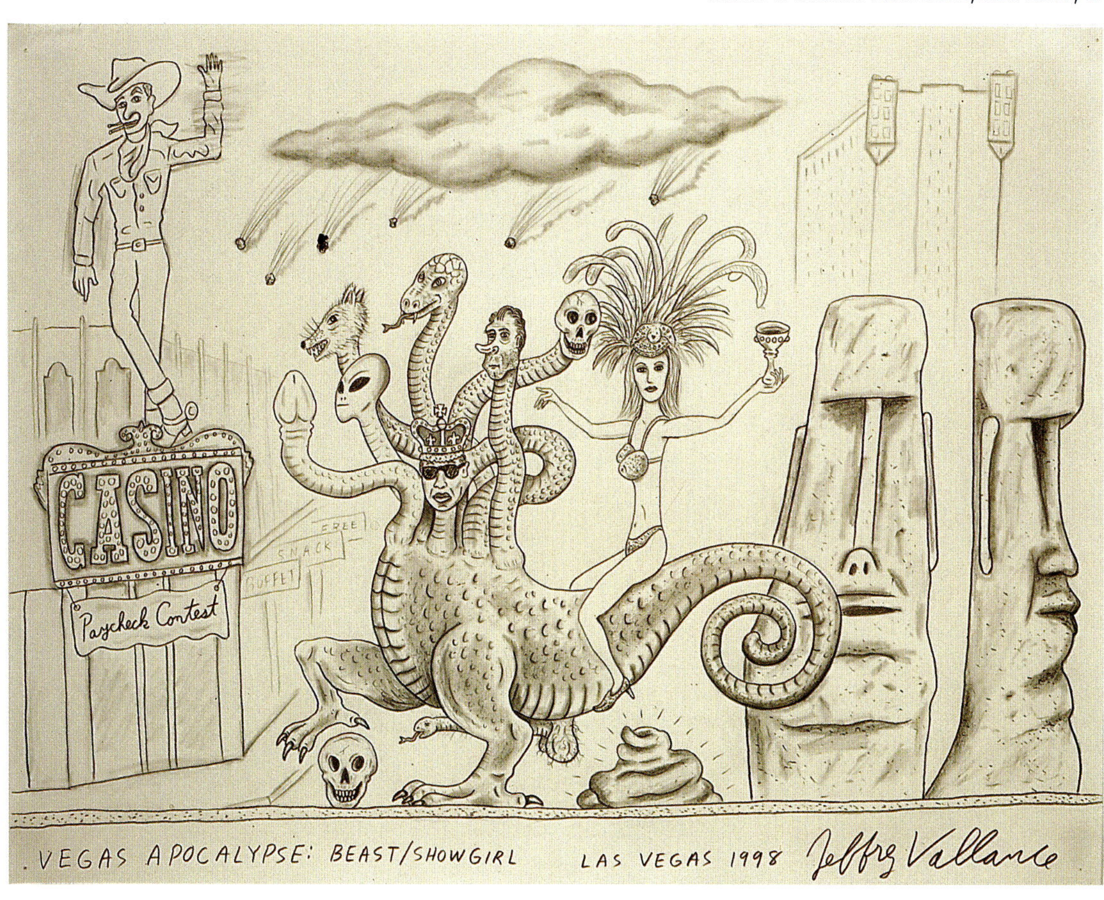

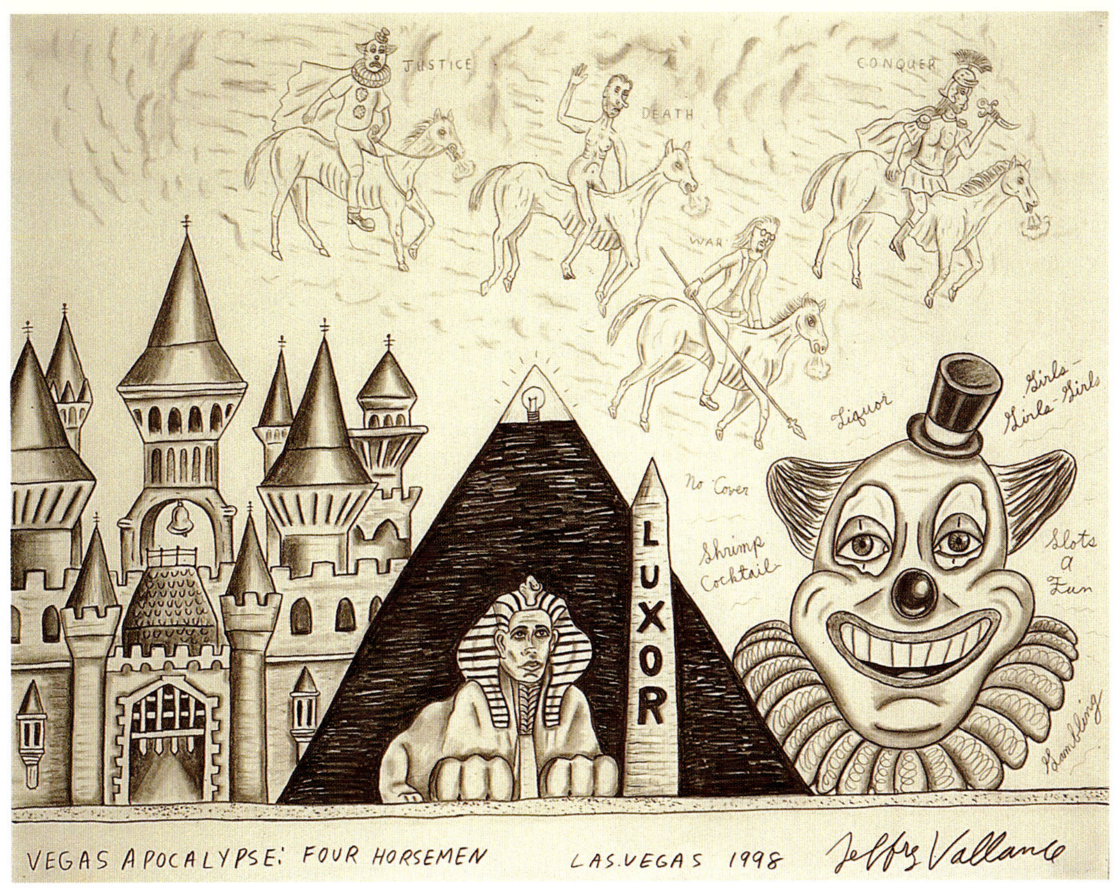

VEGAS APOCALYPSE: FOUR HORSEMEN 1998
PENCIL ON PAPER 45.7 x 60.3 CM
COURTESY OF THE ARTIST ROSAMUND FELSEN GALLERY, SANTA MONICA, CA

VEGAS APOCALYPSE: MOUTH OF HELL 1998
PENCIL ON PAPER 45.7 x 60.3 CM
COLLECTION OF LYNN ALDRICH, LOS ANGELES
COURTESY OF THE ARTIST AND ROSAMUND FELSEN GALLERY, SANTA MONICA, CA

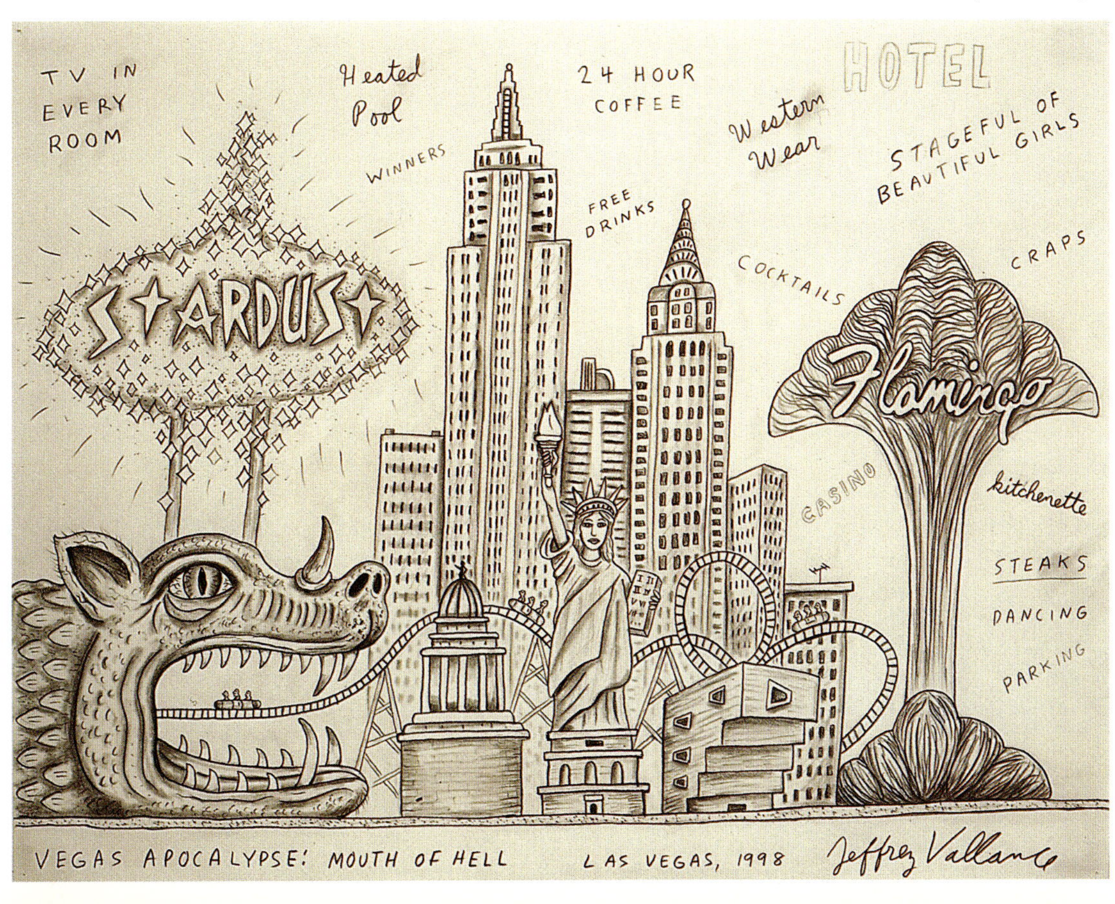

Venice Biennale, *Vegas Style*

The Casino Report, part II

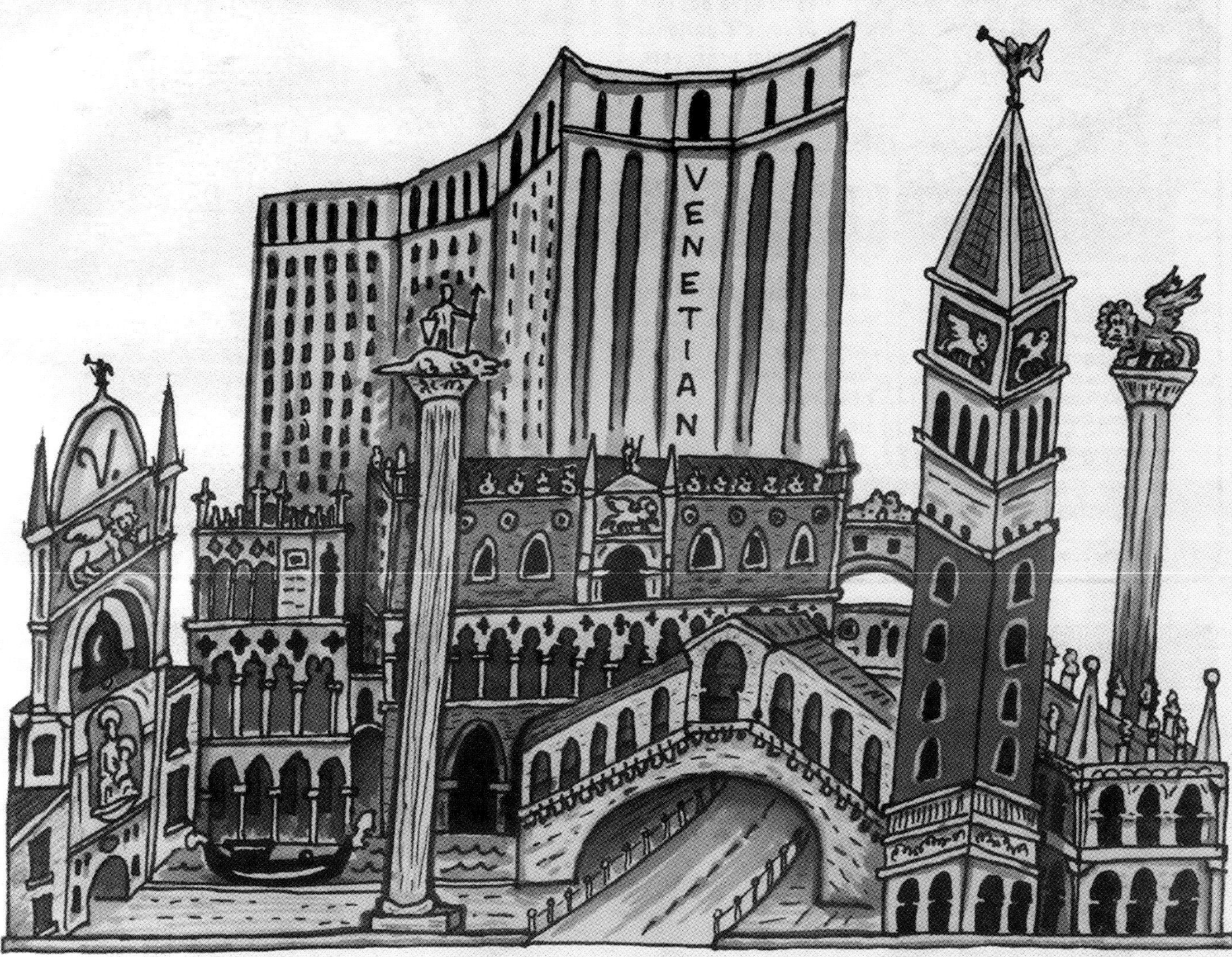

BY JEFFREY VALLANCE

THE FAÇADE OF THE NEW VENETIAN RESORT HOTEL Casino in Las Vegas, the latest casino to feature a "fine art" theme, is a pastiche of Venice, Italy's most famous architectural monuments — all crammed together. The casino imported an architectural historian from Venice to oversee the construction of the building while craftsmen labored for months in the heat of suburban Vegas churning out a horde of faux-marble statuary, sculpted in Styrofoam, coated with fiberglass. The interior of the casino is a conglomeration of "faithful reproductions" of Venice's most esteemed artists from the Golden Age with, for the first time ever in a casino, serious contemporary art. One thing you won't see in Vegas-Venice is statues blackened by years of pollution and pigeons, or murky canals filled with sewage. Everything here is brand spankin' new.

As seen from Vegas Boulevard, the Venetian appears as some kind of weird distortion of the buildings that surround Venice's famous St. Mark's Square (except for the conspicuously missing Basilica San Marco), split by the Grand Canal. The casino entrance is a reconstruction of the Doge's Palace, originally built in the 14th century as the residence of the Venetian head of state, the doge (similar to a duke). This is like using the White House as the entrance to a casino. Adjacent to the Doge's Palace is the baroque Bridge of Sighs, which originally led from the palace to a prison (the "sighs" refers to the wailing of the condemned prisoners); here, the Bridge of Sighs connects the high-limit slots room to a fancy high rollers' lounge. (The sighs now come from gamblers experiencing streaks of bad luck.) In Venice, the picturesque 16th-century Rialto Bridge crosses the Grand Canal. In Vegas, the famous bridge is a moving sidewalk pumping thousands of tourists daily into the facility's majestic entrance.

Also attached to the casino's structure are two 15th-century buildings, the fabulously gothic Ca d'Oro ("House of Gold"), the walls of which were originally embellished with gold; and the Contarini-Fasan Palace, traditionally believed to be the house of Desdemona from Shakespeare's *Othello*. Across the Vegas Grand Canal is a full-size reconstruction of the Campanile, a tower at the base of which lies the Loggetta, or Hall of the Palace Guard, as entryway to the moving sidewalk. Beside the Loggetta, the Marcian Library, ornately decorated with replica statues by world-renowned Venetian sculptors, is also home to Madame Tussaud's Celebrity Encounter wax museum, featuring such legendary Vegas icons as Liberace, Debbie Reynolds, Elvis, Wayne Newton, Tom Jones, Siegfried & Roy and Frank Sinatra. On your way out of the museum, you'll be confronted with an audio-animatronic Elvis, who sings and gyrates until he dies. Elvis' wispy spirit then floats over the audience, terminating in a red, white and blue starburst. This is the first time I've seen the ghost of Elvis presented to a mass audience.

My favorite architectural element, though, is the 15th-century arch of the Torre dell'Orologio, or Clock Tower, which has been turned into the casino's flashing marquee. High atop the fabulous tower, bronze figures of Moors strike a huge bell on the hour. The Vegasy archway includes some remarkable architectural details, including a huge disk with the signs of the zodiac in relief and a magnificent statue of the Winged Lion of St. Mark, whose body, according to 14th-century hagiographers, was packed in a barrel of pork. And the crowning touch is a statue of the Blessed Virgin Mary holding the Baby Jesus. Yes — Baby Jesus on a casino marquee!

Just as the art world has almost recovered from the unveiling of Steve Wynn's Bellagio Gallery of Fine Art, the Venetian Casino delivers its knockout punch: a contemporary gallery with fine art rivaling that of the Venice Biennale. Before you go to the art gallery, I suggest you walk through the Venetian's three resplendent halls of fake masterworks. First, see the *Triumph of Venice* by Bambini on the hotel lobby's ceiling, near the main entrance. Then gaze at four heroic scenes by Tiepolo ➤

ILLUSTRATIONS BY JEFFREY VALLANCE

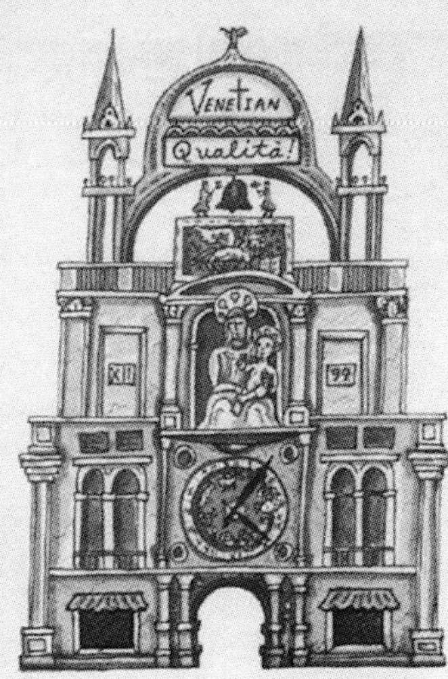

in the grand dome over the golden fountain. As you stroll down the Lobby Colonnade, look up at the barrel-vault overhead to see works by Titian and Tintoretto. In the Doge's Great Room, cast your eyes heavenward for *The Apotheosis of Venice* by Veronese.

The Grand Canal Shoppes, on the second floor, have a second Grand Canal where you can take a gondola ride (courtesy of a singing gondolier) to a second St. Mark's Square. The second Square's second Clock Tower (with a second Blessed Virgin and Baby Jesus) serves as the façade for Qualità Fine Art. Qualità features art by nationally and internationally known artists, but its mark of distinction is that it also shows Vegas artists, including Robert Acuna, Tim Bavington, Jack Hallberg, Victoria Reynolds and Yek. Directed by Nancy Hoffman of Nancy Hoffman Gallery in New York. Qualità is the first contemporary-art space in a casino.

Outside the gallery, masked Carnival characters perform their zany antics beneath a 70-foot ceiling fixed to resemble an early-evening Venetian sky. The Carnival (from the Italian *carne vale*, "farewell to meat") is the last chance for revelry, merrymaking and taboo breaking before Lent, when one must abstain from pleasures of the flesh. Venice was home to the 16th-century Commedia dell'Arte, the theater group that invented such characters as the harlequin and the clown. Pick yourself out a colorful Murano glass clown from one of the Venetian's glass-art shops.

ABOVE ALL ELSE, THE VENETIAN IS HEAVY on Christian apocalyptic iconography. Besides the Winged Lion of Revelation, used as the casino's logo, and the Madonna and Child, the Casino's embellishments include the statue of the Archangel Michael standing with sword drawn — a decorative motif on the Doge's Palace — and a golden Archangel Gabriel perched high atop the Campanile. A monolithic statue of St. Theodore with lance in hand stands triumphantly on a dragon (Satan) on top of one of the casino's entryway columns. Figures of horribly grotesque demons are used as architectural detail.

Some citizens of Vegas believe in a Second Coming, when the golden statue of the Archangel Gabriel will spring to life and blow his mighty horn, heralding the end of the world. Many believe that Vegas is a modern-day Gomorrah that a vengeful God is planning to punish. If in fact Vegas is Sin City and the approaching millennium is the biblical Armageddon, then the Venetian Casino may well be ground zero for the Apocalypse. What a damn town! LA

Professor Vallance divides his time between Las Vegas and Lapland.

The Greatest Art Show on Earth

(Be careful not to splash marinara sauce on the paintings.) **BY JEFFREY VALLANCE**

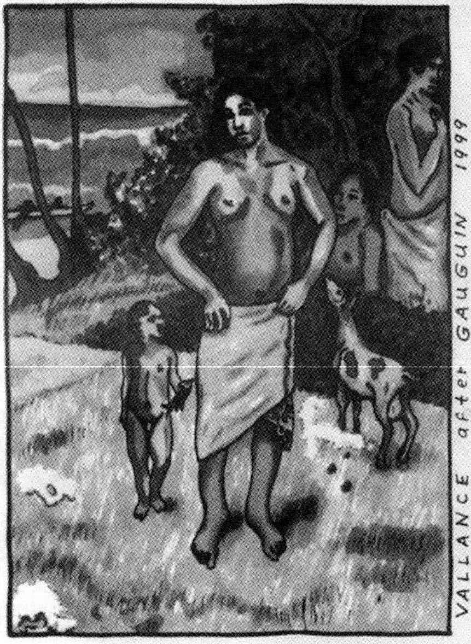

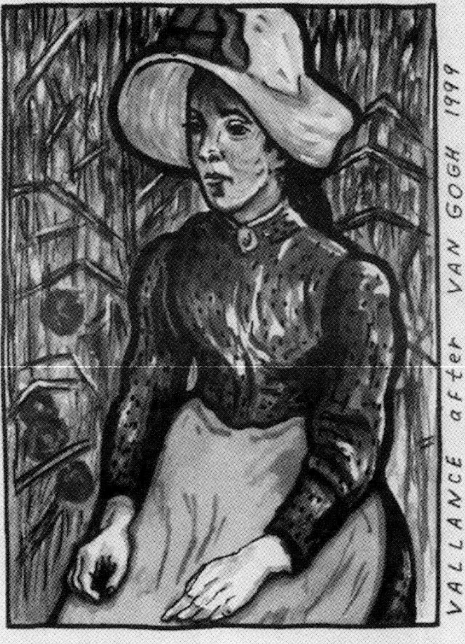

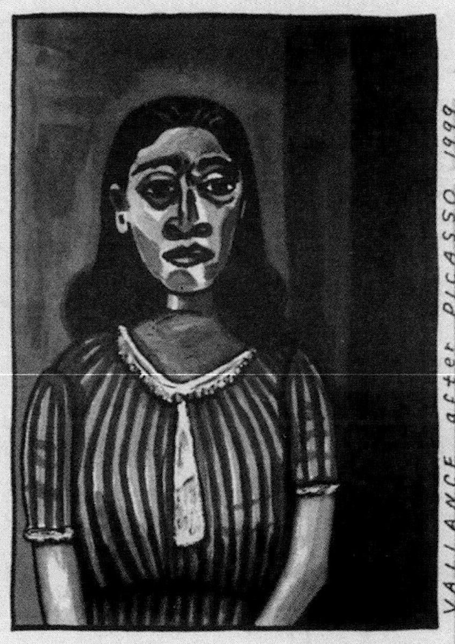

LAS VEGAS CASINO MOGUL STEVE WYNN IS NOT ONLY chairman of Mirage Resorts Inc.; he's also a gallerist. His Bellagio Gallery of Fine Art (in the casino we've been hearing so much about) looks more like a museum, as it is loosely modeled after the Frick Collection in New York and the National Gallery in London. The marquee out in front is a work of art in itself: The old masters' names appear one by one in colored flashing lights like some kind of weird lounge act. Conforming to Vegas aesthetics, the gallery is not a white cube but a resplendent little jewel of a space. Inside, it is filled with works by Cézanne, Degas, Gaugin, Manet, Monet, van Gogh, Picasso, Pollock, Oldenburg and Rauschenberg. (The only thing missing — too perfect for Vegas — is work by Jeff Koons.) The walls themselves are upholstered with a plush, forest-green mohair treatment, accented with stained maple and figured sycamore polished to a high gloss. The mosaic gallery floor is an elegant latticework of crema valencia marble inlaid with rosa aurora. No detail was overlooked, even down to the lighting — special Wendell Lighting framing projectors have been precisely adjusted to illuminate only the artwork, making the paintings so vibrant as to appear hyperreal, like virtual-reality apparitions floating in midair. In a town where fake is the name of the game, seeing something truly authentic seems all the more unreal.

Wynn's notion of bringing art to this desert boomtown has a long, in the context of Las Vegas, history. In 1944, famed pianist Liberace, clad in his bejeweled and rhinestone-studded costumes, brought classical music to regular folk with his first recital at the New Frontier casino. The tradition is carried on today by the Liberace Foundation for the Performing and Creative Arts, which has funded scholarships in the arts since 1976. The foundation runs the Liberace Museum, one of the most popular attractions in town. In the early 1980s, artist Steven Molasky exhibited a series of boxer paintings, including portraits of many renowned prizefighters, at Caesar's Palace. In 1986, sponsored by the Nevada Institute for Contemporary Art, Jenny Holzer found a perfect venue for her work on the Caesar's Palace marquee, flashing the text "Protect Me From What I Want." Throughout the '90s, Vegas artists have exhibited in casinos and other unorthodox locations such as the Debbie Reynolds Casino, the Magic and Movie Hall of Fame at O'Shea's Hilton Casino, the Liberace Museum, Ron Lee's World of Clowns, and the Cranberry Museum. In 1996, the Rio Casino commissioned a series of works by contemporary artists that are currently on display. The Rio just had an exhibition entitled "Treasures of Russia" from the Peterhof Palace of the Czars, featuring various royal objects such as Peter the Great's gilded throne and a Fabergé egg. Harrah's recently commissioned artist Jim Pink to make one of his classic Vegas landscape paintings for its casino.

Heck, right down the street, the Whitney Museum façade is included in the New York, New York Casino skyline. Directly across from the Bellagio at the new Paris casino (now under construction), they're building the damn Louvre. And during the festive holiday season, the Bellagio displayed a majestic 32-foot Christmas-tree sculpture designed by homemaking goddess Martha Stewart.

THE FRENCH IMPRESSIONISTS LOOK PARTICULARLY great in the Bellagio, possibly because they are the blockbusters of high art. But it's equally amazing to see a de Kooning hanging in a casino. The Bellagio's Rauschenberg, a deliciously grubby combine painting (with a strange little globe of lights on top echoing the lights of the Strip), looks especially good amidst the pantheon of masterworks. The Pop artists, too, seem completely at home here — Warhol's now-departed *Orange Marilyn* in the garish lights of Sin City! Oldenburg's monumental *Clothespin — 45-Foot Version (Model)* seems tailor-made for the fantasy architecture. Another Oldenburg sculpture, *Flashlight*, looms over UNLV, its gigantic black shaft pointing down at the ground, its light swallowed by the earth — a contrast to the heavenward lights of the Strip. *Flashlight* refers to the Illuminati symbol of the downturned torch, signifying hidden knowledge. "If Nevada had just one of these paintings," says Dave Hickey, art critic and Vegas cult figure, "the visual culture would improve a thousand percent."

The Bellagio Resort features another venue for fine art, the Picasso Restaurant. The interior is like a giant canvas — the walls are gesso-covered burlap. You dine surrounded by Pablo Picasso paintings, ceramics, tiles and sculptures. Even the freaking carpet is designed by Pablo's son, Claude Picasso. (Be careful not to splash marinara sauce on the paintings.)

One must remember the function of the Bellagio Gallery of Fine Art: It is a Vegas attraction, like the erupting volcano, the pirate battle, the dolphin show and Siegfried & Roy. It's fine art on a par with P.T. Barnum — the greatest art show on Earth. With the population now skyrocketing past a million, Steve Wynn could be a Vegas visionary — casinos may be the exhibition spaces of the future. Get all the art out of stuffy institutions and haul it to Vegas, America's aesthetic capital, the art center of the new millennium. ▣

Professor Jeffrey Vallance divides his time between Las Vegas and Lapland.

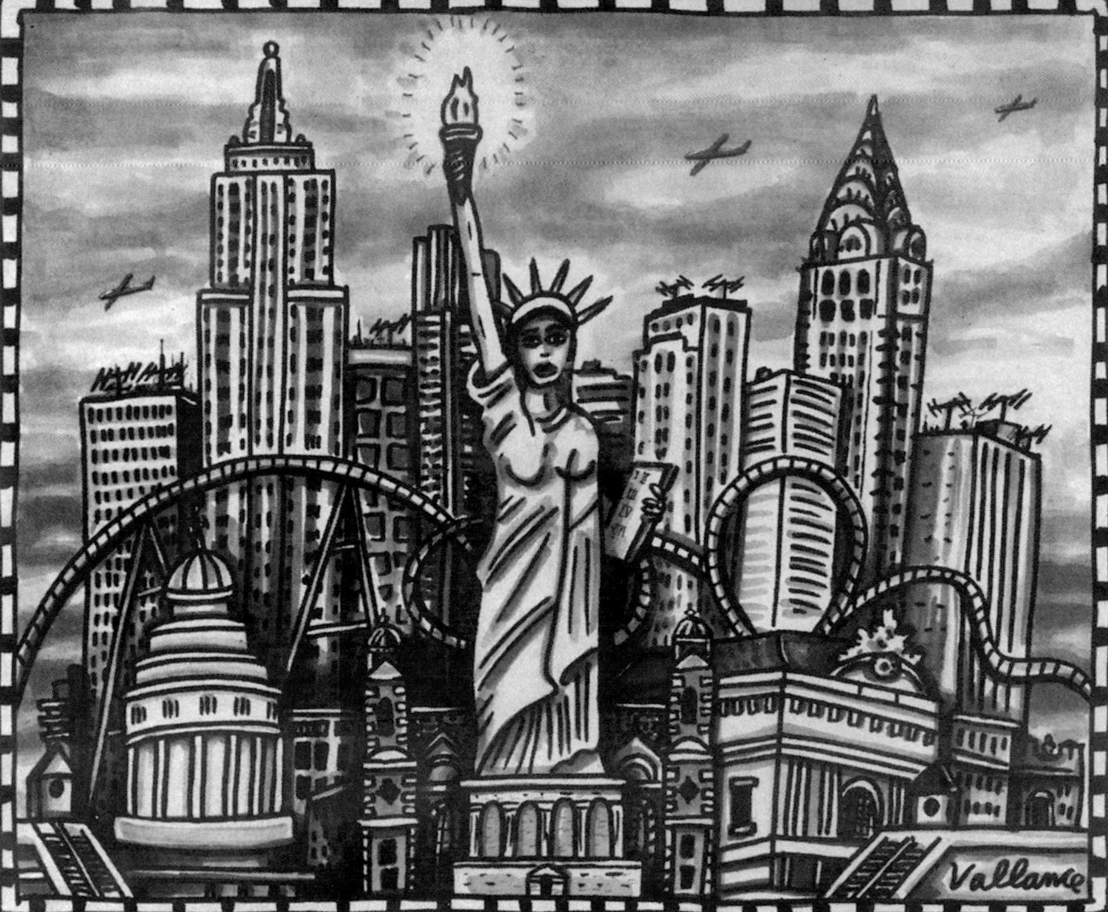

The Arts

New York Art

In Laaas Vegaaaas!

BY JEFFREY VALLANCE

Like Jerusalem, Rome, Lourdes and Mecca, Las Vegas attracts pilgrims from around the world. Each casino is a holy shrine where pilgrims can obtain sacred relics — glittering Vegas souvenirs. At the forefront of the new Vegas attractions is the New York–New York Casino. The Whitney Museum façade, included in the imposing skyline re-creation, seems to make sense here, since this desert gambling fantasyland is fast becoming a mecca for some of the country's most eccentric new artists. (Ralph Rugoff, in *Artforum*, described Las Vegas as "our esthetic capital.") And the casino incorporates many "fine art" references.

The real Whitney, designed by Marcel Breuer (1902–1981), looks rather like a giant chest with its drawers progressively pulled out toward Madison Avenue; constructed of dark-gray granite slats, it is stark and austere. The Vegas version has a swirling, iridescent surface that cantilevers out over the Strip. It's reassuring to know that the doors of the Vegas Whitney serve as the casino's emergency exit; I can picture some disaster at New York–New York — mobs of panic-stricken gamblers stampeding out through the façade of one of America's most prestigious museums.

Upon entering New York–New York, the first thing you see is the Statue of Liberty assuming Marilyn Monroe's famous dress-blowing-up stance from *The Seven Year Itch*. (The actual dress/relic is also found in Las Vegas, at the Debbie Reynolds Hollywood Movie Museum.) Off to one side dangles a monumental apple/disco ball recalling the oversize sculptures of Claes Oldenburg or the work of the Surrealist painter René Magritte. Here, however, the apple is encrusted with Vegas glitter.

Upstairs, in a re-creation of Coney Island, is a series of seven of the finest clown paintings to be seen anywhere, clown paintings that would make John Wayne Gacy cry. (Clown painting seems to be an important genre in Las Vegas — see the Circus Circus Casino and Ron Lee's World of Clowns Museum.) Gallagher's Restaurant has a meat-locker display with a sign reading, "This Is Real Beef Being Dry Aged." It looks like a relic from one of Hermann Nitsch's Actionist performances.

Soho has been turned into a giant gift-shop mall, but if you look through a window above the stand that sells designer pet-food bowls, you can get a glimpse of a Soho artist's studio, complete with brushes, palette and flapping paint rags. Around the corner is the Times Square Camera Shop with a window display of Ansel Adams catalogs and Susan Sontag's book *On Photography*. (No porno stores.)

An area called "The Village" is a maze-like re-creation of a typical New York street scene. At the corner of Greenwich and Bleeker Street is a deli like a giant Julian Schnabel painting: The walls are mosaics of broken plates. Across the street, the window at Houdini's Magic Shop features an artistic display of fake vomit next to a rubber Nixon mask. Above Broadway Burger, at the corner of Sheridan Square and Broadway, is a re-creation of Jackson Pollock's studio, where one can spy a corner of one of his action paintings.

The plaza at the north entrance of the casino features the work of real New York graffiti artists, specially flown in from the city to enhance the casino's urban realism. And then there's the men's room: Painted in the style of Futurist Umberto Boccioni, it features a mural of a locomotive, emphasizing speed, travel and technology — helpful themes to keep in mind while relieving oneself.

At a recent art opening here in Vegas, I overheard someone saying, "Who needs New York? We've got our own Whitney right here."

Viva Las Vegas! LA

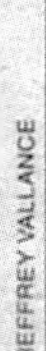
JEFFREY VALLANCE

INSIDE

Robert Venturi, Denise Scott Brown & Steven Izenour

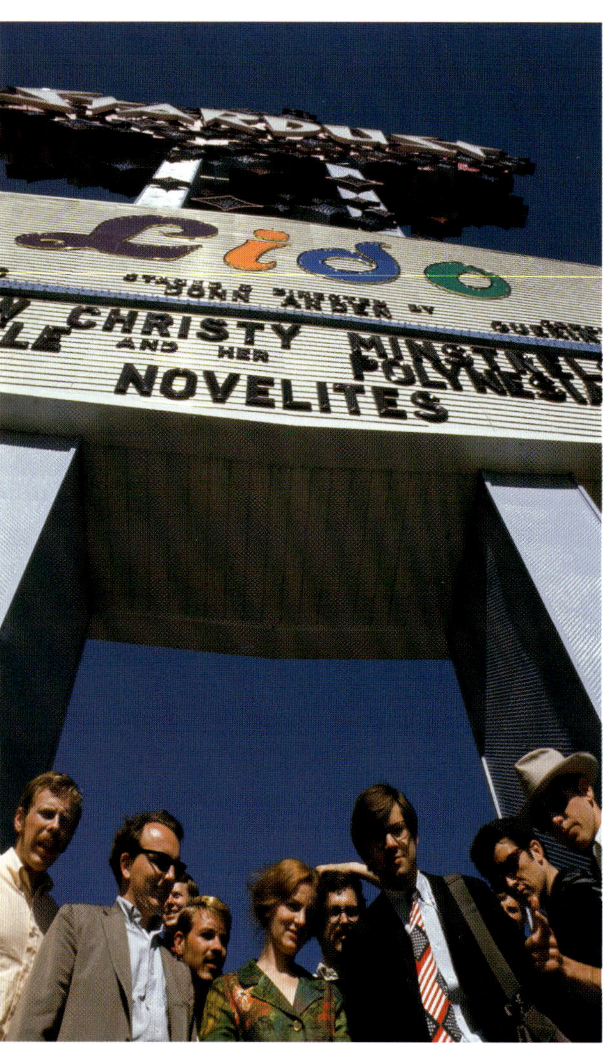

PHOTO BY VENTURI, SCOTT BROWN & ASSOCIATES

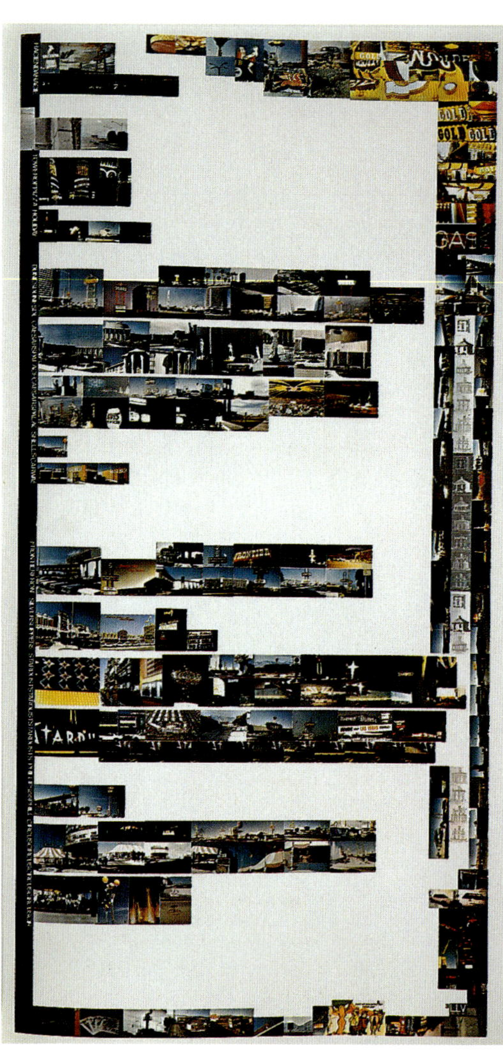

INSTALLATION VIEW
PHOTO BY VENTURI, SCOTT BROWN & ASSOCIATES

PHOTO BY VENTURI, SCOTT BROWN & ASSOCIATES

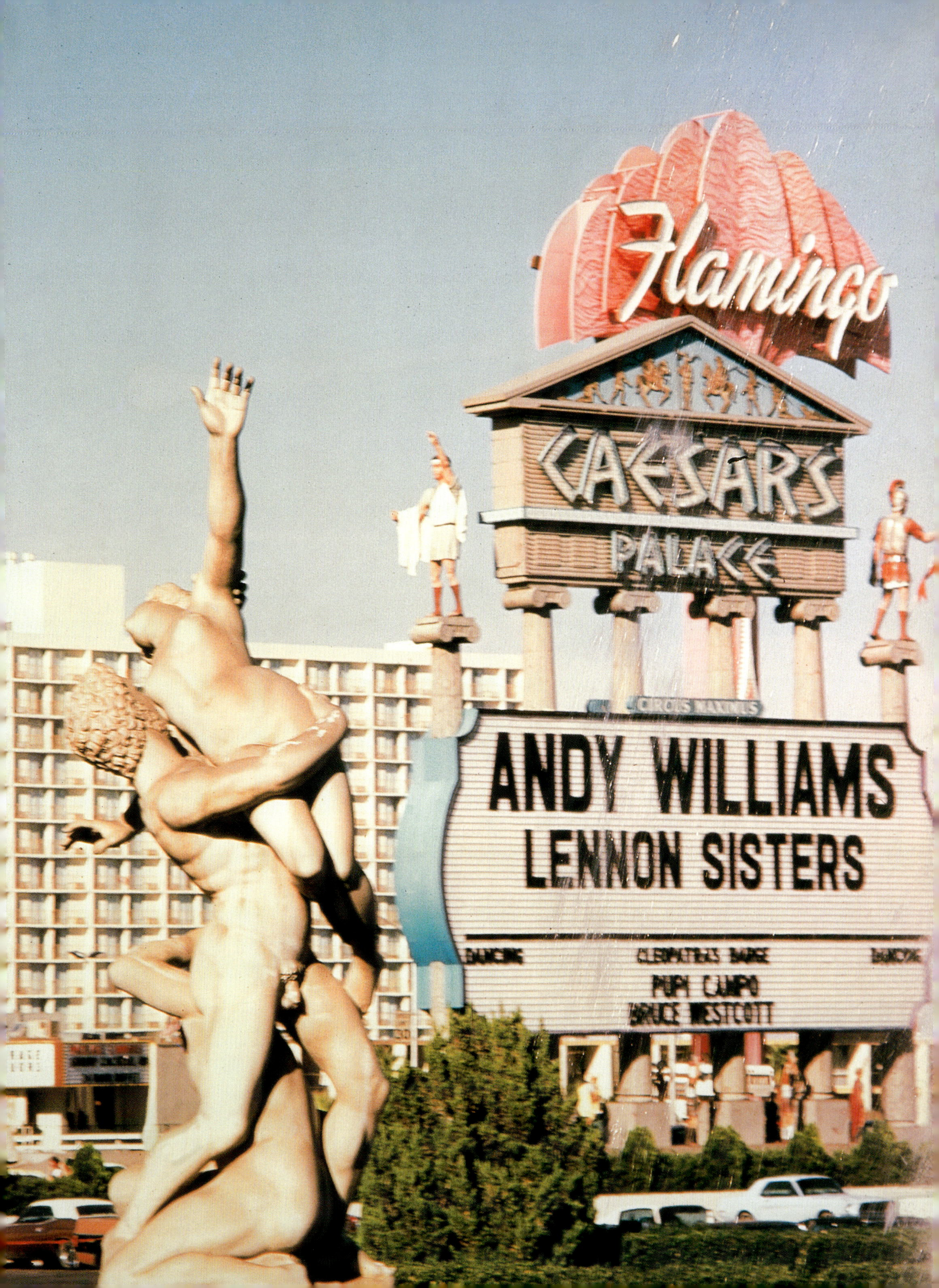
Flamingo
CAESARS
PALACE
CIRCUS MAXIMUS
ANDY WILLIAMS
LENNON SISTERS
DANCING
CLEOPATRAS BARGE
DANCING
PUPI CAMPO
BRUCE WESTCOTT

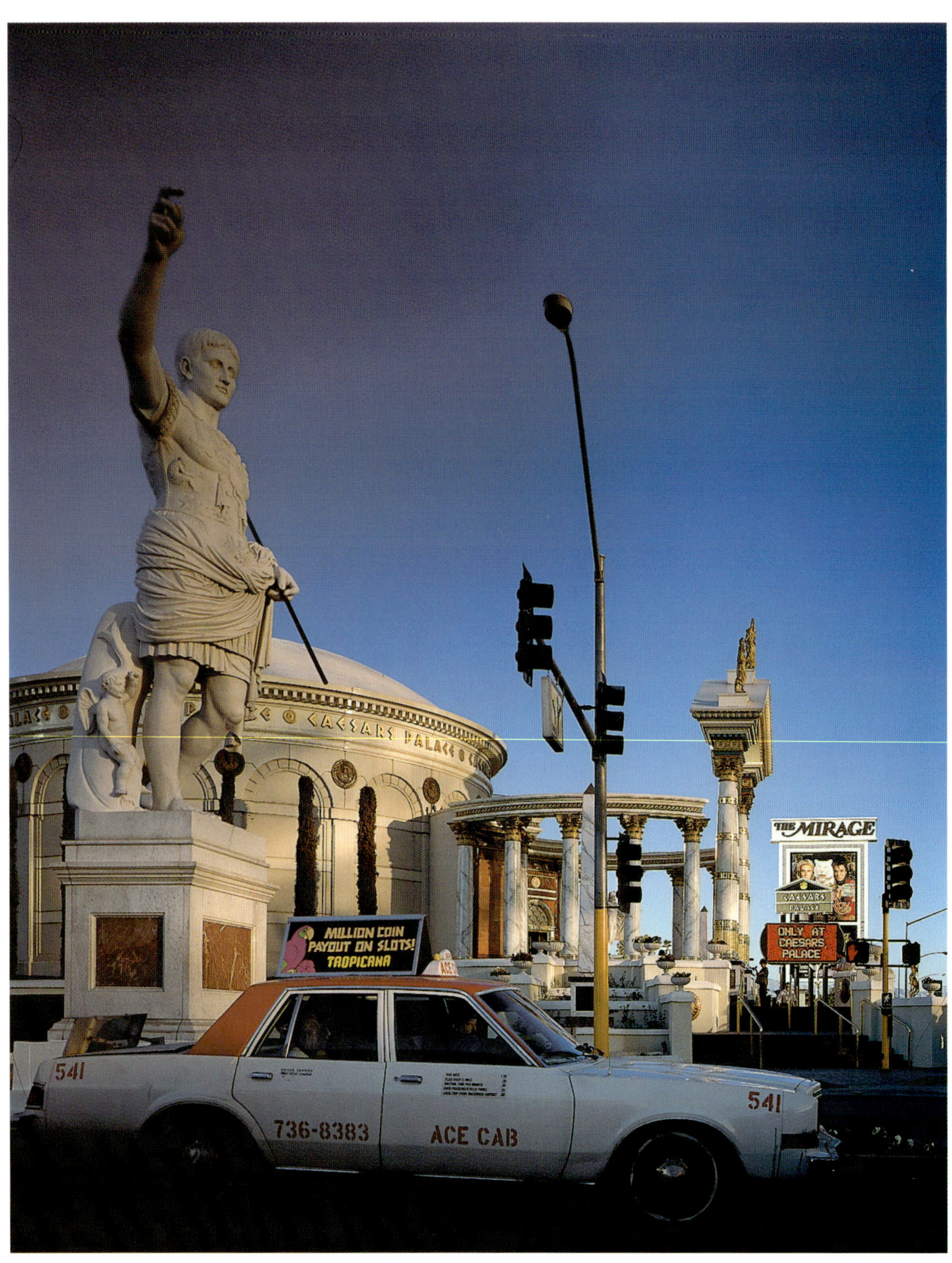

PHOTO BY VENTURI, SCOTT BROWN & ASSOCIATES (MATT WARGO)

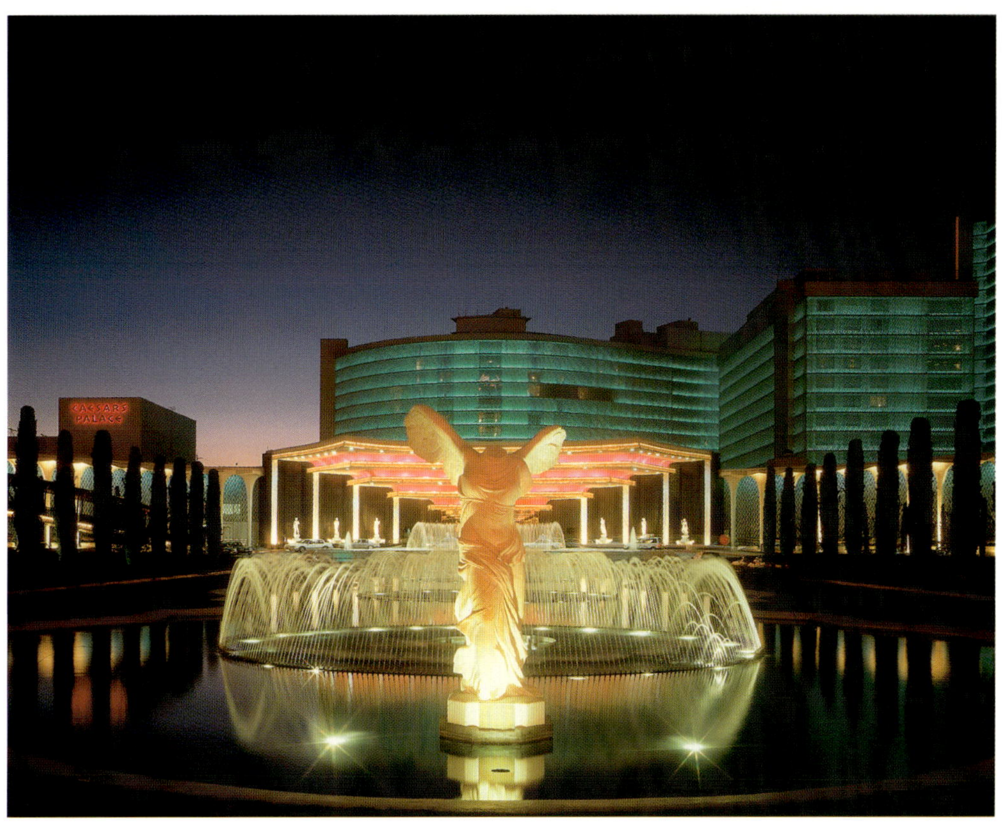

PHOTO BY VENTURI, SCOTT BROWN & ASSOCIATES (MATT WARGO)

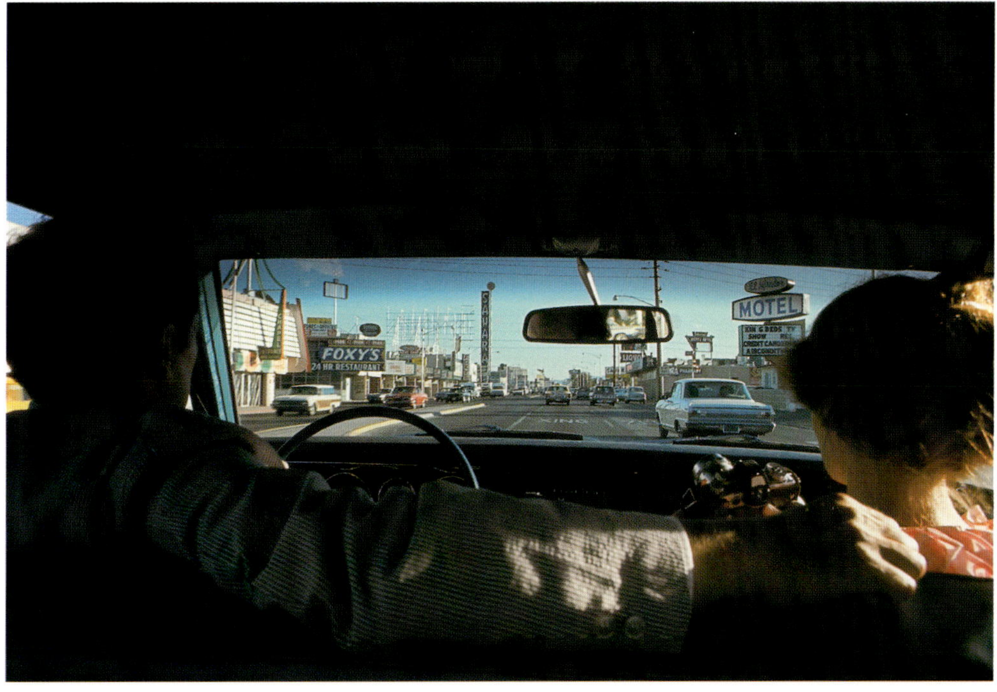

PHOTO BY VENTURI, SCOTT BROWN & ASSOCIATES (MATT WARGO)

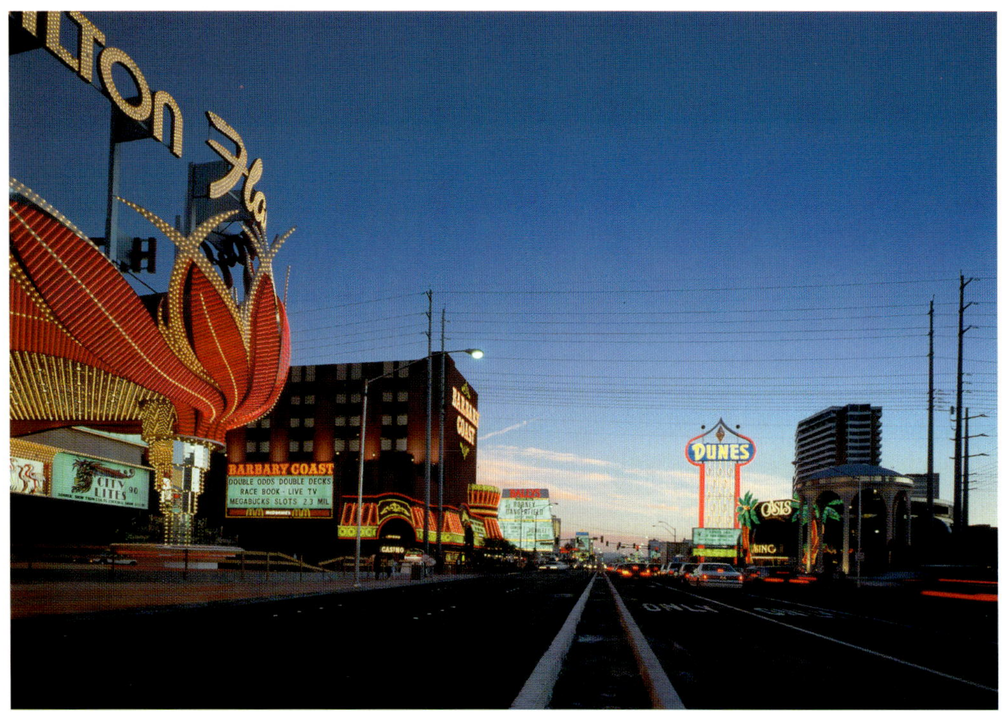

PHOTO BY VENTURI, SCOTT BROWN & ASSOCIATES (MATT WARGO)

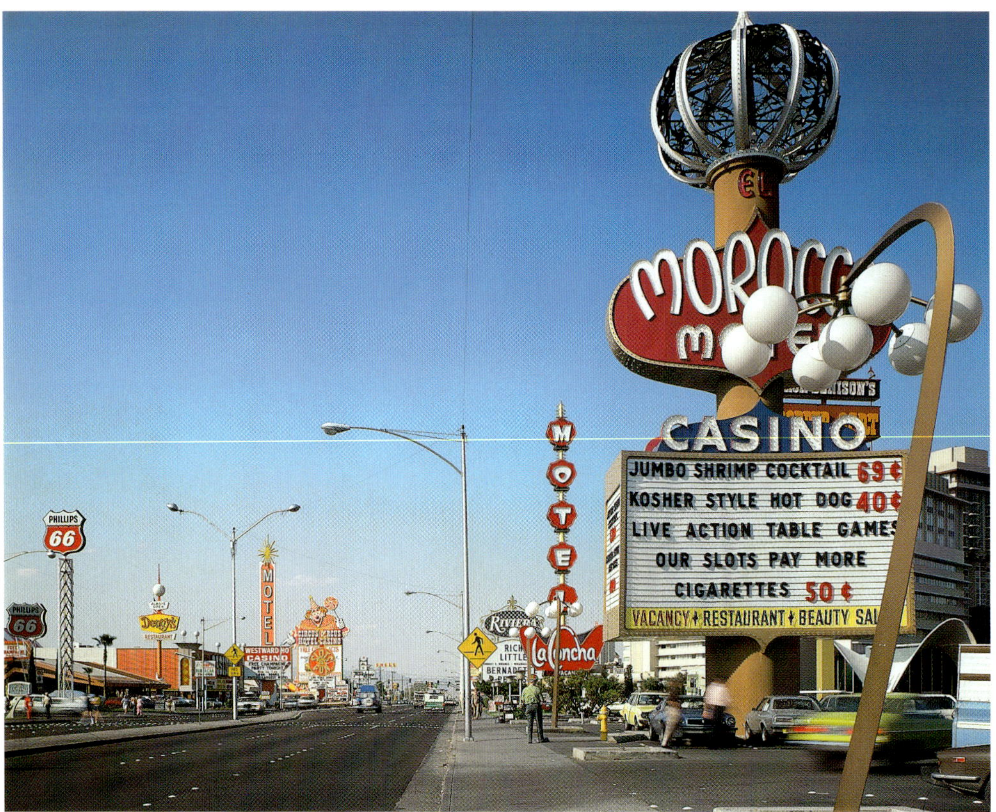

PHOTO BY VENTURI, SCOTT BROWN & ASSOCIATES

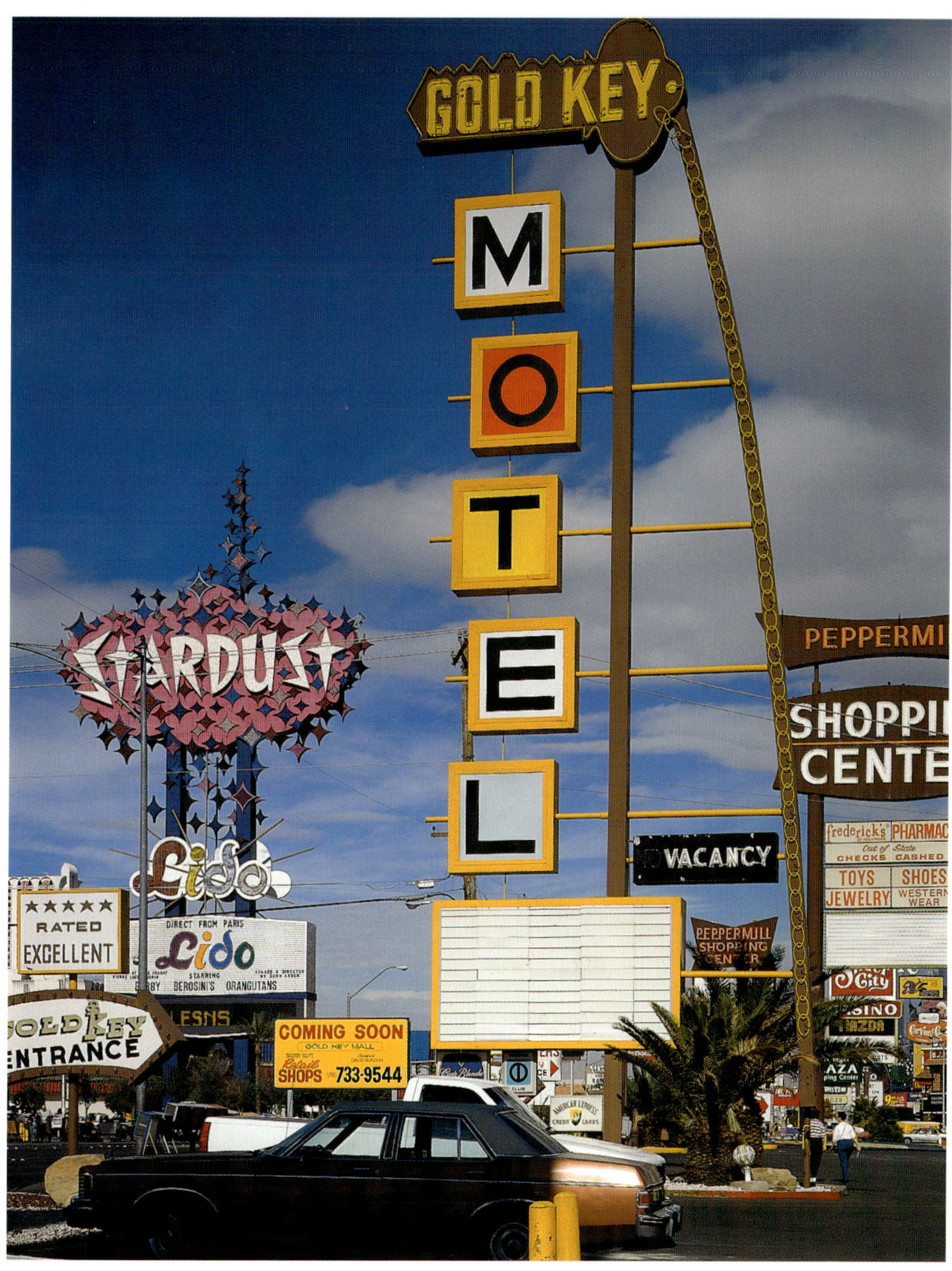

PHOTO BY VENTURI, SCOTT BROWN & ASSOCIATES (MATT WARGO)

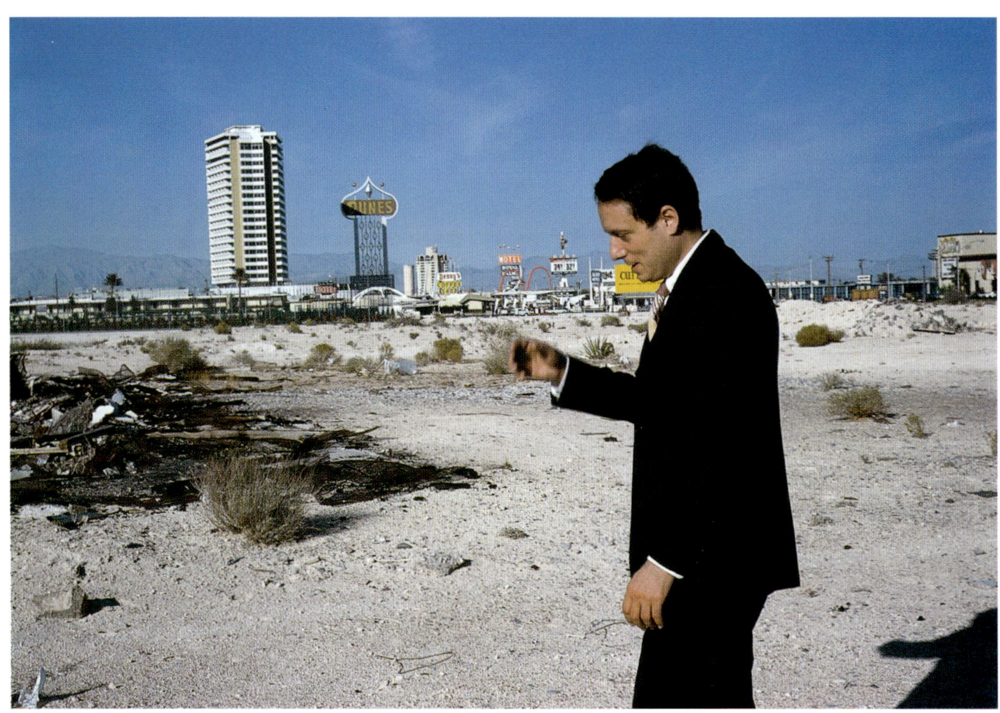

PHOTO BY VENTURI, SCOTT BROWN & ASSOCIATES

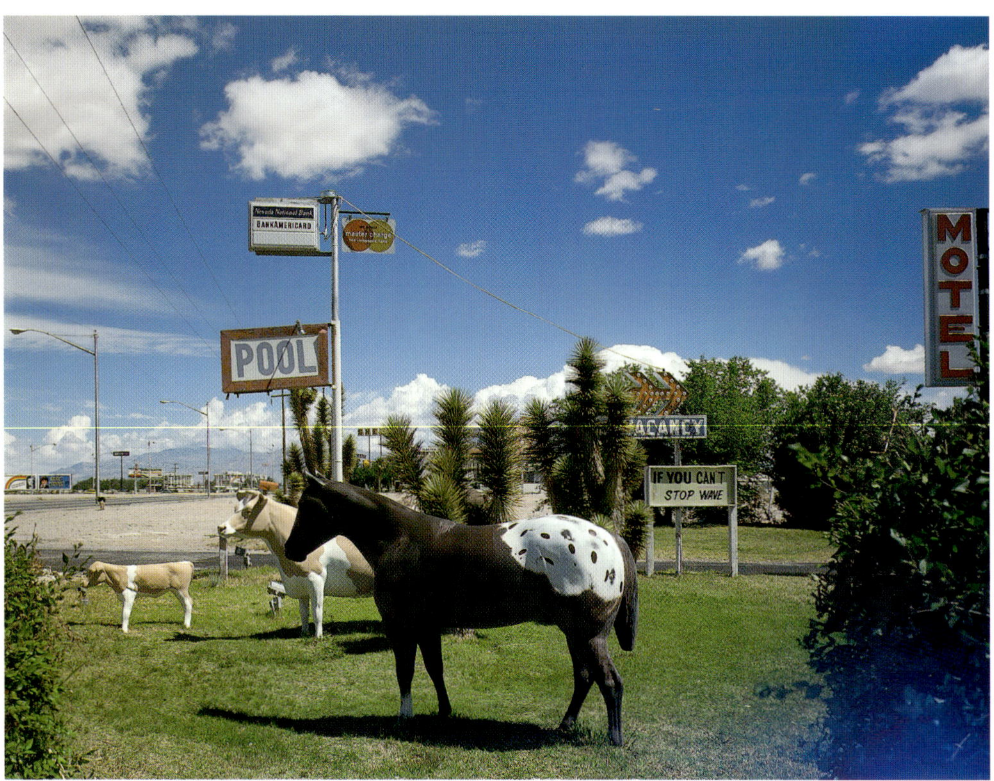

PHOTO BY VENTURI, SCOTT BROWN & ASSOCIATES

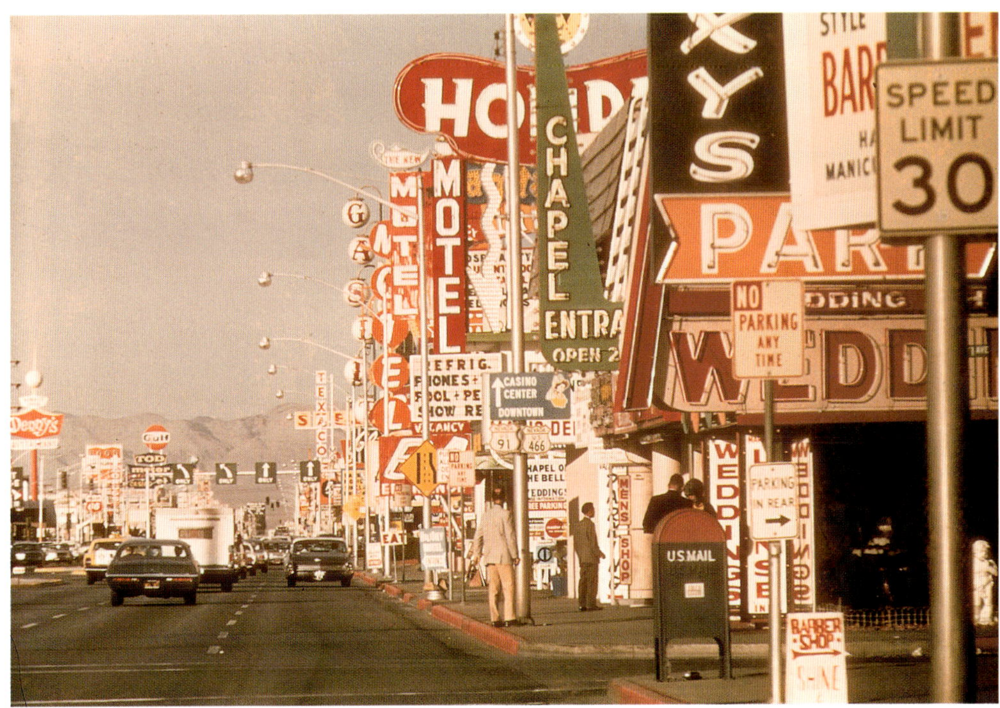

PHOTO BY VENTURI, SCOTT BROWN & ASSOCIATES

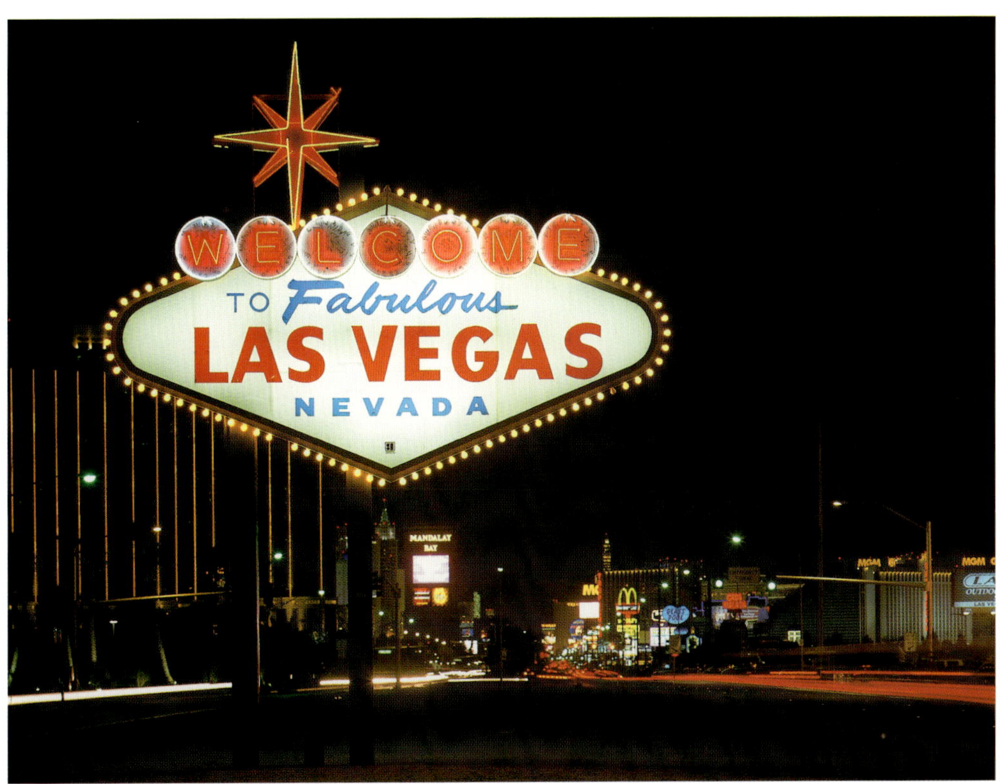

PHOTO BY VENTURI, SCOTT BROWN & ASSOCIATES (MATT WARGO)

Andy Warhol

1928 Born in Pittsburgh, PA
1987 Died in New York, NY

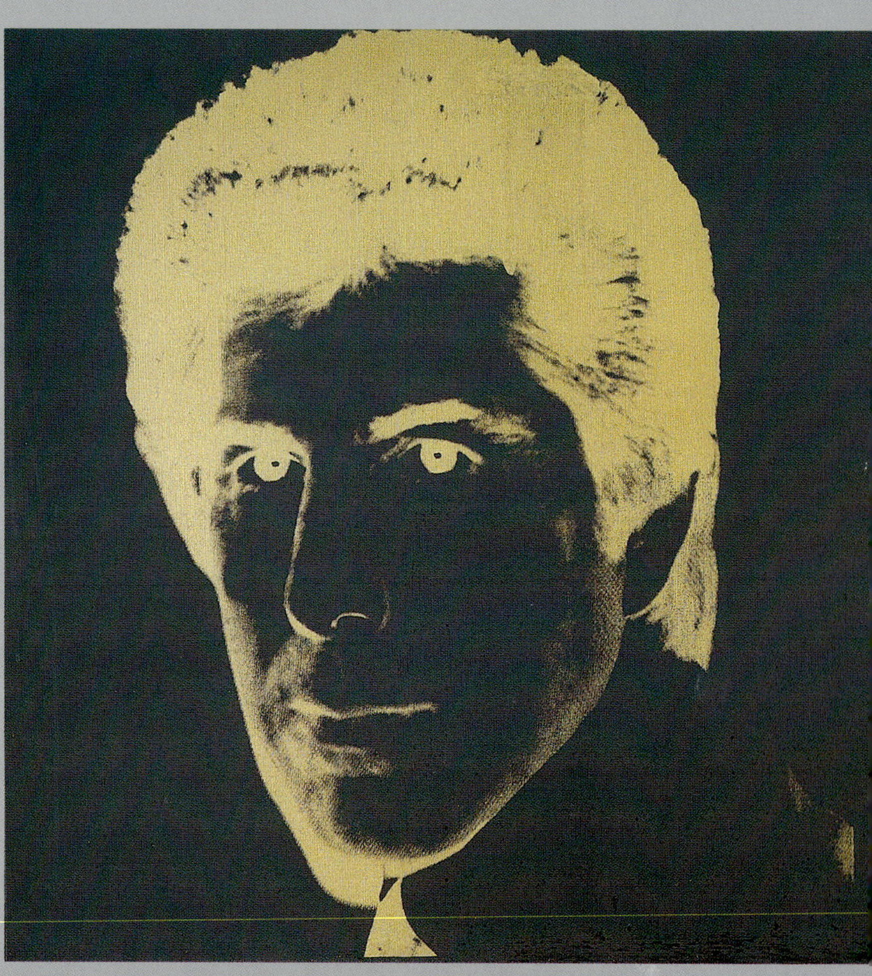

STEVE WYNN 1983
SYNTHETIC POLYMER PAINT AND SILKSCREEN INK ON CANVAS 101.6 x 101.6 CM EACH
COURTESY: THE ANDY WARHOL MUSEUM, PITTSBURGH
FOUNDING COLLECTION, CONTRIBUTION OF THE ANDY WARHOL FOUNDATION OF THE VISUAL ARTS, INC.

PHOTO: RICHARD STONER

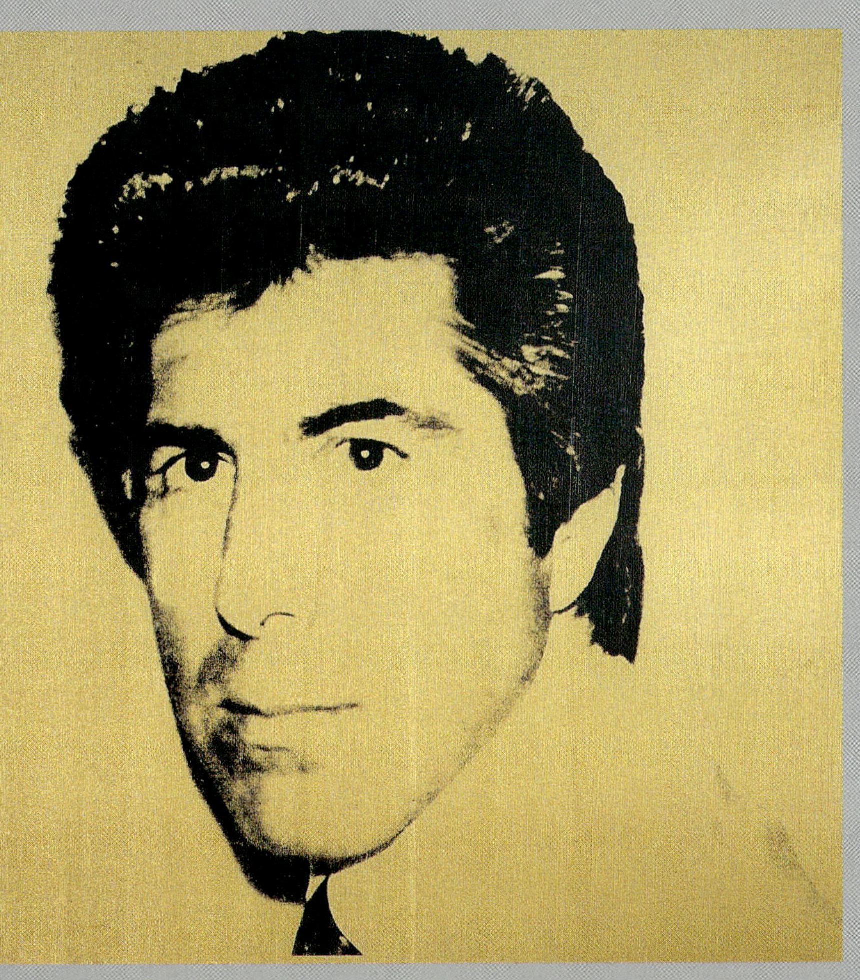

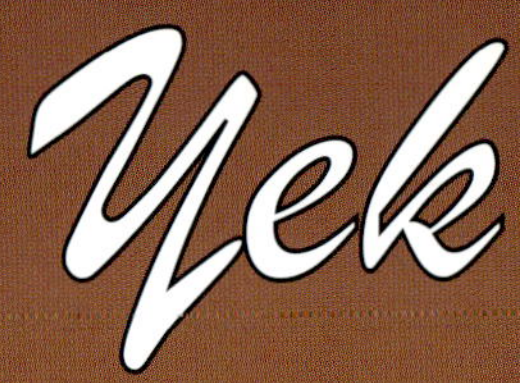

1968 Born in Singapure
1994 B.A. University of Texas at Austin, TX
1997 M.F.A. University of Nevada, Las Vegas, NV
Currently taking chances in Las Vegas, NV

2001
New Paintings, Feigen Contemporary, New York, NY
Smooth, Mark Moore Gallery, Santa Monica, CA
Glee: Painting Now, The Aldrich Museum of Contemporary Art, Ridgefield, CT; traveled to the Palm Beach Institute of Contemporary Art, Palm Beach, FL
Ultralounge: The Return of Social Space, University of South Florida Museum of Contemporary Art, Tampa, FL
1999
Bossa Supernova, Post Gallery, Los Angeles, CA

....In the right is a red pill. In the left, a blue pill ...... You take the blue pill and the story ends ...... You take the red pill and you stay in Wonderland.... (*The Matrix*, shooting script)

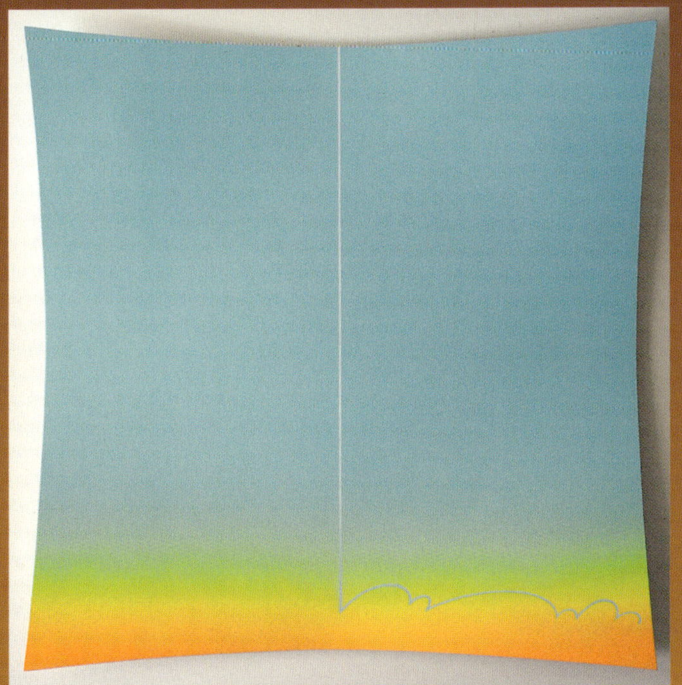

VERY SILLY RAPTURE 1999
ACRYLIC LATEX AND ENAMEL ON PANEL 106.6 x 106.6 x 10.1 CM
PRIVATE COLLECTION, CA

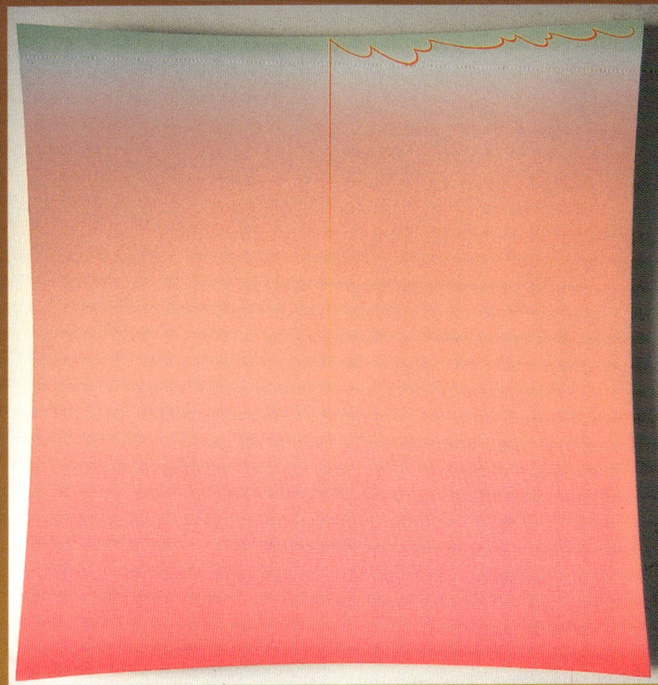

DEMON LOVE 1999
ACRYLIC AND LATEX ON PANEL 76.2 x 76.2 x 7.6 CM
COLLECTION DAVID REED

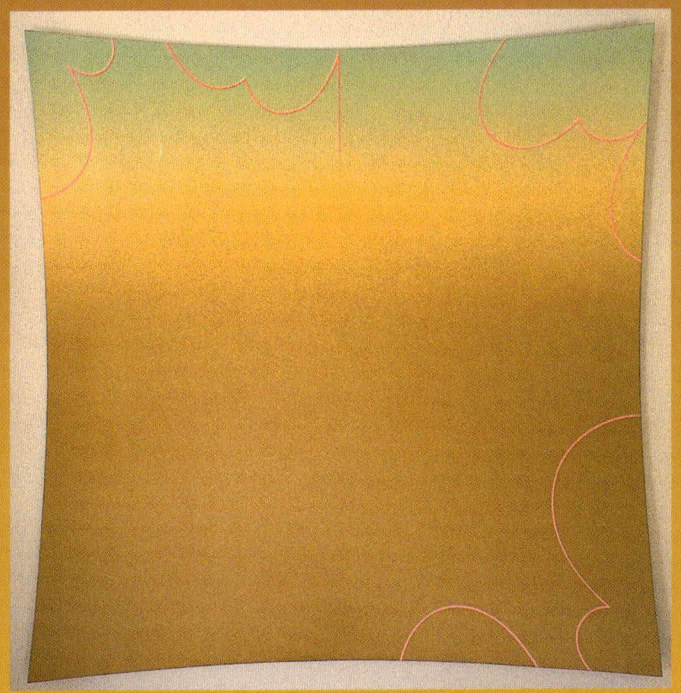

ALL COCONUTS 2000
ACRYLIC LATEX AND ENAMEL ON PANEL 111.7 x 111.7 x 10.1 CM
PRIVATE COLLECTION, TX

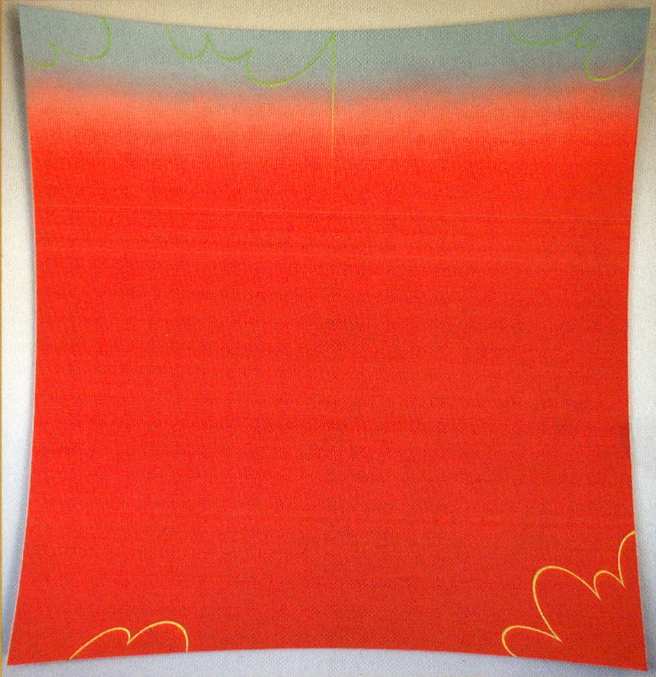

STILL BANANAS 2000
ACRYLIC LATEX AND ENAMEL ON PANEL 111.7 x 111.7 x 10.1 CM
COLLECTION OF CHRISTIAN VENABLE, TX

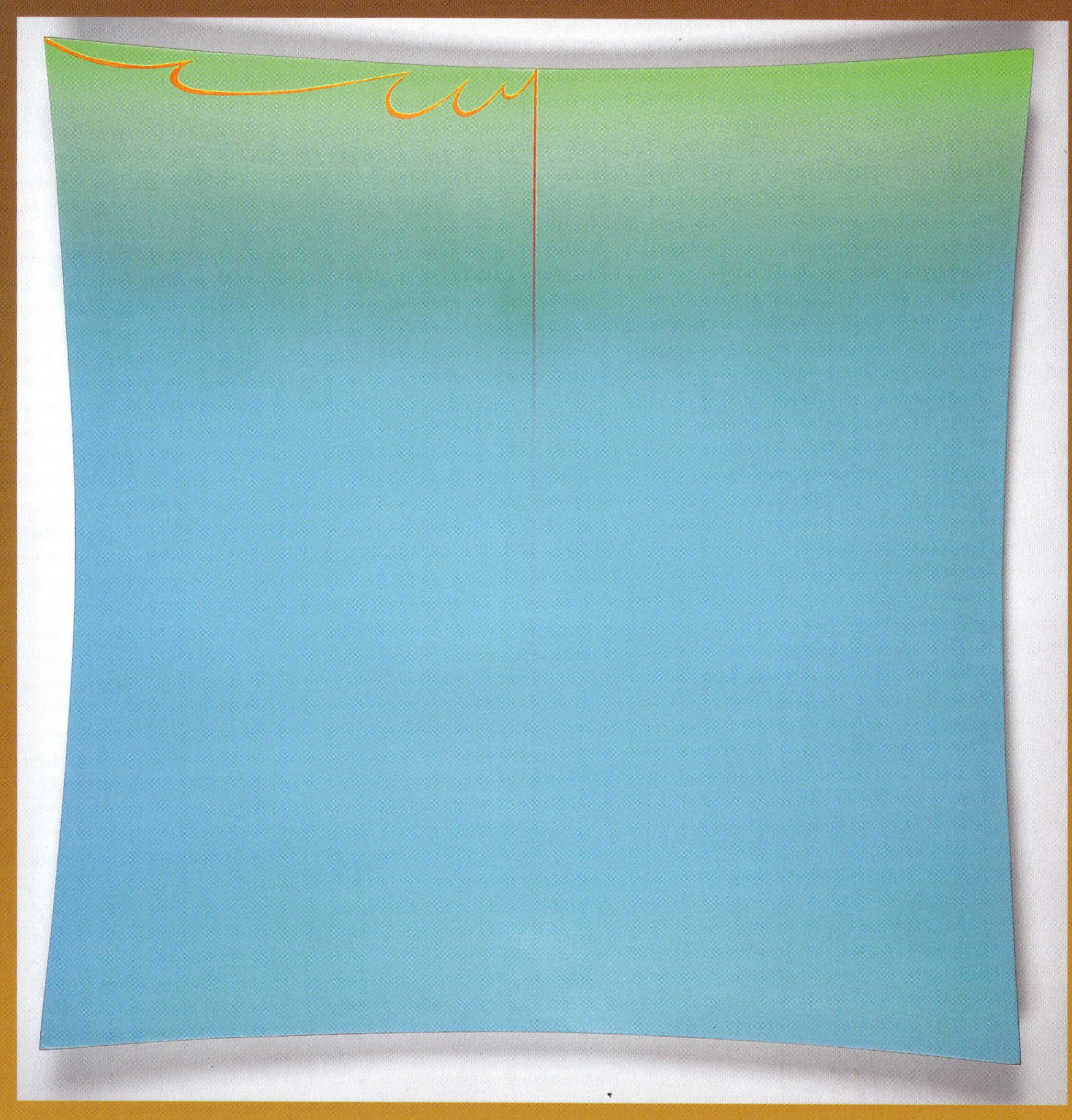

FREEFALLING FAREWELL 1999
ACRYLIC AND LATEX ON PANEL 76.2 x 76.2 x 7.6 CM
COLLECTION DAVID REED

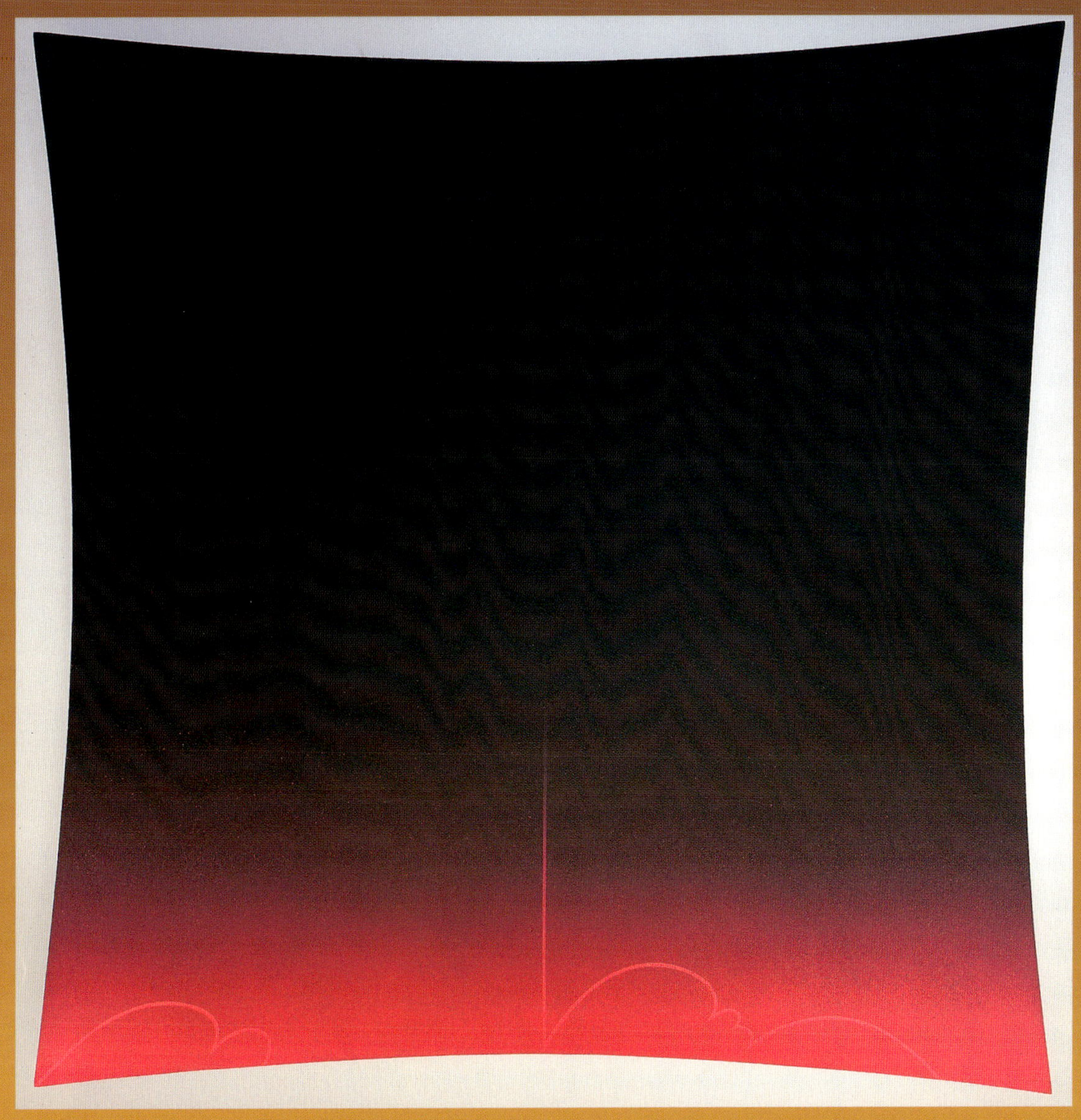

FOR VAMPIRE REASONS 2000
ACRYLIC LATEX AND ENAMEL ON PANEL 121.9 x 121.9 x 15.2 CM
COLLECTION DAVID REED

Timeline

Art and Las Vegas - A Recent Chronology & Bibliography

1990

Dave Hickey is appointed Professor of Art Criticism and Theory at the University of Nevada at Las Vegas

1993

'Viva Las Vegas: Afterhours Architecture' by Alan Hess. Chronicle Books

'The Magic Sign' by Charles Barnard. ST Publications

1994

'The World of Jeffrey Vallance [Collected Writings 1978 - 1994]'. Art Issues Press

'Real Gone', art by Jack Pierson, fiction by Jim Lewis. Artspace Books

'The Showgirl', curated by Mary Warner, at Temporary Contemporary Gallery, Las Vegas

1994-5

Karen Carson at UNLV as Artist-in-Residence & Instructor

1995

Jim Shaw at UNLV as Instructor

'Circus Americanus' by Ralph Rugoff. Verso. (features essays on Las Vegas and Liberace)

'Virtually Las Vegas', BBC2 (U.K.), featuring Steve Wynn, Robert Venturi & Denise Scott Brown, Joel Bergman, Mike Davis, Alan Hess and Ralph Rugoff

The Reverend Ethan Acres receives his Doctorate of Divinity via the Internet

'Liberace! A Visual Tribute to Mr. Showmanship', curated by Jeffrey Vallance, The Liberace Museum, Las Vegas

'The Debbie Reynolds Art Show!', curated by Jeffrey Vallance, Debbie Reynolds Casino-Museum, Las Vegas

'Clown Oasis: An exhibition of works by artists and clowns', curated by Jeffrey Vallance, Ron Lee's World of Clowns, Henderson (Las Vegas)

1995-8

Jeffrey Vallance at UNLV as Instructor

1996

The Neon Museum is inaugurated with the installation of the restored Hacienda horse and rider sign in Downtown Las Vegas.

'The Magic Show', curated by Jeffrey Vallance, Magic and Movie Hall of Fame, O'Sheas Casino, Las Vegas

'The Cranberry Show: An Exhibition of Good Taste', curated by Jeffrey Vallance, Ocean Spray's Cranberry Museum, Henderson (Las Vegas)

1997

'Report from Las Vegas: Art on the Strip' by Alisa Tager in Art in America (February)

'The Vegas Show', curated by Jeffrey Vallance, at Rosamund Felsen Gallery, Los Angeles

'Air Guitar: Essays in Art and Democracy' by Dave Hickey. Art Issues Press. (features essays on Las Vegas, Liberace and Siegfried & Roy)

1998

Steve Wynn opens his Gallery of Fine Art at the new Bellagio resort. Libby Lumpkin is the Gallery's Curator. The collection is believed to be worth some $300 million.

Jeffrey Vallance is dismissed from UNLV for inviting 'Cran-Cran, the Cranberry Girl' from Ocean Spray to model for his life drawing class.

1998-0

'Ultralounge: The Return of Social Space (with Cocktails)', curated by Dave Hickey, tours Housten, Las Vegas and Tampa Bay

1999

Rev. Ethan Acres is shown walking on water in front of the Bellagio on the cover of Art issues magazine (January / February). His sermon on Steve Wynn's Gallery of Fine Art features within.

'Deep Design: Nine Little Art Histories' by Libby Lumpkin. Art Issues Press (includes essays on 'Chance Art' and 'The Showgirl')

'Degas in Vegas' by Arthur C. Danto in The Nation (1st March)

Jim Isermann teaches at UNLV for a semester

2000

'Double or Quits' by Dave Hickey. frieze, issue 50

2001

Guggenheim Museum, designed by Rem Koolhaas, opens in October at the Venetian resort, with 'The Art of the Motorcycle' (exhibition architecture by Frank Gehry) and 'Masterpieces and Mastercollectors: Impressionist and Early Modern Paintings from the Hermitage and Guggenheim Museums'

'The Sermons of Reverend Ethan Acres'. Art Issues Press

Epilogue

Las Vegas
The City – A Place of Consumption in the Post-industrial Information Society

by Peter Weibel

The industrial revolution has generated cities of a size above all prognoses and expectations. Poverty, misery, hygienic deficits, dust and dirt have exploded. The science of Urbanism, invented around 1900, should find a way to give cities a human face again by planning. The classical conception of a city with which these urbanists started was the city as a place of production. In the wake of the industrial revolution the city was conceived as a sequence of phases conditioned by industrial labour. You start with an assembly line. Around the assembly line you build a factory. Around the factory you build the homes of the workers. Around the homes you build shops, restaurants and other services. We can perceive the publication of a large volume entitled 'Une Cité Industrielle' by Tony Garnier in 1907 precisely in that sense. This project is a significant milestone in modern town planning, as Le Corbusier said: "The first example of urban land defined as public space and organized to accommodate amenities for the common benefit of the inhabitants (...) integrating housing, work and contact between citizens." Another title for the project was indeed 'City of Labour.'

So it is very clear, that modern city planning had as its source the idea of labour and production, on the basis of the industrial revolution. Garnier therefore conceives only three main functions for a city: production, housing and health facilities. The tyranny of production turned housing and health into the service of production. Workers had to be healthy and therefore housed well to remain stable and reliable in the production process.

Even revisions of the modern city still designed a city as a set of functions, mainly adding new functions to the classical functions of the city. The famous lecture of 1928 by Cornelis van Eesteren therefore promoted 'The idea of the functional city' (republished in Rotterdam 1997). Habitation, work and traffic are still the dominant factors in the structure of a multifunctional city. But the once fully functioning centres of craft and trade gained an enchanting beauty, which could be used as an environment for recreation. Therefore van Eesteren added to the classical functions of the city, housing, work, and traffic, the new function of the post-industrial city: recreation. To Garnier's main functions, production, housing, and health, he added: consumption.

A post-modern critique realized that the city under the spell of production is not only deteriorating the urban environment but in fact is completely dependent on the environment outside the city. The energy, the food, the water, nearly everything comes from the non-urban environment. The industrial city is not self-dependent, does not sustain itself. Sustainability therefore becomes the central critical argument against the concept of the modern city as a place of production. The urban 'footstep theory' made us realize that the city leaves many footprints in the environment outside the city. An area from ten to twenty times bigger than the area of the city itself is needed to support the city, to make the city survive, to keep the production in the city going, to keep the operating of the city sustained. So it became evident, that a town focused on industry and production cannot survive. It not only destroys its non-urban environment outside the city, but in consequence also the city itself. Therefore the post-modern city moved the shopping area to the periphery of the city and the production and industrial zone even outside in front and far off the city. The centres of the city became vacant. The typical American city was the 'bagel city.'

But naturally the problem of sustainability was only partially solved by the post-modern non-industrial city. Responsibility for the supply of water, gas, electricity, canalisation, information wiring, food, medicine, traffic, sanitary facilities, schools, public services still has to be taken by society, by private or public institutions. Strict reduction of factories and other production sites was a first attempt to reduce the footprints in the environments and make the cities sustainable.

At the historic moment when material products of labour lost their pivotal role in the accumulation of capital in the post-industrial society, when immaterial labour, the acts of communication and services, investing in stocks and shares etc., could generate more profit than material labour, the city also changed from a centre of labour to a centre of immaterial labour such as services and communication. Consumption is part of this new kind of urban communication, just as shopping is part of consumption. As the architect Rem Koolhaas said: "Shopping has become the dominant mode of public activity," or as Mark Ravenhill said in his theatre play, "Shopping & Fucking" (1998) are the main activities in the post-industrial consumer city. A private and a public activity merge in the title, because this is exactly what the consumer city is all about: public space becomes private space. Koolhaas says: "We are witnessing the birth of the post-public, the private city." Manuel Castells has described in his book 'The Informational City' (1989) the rise of the 'dual city' in the wake of the rise of the dual economy. Dual economy means the parallel existence of an economy built on production and an economy built on information technology and the restructuring of capital-labour relationships.

Post-modern contemporary cities are no longer the places of the primary and secondary spheres of economy, that is, the spheres of production, but have become the places of the tertiary spheres of economy, that is, the spheres of communication, services, transactions. The post industrial city in the information age has become the knot in a web of universal transmissions and transactions, e.g. of goods, currencies, messages, information (all kinds of material and immaterial commodities, even cultural commodities). The first to realize this, were the 'Situationists.'[1] Consumption in the form of shopping and other leisure activities and institutions that provide a variety of leisure events have become a main part of the attraction cities today have for visitors. Therefore tourists have become more important for cities than inhabitants. The first city where you can study this phenomenon is Venice, Italy. A former place of craft and trade has become a city completely dependent on tourism. The next step in the urban evolution to a private city, a consumer city, depending completely on the non-urban environment outside of the city, is Las Vegas. Between Venice and Las Vegas are many analogies, but also differences. Venice is a model for Las Vegas as the first consumer city of the old world, as Las Vegas is the first consumer city of the new world. Therefore Las Vegas is architecturally imitating the most famous scenic views of Venice and one of the most famous hotels is called The Venetian Casino Resort Hotel. On the other hand Las Vegas was never a city of craft, production, and trade. It was conceived from the beginning as a place of consumption and recreation. From all the functions of a modern city, recreation and services became the only functions. And above all Las Vegas did not solve the real problem of the modern city; sustainability. In fact, Las Vegas is in that sense the worst modern city. The electricity is produced by coal like in 19th century. The water comes from the environment far away from the city. Therefore Las Vegas on the one hand is the post-modern city par excellence, built on consumption, shopping, fucking, gambling, recreation and leisure, but on the other hand, Las Vegas is the cruellest modern city, completely depending on outside resources.[2] The modern city of production damaged the environment according to the 'footstep theory;' therefore the production units have been dislocated to the periphery of the city to avoid the confrontation with the clouds of pollution. Therefore the cities, emptied of production, turned to cities of consumption, attracting tourists and consumers. It is only consistent, that the post-modern city learned from Las Vegas, since Las Vegas with 30 to 40 million tourists a year is the post-modern city par excellence. Tourists are more cherished than the inhabitants by city planning which is symptomatic for post-modern city planning, which, as I said, is built on consumption instead of production. Everyday millions of information which control the supply of food and news, of the contents of cultural, administrative, productive and consumptive institutions are transacted by the post-modern city in the arising net society in such a complex vertical structure that it can only be maintained with the help of computers. The exchange of information, of services has become the new value, no longer the exchange of products. The exchange of products still exists, but it no longer has the classical function to maximize profit. Profit maximization can be done today much better in the tertiary sphere of economy. The triumph of the New Economy over the old economy is built on this thesis. Cities of consumption have a new way to regulate the contact between citizens. This way is no longer built on labour but on services. This change has also transformed the relation between private and public sphere. Cities of consumption are the final triumph of urbanism and communication built on principles of economy, money and profit. Cultural goods are also subjugated to these laws of economy. Cultural institutions are not measured by the quality of their labour, but by the quantity of their visitors and their profiles for tourist attractions. Cultural institutions under the power of economy turn into institutions of consumption. Event culture, branding, target marketing are not only parts of urban planning but also of cultural institutions. The new cities of the new economy are not only temples of consumption, not only paradises of ecstatic shopping of cultural or material goods, of cultural or commercial enjoyment, e.g. the multiplex cinemas which provide you with food, films, and clothing, they are above all new masks of the market, which make invisible the mechanism of capital. To tear off the urban masks of capital we no longer can rely on culture, because culture has become part of the mask as a privileged way of consumption. Cities of consumption need a constant accumulation of attraction. Institutions, which can guarantee events and spectacles on a high level, like cultural institutions of global branding, become more and more attractive for consumer cities. On the other hand, cultural institutions, which want to attract tourists, are looking for the proximity to cities of consumption. There is a new alliance on the way between institutions of consumption, formerly known as cultural institutions, and cities of consumption, formerly known as places of production.[3] Therefore it follows the logic of the urban evolution in the post-industrial information society that the Guggenheim Museum is opening a new exhibition space precisely in the phantom heart of Las Vegas: the Venetian Casino Resort Hotel.

Las Vegas is the city of the future, because it is the foremost city built completely on recreational, cultural and other services.[4] Las Vegas functions as a city because it reduces the multi-functional modern city to one function: consumption.[5] On the other hand, Las Vegas is the city with no future. Las Vegas is, besides Venice, the foremost city of the world living from tourism, but at the same time, even emptied from production, it is still not sustainable, but just the opposite, polluting a huge environment. Las Vegas is living on an environmental politics of dispossession. It is bound by the chains of the classical industrial city: energy supply. Las Vegas is dependent on the energy and the goods supplied by others. The energy and electricity crisis in California in 2001 is already a symptom of what can happen to Las Vegas. Las Vegas has only a future when its lights and lasers seen from far away eclipse.

1. In their book, 'The Naked City' (1957), Guy Debord and Asger Jorn critisized the modern city à la Corbusier, see Simon Sadler, 'The Situationist City' (Cambridge/Mass.: MIT Press, 1998).
2. Mike Davis, 'The Strip Versus Nature', in Ramesh Kumar Biswas (Ed.), 'Metropolis Now. Urban Cultures in Global Cities' (Vienna: Springer, 2000), pp. 101-110.
3. see Arthur C. Danto, 'Degas in Vegas', in: The Nation, March 1, 1999, pp. 25-28.
4. Jörg Häntzschel, 'Das Paradies in der Wüste – Las Vegas', in Regina Bittner (Ed.), 'Urbane Paradiese. Zur Kulturgeschichte modernen Vergnügens' (Frankfurt/Main: Campus, 2001), pp. 297-302.
5. Las Vegas can claim to have developed a deep structure transformation of consumption, which the managers of Las Vegas call 'junking it up,' as the author Norman Klein has told me in a conversation. 'Junking it up' means that the managers and architects of Las Vegas by intention make mistakes in the buildings to give the consumer the feeling that he is inhabiting an imperfect environment, which allows him to deduce that not only the architecture is occasionally junked, but that the whole Las Vegas gambling system is junked and that therefore he, the gambler, has a chance to be more perfect than the system and that therefore he can beat the system. The dominant exploitative class gives the subordinated exploited class the illusion to be able to be superior by voluntary and intentional deterioration, errors, mistakes, by 'junking it up.' The 'junkie' gets the illusion to be not dependent and governed and ruled by consumption: This is the deep structure strategy of neoliberal consumerism.

Vegaesthetics

by Norman M. Klein

Eras come and go briskly in Las Vegas, like slot machines, or a new ventilation system. That is very difficult for art specialists to grasp. What's worse, this chronic virus is spreading; and mutating. Indeed, in studying Vegas, or any place that operates by its rules, watch out what you wish for. Someone will build it; then tear it down.

For example, we start with an obvious case in point, the Vegas Guggenheims. Then we watch the image of the Guggenheims dissolve – or should I say implode? A quick explanation on imploding: This has a long tradition in Nevada. Old mining towers are regularly imploded, even today, in remote, underpopulated areas. The small town gathers, with guests, as if it were watching a dog chase its tail, then exploding. But the blowout rarely takes more than ten seconds. Don't blink. During the most famous implosion in recent years – at the Dunes in 1993 – the dust literally dropped like a mushroom cloud turned upside down, leaving "a pile of twisted metal and concrete debris."[1] But most of all, removing the Dunes "cleared the way for a new resort."[2] 'Clearing the way' must be understood almost in Hegelian terms, but at hyper speed. The Bellagio – and its era, the 1990s – stand on the Dunes site today. However, Vegas casinos, like the eras that generate them, are designed with a brief shelf life. They carry an expiration date of twenty, or at most forty years. Hegel would have had a stroke just keeping track. I see him staring at his cards, then hyperventilating face first into a blackjack table.

My research indicates that the 1990s Vegas, the eighth or ninth wonder of the world, is already over. What's more, the next decade is already master planned, but under wraps. The best we can do is investigate for symptoms. But there are few signals that we can bank on – one in particular: however sudden, these changes are caused, fundamentally, by Vegas paranoia. This paranoia breeds secrecy, to keep the fright from the paying public. Then, like a cabal, the insiders wait, for a launch date. The wait reminds me of frogs hiding behind a leaf, waiting for a fly at the pond. Vegas is open to the public because it is fiercely secretive.

So I will have to color this essay with a sense of quick-change paranoia, because at the moment, September, 2001, Las Vegas is between fantasias. That amounts to quick-change as theory. It is practically the only way to be honest about what this moment means culturally. But first things first: This essay is part of a museum show about artists responding to Vegas. We should visit a museum first, then stop at the buffet:

Two more Guggenheim franchises, both designed by Rem Koolhaas, are about to open on the grounds of the Venetian Hotel, or "play the Strip."[3] There is something neo-feudal about them, despite all the steel and industrial reference; like cabinets of curiosities for an imaginary Doge. In Las Vegas, they are called 'the Googs,' or "anti-casinos ... practically anti-architecture, at least as that term is understood on the Strip in its Late Megaresort Age."[4] Some architecture critics call it "a courageous act."[5] Others consider it a 'blot' on the Strip. And still others say it brings glory to the four miles of monorail that are in construction, like the city of circulation that Vegas has always claimed to be, on a Strip that was always a road out of town.

The balloon of excitement has already abated by the Fall of 2001; it was even fiercer in January, after the scope of Guggenheim director, Thomas Krens' plans was made public:[6] a three-way collaboration with the Kunsthistorische Museum in Vienna and the financially stricken Hermitage in Saint Petersburg. "McGuggenheim" wrote Mark Honigsbaum, for The Guardian in London, concluding with a quote from Newsweek, that perhaps Krens' "aggressive, global approach may be what high culture needs to survive in our world."[7]

But the response within Las Vegas itself is even more telling. To them, all these monuments are mostly about politics. Unlike critics from outside, they do not treat these casinos as acts of God, cut off from their local problems. If we want to understand how global entertainment actually does its business, we should learn from their native shrewdness, that comes from watching up close for decades. For example, a Vegas columnist grudgingly agrees that the museums are a courageous act; but then asks:[8] "Is it a lasting one? This city, after all, has smoothly incorporated a black-glass pyramid, a Disney-esque castle, a fake skyline and pip-squeak Eiffel Tower into one all-inclusive Vegaesthetic. Can the Googs maintain their autonomy in such a co-optive atmosphere, or will they eventually become just another megaresort come-on?"

Similarly, Chuck Twardy for Las Vegas Life reluctantly praises the Goog-Hermitage as a "Cor-Ten steel box grafted onto the Venetian facade." He even agrees that to arts insiders, it may be the "Jewel Box." However, to visitors, it more likely resembles "a misplaced shipping container from the Venetian harbor."[9]

We've all complained about museum spectacle going too far. In lectures, I promise that one day, next to every Starbucks and Barnes and Noble, there will be a Guggenheim Lite, with one painting. On the other hand, I am equally suspicious of the Neo-Victorian worship of the sublime, of high culture defending itself. Better to let the art world tumble even more, but honestly, fiercely. Perhaps, in some Darwinian way, new forms of art installation and curating will emerge. Perhaps something less fussy, less about blockbusters for the sublime – more engaged.

So I leave the global debate over guggification, even over disneyfication; and try to narrow in on what those local Vegas critics are seeing, on what drives the machine of entertainment. As of August 11, 2001, Nevada gambling had 'eked out' only a 2.2% increase in 2001.[10] There are no new megaresorts opening. Growth next year at the Strip will linger at one to four per cent, below the average 6.6%. Revenues from visitors outside Nevada slowed markedly. And while Reno shows signs of expansion, North Las Vegas, Boulder Strip and South Tahoe markets show double-digit declines.

Signs of slowing are everywhere. As of June, the Southern Nevada Index of Leading Indicators had languished at around 128 for over a year.[11] Recession worries have begun. The building boom of the 1990s has not yet been assimilated. The weakening economy in California is also worrying, since more than half of the gaming profits come from California visitors. While casino profits rise occasionally, as in May, 2001, that implies slowdown as well: slot machine wagering has gone flat, "reflecting economic uncertainty that has plagued the country."[12] Most striking, the top four 'table' games – not slots – were up, baccarat most of all, 26.5%. That means that high rollers are accounting for too much of the increase, a bad signal, because the slot players fill the hotels. They are the bread and butter, the "middle market;"[13] though a drop in high roller profits from Asia helped to bring down Steve Wynn, made him vulnerable to the takeover by MGM in 2000, marking the end of an era.

In short, paranoia is fueling Las Vegas planning. Ironically, the decline is not even a decline, not by European or American standards surely. But in Las Vegas, the patient always keeps one hand on his pulse. In the first quarter, Harrah's Entertainment reported a 15% jump in earnings; but in the same article, worries about the California energy crisis dominate. "Our prognosis for Nevada is (electricity) costs are only going to go higher."[14] Even more troubling, in 1999, California Governor Gray Davis negotiated with 61 California Indian tribes. Thirty-eight of them already run casinos. For these, he approved up to 2,000 new slot machines, to replace the old fashioned 'Nevada-style' slots.[15] In the long run, there may be as many as 200,000 slot machines in California. Professor William Eadington, the doyen of gambling research in Nevada, estimated that by 2010, California gaming may generate more revenue than Las Vegas,[16] in only nine short years – a short fuse indeed, along with concerns about Internet gambling;[17] and flagging investments for casinos around the world, now that the global economy looks sour.

The 'shakeout' in tribal gaming, promised in 1996, has not materialized.[18] Instead, like the downturn in e-commerce, and the anxiety over Bush policies in Europe, there is an unease, an undertow in 2001. Blind faith in Internet businesses and casinos – as recent as 1996 – has evaporated. The paranoia is on, a unique phenomenon in Las Vegas, but an indicator of global problems to come – or should I say, adjustments? In the end, the global process reinvents itself, but with the same power players.

Meanwhile, the bill for immense population growth throughout greater Las Vegas – 85% growth in the past ten years –[19] has come due. Pollution, traffic (particularly the I-15),[20] massive in-migration and foreign immigration have added vastly to the costs of infra-structure, in a city famous for cheap maintenance, in a state without an income tax. How will Vegas adjust, now that it has a world-class, if overcrowded airport, now that Zagut has declared it eighth best in the world for dining,[21] just behind the New York area, ahead of Los Angeles, ahead of much of the world – and expensive. The promise of class acts and world-class prices, gambling for sophisticated adults, has paid off; but left a bill. America West Airlines now waives its stopover fee for flights over Las Vegas, bringing even more crowding. The convention trade in Las Vegas has passed Chicago's, was voted the top US convention city by Tradeshow Magazine in 1999, "though industry experts warn that convention business may decline in 2001, after several years of growth."[22] There are more Vegas hotel rooms than any American city, perhaps than any city in the world. But that means the boom has saturated for the moment. Or has it?

That brings me to the primary lesson that a localized view of Vegas reveals. Seen up close, Vegas paranoia works like a barometer. It regulates the business climate, but in turn, gradually but inevitably, strangles culture. The process is painfully simple: Entertainment businesses specialize in turning wasted space into profit. That can prove maddening. Once a new gimmick fills in what used to be wasted space, then the worry really begins. Public taste wears out faster than crops or machines. The gimmick's appeal often fades in a hurry. But now this space has been noticed. It can never be wasted again. Like a truck, it will never ride empty. It belongs to the larger profit picture, to the brand. It must harvest at 100%. And unlike other businesses (oil, mining, farming, automobiles) there is no easy way to back off. You cannot say: let it go fallow; or the lode has run dry. This space belongs to the stockholders now; it must pay off on schedule – period. The pressure is infernal. Guessing at shelf lives can give you a heart attack.

But never let the paying public know. Never drop your guard when they're watching. The smile is essential to the sell. Eroticize with as much banality, and campy shrewdness as possible, as much cuteness and evasion as the market can bear (bare?). Eroticize the ordinary.

This corrosive syndrome has destroyed cable news (especially CNN) in the US, has turned European tourism into a case of malaria, has driven museums into shopping mall hysterias, has dissolved American publishing into mad searches for anything profitable but literature, has dissolved Hollywood cinema into special-effects, immersive, perpetualized adolescence. Indeed, as Hegel noted while playing blackjack, the dialectic is definitely gone, except as paranoia.

That is the Vegas 'virus' that I mentioned in the opening of this essay. It should be seen as more than simply an evil plot. It is a form of mutation that speeds up time, collapses eras into seasons, and continually silts up the harbor, mixing garbage and fine art indiscriminately, into mounds that, in time, turn into a comic-book version of the Baroque.

An Hyperbole for Global Culture: If an imaginary Hollywood is the stabilizing myth for global culture, then the imaginary Las Vegas is its hyperbole. Both have had a curious run since 1989. I often write about the last twelve years as three separate eras: 1989-93; 1993 to 2000; and now whistling into the next – as yet unknown, but clearly much more unsettling, uneasy, not quite the victory of heroic capitalism. Both Los Angeles and Las Vegas serve as perverse chronometers for these eras, along with the rise and fall of e-commerce. They give us the story line, and the evasions. Trillions of dollars changed hands. But much of this went unnoticed: Thousands of cultural destinations undone and remade, barely noted: museums; theme parks; cities old and new; shopping malls; casinos; the Internet; computer games; palm pilots, and more. When I rummage through my dozens of boxes on cultural history since 1989 – the clippings, the interviews, the headline stories – only Hollywood and Las Vegas were consistently covered, and recovered. There was certainly a flourish about Bilbao, about the new Berlin, and other sites; but they passed out of view quickly. Mostly, my hundreds of documents point toward a vast whitewash, hiding events, keeping the vast shifts in class and power away from the public.

I sift through my Vegas Boxes. Indeed Vegas was the poster child for this new power structure, for the upscaling of global entertainment, like burlesque turning into opera. After 1993, the institutions that justified the new power arrangements were put into place, the skyline on the Strip most of all, along with the vast petting zoo for postmodern, global architecture at the Potsdamer Platz. Somehow, the same process looks awkward in Berlin, an awkward fit elsewhere as well; it Disneyfies great cities of the world. But in Las Vegas, the very same impulse brought masterpieces after 1989. Imagine a snake putting its fangs into Las Vegas; and the snake dies. Somehow Vegas seems immune to globalization. It is a bottomfeeder, one of those fish that like toxic swamp land. And this immunity continues to fascinate the entire world. The hyperbolic, implosive quick change works for the Strip, and seemingly nowhere else quite as well (except perhaps Los Angeles, but not at all the same way). As historian Hal Rothman explained, "Las Vegas is quicksilver. It never freezes."

Rothman also hinted that a new implosive stage was coming, scheduled in eighteen months, some time in 2002. Apparently the casino industry has secret plans to 'revolutionize' visitor experience. As always, the Vegas bomb is being kept under wraps. My guess is that this too will work like a chronometer to match what goes around in global culture. It will reflect, as hyperbole, the next wave of media mergers (AOL/Warner; HP/Compac, etc.) that promise to narrow cultural options even further. Thus, casino planning will marry even closer to globalized entertainment investors, and with e-commerce. Presumably, this 'revolution' will cure the next wave of paranoia.

I love this Vegas nightmare, not the casinos or the buffets, or the pretensions for Zagut greatness. Not even the gambling spirit, or the shows. If anything, the immigrants buried inside Vegas interest me more, like time travelers in a place where time has imploded. I love the literary challenge of Las Vegas. Anything I write today may be old before the ink dries. How do you capture the unease, the blind and deaf lies, the velocity of something that never touches ground? This is Vegaesthetics – ludicrous, hyper-caffeinated, an endless whitewash running on sheer paranoia. It is the hyberbolic aesthetics of the Electronic Baroque – a pan-colonialism, the next ruthless step beyond post-colonial, particularly for Las Vegas.

The Paranoid Brand – I often write that 'global' LA does not exist in southern California, but instead as an imaginary – a brand that is both placeless, transnational, a mix of European fantasies as much as American ones. The Los Angeles that many Europeans 'imagine' does not match its street realities very much at all (almost never) – nor do Hollywood films, the TV coverage of the 1992 uprising, or MTV. Nor do noir films circa 1955, any more than neo-noir today. None of that actually exists. No one I know lives in noir LA.

In a parallel sense, Las Vegas is also a noir imaginary we remember from films, with the opening to Scorcese's 'Casino' a possible exception. But mostly, its criminal myths came in another way – as revenge. Vegas is quite different from the LA brand, infinitely more tied to its local economy than Hollywood, certainly not placeless. Traditionally, that brand is linked to gangsters. However, since the early 1970s, Vegas was no longer a fiefdom for organized crime, or for the Teamster pension fund. And after 1989, it became now the hub of sprawling Clark County, population 1.2 million. At the same time, it is the engine for a state founded by Mormons, colonized by mining companies and LA tourism, with arguably the strongest union movement in the United States.

There lies our clues to 'Vegas noir.' Nevada is part of the Rocky Mountain West. Thus, it was colonized by railroad and mining interests, pillaged by water pirates, forced to absorb the largest nuclear waste dumps in the United States (Yucca Mountain, where uranium waste has to be transmuted into gold).[23] Out-of-towners have sucked it dry for a hundred years. In the 1950s, gamblers on the Strip could watch atomic testing, the flares. The memory of being the vampire's host still affects the local politics; beneath all the boosterism, there is a kind of self-loathing, almost a postcolonial rage, and a paranoic disregard for the environment. That is Vegas noir: imagine investors (gangsters, mining companies, transnational leviathans) loading money on trucks, and sending it out of state. That colonial memory helps explain the fierce over-reactions to anything that looks like a downturn from outside – in California most of all – or to tribal casinos from California crowding out the Strip. Even the Strip itself was out of downtown, away from city taxes and rules. Vegaesthetics is ruthlessly defensive capitalism, but with a smile.

Laboratory Vegas: Thus, implosive time warps aside, Las Vegas is weirdly stable. It is laboratory for new globalized gimmicks, ways to theme and milk the consumer. They have literally, at last, turned the con into an art, and an architecture, and a microprocessed fantasy – in the slots; the 'convergence' of gambling across a dozen markets.[24] The laboratory is covered like a greenhouse effect. In 1999, the mayoral election evoked more excitement in the world press than in Vegas itself.[25] With all the 1990s glitz, Vegas now sells its brand as never before. The town council sued 'Visa Las Vegas,' and like Disney, guards its brand ferociously, what one councilman called "the oomph of the name."[26] In 1996, a hint of more to come, Bally Gaming International merged even more completely with European investors (Alliance), to expand on slot design for uses throughout the world; while running casinos in Vegas, Atlantic City, Mississippi, Louisiana.[27] The Vegas-based consulting firm, Structured Communication (Strucom.com), "with offices, affiliates and partners throughout the world," especially Europe, specializes in training businesses to go global. There is a flock of such companies in Las Vegas. Somehow, when it comes to converging markets, with an aesthetic upscale touch, Vegas is the source. I find it strange indeed. Over the past twelve years, I have been obsessed with finding the grammar of the Electronic Baroque, this vaporous transnational civilization. I have invented various terms to help me interview designers, architects, artists, filmmakers, media experts. I find they fit Vegas almost perfectly; and help map the various epochs that have shaped the Strip:

(1) Scripted Spaces

Imagine walking through a sequence of rooms or alleys. The space between has been scripted for you. By that I mean a street or interior where the spectator imagines herself as a central character in an imaginary story. Baroque churches were scripted spaces, as was Coney Island. Paris has been scripted many times from the eleventh century forward. Presumably the walker experiences free will, though often that is an illusion. Scripted spaces imply a cybernetic freedom – freedom to choose. But that is often an illusion; and the spectator knows it. Nevertheless, you are willing to bow to the authority of the feedback program.

The Fifties: Beginning in 1955, the number of scripted spaces in the developed consumer world has multiplied geometrically. This spawning process began essentially in Southern California and Las Vegas. Disneyland opened on the Fourth of July in 1955, while from April onward, five casinos opened that year on the Vegas Strip.

You might call Disneyland and Vegas the Janus twins. Both converted suburbs into resort destinations. Anaheim had been cheap orchard land before Disney's team installed the great berm there. So too the Strip was undeveloped suburb just outside city limits, a neck of desert on the way to the tiny McCarran Airport. Since 1941, a few casinos had been stuck out on the Strip, mostly to avoid city taxes and city police.

Both tried to lure Angelinos by car. Disneyland linked to the new freeway coming from Los Angeles. The Strip literally ran on Highway 91, a two-lane road from LA. Like many investors across the US, they were trying to capitalize on the federal Interstate Highway plan of 1953. In ten years, billions of government dollars brought a 20,000 mile grid of interlocking freeways from one coast to the other. LA became the hub on the Pacific. Both Disney and casino owners hoped that caravans from Southern California could now drive hundreds of miles for a day's pleasure.

Both projects turned into huge suburban job zones. Both 'Los Angelized' the surrounding metropolitan areas.[28] Of course, newly minted suburbs were transforming rural towns across the country that year, particularly in the San Fernando Valley of Los Angeles. But there were dozens of symbiotic forces at work – nationally and internationally – in 1955. The sum of these started the race for capital that led to the globalized economy by 2000. For example, the television industry came of age by 1955, shifting toward film stock, moving offices from New York to LA, finding European links; as did the airline industry, the credit card industry, the Holiday Inn chain, McDonalds, the dealer system for art in New York; and dozens of new ad agencies only a taxi ride away.

Viennese emigré Victor Gruen designed the first enclosed shopping mall in Minneapolis in 1956. Throughout the country, at the crossing of freeways, thousands of new shopping centers were added within a few years. This was indeed the first stage toward globalization – the consumer expansion around the automobile. By 1980, the era of consumer 'autopia' ends, but by then, it had linked across five continents; and was in the process of globalizing production itself.

By 1955, the Korean War had ended, but the hunger to keep the American economy pumped-up continued. Thus like an athlete on steroids, the US had to remain on constant war alert for another fifty years. With what even Eisenhower called – with grave concern – "the military-industrial complex" came massive investments in miniaturizing energy for missiles, for space flights; and to miniaturize computers, radios; and design advanced telematic hookups by satellite. All of these, ironically enough, fed the globalizing consumer investments, from the US to the newly energized western Europe, to Japan on the edge of Vietnamese overflow of capital. Even the rudiments of the Internet came out of American defense spending (ARPANET, 1965). Indeed the Cold War turned out to be a laboratory for electronic civilization, on behalf of NATO in particular.

The Sixties: In stages, particularly after the Cuban Missile Crisis of 1962, the NATO alliance supported a rapidly growing cultural investment pool. At the center of this flood more than a pool was Global English – 900 words for TV, petrodollars, MTV, computers, NATO, even diplomacy at the EU. This business dialect spoke for the electronic consumer. Year by year, the percentage of overall profit from Global English movies shrank in the US, as it grew in Europe and Asia. Increasingly, investments for these products came from three continents. And for a time, it seemed that Mid-East oil and Japanese export power could rival the NATO entertainment juggernaut. And by the 1980s, a global cultural transformation was essentially in place from Western Europe all the way to Japan. It would shift many times, but mostly, all that was needed next was the Fall of Communism, to open the flood gates of global investment. The military-industrial capital would diminish while the entertainment capital would grow, until at last, all forms of heavy industry shared the same software as the movies, ad agencies, mall architects.

1989: After the Wall came down, electronic consumer culture became the global brand for triumphal capitalism, with Los Angeles and Las Vegas as mythic headquarters – or rather the entire West Coast of the United States. But capital here comes from Europe almost as much as from the US. It is NATO-fied entertainment. German companies funnel hundreds of millions for film-making in Southern California. French investors plan to buy Universal Studios – from Canadians, who bought it from the Japanese. It is mercantilism in web time.

That corrosive speed, with barely any legal oversight, has brought on warlord capitalism, hordes without borders. A data flux has dissolved many institutional controls within the nation state. Data rejects nationality. It erases boundaries blindly, what I call Electronic Feudalism, leading to grim localized wars, narco-capitalism, globalized immigration; transnational eco-blocs; the LA uprising in 1992; Russian cities abandoned to mafiosi. But this erosion with a cybernetic smile has its preferred 'look,' what I call the Electronic Baroque. Since 1989 in particular, 'it' has installed 'its' brands across the world: narratized themed architecture. With the Electronic Baroque, cities, movies, museums and Web sites begin to look like each other. As a result, entertainment has been homogenized as never before. Cultural censorship is more complete than at any time since the Counter Reformation. In fact, I suspect that Ignatius Loyola would have dedicated a hundred Jesuit colleges to the Electronic Baroque. He would have been inordinately impressed. (I shudder to imagine what Hitler would have accomplished with computers.)

The signature of the Electronic Baroque is special effects added to scripted spaces. And since 1989 in particular, this has begun to escape from malls and theme parks, and enter the cityscapes of European cities themselves – the Baroque source finding its source. To accommodate globalized tourism, European town centers have been rehabbed for a catholicity unknown since the pilgrimages of the middle ages; or since the European world's fairs from 1851 to 1900. But nowhere have these experiments in the Electronic Baroque been fiercer than in Las Vegas and Southern California. These two cities become our laboratory (not much of a compliment, more like the victims of a plague that people want to catch).

From 1989 to 1993, it does indeed look like a plague. Corporate downsizing seems to be spreading to entire countries and cities as well. Southern California goes through its worst downturn since the 1930s. One biblical affliction follows another: real estate depression; colossal scandals in policing and public education; the largest urban disturbance in the United States in the 20th century; the most expensive earthquake in American history; the worst fires in half a century; more whites leaving than arriving for the first time in its history.

By contrast, Las Vegas had been preparing since the late 1980s, after another overbuilding and fiscal crisis hit. By 1988, planners in the gaming industry knew that over forty American states were about to legalize gambling. There was no time to lose. A new resort image had to be put in place. But Vegas had been in a financial slump. However, in 1989, just as the Wall went down, that started to turn around. Entrepreneur Steve Wynn opened the Mirage Hotel, costing nearly $650 million – including a working volcano ($30 million); and the gaudiest, most upscale interior yet seen in Las Vegas; until the Bellagio and its Kulturkampf with the Venetian. Wynn's Mirage became the flagship for the Baroque on the Strip. It inspired a flourish of new 'pedestrian friendly' venues in 1992-94 – Caesars Forum, the new MGM Grand, Luxor, Treasure Island, New York/New York. Tens of millions of new tourists were added. By 1997, 52% of all Vegas revenues came from the resorts themselves, rather than gambling.

In 1998, I told Jon Jerde, the architect of Wynn's even grander Bellagio Hotel, that he was a master of the Electronic Baroque. Then Jerde told Wynn, who officially announced to the New York Times that indeed, the new Vegas was Baroque; and that Jerde was its Bernini (Jerde preferred to think of himself as its Borromini).[29] Thus, the newspaper of record officially declared the Baroque era underway.

But that era is already ending in Vegas, even while the recovery in LA – since 1995 – slows down. That means less revenue outsourced from media, e-commerce, or booms like those on west-side LA. The stage after 2000 will involve global corporations swallowing each other, after removing the nickel e-business, and the free-for-all after 1989 – the triumphalism. Now the triumph of mega-mergers outpaces all others. The scale of entertainment has finally – and institutionally – gone imperially global, even in Las Vegas.

In the Spring of 2000, Steve Wynn agreed to sell all his casino interests to the MGM Group (even much of his 'fabled' art collection). The last of the Medici-style freewheelers would no longer dominate what comes next. And like a chronometer, this coincided with the slide in the Silicon Valley as well. The freewheeling is being replaced by freebooting. We have left the 'anarchy' of the early Internet era, and entered a Baroque imperium: the hardening of forms, with an implosion of culture that must be resisted. The land rush after 1989 has run its course, even in Berlin. A culture build around hierarchy as media more than mass ('democratic?') media is upon us.

The industrialization of desire that began in 1955-56 has matured at last. To repeat: the primitive accumulation of entertainment capital took nearly fifty years. It finally reached an institutional takeoff after 1993. And now will pan-colonize on a scale that rivals the Roman Empire – but without an emperor, perhaps even without a Rome. For the first time, the consumerized version of Baroque space will simply invade all public street life. It certainly has in Los Angeles, with the growth of outdoor themed shopping spaces like the Third Street Promenade, Citywalk, Old Pasadena, Media-City Burbank. And in Las Vegas as well, with the lowest ratio of public parks and space per capita of any major city in the US.

On the Strip, many sidewalks adjoining casinos are sold to business. There is essentially no public life in the old industrial urban sense, though amenities will be added: the monorail for orderly circulation; and Kultur. The Googs add a bit of worthiness to the transition, for the "culturati and the average Joe,"[30] one article explains; or in a guide: the Googs prove "the almost mystical link between art and Italian cuisine. (They) should be a boon the hotel's top Italian venue."[31] I imagine Bernini brought back from the dead to design a hotel/casino across from the Googs. With a good translator, would it take more than a few weeks for Bernini to sculpt a maquette? We are witnessing the return of theatricalized Baroque interiors that he would have understood – the outdoors brought inside as theater.

In fact, museums – as well as universities – are being rescripted to serve as indoor city/malls. They commemorate the cities that are gone, like a museum/museum as cultural casino. After all, in the midst of Electronic Feudalism (or Baroque, something hierarchical surely), museum attendance is way up in the US. Imagine a refurbished monastery as cultural service provider after the fall of Rome. It displays what disappears, but also accommodates to the new faith. And it costs less than a movie ticket (though a visit to each Goog runs fifteen dollars).

Museums help map the transition toward this new Baroque, toward the alliances around special effects and the digital. (So many new installations since 2000 are designed as indoor overlapping 'cityscapes.' That would be an essay in itself.) But museums are also under the gun. They must evolve new grammars for how they install objects. Very likely, shows will look more like wunderkammers than they used to. They will overlap and sprawl more, like browsers and search engines. But they remain one of the few areas of spatial critique in a culture built on shoppers consensus. Still, the pressures to make shows that monumentalize the new power relations will be intense.

And more importantly, what will the poetics of these monuments be? What can they tell us about the next ten years? In the few pages remaining, I'll review a few categories that discuss scripted spaces as poetics – channeling through Las Vegas (Vegaesthetics):

(2) Happy Imprisonment: The Labyrinth Effect

A visitor writes about getting lost in the Caesars Palace casino – every time he goes. But it is fun getting lost, 'a challenge.' Also, you always find your way out eventually. "Wish me luck for the next Xtreme Adventure at Caesars I attempt to take."[32]

This is what I call Happy Imprisonment, or a labyrinth effect, standard issue at most casinos. You have infinite choice, but seemingly no way out. Happy imprisonment is essential as well in mega malls, even in video games, and on the Internet. The labyrinths are 'ergonomic.' Entrances and exits are thrillingly inscrutable, with good digital sound, slot machines humming blissfully, as if you were inside a whale.

(3) Slots: Baroque Power in Miniature

Slot machines earn upwards of 70% of all gaming profits, and are possibly the most multiplied use of digital software in the entire entertainment economy. Apparently, the micro-chips set the winners, while sending out feedback to many sources at once. They have a statistical control package[33] for casino owners to make a count, with palm pilots for employees on the floor, wireless tracking of financial records for the desk, polling for the slot club, and for many casinos at once. Since many casino owners expect a slowdown by 2002, slots must have "killer software in an era of slower growth."[34] That means more reward action games built in, a trend pioneered by Odyssey slots in the early 1990s – a 'game within a game' bonus features[35] carefully hidden; and 'pick-a-game' (multigame) choices – up to twelve choices, from keno to poker to various slot games – all on a single machine, like a remote control programmer for gamblers. Finally, the backgrounds behind the slot reels will become far more elaborate. Odyssey[36] specializes in cyber staging for backgrounds: Arabian Riches; bonus vacation maps; banana-rama animated monkey hosts; Fort Knox as an adventure game; Three Wishes magic lantern under glittery sky reminiscent of Disney's Pinocchio; Riddle of the Sphinx, lit like an Indiana Jones mystery; Phantom Belle, a live-action Southern belle deals, then smirks while she hides her cards just above her cleavage; Buccaneer Gold, an atmospheric pirate deck modeled on the woodsy imagery of Myst; a glowing yellow palm reading for Lady of

Fortune; a magic wand coming to life in Top Hat. The slot machine is a metonym for the globalized electronic economy. It stands in for cybernetic controls across many markets at once. New computerized full service digital tracking services perform like a bot for the house: tracking players, slots, tables, revenue sources, demographics, doing the taxes, providing "up to the minute WIN reporting," player photos, electronic signature identification, messages for players on screens in their hotel rooms; and for the trackers on the casino floor, portable handheld tracking devices; for their bosses, multiple casino access.[37] This is indeed a software chimera, the tail of a serpent attached to the head of a lion. It combines business graphics with the Internet, cinematic memory, remote control systems – and banking, franchise capitalism at your fingertips. Increasingly, digital slots will operate without coins (the Cashless Casino), like an ATM gambling machine that simply withdraws from Master Card; or as coinless payout machines that take dollars, and whir quietly (no more jangle).[38] This chimerical screen merges horizontally all the industries that pay for the play on the Strip; as well as casinos across the United States. Even many Indian casinos "from Cherokee, North Carolina to Deadwood, South Dakota"[39] are wired like electronic mailboxes off the main road. In the era of the palm pilot, as the computer monitor spawns in miniature, as genetic technology spawns, the monuments will shrink. Eventually they may be able to inject a slot machine under your skin.

(4) Immersion: Shrinking into the Movie

We wait for the sea battle at Buccaneer Island in front of Treasure Island, for the pirates to sink the British frigate one more time. The entire site was designed around a scenario, like a nineteenth century panorama[40] of the Battle of Waterloo. A Portuguese island in the Caribbean is taken over by the Spanish, then falls to pirates. "That way," explains designer Charles White, "we could rationalize a lot of Middle-Eastern attitude and Moroccan influence." And this (looking at the bottom line) would please the Arabic high rollers; beyond each hidden script, there is a bottom line, with yet another script, the image of Moslem gaming in Vegas. These back-story movie scripts help designers fill in with atmospheric details. Pieces of imaginary shipwrecks turn into pirate lairs. The stern of a pirate wreck clings to the hillside as if from a giant pack horse.

Similarly, Bellagio has a cinematic back story, about a fictional Italian immigrant, the son of chefs, who settles in Las Vegas earlier in the century, then gradually builds a fantasy version of his place of birth; even starts collecting Impressionist art. Bellagio is imagined, therefore, as eighty years old; it simulates a pre-history to a Las Vegas that never was. The integration of cinema and scripted spaces is complete, only in this case, you the spectator are inside the movie – in the masque. The foreground disappears. You disappear, as if you were a miniature yourself.

(5) Condensed Cities

Through Baroque devices (trompe lœil, accelerated perspective, anamorphosis, multiple vanishing points), cities can be shrunk to the scale of a hundred acres or less. Bally's Paris is less than twenty acres, across the street from Lake Como, down the block from Venice, near Rome and New York. Obviously, these are 'condensed' spaces, but not simply because the Chrysler Building is foreshortened against the Empire State Building. They are condensed in Freudian terms: mutual narratives that distract by overlapping the same space, into a comforting vertigo.

There are rumors that a Vegas/Vegas hotel may be built – the entire Strip condensed to 5/8 scale, like Disneyland's Main Street at 7/8 scale; or like Universal Citywalk (1994 – the launching of the next era in LA) where ten LA neighborhoods were squashed on to three curved streets. I've also seen an early design for San Francisco/San Franciso: the entire hill downtown as one loaf of a building. These condensed cities often harken back to shrunken New York streets built in the 1920s for Hollywood Studios. Even today, the old Paramount street really explodes with Baroque trickery (trompe l'œil, etc.). But the camera erases all the distortions. It turns something awry into something comforting. Photos also condense, helps us become tourists inside our own city. In all spatial media, the poetics of archi-miniaturization are crucial to the Electronic Baroque.

(6) Architainment

That is the term used in Vegas to describe the new pedestrian friendly eye candy along the Strip. It reminds us that spatial entertainment will remain the crisis of representation for 2000 to 2010. But let us be surgical in our critique. These spaces are not blurs, not deconstructed or floating signifiers, not simulacra. They are grammar for a new political civilization.

We are witnessing monument building. Inside these monuments, we are expected to feel as thankful as peasants watching the prince throw them a few coins from the window. But concentrate on the politicized paradoxes in architainment and the paranoia behind Vegaesthetics – what this monumentality means. Most monuments were designed to hide the corruptions of the age. In the next decade, we will face a bumper crop of corruptions to work on. But to make surgical cuts, we must never congratulate ourselves for the obvious, never feel superior to the Electronic Baroque, nor worship the mess it brings us. We must be indestructible in our resolve to make these paradoxes as fierce as possible.

1. 'Fiftieth Anniversary,' Las Vegas Sun, 2000.
2. Ibid.
3. Ken White, 'Guggenheim to Play the Strip,' Las Vegas Review-Journal, October 21, 2000.
4. Scott Dickensheets, 'Can the Raw Design of the Guggenheim Mesh with Strip Fantasia to Give Us a Museum Peace?' Las Vegas SUN, Jan. 17, 2001.
5. Ibid., from Nicolai Ouroussoff of the LA Times, when the designs for the casinos were released in 2000 (Oct. 21, 2000).
6. Krens' plans for the Las Vegas 'Googs' were leaked during the summer of 2000, formally released in October; but more information emerged in the months afterward.
7. Mark Honigsbaum, 'McGuggenheim?' The Guardian, Jan. 27, 2001.
8. Ibid. Admittedly, many of the reviews throughout the world were cynical about Las Vegas/Guggenheim. But the Vegas reviews came out of an insider sense of the ironies ahead.
9. Chuck Twardy, 'The Guggenheim: What the Museum Means to the City,' Las Vegas Life, August, 2001.
10. Jeff Simpson, 'Casinos Experience Revenue Slowdown,' Las Vegas Review Journal, August 11, 2001.
11. Hubble Smith, 'Nevada Economy: Slowdown Hits Las Vegas,' Las Vegas Review Journal, July 26, 2001.
12. Jeff Simpson, 'Casino Revenues: May Gaming Win Jumps,' Las Vegas Review-Journal, July 11, 2001.
13. Cy Ryan, 'Evidence of Las Vegas Casino Slowdown Mounts,' Las Vegas Sun, August 10, 2001.
14. Dave Berns, 'Quarterly Revenue Up 15 Percent at Harrah's,' Las Vegas Review-Journal, April 19, 2001.
15. Editorial, 'California's Casino Frenzy Slows,' Las Vegas Review-Journal, June 16, 2001.
16. Conference talk in Las Vegas, by Prof. William Eadington, of the University of Nevada at Reno. 'Professor Says Tribal Casinos Could Overtake Nevada Casinos,' Las Vegas Sun, June 16, 2000.
17. Ed Vogel, 'Assembly Committee: Internet Gaming Gets OK,' Las Vegas Review-Journal, April 17, 2001.
18. Gary Thompson, 'Global Economy to Fuel Boom for New, Existing, Casino Venues, Las Vegas Sun, Oct. 2, 1996.
19. Manuscript of Hal Rothman's 'Neon Metropolis: How Las Vegas Started the Twenty-First Century', due out in the Spring, 2002; from Routledge, chapter 11.

20. Jeff Simpson, 'Beyond Business Las Vegas: Southern Exposure; Casinos in Primm and Jean Face Formidable New Competitor: California Tribal Gambling,' Las Vegas Review-Journal, April 15, 2001.
21. Heidi Knapp Rinella, 'Restaurant Evolution,' Las Vegas Review-Journal, July 18, 2001.
22. 'Business Briefs,' Las Vegas Review-Journal, March 31, 2001.
23. May Manning, 'UNLV Studies May Aid Yucca Fight. Transmutation Could Ease Need to Ship Nuclear Waste,' Las Vegas Sun, August 31, 2001.
24. Gary Thompson, 'Global Economy to Fuel Boom for New, Existing Casino Venues,' Las Vegas Sun, Oct. 2, 1996.
25. Adrienne Packer, 'Mayor's Race has Global Appeal,' Las Vegas Sun, June 8, 1999.
26. Erin Neff, 'City Officials Want a Slice of Visa Las Vegas' Success,' Las Vegas Sun, March 14, 1999.
27. Gary Thompson, 'Bally-Alliance To Go Global,' Las Vegas Sun, April 3, 1996.
28. Eugene P. Moehring, 'Suburban Resorts and the Triumph of Las Vegas,' in Wilbur Shepperson (Ed.), 'East of Eden, West of Zion: Essays on Nevada,' (Reno and Las Vegas: University of Nevada Press, 1989), p. 158. Such a vast literature on Las Vegas. Among the new experts: Hal Rothman.
29. Frances Anderton, 'The Global Village Goes Pop Baroque,' New York Times, Oct. 8, 1898, p. B9.
30. Stacy J. Willis, 'Thinkers Paradise? Philosophers Converge on LV, and Setting Arouses Debate,' Las Vegas sun, March 13, 2001.
31. 'Guide to the Guggenheims,' special issue of Las Vegas Life, August, 2001.
32. Marm's Travels, www.marmsweb.com
33. While the new slots are exceptionally elaborate in their statistical control – and infinitely more complex in their visual games – by the 1970s, much of the essential digital slot machine was already in place. See Jerome H. Skolnick, 'House of Cards: The Legalization and Control of Casino Gambling' (Boston: Little, Brown and Company, 1978), p. 76.
34. '...Slow growth (brings) market share wars. That applies to both (slot machine operators) and manufacturers.' (statement by Jose [Pepe] Charles, executive at Casino Data Systems), John Edwards, 'The Game's the Thing,' Casino Journal, Sept., 1998, p. 84.
35. Examples of game within a game: Treasure Time from Sigma; new games from Bally.
36. Silicon Gaming. Their Product Information packet features a quote from Sam Goldwyn (indicating links particularly to MGM): 'Reach for the Stars. You might not catch one, but at least you're heading in the right direction.'
37. Taken from promotional brochures from slot machine manufacturers, particularly the Quick Track Gaming Company.
38. David Berns, 'Park Place Entertainment to Boost Use of Coinless-Payout Slot Machines,' Las Vegas Review, June 20, 2001.
39. Ibid.
40. See: Stephan Oettermann, 'The Panorama: History of a Mass Medium', tr. D. Schneider (New York: Zone Books, 1997; orig. 1980); and Richard Altick, 'The Shows of London' (Cambridge: Harvard/Belknap Press, 1978. However, I have not encountered much direct use of 19th century panoramas or cycloramas in Las Vegas design, except in the immersive positioning of the viewer – slightly higher than the illusion in the round (i.e. Luxor; inside the Showcase on the Strip [shaped like a Coke outside, similar to old panorama buildings]). But the amount of literal appropriation of Baroque perspective 'awry' (1480-1750) is staggering.

The Strip Versus Nature

by Mike Davis

It was advertised as the biggest non-nuclear explosion in Nevada's history. On October 27, 1993, Steve Wynn, the state's official god of hospitality, flashed his trademark smile and pushed the detonator button.

As 200 000 Las Vegans cheered, the Dunes Hotel, former flagship of the Strip, slowly crumbled to the desert floor. The giant dust plume was visible from the California border. Nobody in Nevada found it the least bit strange that Wynn's gift to the city he adores was to blow up an important piece of its past. This was simply urban renewal Vega-style: one costly facade destroyed to make way for another, indeed, the destruction of the Dunes merely encouraged other casino owners to blow up their obsolete properties with equal fanfare: the Sands, of Rat Pack fame, came down in November 1996, while the Hacienda was dynamited at the stroke midnight that New Year's Eve. Extravagant demolitions have become Las Vegas's version of civic festivals.

In place of the old Dunes, the Mirage Resort is completing the €1.25 billion Bellagio, a super-resort with lakes large enough for jet-skiing. No one bothered to explain where the water would come from. Neither did those who built the €2 billion, 6000-room Venetian Casino Resort, with gondolas along artificial canals; or has Circus Enterprises, which is transforming the old Hacienda into Project Paradise, 'an ancient forbidden city on a lush tropical island with Hawaiian-style waves and a swim-up shark exhibit.' €8 billion has been invested in thirteen major properties along the Strip alone. As a result, the Sphinx now shares a street address with the Statue of Liberty, the Eiffel Tower, Treasure Island, the Land of Oz and the Piazza San Marco. The boom, still breaking all records, shows every sign of continuing.

By obscure coincidence, the demolition of the Dunes happened on the centenary of Frederick J. Turner's legendary 'end of the frontier' address to the World's Exposition in Chicago, where the young prairie historian ruminated on the fate of American character in a conquered, rapidly urbanising West. Turner questioned the survival of frontier democracy in the emergent epoch of giant cities and wondered what the West would be like a century hence.

The robber barons of the Strip think they know the answer: Las Vegas is the terminus of Western history, the end of the trail. As an overpowering cultural artefact it bestrides the gateway to the twenty-first century in the same way that Burnham's 'White City' along the Chicago lakefront was supposed to prefigure the 20th. At the edge of the millennium, this strange amalgam of boomtown, world's fair and highway robbery is the fastest growing metropolitan area in the US. It is also the brightest star in the neon firmament of postmodernism.

More than 32 million had their pockets picked by its one-arm bandits in 1999: a staggering 33 percent increase since 1990. (By the time you read this, Vegas should be hard on the heels of Orlando, Florida, the world's premiere tourist destination with 35 million visitors to Disney World, Universal- and MGM Studios). While southern California has suffered its worst recession since the 1930s, Las Vegas has generated tens of thousands of new jobs in construction, gaming and security services. As a consequence nearly a thousand new residents, half of them

Californians, arrive each week. Some of the immigrants are downwardly mobile blue-collar families seeking a new start in the Vegas boom. Others are affluent retirees headed for a gated suburb in what they imagine is a golden sanctuary from urban turmoil. Increasing numbers are young Latinos, the new sinews of the casino-and-hotel economy. In spring 1995, Clark County's population passed the one million mark, and anxious demographers predicted that it will grow by another million before 2010.

This explosive growth has dramatically accelerated the environmental deterioration of the American Southwest. Las Vegas long ago outstripped its own natural-resource infrastructure, and its ecological 'footprint' now covers southern Nevada, parts of California and Arizona. The hydrofetishism of Wynn (he once proposed turning downtown's Fremont Street into a pseudo-Venetian Grand Canal) sets the standard for the Las Vegan's profligate overconsumption of water: 1800 litres daily per capita versus 1055 in Los Angeles, 800 in Tucson, and 550 in Oakland. In a desert basin that receives only 10 cm of annual rainfall (less than 30 percent of L.A.'s precipitation), irrigation of lawns and golf courses (60 percent of Las Vegas's total water consumption) – not to mention artificial lakes and lagoons – ads the equivalent of another 50 to 75 cm of rainfall.

Yet southern Nevada has little water capital to squander. As Johnny-come-lately to the Colorado Basin water wars, it has to sip Lake Mead through the smallest straw. At the same time, reckless groundwater overdrafts in the Valley are producing widespread subsidence of the city's foundations. The Strip is several metres lower today than in 1960, and some subdivisions have had to be abandoned.

Natural aridity dictates fastidiously conservative water ethic. But Las Vegas haughtily disdains to live within its means. Instead, it is aggressively turning its profligacy into environmental terrorism against its neighbours. 'Give us your water, or we will die,' developers demand of politicians grown fat on campaign contributions from the gaming industry. Las Vegas is currently pursuing two long-term, fundamentally imperialist strategies for expanding its water resources.

First, the SN Water Authority is threatening to divert water from the Virgin River or steal it from ranchers in sparsely populated central Nevada. In 1989 the Authority stunned rural Nevadans by filing claims on more than 800,000 units of surface and groundwater rights. This infamous water grab ('cooperative water project' in official parlance) brought together an unprecedented coalition of rural Nevadans against it: ranchers, miners, farmers, the Moapa Band of Paiutes and environmentalists. Their battle cry has been 'Remember Owens Valley,' in reference to L.A.'s notorious annexation of water rights in the once-lush valley in the Sierra Nevada: an act of environmental piracy immortalised in the film 'Chinatown'. Angry residents of Owens Valley blew up the L.A. Aqueduct during the 1920s, and some central Nevadans have threatened to do the same to any pipeline hijacking local water to Las Vegas. Las Vegas and the Los Angeles area want to divert the allocation of Colorado River water away from agriculture and toward their respective metropolitan regions.

Finally, to return to yet another 'Chinatown' parallel, watchdog groups such as the Nevada Seniors Coalition and the Sierra Club are increasingly concerned that the Water Authority's €1.7 billion delivery system from Lake Mead may be irrigating huge speculative real estate profits along metropolitan Las Vegas's undeveloped edge. One major pipeline runs near the suburb of Henderson where private investors recently acquired huge parcels in a complicated land swap with the Bureau of Land Management, which controls most of the desert periphery. This is the same equation – undervalued land plus publicly subsidised water – that made instant millions for an 'inside syndicate' when the L.A. Aqueduct was brought to the arid San Fernando Valley in 1913.

Southern Nevada is as thirsty for fossil fuels as it is for water. Tourists naturally imagine that the world's most famous nocturnal light show is plugged directly into the turbines of nearby Hoover Dam. In fact, most of the dam's output is exported to California. Electricity for the Strip, as well as for the two million lights of the new and disconcerting 'Fremont Street Experience', is provided by coal-burning and pollution spewing plants on the Moapa Indian Reservation and along the Colorado River. Only 4% of Las Vegas's current electricity comes from 'clean' hydropower. Cheap power for the gaming industry, moreover, is directly subsidised by higher rates for residential consumers.

Automobiles, of course, are the other side of the fossil fuel problem. As Clark Country's transportation director testified in 1996, the county has the 'lowest vehicle occupancy rate in the country' in tandem with the 'longest per person, per trip, per day ratio.' Like Phoenix and Los Angeles before it, Las Vegas was once a Mecca for those seeking the restorative powers of pure desert air. Now, according to the Environmental Protection Agency, Las Vegas has supplanted New York as the city with the fifth highest number of days with 'unhealthy air'. Its smog already contributes to the ochre shroud over the Grand Canyon and is also reducing visibility in California's East Mojave National Recreation Area.

Las Vegas, moreover, is a major base camp for the panzer divisions of motorised toys – dune buggies, dirt bikes, speed boats, jet-skis – that make war each weekend on the fragile desert environment. Few western landscapes are more degrades than the lower Colorado River Valley, which is under relentless attack by the leisure classes.

Skyscraper casinos and luxury condos share the west bank with the mega-polluting-Mojave Power Plant, which devours coal slurry pumped with water stolen form Hopi mesas hundreds of miles to the east. Directly across the river, sprawling and violent Mohave County, Arizona provides trailer-park housing for the non-union, minimum-wage workforce, as well as a breeding ground for antigovernment militias à la McVeigh. The Las Vegas 'miracle' demonstrates the fanatical persistence of an environmentally and socially bankrupt system of human settlement and confirms Edward Abbey's worst nightmares about the emergence of an apocalyptic urbanism. Although postmodern philosophers (who don't have to live there) delight in the Strip's 'virtuality' or 'hyperreality', most of Clark County is stamped from a monotonously real and familiar mould. Las Vegas, in essence, is a hyperbolic L.A. – the Land of Sunshine on fast-forward.

The historical template for all low-density, resource-intensive southwestern cities was the great expansion of the 1929s that brought two million midwesterners and their automobiles to L.A. County. This was the 'Ur' boom that defined the Sunbelt. Despite the warnings of an entire generation of planners and environmentalists. regional planning and open-space conservation again fell by the wayside during the post-1945 population explosion. In a famous article for 'Fortune' in 1956, sociologist William Whyte described (flying from Los Angeles to San Bernardino) 'an unnerving lesson in man's infinite capacity to mess up his environment – the traveller can see a legion of bulldozers gnawing into the last remaining tract of green between two cities'. He baptised this insidious growth-form 'urban sprawl'.

Although Las Vegas's third-generation sprawl incorporates some innovations (casino-anchored shopping centres, for example), it otherwise recapitulates with robot-like fidelity the seven deadly sins of L.A, and its Sunbelt clones such as Phoenix and Orange County. Las Vegas has

1 abdicated a responsible water ethic;

2 fragmented local government and subordinated it to private corporate planning;

3 produced a negligible amount of useable public space;
4 abjured the use of 'hazard zoning' to mitigate natural disaster and conserve landscape;
5 dispersed land uses over an enormous, unnecessary area;
6 embraced the resulting dictatorship of the automobile; and
7 tolerated extreme social and racial inequality.

Why all this talk about water? In 'mediterranean' California or the desert Southwest, water use is the most obvious measure of the environmental efficiency of the built environment. Accepting the constraint of local watersheds and groundwater reservoirs is a powerful stimulus to good urban design. It focuses social ingenuity on problems of resource conservation, fosters more compact and efficient settlement patterns, and generates respect for the native landscape. In a nutshell, it makes for 'smart' urbanism, as seen in modern Isreal or the classical city states of Andalucia and the Maghreb, with a bias toward continual economies in resource consumption.

Southern California in the early Citrus era, when water recycling was at a premium, was a laboratory of environmental innovation, as evinced by such inventions as solar heating (widespread until the 1920s) and state-of-the-art wastewater recovery technologies. It's departure from the path of water rectitude, and thus smart urbanism, began with the Owens Valley aqueduct and culminated in the 1940s with the arrival of federally subsidised water from the Colorado River. Hoover Dam extended the sub-urban frontier deep into California's basins and underpriced traditional conservation practices such as sewer-farming and stormwater recovery out of existence.

Unlike L.A., Las Vegas has never practised environmental conservation or design on any large scale. It was born dumb. Cheap water has allowed it to exorcise even the most residual semiotic allusion to its roots. Visitors to the Strip, with its tropical islands and Manhattan skylines, will search in vain for any reference to the Wild West (whether dude ranches or raunchy saloons) that themed the first generation casinos of the Bugsy Siegel era. The desert has lost all positive presence as landscape or habitat; it is merely the dark, brooding backdrop for the neon Babel. Profligacy likewise dissolves many of the traditional bonds of common citizenship. L.A. County is notorious for its profusion of special-interest governments – 'phantom cities,' 'county islands,' and tax shelters – all designed to concentrate land use and fiscal powers in the hands of special interests. Clark County, however, manages to exceed even L.A., in its radical dilution and dispersal of public authority.

The city limits encompass barely one-third of the metropolitan population (versus nearly half in L.A.). The major regional assets – the Strip, the Convention Center, McCarran Airport and the University of Nevada – are located in an unincorporated township aptly named Paradise, while poverty, unemployment and homelessness are disproportionately concentrated within the boundaries of the cities of Las Vegas and North Las Vegas. This is a political geography diabolically conceived to separate tax resources from regional social needs. Huge, sprawling county electoral districts weaken the power of minorities and working-class waters. Un-incorporation, conversely, centralises land-use decision making in the hands of an invisible government of gaming corporation and giant developers. In particular, the billion-dollar corporate investments along the Strip – with their huge social costs in terms of congestion, water and power consumption, housing and schools – force the fiscally malnourished public sector to play constant catch-up. This structural power asymmetry between the gaming corporations and local government is most dramatically expressed in the financing of new public infrastructure to accommodate casino and tourism expansion. Contrary to neo-classical economic dogmas and trendy 'public choice' theory, corporate-controlled economic development within a market-place of weak, competing local governments is inherently inefficient. Consider the enormous empty lots in the urbanised fabric of Las Vegas, dramatically visible from the air, that epitomise the leapfrog pattern of development that planners have denounced in California because it unnecessarily raises the costs of streets, utilities and schools. Crucial habitat for humans as well as for endangered species, in the form of parks, is destroyed for the sake of vacant lots and suburban desolation.

Similarly, both L.A. and Las Vegas zealously cultivate the image of infinite opportunity for fun in the sun, in reality, however, free recreation is more accessible in older eastern and mid-western cities that cherish their parks and public landscapes. Although the beach crisis was partially ameliorated in the 1950s L.A. remains the most park-poor of major American cities, with only one-third of the usable per capita open space of New York City.

Las Vegas has virtually no commons at all: just a skinflint 0,7 hectares per thousand residents, compared with the national minimum of 4.05 hectares. This park shortage may mean little to the tourist jet-skiing across Lake Mead or lounging by the pool, but it defines a impoverished quality of life for low-wage service workers who live in the stucco tenements that line the side streets of the Strip Boosters' claims about hundreds of thousands of acres of choice recreational land in Clark County refer to car-trip destinations, not open space within walking distance of homes and schools.

One its not a substitute for the other.

in Ramesh Kumar Biswas (Ed.), 'Metropolis Now: Urban Cultures in Global Cities' (Vienna: Springer, 2000), pp. 101-110.

Biographies of the authors

Joel Bergman is President of Bergman, Walls & Associates, an architectural planning and design firm (est. 1995, Las Vegas) specialising in gaming resort hotels and entertainment complexes. His portfolio boasts award-winning, premier casino resorts including the Paris Casino Resort in Las Vegas, for which he won Casino Executive's Gold Medallion Design Award, 1999, and The Mirage in Las Vegas for which he won the Silver Award in 1991. Other well-known properties he has designed include Treasure Island in Las Vegas, Palace Tower at Caesars Palace in Las Vegas, and the Golden Nugget properties in Las Vegas, Laughlin and Atlantic City. With the Indian Gaming rush on, Bergman has worked extensively in this arena as well. His professional affiliations include AIA, NCARB, CSI and ICBO.

Mike Davies, a former meatcutter and long distance driver, now teaches Urban Theory at the Southern California Institute of Architecture in Los Angeles. He is co-editor of 'The Year Left: An American Socialist Yearbook' and the author of 'Prisoners of the American Dream' (Verso), 'City of Quartz: Excavating the Future in Los Angeles (Verso), and 'Ecology of Fear: Los Angeles and the Imagination of Disaster' (Vintage).

Dave Hickey is a writer, curator and lecturer living in Las Vegas, where he is Professor of Art Criticism and Theory at UNLV. He is the author of 'Air Guitar: Essays in Art and Democracy' (Art Issues Press), 'The Invisible Dragon: Four Essays on Beauty' (Art Issues Press) and 'Stardumb' (Art Space Books). He curated Site Santa Fe in 2001, entitled 'Beau Monde', and prior to that, 'Ultralounge', at various U.S. venues, which featured numerous artists from Las Vegas. His writing can be found in Art Issues, Artforum, Parkett and other journals on art and other subjects.

Norman Klein is a professor at the California Institute of the Arts. He has written 'The History of Forgetting: Los Angeles and the Erasure of Memory' and 'Seven Minutes: The Life and Death of the American Animated Cartoon.' At the moment, he is completing his next book, 'The Vatican to Vegas: The History of Special Effects;' and is at work on a DVD-ROM about the erasures of memory and cinema, to be published by ZKM, and the Annenberg (USC).

Libby Lumpkin is author of 'Deep Design: Nine Little Art Histories' (Art Issues Press) and 'Ingrid Calame' (Deitch Projects), and currently teaches art history at the University of Nevada at Las Vegas. She is a contributing editor of Art Issues magazine and a regular contributor to Artforum. She was the founding curator of the Bellagio Gallery of Fine Art, Las Vegas, 1997-1999. She is the curator of 'Tim Gardner: Watercolors 1999-2000' at the Donna Beam Fine Art Gallery, Las Vegas, Sept-Nov 2001.

Ralph Rugoff is Director of the CCAC Institute, a contemporary exhibition space in San Francisco and Oakland. He is the author of 'Circus Americanus' (Verso) and co-author of 'Paul McCarthy' (Phaidon). He was co-curator of 'The Greenhouse Effect' (2000) at the Serpentine, London, and curator of 'Scene of the Crime' (1997) at Armand

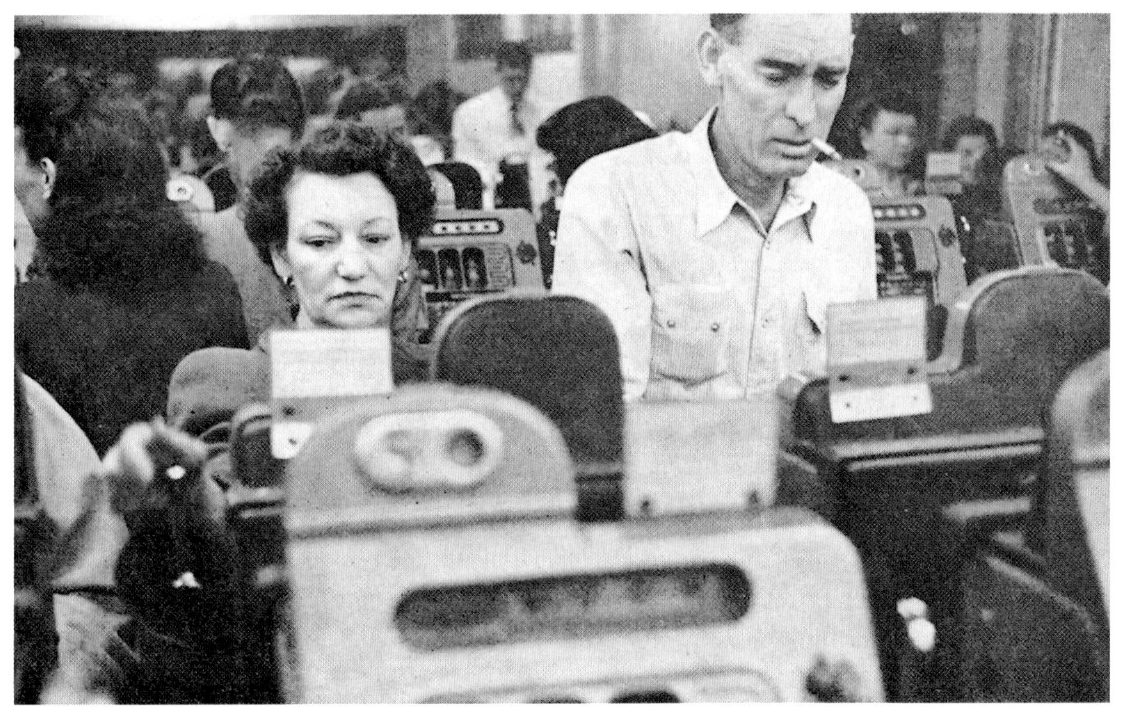

Acknowledgements

The Neue Galerie Graz am Landesmuseum Joanneum and the curator would like to thank all the following lenders:

Lynn Aldrich, Los Angeles
Kim and Tim Bavington, Las Vegas
Enron Corporation, Texas
Beverly and Stanley Erdreich, Birmingham, Alabama
Patricia Faure Gallery, Santa Monica
Rosamund Felsen Gallery, Santa Monica
Frith Street Gallery, London
James Hinderer and Dawn Saari, Los Angeles
Günther Holler-Schuster, Graz
Instrumentenmuseum Schloß Kremsegg, Kremsmünster
Klaus Kempenaars, New York
Libby Lumpkin, Las Vegas
Lehmann Maupin Gallery, New York
Mark Moore Gallery, Santa Monica
Neon Museum, Las Vegas
Patrick Painter Gallery, Los Angeles
David Reed, New York
Regen Projects, Los Angeles
Christine Siemens, Los Angeles
Richard Telles Fine Art, Los Angeles
Texas Gallery, Houston
Dario Urzay, Bilbao
Jeffrey Vallance, Las Vegas
Venturi, Scott Brown & Associates, Philadelphia
The Andy Warhol Museum, Pittsburgh – Founding Collection, Contribution of
Andy Warhol Foundation for the Visual Arts, Inc.
Shoshana Wayne Gallery, Santa Monica
Anthony Wilkinson Gallery, London
Linda Yeaney, Los Angeles
Young Electric Sign Company, Las Vegas

We would like to thank the following for assisting the development of this exhibition and publication in a whole variety of ways: Charles Barnard, Kim Bavington, Paul Bayley, Wendy Brandow, Roy Dowell, Lari Pittman, Guy Fisher, Bruce Haines, Alan Hess, Dave Hickey, Libby Lumpkin, Mark Holborn, Christopher Knight, Emma Posey, Ralph Rugoff, Roger Thomas; Joel Bergman & Heidi Cunningham (Bergman, Walls & Youngblood), Richard Hooker (Neon Museum), Charles Silverman (Yates & Silverman), Robert Venturi, Denise Scott Brown, Jamie Kolker & Sue Scanlon (VSBA), Steve Weeks (YESCO), Andrea Wood (The Andy Warhol Museum), Tom Christie (LA Weekly), George Perkins (Pierson studio), Dean Daderko & Andrea Geyer (Reed studio), Patricia Faure & Alka Agrawal (Patricia Faure Gallery), Rosamund Felsen & Gordon Haines (Rosamund Felsen Gallery), Rose Lord (Frith Street Gallery), Juliet Gray (Lehmann Maupin Gallery), Shaun Caley (Regen Projects), Richard Telles (Richard Telles Fine Art), Ian Glennie and Fredericka Hunter (Texas Gallery) and Shoshana Blank (Shoshana Wayne Gallery). We are also very grateful to the lenders, whose names, unless requested, appear elsewhere in this catalogue. Above all we would like to thank all the artists for the works they have contributed to 'The Magic Hour,' and for sharing with us their visions of Las Vegas.

Impressum / Colophon

Ausstellung / Exhibition:

THE MAGIC HOUR
The Convergence of Art and Las Vegas
Die Konvergenz von Kunst und Las Vegas

23/09/2001 - 4/11/2001

Neue Galerie Graz am Landesmuseum Joanneum
Sackstraße 16, A-8010 Graz
Tel ++43-316-82 91 55
Fax ++43-316-81 54 01
post@neuegalerie.stmk.gv.at
http://www.neuegalerie.at
Leitung: Christa Steinle, Peter Weibel

Kurator / Curator:
Alex Farquharson

Organisation:
Günther Holler-Schuster
Assistenz / Assistence: Sabine Schöck

Ausstellungsgestaltung / Exhibition design:
Alex Farquharson, Günther Holler-Schuster
Teppich / Carpet: Jim Isermann
Wandmalerei / Wallpainting: Yek
Ausführung / Realisation: Gerhard Pinter

Ausstellungseinrichtung / Construction:
Andreas Hochegger, Walter Rossacher, Nikolaus Vodopivec, Alois Weitzer, Kasimir Werschitz, Franz Zollner

Konservatorische Betreuung / Conservator:
Walter Rossacher

Kunstvermittlung /Mediation
Christine Kostka & Team: Franz Jud, Martin Pfitscher, Annette Rainer, Sylvia Schneider

Public Relations:
Elisabeth Fiedler

Katalog / Catalogue:

THE MAGIC HOUR
The Convergence of Art and Las Vegas
Die Konvergenz von Kunst und Las Vegas

Herausgeber / Editor:
Alex Farquharson

Grafik-Design / Graphic design:
Günther Holler-Schuster

Redaktion / Editorial support:
Günther Holler-Schuster, Karin Buol-Wischenau, Peter Weibel

Lektorat / Proof reading:
Karin Buol-Wischenau

Layout, Satz / Typesetting:
Karin Buol-Wischenau

Reproduktion / Reproduction:
Reprozentrum Klagenfurt

Druck / Printing:
Universitätsdruckerei Klampfer, Weiz

Erschienen im / Published by
Hatje Cantz Verlag
Senefelderstraße 12
73760 Ostfildern-Ruit
Tel. +49/7 11/4 40 50
Fax +49/7 11/4 40 52 20
Internet: www.hatjecantz.de

DISTRIBUTION IN THE US
D.A.P., Distributed Art Publishers, Inc.
155 Avenue of the Americas, Second Floor
New York, N.Y. 10013-1507
USA
Tel. +1/2 12/6 27 19 99
Fax +1/2 12/6 27 94 84

ISBN 3-7757-1153-8

Printed in Austria

CASINO GRAZ

Das Land Steiermark

.KUNST bundeskanzleramt

As I was falling asleep, I wrote the introduction to In Dreams – 'A candy-colored clown they call the Sandman / Tiptoes to my room every night / Just to sprinkle stardust and to whisper / Go to sleep, everything is all right'. I went to sleep, got up the next morning and I already had the lyric. All songs are gifts, but that was really a gift.

Roy Orbison

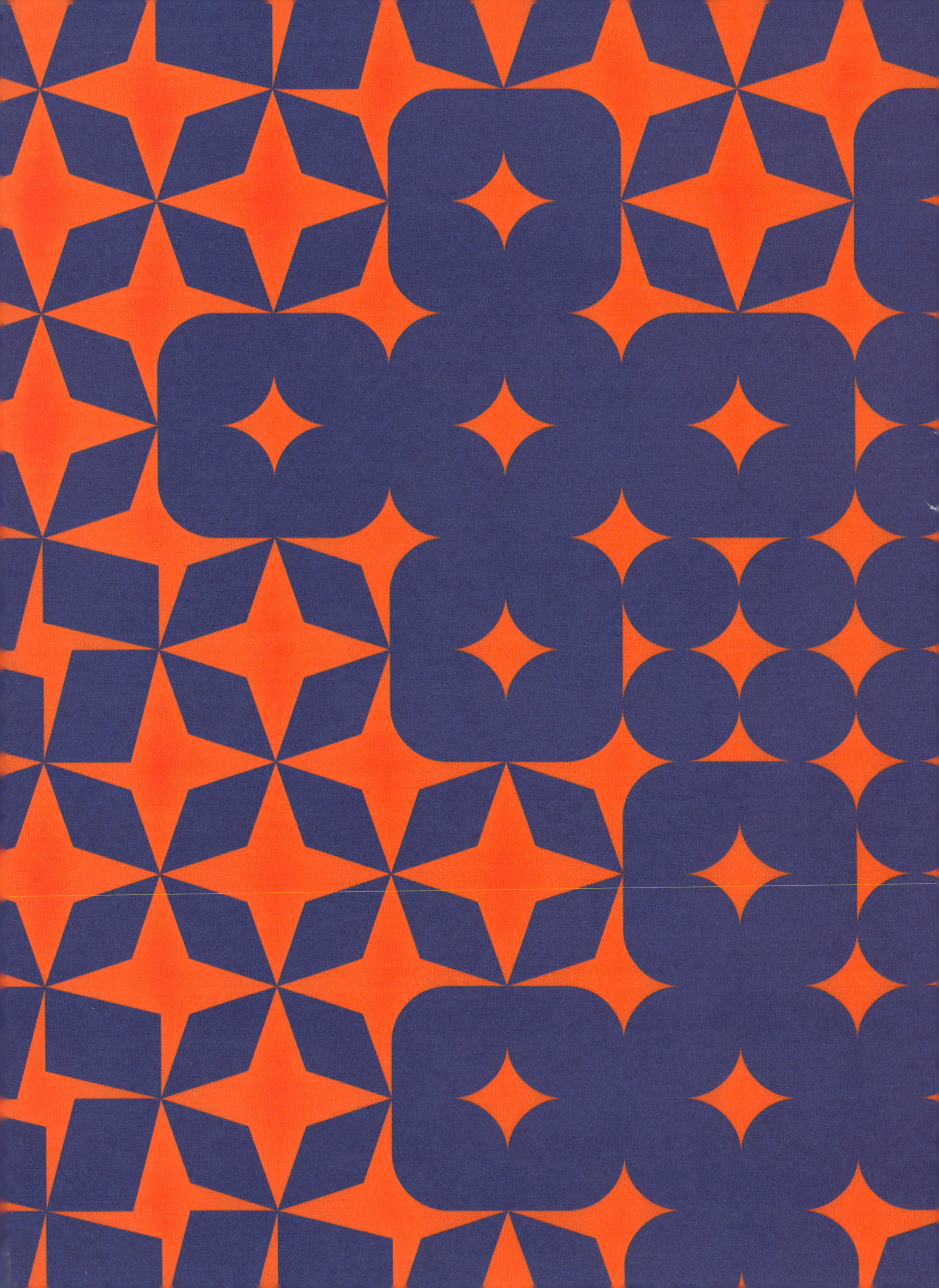